WORKING WOMEN
in CANADA

WORKING WOMEN
in CANADA

An Intersectional Approach

Edited by Leslie Nichols

WOMEN'S
PRESS

Toronto | Vancouver

Working Women in Canada: An Intersectional Approach
Edited by Leslie Nichols

First published in 2019 by
Women's Press, an imprint of CSP Books Inc.
425 Adelaide Street West, Suite 200
Toronto, Ontario
M5V 3C1

www.womenspress.ca

Library and Archives Canada Cataloguing in Publication

Title: Working women in Canada : an intersectional approach / edited by Leslie Nichols.
Names: Nichols, Leslie, 1988- editor.
Description: Includes bibliographical references and index.
Identifiers: Canadiana (print) 20190119365 | Canadiana (ebook) 20190119403 | ISBN 9780889616004 (softcover) | ISBN 9780889616011 (PDF) | ISBN 9780889616028 (EPUB)
Subjects: LCSH: Women employees—Canada. | LCSH: Women—Employment—Canada. | LCSH: Intersectionality (Sociology)
Classification: LCC HD6099 .W67 2019 | DDC 331.40971—dc23

Page layout by S4Carlisle Publishing Services
Cover design by Lauren Wickware
Cover image by Alexey Kuznetsov on Adobe Stock

19   20   21   22   23   5   4   3   2   1

Printed and bound in Ontario, Canada

Canadä

CONTENTS

Acknowledgements   *vii*

Chapter 1   Women, Work, and Intersectionality: An Introduction   1
Leslie Nichols

Chapter 2   Unions Are Definitely Good for Women—But That's Not the Whole Story   23
Anne Forrest

Chapter 3   Women's Occupational Health and Safety   51
Katherine Lippel and Stephanie Premji

Chapter 4   Unemployed and Underemployed Women in Canada   67
Leslie Nichols

Chapter 5   Immigrant Women's Work: Paid and Unpaid Labour in the Neoliberal Economy   95
Leslie Nichols, Vappu Tyyskä, and Pramila Aggarwal

Chapter 6   "Not Just a Job": Disability, Work, and Gender   111
Esther Ignagni

Chapter 7   Young Women: Navigating the Education-Employment Divide   137
Leslie Nichols

Chapter 8   Childcare: Working in Early Childhood Education and Care in Canada   157
Susan Prentice

Chapter 9   Minoritized Faculty in Canada's Universities and Colleges: Gender, Power, and Academic Work   177
Sandra Acker and Linda Muzzin

Chapter 10   Black Women's Small Businesses as Historical Spaces of
Resistance   203
Melanie Knight

Chapter 11   Black Women in Canadian University Sports   223
Danielle Gabay

Chapter 12   The Public Women of Canada: Women in Elected Office   247
Jocelyne Praud, Alexa Lewis, and Jarod Sicotte

Chapter 13   Women, Aesthetic Labour, and Retail Work: A Case Study
of Independent Fashion Retailers in Toronto   269
Deborah Leslie and Taylor Brydges

Chapter 14   From the Woman's Page to the Digital Age: Women in
Journalism   287
Andrea Hunter

Chapter 15   Equity Shifts in Firefighting: Challenging Gendered and
Racialized Work   303
Susan Braedley

Chapter 16   Women in Manufacturing: Challenges in a Neoliberal
Context   323
June Corman

Chapter 17   The Nonprofit Sector: Women's Path to Leadership   339
Agnes Meinhard and Mary Foster

Chapter 18   Understanding the Work in Sex Work: Canadian Contexts   359
*Kara Gillies, Elene Lam, Tuulia Law, Rai Reece, Andrea Sterling,
and Emily van der Meulen*

Glossary   *381*

Contributors   *387*

Index   *393*

ACKNOWLEDGEMENTS

This book has been under development for several years and involved the efforts of many dedicated individuals who supported its progress. The idea for the book grew out of a discussion with my colleague Vappu Tyyskä (Ryerson University, Professor Emerita, Sociology) about the lack of an updated textbook for a course I was instructing at Wilfrid Laurier University called Women, Gender, and Work—the assigned textbook was from the late 1990s. Vappu played a critical role in the development of the book and contributed to the first draft. I am grateful for her continued support throughout the entire project.

First and foremost, I owe a deep debt of gratitude to the authors of this book, who persisted patiently through a long process of editing and revising to make the book as good as we could get it.

Thank you to research assistants Taraneh Etemadi, Mounica Gudivada, Mia Hershkowitz, and Pouyan Tabasinejad for their support with research for the book, and to Michael Steeleworthy, data librarian at Wilfrid Laurier University, who provided substantial technical assistance with locating key statistical data.

This book was produced with the support of professional development funds from Wilfrid Laurier University and Trent University. Canadian Scholars/Women's Press provided invaluable assistance and timely support from the acquisitions phase through final production. I would particularly like to thank acquisitions editor Kerrie Waddington and production manager Lizzie Di Giacomo for their wisdom and patience.

My long-time editor, Margaret Copeley, provided incisive input on all aspects of this book, from development and content editing of the chapters to chapter reviews and final copyediting.

I am grateful to my parents, Jane and Darrell Nichols, for their continual support—to my father for instilling in me the importance of education and giving me the freedom to study what I was interested in, and to my mother for being my inspiration for exploring the lived experiences of Canadian working women. Finally, I thank my husband, Chris Curtis, for his love and encouragement.

CHAPTER 1

Women, Work, and Intersectionality: An Introduction

Leslie Nichols

Out of a total Canadian population of 36 million people, 9 million are working women ages 15 and older (Statistics Canada, 2018c). Working women and their dependents are strongly impacted by labour conditions such as salary, work hours, benefits, promotions, employment insurance, discriminatory hiring practices, **harassment**, and many other workplace issues as well as federal and provincial policies that regulate work. Given that working women make up such a large proportion of the population, it is vital to have a full picture of the role of work in their lives and how gender affects their work experience.

The experience of work is not the same for everyone. Two individuals, even if they perform the same type of work, can have very different experiences in the labour market depending on their gender, age, class, race, ethnicity, disability, and other social categories. These categories and social conditions *intersect*— that is, they operate together—to improve or worsen women's working lives and their ability to care for themselves and their families. Using an intersectional approach, this book investigates how Canadian women experience work by taking these categories and conditions into account and observing how they work together. The rationale for focusing on gender is that women and men experience work differently. For example, men and women tend to have different educational paths, leading to different career paths. Women's engagement in the labour force is also greatly impacted by their role in bearing and raising children and their unpaid domestic labour, which are still socially reinforced today despite more than a century of Canadian women working to achieve equality in all spheres of life. This book explores the many implications of these gender differences for women in their paid and unpaid labour.

We begin by trying to differentiate between *gender* and *sex*, which is more complex than might appear on the surface. **Sex** is biologically determined, while **gender** is a social construct created by a variety of socialization agents such as family, friends, schools, the media, and religion. The traditional belief was that sex and gender were one and the same, with no ambiguity. There were just two genders, male and female, with biological traits and behavioural norms established for each for physical makeup, appearance, speech, demeanour, and many life choices related to partners, sexual relationships, family, and work. Individuals who did not conform to those norms were viewed as outliers and were often ostracized. But with the political, sexual, and cultural revolution of the 1960s, sociologists, psychologists, and advocates of oppressed groups began to broaden the definitions of gender. For example, the Bem Sex Role Inventory Test (Bem, 1974) clusters personality traits in four rather than just two groups: (1) androgynous (high levels of femininity and masculinity), (2) feminine, (3) masculine, and (4) undifferentiated (low levels of both femininity and masculinity). On the biological side, scientists have now identified at least six different combinations of X and Y chromosomes that determine sex, meaning that many millions of people—referred to as *intersex* individuals—do not have the typical XY (male) and XX (female) chromosomes. Moreover, it is now known that the brain may identify with one sex when the body has characteristics of the opposite sex, confirming transgender identity.

Recently there has been a growing movement among social groups and scholars to advocate for a more inclusive perspective on both sex and gender that takes into account the widely divergent ways that they are manifested across the human spectrum. Individuals who don't conform to traditional biological sex and **gender norms** are increasingly becoming viewed not as deviant outliers but as part of a broad continuum of biological and behavioural traits. These present-day trends grew out of liberation movements that developed in the mid-20th century, including the women's movement, the US civil rights movement, and the **LGBTQ** movement. The goal of these efforts is to create greater equality and freedom of choice for all individuals in society, free of confining stereotypes, and to lessen social stigmatizing and discrimination, which have major impacts in the area of work.

This book focuses specifically on working women in Canada from historical and contemporary persepctives. To maintain that focus, and for simplicity, we use the terms *men* and *women* to differentiate two basic sexes and genders, while acknowledging that the range of sexes and genders cannot be fully captured by two categories. Most people continue to think and act in a binary (male and female) fashion, and most research, including official statistics issued by the government of Canada, continues to be based on these two categories. Thus, work tends to also be considered in a binary fashion as male and female employment or male and female gender roles and tasks in the workplace and at home. This approach excludes transsexual and intersex people, and it is hoped that future research will investigate the workplace experiences of these groups.

Gender as it has been traditionally understood had led to enduring, limiting stereotypes of women as dependent, emotional, nurturing, and impractical, while men have been viewed as loyal, strong, adventurous, and logical. These gender stereotypes influence women's daily tasks and roles in society, including the type of work they do, where and how much they work, how much they earn, and how others relate to them in the workplace. Viewing women as natural caregivers and men as providers (Nelson, 2010) immediately classifies men as workers and women as nonworkers. These notions of gender must be uncovered and questioned because they have such a large impact on women's position in the labour market and the messages conveyed to young girls as they imagine their future possibilities.

Work is an inherently human activity that is the root of survival for both individuals and society. Our quality of life and our social status are directly connected to work. Both paid and unpaid work, whether manufacturing cars or caring for a family, provide value for the economy and for the advancement of society. But in order to be considered part of the official **labour force**, one must be doing paid work or searching for paid work. This book will use the term *work* in the broader sense to include paid and unpaid work to explore how women engage with work in Canada.

AN INTERSECTIONAL APPROACH TO UNDERSTANDING WOMEN AND WORK

Approaches to studying gender differences in employment have been based largely on three different understandings of those differences as caused by (1) women's lower education and skills due to their role in bearing children, (2) discriminatory preferences of individual employers, and (3) employers' generalizations about male and female job candidates, arrived at without having met the candidates (Kabeer, 2012). Beginning in the 1980s feminist scholars found these explanations unsatisfactory. They pointed instead to structural factors in the labour market that ensured that women occupied an inferior position. In their view, both employers and male employees, especially those who are unionized, seek to exclude women from high-paying jobs. Employers exploit gender differences to reduce class solidarity and gain a reserve army of labour, while male workers have a stake in protecting their privileges as the core of the labour force, relegating women to a marginal position (Folbre, 1994). Feminist economists explain that while women make choices and exercise agency in their lives, they do so within structural constraints, including barriers and preferences maintained by employers and institutions as well as those enforced by social norms (Kabeer, 2012).

These discriminatory practices have been well documented over time. Regarding the placement of women in different occupations, Bergmann's (1974) concept of *crowding* has been influential. He asserted that certain marginal groups, including women and black people, were excluded from many occupations, limiting their choices to a relatively small cluster of jobs with the ultimate goal of insulating privileged workers from competition from outside groups. Regarding wages, Treiman and Hartmann (1981) were among the first scholars to show that the larger the percentage of women in an occupation, the lower the average wages of that occupation were. Phillips and Taylor (1980) asserted that the wages of an occupation are not based on the complexity of the job or the skill required to do it, but on the identity of the individual doing the job. This means that women's work is considered inferior not because their occupations are inferior or require less skill, but because women as a group are considered inferior.

Studying women's experiences in the labour market by focusing only on gender is problematic because people, their life circumstances, and relationships among social groups are very complex and cannot be captured by investigating a single variable. Two women—one white, age 25, Canadian born, with a university degree, and one an African immigrant to Canada, age 46, without a university education and with no English skills—will have dramatically different experiences looking for and securing work and negotiating for raises and promotions. Race, gender, class, location, family status, education, language, and ethnicity—singly and combined together—give rise to a vast number of different pictures of individuals' lives, each with a different outcome in the workplace. It is difficult to examine gender without simultaneously examining these many other factors that impact women and how these variables interact. Ultimately, we study women's lives in order to create greater equality via laws, policies, and assistance programs such as job training. Prioritizing one social condition and excluding others results in an incomplete and inaccurate understanding that may lead to inequitable social policies that don't match the reality of women's lives.

But how can all of these dimensions of identity and social conditions be taken into account simultaneously? To meet this challenge, feminist scholars developed *intersectionality*, which is both a theory and a methodology that can be applied to specific studies. The main argument of **intersectionality** is that it is not solely gender that leads to social inequality for women; rather, inequality results from the impact of a number of overlapping (intersecting) basic traits (such as race and gender) and social conditions (such as poverty and education).

These traits and conditions are created by overlapping systems of power, status, and privilege designed to benefit specific groups (such as white upper-class males) to the detriment of others (such as poor women of colour). For example, dividing people into a *gender binary* of male and female and attempting to align sex, gender, gender roles, sexuality, and behaviours with this strict division allows males to benefit from privileges associated with maleness. Dividing people into racial categories creates a dominant white social group that contrasts with all other racial identities. These divisions are taught and enforced by powerful social forces such as religion and schools.

Social categories then become controlling forces in the labour market that lead to different results for individuals based on their social identities rather than their skills. Intersectional scholars study the factors that create these power relations in order to understand oppression and marginalization, inclusion and exclusion, in social locations such as the workplace (Hankivsky, 2007). This approach also helps to understand the choices that people make—why, for example, a single mother with three children might feel forced to work part-time instead of full-time.

Intersectionality has its roots in black feminist scholarship (Combahee River Collective, 1977). The term was coined by US legal scholar Kimberlé Crenshaw in 1989. As a theory and research method it has now expanded beyond feminist studies and is used in sociology, anthropology, social justice, demography, education, health care, and employment (Christensen & Jensen, 2012). Intersectionality is more than exploring "individual factors such as biology, socioeconomic status, sex, gender, and race. Instead, it focuses on the relationships and inter-actions between such factors, and across multiple levels of society" (Kapilashrami & Hankivsky, 2018, p. 2589). This book adopts an intersectional approach in order to render an account of women's working lives that is both broad and detailed.

Intersectionality is a tool for studying diversity (Rodriguez, 2018), but some scholars question whether it is a theory or a method. Intersectionality as a theory has been well developed and is a popular approach among feminist scholars (Hillsburg, 2013). Intersectionality as a method is less well developed, resulting in trial and error for researchers attempting to use it (Hillsburg, 2013). Key intersectionality scholars Cho, Crenshaw, and McCall (2013, p. 788) refer to intersectionality as the "field of intersectionality studies" rather than a method or concept. As this debate continues to unfold, in this book intersectionality will be applied as a theory.

GLOBALIZATION AND WOMEN'S WORK

While the focus of this book is Canada, a good starting point is to situate the experience of work in the global context. Rather than dividing the world into four geographical hemispheres, economists now divide the globe into two economic regions. The **Global North** includes the United States, Canada, Western Europe, Australia, New Zealand, and the developed parts of Asia, such as Japan and Israel. The **Global South** includes Africa, Latin America, and developing countries in Asia, including the Middle East. In general the Global North is much more prosperous and developed than the Global South. While only one-quarter of the world's population lives in the Global North, the vast majority of industries are owned by the Global North and the majority of income is earned by residents of the North. The economic divide between the North and South is in part a product of history, as many countries in the South were colonized and controlled by the North from the 16th to the mid-20th century. As during the colonial period, the South continues to provide the raw materials that support Northern prosperity. Due to lack of development and the flow of wealth to the North, countries in the Global South suffer higher levels of extreme poverty, hunger, child mortality, and disease and have lower levels of education. Women's equality is very problematic in many countries in the Global South.

In the economic sphere globalization is broadly defined by (1) an increasing interrelationship between national economies, (2) an increase of international trade, (3) the free flow of direct investments between countries, (4) the globalization of financial markets as markets around the world open up to competition from other countries, and (5) the flow of technology between nations (Reinecke, 2006). Examples of globalization are the outsourcing of cheap labour in the Global South by companies located in the Global North, the ease with which Western consumers purchase goods from China via Amazon, and the movement of people from the Global South to the Global North to escape poverty, political instability, and war.

Those who advocate for globalization point to the benefits it offers for advancements in technology and the economic market, particularly for reducing the gap of inequality between developed and developing countries (Shin, 2009). But opponents believe that globalization has actually increased inequality between countries (Banerjee & Linstead, 2001; Shin, 2009).

As manufacturing has moved to the Global South, women there have become a source of cheap labour, benefiting companies in the Global North (Bair, 2010; Caraway, 2007; Desai & Rinaldo, 2016). Other Southern women have moved to the North to take on low-paid, often undocumented domestic positions as housekeepers and nannies for wealthy Northerners (Desai & Rinaldo, 2016). Thus, the emancipation of women in the North is connected with reinforcing inequality for women in the South.

INDIGENOUS WOMEN IN CANADA

There are 1.7 million Indigenous people in Canada, making up 4.9%[1] of the population, including 860,265 women (Statistics Canada, 2017a, 2018a). The status of Indigenous women in Canada's workforce today cannot be understood without understanding their history of oppression dating to the country's beginnings. **Colonialism** did not only occur in the Global South. Canada's colonization by France and Britain has left a legacy of violence, exploitation, and marginalization for Indigenous Peoples, particularly women. *Settler colonialism* allowed large numbers of Europeans to seize Indigenous lands for their own use until Europeans outnumbered Indigenous Peoples and forced cultural assimilation on them. Their subjugation was codified in laws such as the Gradual Civilization Act (1857), which aimed to remove Indian status from Indigenous people and turn them into British subjects. The Indian Act of 1876, still in force today with amendments, defined relations between the government of Canada and Indigenous Peoples, including many aspects of life on reserves, such as education, land use, health care, and governance. Although the act was based on previous treaties, it was not a mutual agreement between the government and Indigenous Peoples, but rather imposed by the government. Legal discrimination against Indigenous women that was built into the original Indian Act continues today despite amendments to the act (Smiley, 2016).

Violence against Indigenous women is so widespread that in 2015 Prime Minister Justin Trudeau ordered the National Inquiry into Missing and Murdered Indigenous Women and Girls to investigate more than 1,000 cases that occurred between 1980 and 2012. A 2014 analysis of these cases by the

Royal Canadian Mounted Police concluded that Indigenous women make up 4.3% of the population of women in Canada but 16% of murdered women and 11.3% of those reported missing (Royal Canadian Mounted Police, 2014).

The high incidence of violence against Indigenous women stems from their historical and current socioeconomic and political marginalization and gender discrimination, as well as abuse in residential schools that 150,000 Indigenous children were forced to attend from the late 1800s to 1990 under Canada's assimilation project. The schools were funded by the government and run by churches. In 2008 the Truth and Reconciliation Commission of Canada was established to investigate the history of the Indian residential school system. In its final report (2015) it described the schools as "badly constructed, poorly maintained, overcrowded, unsanitary fire traps. Many children were fed a substandard diet and given a substandard education, and worked too hard. For far too long, they died in tragically high numbers. Discipline was harsh and unregulated; abuse was rife and unreported. It was, at best, institutionalized child neglect" (p. 46). As many as 6,000 children died in these schools, and one in five were sexually abused (Naumetz, 2009) in a pattern that has been repeated from one generation to the next in Indigenous communities as those who were victimized as children go on to become victimizers. Present-day mental health problems, suicide, and alcohol and substance abuse in these communities are considered to be directly linked to the residential schools.

As a direct result of oppression and violence, many Indigenous women today struggle with poverty, unemployment, substandard housing, and raising children as single mothers. While indivdual women and grassroots movements work to gain political power for Indigenous women, they continue to face obstacles to equality in the workforce even at the highest levels. Strongly embedded cultural prejudices, legal codes, and institutional practices continue to marginalize them in both the workforce and society.

WOMEN AND WORK IN CANADA: GENERAL TRENDS

In the Global North, including Canada, neocolonialism is accompanied by pressure to diminish the role of the state in remedying income inequality and the ill effects of changing economies. From the end of World War II until the 1980s, Canada was developing as a social welfare state guided by a commitment to the well-being of all citizens and shared responsibility for caring for people who needed assistance in major life areas such as employment, financial security, health, housing, and childcare. While these programs did not cover all needs in all areas, especially housing and childcare, prosperity during the postwar economic boom supported the expansion of social welfare programs. In the 1970s many Western countries went through an economic recession caused in part by a steep rise in the price of oil during an oil embargo enacted by the Organization of the Petroleum Exporting Countries (OPEC) against the United States during the Arab-Israeli War. The recession became the impetus for a return to 19th-century laissez-faire capitalism—the doctrine that the economy should be free of government interference—and a retreat from the commitment to national responsibility for the social welfare of citizens under criticisms of excessive government spending. By the 1980s the social and economic ideology of neoliberalism came to replace the social welfare ideology across the West with the support of world leaders like US President Ronald Reagan and British Prime Minister Margaret Thatcher.

Neoliberalism holds individuals, rather than the government, responsible for their own well-being—a dramatic change from the social thinking that had dominated Canadian government policies since the 1940s. In the neoliberal paradigm, the adverse effects of events and social conditions that can befall virtually anyone—illness, accidents, loss of a job for whatever reason, divorce, disability, poverty—as well as the burdens of parenting are borne by individuals, not the state. The priority under neoliberalism is no longer the welfare of citizens but economic profit, leading to a new view of work and workers. The model of full-time permanent jobs and associated benefits that fulfilled the economic and social needs of workers and their families, along with the belief that workers deserved stable full-time employment, gave way to an increase in part-time, temporary jobs (referred to as **precarious employment**) that serve corporate profit without regard for the needs of workers and families. Under neoliberal policies, social services are reduced or rescinded, while labour laws and labour organizations are weakened (Pulkingham & Ternowetsky, 2006).

The neoliberal approach to work and the economy has resulted in financial hardship and insecurity for Canadians, accompanied by a reduction in social services to assist people during periods of hardship. It has also led to high rates of unemployment, causing workers to move from job to job and to emigrate from Canada to other countries in search of work. These pressures have undermined family stability (Pupo, Duffy, & Glenday, 2017).

At the same time, the economy has been shifting from a manufacturing and resource base to a knowledge base, in which value is created by the availability of information. This "new economy" has moved from industrial jobs to service-sector jobs (Pupo et al., 2017). At the beginning of the industrial age in the mid-18th century, few women worked in the paid labour market, a trend that continued until the cultural revolution and women's liberation movement in the late 1960s. It can be difficult to compare early 20th-century employment to today, because methods of measuring employment were less sophisticated than today and inconsistent from year to year, but the following figures convey an idea of the large discrepancy between the numbers of female and male workers. It is estimated that in 1911, about 13% of gainfully employed people were women and 86% were men (Denton, 1999). Most of these women were single and left the labour market once they married (Pupo et al., 2017). In 1941, 19.8% of women were gainfully employed (Denton, 1999). This low percentage of women workers may have been related to efforts to separate women from the public sphere and paid labour. For example, female teachers were expected to resign when they got married (Ontario Federation of Labour, 2007). World War II propelled women into the labour market as factories retooled to produce weapons and materials to support the war effort. The total labour force is now defined by Statistics Canada as the number of people who are employed plus those who are unemployed, available for work, and searching for work. The proportion of women in the labour force increased dramatically from 22% in 1951 to 47.5% in 2018 (Denton, 1999; Statistics Canada, 2018b). Today dual-earner households are the norm (Pupo et al., 2017).

Historically, in both the industrial and service economies, all members of the family have had to work, whether at paid or unpaid work. Most people must work to survive. During the early industrial age, women of the lower socioeconomic classes often took in other families' laundry for a wage (Krahn, Lowe, & Hughes, 2015). The choice to engage in paid work has never been a real one for women, except for those of the wealthier classes.

During the 19th century women's work was mostly household labour, that is, in the private sphere, while men worked in the public sphere. The **gendered division of labour** was based on a belief that men should be supporting the family (even though often they did not earn enough money to do so) while women were responsible for the reproduction and raising of children that was essential to ensure the availability of future labourers (Krahn et al., 2015). A century later, during the era of economic globalization, Western industries were able to obtain cheaper labour by moving production overseas. Deindustrialization brought deep social changes as stable jobs with high wages and good benefits were lost and replaced with insecure temporary and part-time service-sector jobs (Pupo et al., 2017).

Women are overrepresented in the service sector, sometimes referred to as the *female job ghetto*, that grew during the onset of neoliberalism and globalization. These jobs offer little economic security or opportunities for promotion because they are usually precarious low-wage, temporary, or part-time positions. They are also often unpleasant, physically demanding, and repetitive. The nature of these jobs reflects social values about femininity and masculinity, resulting in gender labelling of jobs (Pupo et al., 2017). Thus, although neoliberalism and globalization of the Canadian labour market have impacted both women and men, women continue to carry an added burden of being consigned to lower-status jobs.

The Paid/Unpaid Labour Divide

Domestic work and social reproduction are unpaid labour, which includes (1) household labour—cooking, cleaning, and laundry; (2) care work, including bearing and rearing children, caring for elders, and tending to family members' emotional needs; and (3) kin and community work—communicating and maintaining a network with extended family and neighbours. Traditionally these tasks were deemed women's work, and that norm has been maintained to the present day as women now do both unpaid domestic work and paid work, termed women's *double day* or *second shift*. Time-use studies find that women with young children do more household labour, which diminishes as the children grow older. University-educated and younger couples tend to favour more egalitarian relations (Krahn et al., 2015). Despite this, overall Canadian women spend 38% more time on unpaid labour compared to men. Women work 3.9 hours per day in the household, compared to men's 2.4 hours, which amounts to a difference of 10.5 hours per week—the equivalent of more than a full work day each week or 52 extra days per year that women are doing household work (Moyser & Burlock, 2018).

As women have increased their paid work hours, some dual-earner couples are paying for household services, such as food preparation, caring for children, and cleaning, that were previously done without pay by mothers and wives (Krahn et al., 2015). However, even here a gendered labour division is in force: the majority of hired household labourers are women, and they are paid low wages due to the social devaluation of this type of work. This has given rise to a class of women household labourers who serve wealthier women, marked by a racial divide as this is a work niche for racialized women and those from the

Global South. But most women cannot afford to hire household help, and they do both paid and unpaid labour.

It is important to acknowledge that although household labour is in a sense invisible—because it is taken for granted and unpaid—it is labour nonetheless. Moreover, although the fact that it is unpaid reflects the low value that society places on this work, it is essential for the maintenance of society. It has been argued that if women went on strike worldwide, the consequences would be devastating since women perform the majority of both paid and unpaid labour (Tuttle, 2017).

OVERVIEW OF WORK EXPERIENCES OF DIVERSE CANADIAN WOMEN

Impact of Diversity on Women's Employment Rate

The jobs that women do, their work hours, salary, benefits, and other working conditions are impacted by a number of traits and social conditions. Data provided by Statistics Canada allows us to detect patterns of differential treatment and outcomes for women in the labour market with respect to factors such as age, race, ethnicity, and immigration status. The main guiding principle of this book is that when we make arguments about the status of all women, these must always be qualified by bringing attention to differences in experience that result from belonging to different social categories.

Age

Official statistics show that in 2015, 77.5% of women and 85.3% of men of the core working age (25–54) worked, reflecting a narrowing gender gap in the labour force. The gap is greater among older workers: 40.8% of men 55 years and older are employed, while 30% of women in that age group are employed. By contrast, in the 15- to 24-year-old group, more women (57.2%) are employed than men (54.4%), showing the growing trend of young women joining the workforce (Moyser, 2017).

Age impacts women workers in the form of discrimination in hiring, sexual harassment, and sexual assault on the job, pay, and devaluing of older women due to a double standard regarding aging (Ainsworth, 2002; Nelson, 2010). Older women are vulnerable to poverty after a lifetime of caring for children and the household, which makes it difficult for them to develop financially rewarding careers (Nelson, 2010). They may find themselves relegated to low-skilled, low-wage jobs that leave them with insufficient retirement funds, particularly if they are widowed, divorced, or single (Nelson, 2010; Satter, 2017).

Race

Race as a social category has a significant impact on employment. While race may seem like a simple concept on the surface, attempting to define it reveals its complexities. In the 18th century race was thought of as an obvious division of people by colour, facial features, hair type, and other physical attributes into five main groups (white, black, yellow, red, and brown). This simplistic definition is problematic for several reasons: First, it is based on perceptions, which may be subjective. Second, since the original racial categories were conceived, large-scale migration of people around the globe has resulted in racial intermarriage and mixing, so that it is no longer possible to divide people into five distinct races. As the lines between the races become blurred, the biological classification of races becomes less valid and less useful. Third, a simplistic definition of race does not take into consideration how people identify themselves. People of mixed-race heritage may choose a racial identity that is different from the one ascribed to them by others, or they may favour one racial identity over the other. A well-known example of this is former US President Barack Obama, who is of equal black and white heritage but is universally identified and self-identifies as black, pointing less to his biological race and more to sociological factors that govern racial identification.

These complexities of external perceptions and self-identification show that race is as much a *social construct* as a biological category. The scientific and biological bases of racial categorization are weakening. There is evidence that there are greater differences between individuals of the same race than between people of difference races, and all humans share 99.9% of their DNA regardless of their race (National Human Genome Research Institute, 2018). It is important to recognize the social origins of race because subjective perceptions of race that claim superiority of one race over another are used to justify racism, such as white supremacy, and to portray social inequalities like poverty as arising naturally from racial differences.

Understanding patterns of racialized women's employment relies heavily on the Canadian census, which uses the term *visible minority* rather than *race* in its questions. The census uses the definition of *visible minority* expressed in the Employment Equity Act: "persons, other than Aboriginal peoples, who are non-Caucasian in race or non-white in colour." The 13 visible minorities on the census are South Asian, Chinese, Black, Filipino, Latin American, Arab, Southeast Asian, West Asian, Korean, Japanese, Visible minority, n.i.e. (not included elsewhere), and multiple visible minorities (Statistics Canada, 2017b).

Race impacts women significantly more than men in the job market (table 1.1; Statistics Canada, 2018d). Racialized women have an employment

Table 1.1: Employment Rate by Race, Immigrant Status, Age, and Gender, 2016

Age	Total		Canadian-born		Immigrants	
	Women	Men	Women	Men	Women	Men
15 and over						
Racialized	56.0	65.2	61.2	60.3	55.5	67.6
Nonracialized	56.9	63.4	58.5	64.3	45.1	56.4
15–24						
Racialized	41.2	39.1	44.7	40.3	40.7	40.5
Nonracialized	57.5	55.0	58.0	55.3	49.2	51.4
25–34						
Racialized	68.1	79.6	79.8	80.4	65.3	81.6
Nonracialized	78.1	83.4	78.8	83.3	70.6	85.7
35–44						
Racialized	70.4	84.9	81.8	86.4	69.2	85.3
Nonracialized	80.8	86.5	81.7	86.4	74.8	88.6
45–54						
Racialized	72.0	83.3	78.8	82.6	72.1	83.7
Nonracialized	79.5	83.5	79.6	83.1	78.7	87.5
55–64						
Racialized	54.5	70.9	60.3	67.9	54.5	71.2
Nonracialized	56.1	65.0	55.8	64.1	58.8	71.8
65–74						
Racialized	14.6	25.9	18.6	26.4	14.5	26.0
Nonracialized	15.4	25.2	15.1	24.5	16.9	28.2
75 and over						
Racialized	1.8	5.2	3.6	7.4	1.7	5.0
Nonracialized	2.5	6.9	2.6	7.2	2.3	6.2

Source: Adapted from Statistics Canada, 2018d.

rate of 56%, compared to 65% for racialized men. The impact of race is particularly strong for women in the 15 to 44 age group, where there is a difference of 10% to 16% (depending on age) in the employment rates of racialized and nonracialized women. Younger racialized women (15 to 24) experience a particularly large employment gap with their nonracialized peers. The effect of race on employment appears to be less important for women over 65.

Immigrant Status

Immigrant status may create a greater disadvantage for women than for men—there is a difference of 11.7% in their employment rates—and for racialized versus nonracialized women across all age groups. The employment rate also varies across different national origins. Filipino women in the core working group of 25 to 64 years of age had an employment rate of 84.5% in 2016—even higher than nonracialized immigrant women at 70%. Arab, Korean, South Asian, and West Asian women 25 to 64 were least likely to be employed. Racialized women were more likely to be employed if they were Canadian born (Statistics Canada, 2018d).

Full-Time versus Part-Time Employment

Overall, women's full-time employment rate has increased dramatically in the last 40 years. In 1976, 38% of women worked full-time, compared to 89.8% of men. In 2014, 64.2% of women and 82% of men worked full-time (table 1.2). This is consistent with the growth of dual-earner households and the loss of manufacturing jobs traditionally held by men.

There are a variety of reasons why workers may choose part-time jobs, including attending school, having to care for children or elders, illness or disability, or inability to find full-time work. Women predominate in part-time employment for a combination of these reasons. In 2015, 18.9% of women compared to 5.5% of men worked part-time (Moyser, 2017). Racialized women were slightly less likely to engage in part-time work than nonracialized women (27.7% compared to 29.5%; Hudon, 2016).

Unemployment and Underemployment

Unemployment is an increasing concern in the new economy as many jobs lack long-term security. The unemployment rate for all workers in late 2018 was 5.6%. By gender it was 6% for men and 5.3% for women (Statistics Canada, 2018e).

Table 1.2: Full-Time Employment Rate by Gender, Ages 25–54, 1976–2014

Year	Both genders	Men	Women
1976	64.0	89.8	38.0
1981	66.6	88.5	44.5
1989	70.4	86.2	54.6
1992	66.8	79.8	53.8
1995	67.9	80.9	54.9
1997	68.3	81.3	55.4
2007	74.3	83.8	64.7
2014	73.1	82.0	64.2

Note: Employment rate includes self-employed.
Source: Adapted from Morissette, Hou, & Schellenberg, 2015.

Women bear a large burden of the loss of full-time permanent jobs and of being forced into underemployment, suffering disproportionate financial hardship and impacts to their physical and mental health when they become unemployed. How women are impacted by unemployment varies among different social categories, depending on their degree of marginalization, social supports, and financial resources to weather a job loss. Their vulnerability increases with the addition of more than one of these social categories, and their hardship is compounded by federal employment insurance policies that disadvantage them.

OCCUPATIONS OF CANADIAN WOMEN

In Canada, women commonly work in service jobs in sectors such as retail, real estate, education, health care, and food services. Only 10% of women worked in the goods-producing sector compared to 90% in services in 2015. Men more commonly work in goods-producing jobs in sectors such as agriculture, forestry, fishing and hunting, mining, construction, and manufacturing (Moyser, 2017).

More than half (56%) of women work in what is called the "5Cs": caring, clerical, catering, cashiering, and cleaning. There has been little change in this pattern in the last 30 years—in 1987 59.2% of women worked in the 5Cs (table 1.3; Moyser, 2017). The 5Cs have considerably lower status and salaries than the occupations that men tend to work in, including natural and applied

Table 1.3: Top Occupations by Gender, Ages 25–54

	Women		Men	
	1987	**2015**	**1987**	**2015**
Total (percentage)	59.2	56.1	15.7	17.1
Secondary & elementary school teachers, educational counsellors	3.8	5.3	2.0	1.6
Paraprofessional occupations in legal, social, community, & education services	2.8	4.7	0.4	0.6
Administrative & regulatory	2.5	4.6	1.5	1.2
General office workers	7.1	4.2	1.0	0.4
Nursing professionals	4.7	3.9	0.3	0.4
Nursing assistants	1.5	3.4	0.2	0.5
Auditors, accountants, & investment professionals	2.0	2.9	2.3	2.5
Financial, insurance, & related administrative support workers	2.9	2.8	0.4	0.4
Cleaners	2.6	2.6	2.0	2.1
Home care providers & educational support	3.7	2.4	0.4	0.2
Retail salespersons	4.0	2.3	1.8	1.5
Human resources & business service professionals	0.7	2.3	0.8	1.2
Customer & information services	2.1	2.1	0.2	0.9
Finances, insurance, & related business administrative occupations	2.4	2.1	0.4	0.6
Office administrative assistants—general, legal, & medical	9.5	2.0	0.2	0.1
Social and community services professionals	0.8	1.8	0.7	0.6
Cashiers	2.3	1.8	0.2	0.3
Food and beverage services	1.8	1.7	0.4	0.6
Policy & program researchers, consultants, and officers	0.4	1.7	0.4	1.0
Other technical occupations in health care	1.7	1.6	0.2	0.4

Source: Adapted from Moyser, 2017.

sciences, in which only 24.4% of employees are women (Moyser, 2017). The dearth of women in the sciences begins with the education of young girls, when gender stereotypes steer them away from science, technology, engineering, and mathematics (**STEM**) programs. Women's absence from these well-paid fields increases the gender wage gap, and progress toward bringing more women into STEM professions has been slow: from 1987 to 2015, female employment in this sector grew by only 7% (Moyser, 2017).

Racialized women have been even more likely to be employed in tradition-ally male occupations. This may be the result of their higher educational attain-ment: 38% of racialized women have a university degree, compared to 25.8% of nonracialized women (Hudon, 2016).

Regardless of what occupation women work in, they experience discrimi-nation and inequality. On the one hand, men who work in female-dominated occupations may experience the "glass escalator," receiving preferential treatment in hiring, promotion, access to desirable work assignments, and higher wages. On the other hand, women and minorities often experience the "glass ceiling," an invisible socially created barrier that prevents them from accessing positions with high status and wages (Nelson, 2010). Both the glass escalator and the glass ceiling are maintained by gender stereotypes, namely that men are innately more qualified for higher administrative and leadership positions.

CONCLUSION: THE FUTURE FOR WOMEN AND WORK IN CANADA

The new economy has changed the way that many Canadians work, and women have been uniquely impacted by this change due to the persistence of traditional gender inequalities, norms, and stereotypes. Despite their advancement in some areas over the years, women have lost ground in others. Their rate of precarious employment is higher than men's. Older women have been pushed out of the long-term job market and lost their union representation, while younger women deal with a perpetual cycle of precarious work arrangements (Khosla, 2014). Women's wages have stagnated or fallen. Women in administrative positions are trapped in a "pink ghetto" with low wages, status, and benefits. Further inequi-ties can be seen in the work experiences of younger and older women; Indige-nous, racialized, and immigrant women; and women with disabilities, as will be shown in more detail in the chapters of this book.

There is a pressing need to move beyond traditional gender norms and their impact on occupational choices, for example by encouraging girls and young women in STEM programs and then supporting gender equality in STEM and other nontraditionally female occupations in the workplace. Glass ceilings that prevent women's advancement need to be removed, women's labour rights need protection, and workplaces need to adopt policies like on-site childcare and flexible work schedules that support women's dual roles as workers and mothers. All policies need to become sensitive to differences among women in order to do justice to claims for equitable treatment.

If precarious employment is inevitable in the new economy, the social infrastructure must be redesigned to meet the needs of all precarious workers, including women and their families. This implies united efforts by employers, unions, community advocates, and governments and acknowledgement that as the nature of labour and production are reorganized in order to benefit employers, it is still workers who make profits possible, whether they work part-time or full-time, and whether their work is paid or unpaid.

NOTE

1. Percentages in this book are rounded to the nearest 1/10 of 1%. In some cases, this may mean that totals don't add up to exactly 100%.

REFERENCES

Ainsworth, S. (2002). The "feminine advantage": A discursive analysis of the invisibility of older women workers. *Gender, Work, and Organization, 9*(5), 579–601.

Bair, J. (2010). On difference and capital: Gender and the globalization of production. *Signs, 36*(1), 203–226. doi:10.1086/652912

Banerjee, S. B., & Linstead, S. (2001). Globalization, multiculturalism and other fictions: Colonialism for the new millennium? *Organization, 8*(4), 683–722. doi:10.1177/135050840184006

Bem, S. L. (1974). The measurement of psychological androgyny. *Journal of Consulting and Clinical Psychology, 42*(2), 155–162.

Bergmann, B. R. (1974). Occupational segregation, wages and profits when employers discriminate by race or sex. *Eastern Economic Journal, 1*(2), 103–110.

Caraway, T. L. (2007). *Assembling women: The feminization of global manufacturing.* New York: Cornell University Press.

Cho, S. K., Crenshaw, K. W., & McCall, L. (2013). Toward a field of intersectionality studies: Theory, applications, and praxis. *Signs, 38*(4), 785–803.

Christensen, A.-D., & Jensen, S. Q. (2012). Doing intersectional analysis: Methodological implications for qualitative research. *NORA: Nordic Journal of Feminist and Gender Research, 20*(2), 109–125.

Combahee River Collective. (1977). The Combahee River Collective statement. In B. Smith (Ed.), *Home girls: A black feminist anthology* (pp. 264–274). New Brunswick, NJ: Rutgers University Press.

Crenshaw, K. (1989). Demarginalizing the intersections of race and class: A black feminist critique of antidiscrimination, feminist theory, and antiracist politics. *University of Chicago Legal Forum, 1*, article 8, 141–150.

Denton, F. T. (1999). Section D: The labour force. *Historical Statistics of Canada*. Retrieved from https://www150.statcan.gc.ca/n1/pub/11-516-x/sectiond/4057750-eng.htm

Desai, M., & Rinaldo, R. (2016). Reorienting gender and globalization: Introduction to the special issue. *Qualitative Sociology, 39*(4), 337–351.

Folbre, N. (1994). Who takes care of the kids? Gender and the structures of constraint. New York: Routledge.

Hankivsky, O. (2007). Gender mainstreaming in the Canadian context: "One step forward and two steps back." In M. Orsini & M. Smith (Eds.), *Critical Policy Studies* (pp. 111–36). Vancouver: UBC Press.

Hillsburg, H. (2013). Towards a methodology of intersectionality: An axiom-based approach. *Atlantis: Critical Studies in Gender, Culture & Social Justice, 36*(1), 3–11.

Hudon, T. (2016). Visible minority women. In *Women in Canada: A gender-based statistical report*. Ottawa: Statistics Canada. Retrieved from www.statcan.gc.ca/pub/89-503-x/2015001/article/14315-eng.htm

Kabeer, N. (2012). Women's economic empowerment and inclusive growth: Labour markets and enterprise development. Ottawa: International Development Research Centre. Retrieved from https://www.idrc.ca/sites/default/files/sp/Documents%20EN/NK-WEE-Concept-Paper.pdf?lbw=1

Kapilashrami, A., & Hankivsky, O. (2018). Intersectionality and why it matters to global health. *The Lancet, 391*(10140), 2589–2591.

Khosla, P. (2014). *Working women, working poor*. Toronto: Women and Work Research Group. Retrieved from http://www.unifor.org/sites/default/files/documents/document/workingwomenworkingpoor_letter_web.pdf

Krahn, H. J., Lowe, G. S., & Hughes, K. D. (2015). *Work, industry and Canadian society* (7th ed.). Toronto: Nelson Education.

Morissette, R., Hou, F., & Schellenberg, G. (2015). Full-time employment, 1976 to 2014. Statistics Canada Economic Insights, Catalogue no.11-626-x, no. 049. Retrieved from http://www.statcan.gc.ca/pub/11-626-x/11-626-x2015049-eng.pdf

Moyser, M. (2017). Women and paid work. In *Women in Canada: A gender-based statistical report*. Ottawa: Statistics Canada. Retrieved from http://www.statcan.gc.ca/pub/89-503-x/2015001/article/14694-eng.htm

Moyser, M., & Burlock, A. (2018). Time use: Total work burden, unpaid work, and leisure. Ottawa: Statistics Canada. Retrieved from https://www150.statcan.gc.ca/n1/pub/89-503-x/2015001/article/54931-eng.htm

National Human Genome Research Institute. (2018). Frequently asked questions about genetic and genomic science. Retrieved from https://www.genome.gov/19016904/faq-about-genetic-and-genomic-science/

Naumetz, T. (2009, January 17). One in five students suffered sexual abuse at residential schools, figures indicate. *Globe and Mail*. Retrieved from https://www.theglobeandmail.com/news/national/one-in-five-students-suffered-sexual-abuse-at-residential-schools-figures-indicate/article20440061/

Nelson, A. (2010). *Gender in Canada*. Toronto: Pearson Canada.

Ontario Federation of Labour. (2007). 1900–2000: A century of women and work. Retrieved from https://ofl.ca/wp-content/uploads/2007.01.01-Publication-WomenandWork.pdf

Phillips, A., & Taylor, B. (1980). Sex and skill: Notes towards a feminist economics. *Feminist Review, 6*, 79–88.

Pulkingham, J., & Ternowetsky, G. (2006). Neo-liberalism and retrenchment: Employment, universality, safety net provisions and a collapsing Canadian welfare state. In V. Shalla (Ed.), *Working in a global era: Canadian perspectives* (pp. 278–292). Toronto: Canadian Scholars' Press.

Pupo, N., Duffy, A., & Glenday, D. (2017). *Crisis in Canadian work: A critical sociological perspective*. Toronto: Oxford University Press.

Reinecke, G. (2006). Is globalization good for workers? Definitions and evidence from Latin America. *International Labor and Working-Class History, 70*, 11–34.

Rodriguez, J. K. (2018). Intersectionality and qualitative research. In C. Cassell, A. L. Cunliffe, & G. Grandy (Eds.), *The Sage handbook of qualitative business and management research methods: History and traditions*. London: Sage.

Royal Canadian Mounted Police. (2014). Missing and murdered Aboriginal women: A national operational overview. Retrieved from http://www.rcmp-grc.gc.ca/en/missing-and-murdered-aboriginal-women-national-operational-overview#sec3

Satter, M. Y. (2017, December 11). Older women workers face tough economics. *BenefitsPRO*. Retrieved from https://www.benefitspro.com/2017/12/11/older-women-workers-face-tough-economics/?slreturn=20190005182252

Shin, S. (2009). A study on the economic benefits of globalization: Focusing on the poverty and inequality between the rich and the poor. *International Area Studies Review, 12*(2), 191–214. doi:10.1177/223386590901200210

Smiley, C. (2016). A long road behind us, a long road ahead: Towards an Indigenous feminist national inquiry. *Canadian Journal of Women and the Law, 28*(2), 308–313.

Statistics Canada. (2017a). Aboriginal peoples in Canada: Key results from the 2016 census. Retrieved from https://www150.statcan.gc.ca/n1/daily-quotidien/171025/dq171025a-eng.htm

Statistics Canada. (2017b). Visible minority and population group reference guide, census of population, 2016; definitions and concepts. Retrieved from https://www12.statcan .gc.ca/census-recensement/2016/ref/guides/006/98-500-x2016006-eng.cfm

Statistics Canada. (2018a). Aboriginal identity population by both sexes, total—age, 2016 counts, Canada, provinces and territories, 2016 census—25% sample data. Retrieved from https://www12.statcan.gc.ca/census-recensement/2016/dp-pd/hlt-fst/abo-aut/Table.cfm?Lang=Eng&T=101&S=99&O=A

Statistics Canada. (2018b). Labour force characteristics by sex and details age group, annual. Retrieved from https://www150.statcan.gc.ca/t1/tbl1/en/tv.action?pid=1410001801& pickMembers%5B0%5D=1.1&pickMembers%5B1%5D=2.10

Statistics Canada. (2018c). Labour force characteristics, seasonally adjusted by province (monthly) (Newfoundland and Labrador, Prince Edward Island, Nova Scotia, New Brunswick). Retrieved from http://www.statcan.gc.ca/tables-tableaux/sum-som/l01/cst01/lfss01a-eng.htm

Statistics Canada. (2018d). Labour force status (8), visible minority (15), immigrant status and period of immigration (11), highest certificate, diploma or degree (7), age (13a) and sex (3) for the population aged 15 years and over in private households of Canada, provinces and territories, census metropolitan areas and census agglomerations, 2016 census—25% sample data. Retrieved from https://www12.statcan.gc.ca/census-recensement/2016/dp-pd/dt-td/Rp-eng.cfm?LANG=E&APATH=3&DETAIL=0&DIM=0&FL=A&FREE=0&GC=0&GID=0&GK=0&GRP=1&PID=110692&PRID=10&PTYPE=109445&S=0&SHOWALL=0&SUB=0&Temporal=2017&THEME=124&VID=0&VNAMEE=&VNAMEF=

Statistics Canada. (2018e). Labour force survey estimates (LFS), by sex and age group, seasonally adjusted and unadjusted. Retrieved from http://www5.statcan.gc.ca/cansim/a26?id=2820087

Treiman, D. J., & Hartmann, H. I. (1981). *Women, work, and wages: Equal pay for jobs of equal value* (vol. 2101). Washington, DC: National Academy Press.

Truth and Reconciliation Commission of Canada. (2015). Honouring the truth, reconciling for the future: Summary of the final report of the Truth and Reconciliation Commission of Canada. Retrieved from http://publications.gc.ca/site/eng/9.800288/publication.html

Tuttle, B. (2017, March 7). What a day without women would really do to the economy. *Time.* Retrieved from http://time.com/money/4693662/day-without-women-statisics-workforce-privilege-income/

CHAPTER 2

Unions Are Definitely Good for Women—But That's Not the Whole Story

Anne Forrest

INTRODUCTION

Unions are definitely good for women. Full stop. All women—mothers and nonmothers, full-time and part-time workers, white and racialized, lesbian and straight, professional and blue-collar—are better off when represented by a union. By comparison with women in nonunion workplaces, organized women earn more money, have better health benefits, enjoy more job security, and receive more respect for their rights as workers and as women. Unions limit management's right to dictate how work is done, by whom, and under what conditions, and give women a voice in determining their terms and conditions of employment. Organized women also have someone who will speak up for them in a crisis and defend their right to challenge what management has said or done, without cost and without fear of losing their job. There is no question that unionism has made Canada a fairer and more equitable society and narrowed the gender gap in pay (Fortin, Green, Lemieux, Milligan, & Riddell, 2012).

Clearly, this is a good news story, but it is not the full story. Women and unions have a complicated and often troubled past that continues to shape women's economic opportunities. Today's ethos of inclusion and equality contrasts sharply with the attitudes, policies, and practices of the 1940s, 1950s, and 1960s, when unions unashamedly put men's needs ahead of women's. The centrality of men's issues—which unions conceptualized as "workers' issues"—reflected the mostly male demographics of union membership, the all-male union leadership, and the patriarchal social mores of those times that championed the needs and expectations of the male breadwinner and normalized discrimination against women. Sugiman (1994, p. 172) argues that the International Union, United Automobile, Aerospace and Agricultural Implement Workers of America (UAW; now Unifor in Canada) "adopted a narrow definition of unionism that advanced the general principles of democracy, equality, and worker unity, yet failed to question the blatant sex-based inequalities in employment." This was true for the movement as a whole, including the most progressive union of that era, the United Electrical, Radio and Machine Workers Union (UE) (Guard, 1996).

Union women were not neglected as long as their needs fit within the male-centred vision of fairness and equality. They were substantially better paid than nonunion women, more secure in their jobs, and assured of strong representation if their pay was short or they faced discipline for shoddy work, pilfering, or other breaches of workplace rules. But union women were not the equals of union men. When women's needs diverged from or were in conflict with men's—when women claimed the right to be promoted to better-paying "men's jobs" or return to work after the birth of a child with their **seniority** intact—they commonly faced indifference or outright resistance. From the union point of view, working women were not real workers; they were secondary earners, not family breadwinners, so less entitled to full union support (Creese, 1999).

The masculinist ethos of mid-20th-century unionism was soon challenged by women and men whose vision of solidarity and democracy made room for women's voices and women leaders. The long process of reform began in the 1960s and remains unfinished business. Influenced by second-wave feminism and left-leaning political groups, union women developed a growing consciousness of their rights as women and as workers (Luxton, 2001; Sangster, 2011). Important milestones toward gender equality were the Royal Commission on the Status of Women in Canada (1967–1970), amendments to human rights codes to prohibit discrimination on the basis of sex and marital status (early 1970s), the rapid growth of public-sector unions (1970s), the fight to ensure women's full inclusion in the Canadian Charter of Rights and Freedoms (late 1970s to early 1980s), and a new, substantive vision of gender equality (1985 to present). Along the way, women activists' interactions with the gay liberation, antiracism, and disability rights movements broadened and refined the meaning of gender equality in the workplace and society at large.

This ferment has changed our ideas about women as workers and union members dramatically. In the 1950s and 1960s, many women agreed that men should be given priority for good jobs, only 16% of working women were union members, and union men outnumbered union women by five to one. Today, most women believe they are fully entitled to any job they can perform, 30% are union members, and women outnumber men in unions (Akyeampong, 1998; Statistics Canada, 2016). Clearly, women should expect unions to put gender equality at the centre of the union project.

This chapter investigates the extent to which union collective bargaining policies and practices have kept pace with women's changing expectations. In the Canadian context, **unions** are workers' recognized voice and empowered to act on their behalf. By law, unions are authorized to negotiate with employers over pay, job security, and working conditions, and to use their bargaining power, including threats of work stoppage, to secure favourable outcomes. Unions are similarly legally empowered to use the grievance-arbitration process to challenge employers' decisions to reorganize the work process, grant or allocate benefits or privileges, and discipline or dismiss workers. How unions exercise this power is a strong measure of their commitment to gender equality.

What unions do in **collective bargaining** is "a tough and important guide to the seriousness of union engagement with an issue" (Hunt & Eaton, 2007, p. 137). Many unions actively campaign for pro-equality legislative action. However, it is the terms and conditions of employment secured at the bargaining table and unions' defence of those rights through the grievance-arbitration process that provide the most meaningful way of evaluating union commitment to solidarity, democracy, and gender equality. Like all organizations, unions must set priorities and make trade-offs, and there are many considerations: bargaining power, scarce resources (time, money, talent), and the competing demands and expectations of majority and minority group members. Consequently, union action or inaction on behalf of women says a great deal about the movement's commitment to gender equality.

The next three sections examine how unions have conceptualized women's place as workers and union members by analyzing how "women's issues" have been taken up at the bargaining table and in grievance-arbitration. The chapter traces the evolution of union thinking and practice on four key concerns: access to good jobs, fair pay, maternity rights, and dignity on the job. It does not consider how union politics have led to changes in collective bargaining practices, which has been the subject of a number of academic studies from different perspectives (Briskin & McDermott, 1993; Foley & Baker, 2009).

The chapter concludes by reflecting on the usefulness of collective bargaining as a means for achieving gender equality. There is no doubt that union women are better off than other women, but this is a low bar. A more appropriate question is whether unions have closed the gender gap in job opportunities, pay, and working conditions. The analysis offered here reveals a mixed record. At times, unions have used their bargaining power to support women's demands for more equitable terms and conditions of employment; at others, their action (or inaction) has narrowed women's rights in relation to union men's. With the benefit of hindsight, it is clear that the past is very much with us. On the one hand, the sexist, racist, and homophobic attitudes of union members and union leaders of mid-20th-century Canada have been pushed to the side; on the other hand, the choices available to women and unions today continue to be constrained by the structures and practices created in that era.

As you read this chapter, it is important to remember the mores of the times. Eighty years ago, unions were not uniquely sexist organizations. Employers actively discriminated against women in their hiring and pay practices, public policy favoured the male breadwinner, and few laws protected women's rights. Unions reflected and solidified aspects of this discriminatory system. However, they have also enhanced women's economic rights and opportunities and have been at the forefront of efforts to challenge and change this system.

WOMEN'S ACCESS TO BREADWINNER JOBS

Canadian women today believe they are entitled to any job they are qualified to perform, and this expectation is affirmed by legislation. Yet obstacles to women's equality in the workforce clearly remain. Notwithstanding new attitudes and aspirations, job segregation by gender within and between industries is widespread in both the union and nonunion sectors and the source of the gender gap in pay. Most women—union and nonunion; white, racialized, and Indigenous—continue to work with other women and to perform versions of "women's work" that are as complex and demanding as men's work, yet pay less, are less secure, and offer fewer promotional opportunities (Arcila, Ferrer, & Schirle, 2017). Job segregation by race is also widespread. Racialized workers are overrepresented in poorly paid, precarious service jobs and less likely to be represented by unions than white workers, which explains why workers of colour, on average, were paid only 81 cents for every dollar earned by all Canadians in 2006 (Block & Galabuzi, 2011; Jackson, 2005; Reitz & Verma, 2004).

Union Support for Job Segregation by Gender

Prior to 1970, when overt discrimination against women was lawful, employers, unions, and governments all championed a regime that reserved "breadwinner jobs" for men—secure jobs that could support a family and offered better opportunities for advancement. In light manufacturing, food processing plants, offices, grocery stores, and hotels—the industries where most union women worked— job titles were routinely gendered, for example, "assembler-male/assembler-female," or "janitor" for men's work and "housekeeper" for women's work. Women (referred to as "girls" in that era) were also assigned to a separate job category for women, boys, and disabled workers. In male-dominated workplaces such as resource extraction, heavy manufacturing, construction, transportation, and utilities, labelling jobs by gender was unnecessary: women were simply not hired to perform these blue-collar jobs. Both employers and unions believed that women were not fit to be steelworkers, bus drivers, electricians, or miners.

Hiring decisions were (and are) also influenced by race. In mid-20th-century Canada, the racialized workforce was predominantly composed of Jews and immigrants from Eastern and Southern Europe. Racialized women were steered toward labour-intensive industries such as garment-making and food processing; men were placed in unskilled, physically demanding jobs in both the union and nonunion sectors. All were quickly integrated into a wide range of industries, and many made significant personal sacrifices to help establish unions in their workplaces. But not all racialized workers were on an equal footing. Some were all but excluded from the union sector. Until the 1980s, it was exceptional for black, brown, and Indigenous workers in Canada—particularly women—to have access to better-paying jobs in unionized workplaces (Creese, 1999; Sugiman, 1994).

Formal job segregation by gender came under challenge in the 1960s, and union women led the way. Sugiman (1994) recounts how the reorganization of the auto industry led union women to press their case for reform with their union and the Ontario government. General Motors' (GM) decision to close its cutting and trim department in Oshawa led to layoffs of women even as men were being hired elsewhere in the plant. When laid-off women tried to use their seniority to bump into jobs in other departments, they learned they could not: their seniority was tied to jobs set aside for women, and those jobs were being eliminated. The UAW would not commit to rethinking this gender division of labour and refused to pursue grievances filed by its women members.

Frustrated and angered by their union's inaction, a group of activists joined with other women's groups to demand a change to the Ontario Human

Rights Code, which at that time did not prohibit discrimination on the basis of sex (or marital status). The campaign was timely—denying women access to better-paying jobs simply because they were women was out of step with public sentiment—and garnered widespread support, including support from unions. The law was changed in 1970, and the GM women got what they wanted: the women-only job class was eliminated and women workers acquired plant-wide seniority, which some used to secure jobs in previously men-only departments.

But other women did not fare so well. In most workplaces, the impact of the new law was not a thoroughgoing change in hiring and promotion practices. After 1970 all jobs were technically open to both women and men, but in practice, this was not the case. Most employers continued to hire men for jobs tradition- ally performed by men and women for jobs traditionally performed by women. Well into the 1970s, some collective agreements continued to identify jobs by gender with union support (Guard, 1996; Tillotson, 1991; Townson, 1975). In some workplaces, compliance with the law was achieved by the simple expedient of renaming jobs. For example, "assembler-male" became "assembler-heavy" and "assembler-female" became "assembler-light," but the pay differential was left intact. In other workplaces, where jobs were implicitly but not explicitly gen- dered, there was no ostensible need for change. Job titles such as "janitor" and "housekeeper" and the gender gap in pay did not violate the new law, as long as the duties were different, even in small ways, such as requiring janitors to use larger mops or do occasional heavy lifting (Tillotson, 1991).

The revised human rights code prohibited overt gender discrimination, but left many forms of indirect discrimination untouched. While it was no longer lawful to refuse to hire a woman into a formerly male job class, most employ- ers continued to assign new women employees to entry-level jobs in lower- paid "women's work." Once hired, they commonly found their opportunities for advancement restricted by union-negotiated seniority systems that gave long-tenure employees priority for promotions and better protection from layoffs within well-defined "seniority districts" (job clusters).

Failure to tackle the thorny issue of seniority rights disadvantaged women by constraining their opportunities for advancement. In unionized workplaces, job vacancies are filled by existing employees according to their seniority in the seniority district. As a result, although seniority systems were gender neutral on their face, they reinforced the existing gender-linked patterns of job segregation by ensuring that job vacancies in better-paying job classes were filled by men and vacancies in lower-paid "women's work" by women. Consequently, after 1970, as before, union women who were hired into entry-level jobs in a "women's work" job class continued to be caught by seniority systems that locked them into narrowly constructed, lower-paid job sequences with fewer possibilities for promotion. (The same restrictive dynamic affected racialized men as well insofar as their jobs were grouped into narrowed defined seniority districts that confined them to the hottest and dustiest departments.)

Implementing the spirit (rather than the letter) of the new law would have required a radical rethinking of women's economic rights and significant modifications of seniority systems. At a minimum, truly opening breadwinner jobs to women would have necessitated the creation of broader, gender-inclusive seniority districts, as was done at GM. For the most part, however, this did not happen. Dominion Stores, a grocery store chain, was typical. The new law provoked no fundamental change in its gender division of labour. After 1970, with the union's agreement of the Retail, Wholesale, and Department Store Union (RWDSU), the company retitled "clerk-female" as "clerk A" and "clerk-male" as "clerk B." Clerk A continued to be a female-dominated job class with a shorter seniority list and a maximum wage that was 10% lower than that of clerk B (*Dominion Stores Ltd.*, 1976). Because the seniority system was left untouched, Dominion Store women who sought promotion to the higher-paying, male-dominated clerk B job class could not displace a clerk B worker with less seniority. Union representation gave clerk A women a path forward, but they were required to take the lowest-paid entry-level job in the clerk B seniority district, even if they had many years of service with the firm.

Seniority rights were (and are) among the most coveted of union benefits and jealously guarded. Then, as now, any proposal to reconfigure seniority districts to advance women's economic opportunities would be opposed by some as unfair "reverse discrimination" against men and undermine support for gender equality (Sheppard, 1984). Even the UE (United Electrical, Radio and Machine Workers of America), which publicly championed women's economic equality, failed to deliver. The union did not prioritize "equal seniority rights for women or the elimination of the sex-specific job classifications that prevented women from 'bumping' into men's jobs as bargaining issues" (Guard, 1996, p. 167) and often resisted women using their seniority rights to claim jobs over men. These complexities explain why even some women's rights advocates are cautious about improving women's economic opportunities by modifying seniority rights (Sheppard, 1984). By contrast, Das Gupta (1996, p. 100) questions whether seniority rights should be left intact if doing so amounts to discrimination against marginalized workers. She speaks approvingly of a United Steel Workers (USWA) collective agreement that gives preference to Indigenous workers in layoff and recall situations, regardless of their seniority.

Union Support for Women Doing Men's Work

The 1970s and 1980s saw a number of "firsts"—first woman in a steel mill, first woman on a construction site, first woman bus driver, first woman police officer (all white)—some with active union support. Unions at Stelco (a steel producer in Hamilton, Ontario, now US Steel), CN, Gaz Métropolitain, and elsewhere publicly championed women's rising economic aspirations and supported their right to hold any job they were qualified to perform. But that willingness was (and often continues to be) contingent on the formal equality expectation that women will do a job in exactly the same way and under exactly the same conditions as men. Accordingly, when women raise concerns about their working conditions or appear to fall short in job performance, their gender difference is commonly taken as evidence that they are not fit for these jobs.

This formal equality proposition is not realistic. If women are to succeed in jobs created by men for men, some accommodation must be made. Among other things, a separate locker room must be built, correctly sized safety equipment must be provided, and consideration must be given to the woman whose baby-sitter does not show up. As Luxton and Corman (1991) observed about the integration of women into Stelco in the late 1970s, "It was impossible for the women simply to be workers. They were always women first, women working in a male workplace" (p. 67). This dynamic applied everywhere. The fact that women are not "like men" has made it difficult for some to succeed in jobs structured for men's bodies or men's social practices.

Neither managers nor male workers have found the hiring of women into male-dominated workplaces easy to navigate. In her study of women guards in a US men's prison, Zimmer (1987) discovered that newly hired women were given poor performance reviews because they used different techniques to gain prisoners' compliance with the rules. In contrast to male guards, who used shows of force to secure prisoners' cooperation, female guards were more likely to establish friendly relationships that proved to be just as effective in an emergency. The fact that women chose a different approach because they could not count on the support of their male coworkers was overlooked. Similarly, GM and Inco, a nickel and copper mining company in Sudbury, Ontario (now called VALE), soon found themselves in dispute with their unions over their decisions to exclude women (but not men) from production jobs that exposed workers to chemicals like lead that are particularly injurious to the fetus. In this instance, concerns for women's reproductive health raised awkward questions about the impact of hazardous materials on men (Fudge, 1991).

The integration of women into previously all-male work spaces and processes has challenged union leaders as well as managers to question their belief that workers whose skills and abilities do not mirror those of the existing workforce would necessarily underperform. This has proven to be a false assumption, yet it remains a lively point of contention in industries such as forestry where physical strength and willingness to work in dangerous conditions are highly prized (Mills, 2011). The necessity of representing these "new" groups has pushed unions to think in new ways about women workers' rights. How, why, and to what extent gender differences should be accepted and supported is an ongoing project. Gradually, through practice (not theory), many unions have come to see that a strict application of formal equality thinking—the principle that all workers must always be treated alike—addresses some but not all of the challenges faced by women members. Resolving practical problems such as mothers' need to be available to children in case of emergency edged unions toward substantive equality thinking. This approach does not accept that gender equality is achieved when women are treated just like men, but asks rather whether women are disadvantaged by workplace policies or practices. This would be the case in many factories where workers are not permitted to call out or receive phone calls during work time. Negotiating permission for women to check on their children's welfare would be a sensible accommodation of their family-care responsibilities. However, such a proposal could be seen as unfair, as special rules for women, by workers who adhere to a strict formal-equality definition of fairness. An astute union could avoid this outcome by advocating that all workers with family-care responsibilities be permitted to receive calls from children when needed—a substantive equality solution that would benefit many fathers as well as mothers.

The shift from formal to substantive equality thinking is critical for gender equality, as Tawnney Meiorin's grievance demonstrates. In 1994, Meiorin was dismissed from her job as a firefighter for the British Columbia Ministry of Forests after three years on the job because she failed a newly instituted physical fitness test. Her employer believed that Meiorin's lesser physical fitness would jeopardize her safety and the safety of her coworkers and the public. Her union disagreed and filed a grievance on her behalf, which it pursued aggressively and successfully, all the way to the Supreme Court of Canada (*British Columbia [Public Service Employee Relations Commission] v. BCGSEU*, 1999).

The support of the British Columbia Government and Service Employees Union (BCGSEU) for Meiorin was both ordinary and remarkable: ordinary because unions almost always fight dismissal cases, and remarkable because it defended Meiorin's right to a job that required a standard of physical fitness that she could not attain, even with practice. The union's challenge was remarkable as well because it rejected the argument that women must be "like men" to be employed in "men's work." When, as in this case, women don't measure up to employer expectations, a substantive equality analysis questions whether the qualifications demanded by the employer are actually necessary to perform the job successfully or just happen to be those of the men currently doing the job. In its defence of Meiorin, the union argued that the fitness requirement discriminated against women, who, on average, are physiologically less able to do aerobic work than men. They also critiqued the lack of evidence to support the employer's claim that its new standard of physical fitness was necessary for firefighters to perform their jobs safely.

This case made legal history—we now have the "Meiorin test" to determine whether job requirements are truly necessary to perform the job successfully. If not, they can be challenged, putting another crack in the wall of job segregation by gender. This approach is now used in grievance arbitration and by human rights tribunals across Canada. Thus, the beneficiaries are not just union women, but also nonunion women, racialized workers, disabled workers, and others who may not be hired because they are stereotyped by employers who assume they are less able to perform the job than white or male applicants.

Willingness to reconsider established policies and practices is not universal. Mills's (2011) investigation of an employment equity initiative at a Saskatchewan forestry firm reveals limited union support. The union went along with targeted hiring of white and First Nations women (and men) for production jobs, but was unwilling to consider part-time work for women with children and voted against a proposal to expand apprenticeship training if two positions were filled by "diversity" hires. The apprenticeship proposal was rejected, Mills argues, because the majority of the members believed that seniority is a fair, nondiscriminatory mechanism for allocating scarce job opportunities. Reality is more complex: seniority is a fair way to reward the contributions of longer-service workers, but it cannot correct for years of discriminatory hiring practices.

Modifying seniority systems to correct for past discrimination is a highly controversial and as yet unused remedy on behalf of a class of workers in Canada. Dulude (1995) pointed out that the failure to give women retroactive seniority in the *Action Travail des Femmes* case against CN meant that women's progress had been minimal. As new employees, women were placed at the bottom of the seniority list and therefore were vulnerable to layoff and not likely to be recalled. This was not an isolated outcome. In all the male-dominated firms that opened their doors to women in the 1980s, women's place at the bottom of seniority lists and application of the "last in, first out" principle meant that almost all were soon back on the street because of restructuring and downsizing (Sheppard, 1984).

WOMEN'S ACCESS TO BREADWINNER WAGES

Union fair-pay practices, past and present, have both advanced and blocked women's economic aspirations. There is no question that union women today are far better off than their nonunion counterparts. The Canadian Labour Congress (2018) reported an average pay advantage of $6.89 per hour for union compared to nonunion women in 2013. Union women, including racialized women, also earn more in relation to union men. In 2013, the gender gap in pay was 16% in the union sector versus 29% in the nonunion sector.

Protecting the Breadwinner Advantage

Union fair-pay practices in the 1940s, 1950s, and 1960s were purposefully designed to ensure that all male members, including the unskilled, earned a wage sufficient to support a family. This focus, which made it possible for racialized as well as white men to earn breadwinner wages, was widely popular in post–World War II Canada. At that time, relatively few women were employed outside the home and typically only until they married. Most Canadians, women and men, union and nonunion, agreed that good jobs should go to men, and they did not expect women to earn a man's wage.

The gender gap in pay in unionized workplaces was significant—often the highest-paid woman earned less than the lowest-paid man (Guard, 1996; Sugiman, 1994)—yet union women were substantially better paid than their nonunion counterparts. In the late 1960s, the wage difference between women and men who performed the same jobs in the same manufacturing establishments was 11% in unionized workplaces compared with 22% in nonunion workplaces (Gunderson, 1975). This considerably smaller gender gap in the union sector resulted from the bottom-up wage policy adopted to increase the wages of unskilled and semiskilled men; it also reflected industrial unionism's commitment to building worker solidarity and fairness (Forrest, 2007).

Union women were also more likely to have access to fringe benefits and family benefits. Securing and expanding these benefits was a union priority, and the needs of the male breadwinner topped the list. Medical and dental coverage, vacations with pay, and retirement pensions were central concerns; pregnancy leave with or without pay was not. As with many government programs, women did not always have equal access to union-negotiated benefits packages (Bossen, 1975). But even when women were covered on the same basis as men, they were disadvantaged when benefits were related to seniority or pay. Pensions are a good example. Mothers who left the workforce or worked part-time to accommodate their families' needs earned fewer years of pension credit, which, when coupled with women's lower wages, resulted in substantially smaller retirement benefits.

The breadwinner focus of union fair-pay bargaining also disadvantaged gay men (and doubly disadvantaged lesbians), who could not claim family benefits such as bereavement leave, dental coverage for dependants, or survivor benefits for their same-sex partners. Union attitudes toward lesbian and gay members started to shift in the 1980s. LGBTQ+ activists came out in their workplaces and pushed their unions to address their unequal status. Initially, their key demand was the inclusion of sexuality in no-discrimination clauses in collective agreements, which unions in the 1980s needed to file grievances on behalf of their LGBTQ+ members. Some unions also supported complaints to human rights tribunals or defended the claims of their LBGTQ+ members in the courts (Hunt & Eaton, 2007). Another strategy was to negotiate a wider definition of *spouse*, for example, "a spouse of either gender," which would automatically extend family benefits to same-sex partners and their children.

Today, protection for LGBTQ+ workers is provided by human rights codes and available to all employees, union and nonunion. Technically, this means that same-sex benefits coverage is universal: where family benefits are provided, coverage must extend to LBGTQ+ families. But entitlement is not the same as access. Same-sex benefits can be claimed only if workers come out, and it is doubtful that all LBGTQ+ workers feel safe revealing their sexuality. In this respect, union members are undoubtedly better off than their nonunion counterparts. Many unions are formally committed to LBGTQ+ inclusion and run educational campaigns encouraging visibility and acceptance. In these workplaces, LBGTQ+ workers should expect to be supported by their union if they encounter harassment or discrimination. By contrast, LBGTQ+ workers in nonunion workplaces often have no one to speak or act on their behalf.

Pay the Job, Not the Worker

"Pay the job, not the worker" was (and is) foundational to the union concept of fair pay. By contrast with nonunion workplaces, where pay is often individualistic and secret, pay systems in unionized workplaces tie wages to jobs and wage rates are published in collective agreements. This approach was designed to ensure that workers who perform the same job are paid the same wage. Women as well as men have benefited from the strict application of this principle. Any hint that one seamstress or payroll clerk might be earning less than her coworker for reasons not provided for in the collective agreement would be investigated. If the discrepancy was not resolved quickly, unions routinely filed grievances on the lower-paid worker's behalf.

Rigorous application of "pay the job" has minimized managerial bias and pay discrimination against immigrant, racialized, and Indigenous women, who are often disadvantaged in the hiring process. The extent of this bias is well established. Das Gupta (1996, pp. 35–40) describes the struggles of black health-care workers, who are commonly stereotyped as infantile or troublesome, hired to perform jobs below their skill level, or subjected to overly vigilant supervision.

Union application of the "pay the job" principle has been good for union women, for example, when unions pressed employers to pay women the established rate for the job when they were temporarily assigned to do men's work (to avoid downward reclassification of men's work once it had been successfully performed by a woman, Tillotson [1991] argues). In other situations, unions were not so quick to act. It was not until 1976 that the RWDSU took up the complaint of a Dominion Store worker who had been performing the job of male clerks for five years but was paid the female rate (*Dominion Stores Ltd.*, 1976). It took the Service Employees International Union (SEIU) until 1978 to correct the pay difference between female nurse's aides and male orderlies employed by the Sunnyside Home in London, Ontario, whose job duties were the same but for the gender of the patient (*Waterloo [Regional Municipality]*, 1978).

The union movement's lack of focus on gender equality is also evident in the treatment of part-time workers, two-thirds of whom are women (Organisation for Economic Co-operation and Development [OECD], 2018). While it is true that organized part-time workers are substantially better off than their non-union counterparts—on average, the hourly wage of unionized part-time work is one-third higher (Uppal, 2011)—part-time work is often a female job ghetto, even in unionized workplaces. Many part-timers perform the same work as their full-time counterparts and would have benefited from the "pay the job" rule; however, this is not what has happened. In most industries, part-time workers' wages were (and are) lower and their benefits fewer than their full-time counterparts. By union practice and public policy, part-time jobs are often in part-time-only bargaining units and seniority districts, which institutionalizes the "lesser-than" status of part-time workers and limits their access to full-time jobs.

These outcomes reflect the long-standing union belief that part-time workers are a threat to the standard of living and job security of full-time workers. This is a legitimate fear, as more and more employers seek to lower wage costs by substituting part-time for full-time labour. One solution to this dilemma would be to significantly reduce the wage differential between full- and part-time workers, which would counterbalance the economic incentive to hire more part-time labour. But in most industries, this has not been the solution chosen.

Equal Pay for Equal Work

In mid-20th-century Canada, equal pay for equal work was a men's, not a women's, issue. How jobs are paid in relation to each other was (and is) of critical importance to workers, and unions sought to negotiate wage structures that reflected differences in job duties rather than employers' sense of job worth. In the immediate post–World War II years, industrial unions focused on raising wages from the bottom up, which increased the wages of the lowest-paid workers most. The result was a smaller wage differential between skilled and unskilled workers and a narrower pay gap between racialized and white men. These efforts were successful. Many studies demonstrate that men's wages are less variable in the union than in the nonunion sector of the economy, even though nonunion men are more alike in their income-earning characteristics (Fortin et al., 2012).

The evolution of equal pay for equal work as a women's issue began with the fair-pay laws of the 1950s, but did not come to the fore until the rise of the women's movement 20 years later. As late as 1969, only 5% of 500 collective agreements covering 500 or more employees included equal pay language (*Report of the Royal Commission on the Status of Women*, 1970, para. 207). In the interim, neither women nor men expected women to earn a man's wage. In unionized workplaces, as everywhere, pay for women was set below that of men and in relation to what other women earned. This difference was justified in part by the breadwinner ideology and in part by the belief that women's jobs were inherently less skilled and less demanding than men's. Defenders of this system argued that to earn men's wages, women must be "like men" and perform jobs that required the same skill sets and the same forms and degree of effort and responsibility, under the same working conditions.

As interpreted and applied by most governments, employers, and unions, the "equal pay for equal work" principle protected only women whose jobs were the same as or similar to jobs routinely performed by men in the same establishment. The "same or similar"—not identical—test offered room to argue on behalf of women; in practice, however, even small differences were used to justify higher wages for men. One advocate for equal pay explained how this loophole undercut the value of fair-pay legislation: "A man and a woman worked beside each other on a machine, and turned out the same number of parts. … But in the last five minutes or so, the man's job was to wheel away the truck load of finished parts, and the women's job was to clean up the machine." This was an insubstantial difference, he argued, yet commonly used to discriminate against women (cited by Tillotson, 1991, p. 543).

Differences in the physical demands of men's and women's work were commonly asserted to suppress women's wages. The pay gap between male nursing orderlies and female nonregistered nursing assistants is a well-known example. In *Riverdale Hospital v. Ontario* (1973), the hospital sought to maintain a lower women's wage on the grounds that only men were required to lift patients. However, the inquiry in the case learned that women also did a great deal of lifting and that women and men worked cooperatively to accomplish heavy lifts. In the adjudicator's opinion, the greater use of physical strength by male orderlies, if it existed, was a marginal difference in the context of the job as a whole. But in 1971 the Hotel and Restaurant Employees and Bartenders International Union lost its grievance on behalf of female waiters employed by MacDonald Tavern in Edmonton who were paid less than male waiters because the waiters were expected to act as bouncers from time to time. However, there were no written job descriptions and the union claimed that managers, not workers, were responsible for keeping order. Nonetheless, the possibility that waiters occasionally acted as bouncers led the arbitrator to decide in management's favour without considering how the waitresses also helped maintain order (*MacDonald Hotel*, 1971). This justification of differences in duties continues to influence pay decisions. As a case in point, Soni-Sinha and Yates (2013) report that even today unionized women janitors are often paid less than men in industrial cleaning because the women's responsibilities—dusting, vacuuming, and arranging furniture—are labelled "light duty" compared to the "heavy duty" sweeping, buffing, and waxing done by men.

The "equal pay for equal work" standard entitles women to be paid like men only when their jobs are the same or very nearly the same as those performed by men. But this was and is rarely the case. Most women perform jobs that require a different complement of skill, effort, responsibility, and working conditions than men's jobs. Women's jobs are no less complex or demanding, but comparability is often difficult to see when the measuring rod uses men's work as the marker of value. This dilemma is best illustrated by the case of Beatrice Harmatiuk, who in

1983 was forced to take her pay complaint to the Saskatchewan Human Rights Commission because her union twice refused to file a grievance on her behalf. Harmatiuk's all-female housekeeper job was paid less than the all-male caretaker job, even though it was similar in skill, responsibility, and working conditions. The caretaker job scored ahead of the housekeeper job in the hospital's job evaluation scheme because of its marginally greater physical demands, while the extra mental effort required of housekeepers who interacted with patients was invisible to both the union and the employer (*Harmatiuk v. Pasqual Hospital*, 1983).

Pay Equity

By the 1980s, it was clear to union women that no amount of "pay the job" or "equal pay for equal work" would close the pay gap rooted in job segregation by gender. Trained to see the world through men's eyes, male union leaders were not sensitive to the value inherent in traditional women's work, nor could they imagine comparing white-collar, production, or service jobs performed by women to blue-collar jobs performed by men. True fair pay for women required a different lens: equal pay for work of equal value.

Pay equity makes it possible to compare jobs across the gender gap in occupations. This is accomplished by replacing traditional male-centred definitions of skill, effort, responsibility, and working conditions with a gender-inclusive schema and by setting wages for female-dominated jobs in relation to male-dominated jobs of comparable worth. This approach takes into account the full complement of skill, effort, responsibility, and working conditions, making it possible to compare school secretaries, whose jobs require multi-tasking, patience, attention to detail, and responding to the needs of distraught students and parents, with school janitors, whose jobs require more physical activity and technical skill, notwithstanding the significant differences in women's and men's work.

Pay equity quickly became the bargaining demand of choice for women unionists. Where it has been implemented, outcomes have been good. The final report of the Pay Equity Task Force (2004, pp. 111–140), appointed by the federal government to review the pay equity provisions of the Canadian Human Rights Act, provides ample evidence of benefits. In the Canadian public service, pay equity bargaining has raised the wages of many predominantly female job classes: librarians, x-ray technicians, clerks, typists, and cashiers have all received substantial pay increases. Haiven (2007) describes many more successes. For example, in 2003, after 17 years, female emergency dispatchers in the Vancouver Police Department won pay increases of $22,000 to $33,000 based on their comparison with male fire dispatchers. In that same year a group of five unions won a $414 million settlement on behalf of women whose path to pay equity was blocked by the Ontario government when it changed the law and made it impossible for many public sector workers to identify male comparators in different bargaining units. Union leadership and professional expertise have been essential to these successes. Implementation of pay equity is technical and time-consuming—new job descriptions must be written, a gender-neutral wage evaluation system created, and male-dominated comparator jobs identified. Only then can the skill, effort, responsibility, and working conditions in women's jobs be compared with those of men. Unrepresented workers cannot take on these tasks independently of management, nor do they have the resources to pursue a case year after year or chase management through the legal system, as the Public Service Alliance of Canada (PSCA), the Canadian Union of Public Employees (CUPE), and other unions have been forced to do (Haiven, 2007).

But the news is not always good. Pay equity, which could close the gender pay gap in workplaces where men hold the majority of full-time positions and women the majority of part-time jobs, has not been consistently pursued with this end in mind, Kainer (1998) discovered. Her investigation of the pay equity process in grocery stores led her to conclude that the United Food and Commercial Workers (UFCW) union was more interested in wage gains for full-time men than part-time women, even though part-timers were the majority of employees and performed exactly the same jobs as full-timers. The union saw part-time workers as temporary and less committed to the workplace, so thought it entirely proper that part-time jobs be compared with other part-time jobs, which preserved the gender gap in pay.

Overall, the principle of equal pay for work of equal value has taken root only where it has been mandated by law, Bentham (2007) argues. By 2005, only one-quarter of collective agreements in Canada contained pay equity clauses, and most were in the public sector (Bentham, 2007). Union leaders, particularly those at the local level, were slow to see closing the gender gap in pay as a social justice issue, rather than a narrow women's issue, and some have been hesitant to pursue pay equity at the bargaining table. Prioritizing pay increases for women workers can be divisive in economically tough times. Unions also fear backlash from their male members who believe their work is inherently more demanding than "women's work" and, so, deserving of higher pay. Haiven (2007) recounts a successful application of pay equity by CUPE in a Saskatchewan school board that was resisted by school caretakers (a predominantly male job classification pertaining to janitorial and building maintenance services) who simply could not believe their jobs were less skilled than those of teacher assistants and secretaries! As a sign of their disgust, the men sought and were granted permission to create a separate CUPE local.

WOMEN'S ACCESS TO BREADWINNER STATUS

Today, women expect unions to represent their interests as workers and as women. This is a significant shift in expectations. Unions were built by men for men on the assumption that men were family breadwinners and women were secondary workers who would always put home and children ahead of their jobs. In that worldview, men's economic and social interests defined workers' issues and set the union collective bargaining agenda. By contrast, issues of particular concern to women, such as maternity leave and sexual harassment, were less important "women's issues." When exercised, the union voice on behalf of women has been a force for change. But the framework of male privilege and the ethos of worker solidarity also mean that union commitment to women members has been less than wholehearted.

Maternity Rights

There is no clearer marker of women's gender difference than pregnancy. In a society like ours, which disproportionately loads responsibility for children's well-being onto women's shoulders, motherhood shapes women's life choices and economic opportunities.

Prior to 1971, pregnant women were on their own: only British Columbia and New Brunswick guaranteed six weeks of leave before and after birth, and no jurisdiction provided income supports while women were unable to work or guaranteed their right to return to work. Most employers viewed pregnancy as a woman's private decision and saw no reason to accommodate her situation. A 1966 survey (Woodsworth, 1967) found that one in four employers granted no leave, and then only at the employer's discretion. Most employers expected pregnant women to resign and fired those who did not. Whether a woman would be reemployed after the birth of her child was also a matter of employer discretion. If she was rehired, it was likely as a new employee in a lower-paying entry-level position.

Union attitudes were somewhat more generous. Most of the dismissal grievances filed on behalf of women in this era involved marriage and pregnancy, which suggests that women wanted to contest management's inflexibility and their union's failure to negotiate protections (Sangster, 2011). When unions pressed the matter to arbitration their arguments varied: if the policy requiring pregnant women to resign was unwritten, the union claimed the dismissal was without cause; if the collective agreement permitted leaves for legitimate personal reasons, the union claimed that refusing to grant leave was an unreasonable exercise of managerial discretion. There was no talk of women's rights at arbitration—there were none—so challenges to the status quo were largely unsuccessful. As long as the language in the collective agreement did not expressly give rights to pregnant women, most arbitrators believed they did not exist (*Loblaw Groceterias Co. Ltd.*, 1962; *Quaker Oats Co.*, 1960).

By the mid-1960s, the union movement was publicly pro-woman. Addressing the Royal Commission on the Status of Women in Canada in 1968, both the Canadian Labour Congress (CLC, 1968) and the Ontario Federation of Labour (OFL, 1968) affirmed their support for women's equality and called for legislation protecting married or pregnant women from dismissal. They also advocated for paid maternity leave and women's right to return to work after pregnancy.

Even so, unions were slow to take up the matter at the bargaining table. Neither the CLC nor the OFL spokesperson would commit to more aggressive bargaining on these issues. Negotiating protections for pregnant women was a low priority for most union negotiators in the 1950s and 1960s because they saw pregnancy as a women's issue, not a workers' issue (Guard, 1996; Sangster, 2011; Sugiman, 1994). Where unions did act, they improved women's job security. Though few in number, most of the workplaces that assured pregnancy leave in the 1966 survey did so under the terms of a collective agreement. Employers bound by collective agreements were also more likely to provide partial income support and maintain workers' seniority (Woodsworth, 1967).

The lives of working women in Canada were made immeasurably easier in 1971 when the Unemployment Insurance Act was amended to guarantee 17 weeks of maternity leave subsidized through the unemployment insurance system. Related changes to employment standards acts also assured women of their right to return to their previous job or a comparable job following leave. In some jurisdictions seniority was retained but not increased; in others, seniority accumulated during the period of leave (Pulkingham & Van Der Gaag, 2004).

These rights have been expanded by union action. In 1979 the Québec Common Front of public sector unions prioritized improved maternity benefits in its negotiations with the government of Quebec. The final settlement, which covered one-fifth of the province's female workforce, extended unpaid maternity and parental leave to two years, required the employer to top up unemployment insurance benefits to 93% of regular pay for up to 20 weeks, and ensured the continuation of benefits during leave (Labour Canada Women's Bureau, 1985). Two years later, the Canadian Union of Postal Workers (CUPW) won 17 weeks of fully paid maternity leave (that is, the employer agreed to top up unemployment insurance benefits) after a six-week strike. The CUPW win was particularly significant because women were not a majority of the membership. The union worked hard to gain members' support for paid maternity leave as a bargaining priority, and then, more contentiously, as a strike issue, even as many members questioned why the union would prioritize a benefit for one group of workers (White, 1990).

These wins were seen as breakthroughs that would open the way for many more successes at the bargaining table. This did not happen, however. By 1986, just over 40% of the workers covered by a sample of collective agreements were entitled to some employer top-up of employment insurance benefits during pregnancy leave; 30 years later, this proportion was 50%. This is a slow pace of progress, Bentham (2007) argues. In her view, better supports for child-bearing women continue to be viewed as "separate and secondary" to the main business of unions. Come bargaining time, these and other women's issues are less likely to be on the priority list and more likely to be among the first demands dropped.

This assessment is more positive if we also consider how unions have used the grievance arbitration process to ensure that the law is fully and generously applied. In one instance, the union successfully challenged the 1998 firing of an Ontario woman employed by Parry Sound Social Services when it was discovered that she was pregnant, even though the collective agreement did not permit the union to grieve on behalf of employees dismissed during their probationary period (Mitchnik & Etherington, 2012). The case was sent all the way to the Supreme Court of Canada and was not decided until 2003, five years after the woman was dismissed (Mitchnik & Ethington, 2012). In another case the Ottawa Police Association secured the grievor's right to return to her previous job as a court liaison case manager after her maternity leave over management's objection (*Ottawa Police Services Board v. Ottawa Police Assn.*, 2007). For the most part, the beneficiaries of these wins have been other union members. From time to time, arbitration decisions also improve the working conditions of non-union women as well, as happened when arbitrators ruled that employers could not reduce benefits such as paid vacation or sick leave because workers had taken pregnancy/parental leave. Following this decision, the Ontario government amended the Employment Standards Act to protect all workers (Mitchnik & Etherington, 2012).

Dignity on the Job

Women's status as workers and union members has expanded significantly over the last 80 years. Changing social mores and innovative ideas about gender equality offer today's women more freedom of choice with respect to their personal and career decisions. Not that long ago, wearing pants, a hijab, Afro hairstyles, and tattoos that did not conform with an employer's definition of professionalism or provoked complaints from customers or clients would have been grounds for discipline or dismissal. Consider the situation of women at Wardair, a successful privately held charter airline whose owner imposed his heterosexist ideas about appearance on his employees. In the 1980s women flight attendants were required to wear high heels and company-approved brassieres; their makeup, hairstyles, and weight were monitored by management; and they were not permitted to wear glasses or pants on the job. Women who did not conform to these rules were disciplined (*C.U.P.E. v. Wardair Inc.*, 1988).

In a nonunion workplace, these indignities would generate resentment, but workers would comply because they feared losing their jobs. At Wardair, however, CUPE filed both a human rights complaint contesting these unreasonable and sexist rules and a grievance challenging management's decision to suspend an outspoken union official for two weeks without pay because she talked to the press (*C.U.P.E. v. Wardair Inc.*, 1988). No woman or group of women would have the resources to hire a lawyer, find expert witnesses, and devote the time needed to pursue such violations of their rights.

Organized women are also better protected when they experience sexual harassment. In 1989, the Supreme Court of Canada ruled that sexual harassment was a form of gender discrimination and therefore unlawful. The employer's claim that the harassment was about women's attractiveness, not gender, was dismissed and the connection to male power and abuse of power established (*Janzen v. Platy Enterprises Ltd.*, 1989). This was an important gain for women that unions have helped solidify. Cases such as *Osprey Care Inc.* (2012), in which a male coworker at a long-term care home in Penticton, British Columbia, followed the victim home and then made sexual advances, and *Alberta (Solicitor General)* (2011)—in which a woman guard in a correctional institution was picked up by her male coworkers and carried to the men's locker room, where her pants were forcibly undone before the incident was interrupted—demonstrate the need for protection from sexual harassment.

But the advantage of union representation comes with a caveat: unions leaders are willing to pursue harassment grievances against managers without reservation, but when the allegation is laid against male coworkers, women cannot always count on the unequivocal support of their union. In these situations, union leaders face complicated cross-cutting loyalties. On the one hand, they are obligated by law to represent all workers, even those who are in the wrong. On the other hand, they are also obligated to defend women's right to work free from behaviours that can range from annoying to frightening.

How these tensions play out is difficult to discern. Hart's (2012) analysis of grievance arbitration cases from 1992 to 2008 led her to conclude that many unions were biased in favour of the accused. She points to union arguments that underplayed the seriousness of the offender's behaviour, for example, by calling it rude rather than harassing or by denying that the behaviour was harassment because the accused did not have organizational power over the victim. In other cases documented by Hart, the union attacked the victim's credibility in a manner that left her feeling humiliated, claimed that the victim had imagined the incident, or claimed that the complainants were conspiring against the accused because he faced allegations from a number of women. In a separate analysis, Haiven (2006) found that unions were more likely to adopt an aggressive defence on behalf of the accused in workplaces with zero-tolerance policies, which increase the likelihood of dismissal.

Hart's analysis suggests that unions side too readily with the accused and sometimes do so in ways that reinforce antiwoman stereotypes and rape myths. But this would be an incomplete conclusion. In real-life labour relations, relatively few grievances go to arbitration; most are settled informally between the union and the employer and the outcome is unknown. Another complicating factor is the role of lawyers. Arbitration as a process is legalistic and conflictual. Technically, lawyers take their instructions from the union or client, but this rarely happens in practice. The lawyer's expertise coupled with the union leaders' desire to distance themselves from complicated and controversial cases means that lawyers' tools of the trade such as aggressive cross-examination can be used against complainants.

Unions are aware of their dual roles, and more than a few leaders have experienced crises of conscience in harassment cases. Some unions are taking steps to ensure that both the victim and the accused are fully represented (White, 1993). Examples include the CUPE, which now assigns two grievance officers—one to the complainant and one to the accused—who report independently to the local union president; USWA, which now encourages union-led mediation (rather than adjudication) of harassment disputes; and the Public Service Alliance of Canada (PSAC), which, by contrast, advises its members to file a grievance against the employer, even if the harasser is a coworker. Notably, both PSAC and Unifor have decided that the union has the right to refuse to represent a member who has been disciplined for sexual harassment when the employer's decision is warranted.

Assessing the quality and effectiveness of union representation of racialized women members working in hostile environments or subjected to racial harassment is even more challenging. We know these problems exist. Examples of everyday racism abound (Das Gupta, 1996; Irish, 2016; Seputis, 2012; *Working While Black in Nova Scotia*, 2018), yet grievance arbitration cases are difficult to identify. It may be that unions have been successful in getting these matters resolved informally, without resorting to arbitration. It is much more likely that union leaders, like many Canadians, are in denial about the extent of racism and white privilege in the workplace. Backhouse (1999), following Dionne Brand (1994), argues that Canadians hold determinedly to the "mythology of racelessness" and often demonstrate "stupefying innocence" (pp. 13–14) in the face of overtly racist behaviour. Thus, it is very possible that union officials simply cannot see racial harassment for what it is, and do not pursue grievances on behalf of racialized women workers.

Das Gupta's (1996) description of workplace racism supports this analysis. She summarizes the findings of two external investigations of racism in health-care settings conducted in 1985 and 1994 that documented unjust dismissals and layoffs, accusations that racialized staff use allegations of racism to avoid accountability for shoddy work, discipline for disagreeing with a supervisor and suspension without pay for arguing with a white colleague (who was not disciplined), heavier duties in less specialized areas, and institutional failure to fairly investigate and resolve complaints against black health-care workers, among others. Das Gupta's own interviews with nursing staff echoed these experiences. The women described many undermining and humiliating encounters with white supervisors, including the targeting of outspoken nurses of colour, a performance review that labelled a black nurse "incompetent" despite her unblemished work record, discipline for mistakes for which white nurses were offered help to improve, and the refusal to accommodate black nurses' requests for time off during Caribana, an annual celebration of Caribbean culture. Yet Das Gupta barely mentions these nurses' unions. In some situations, workers filed complaints with the Ontario Human Rights Commission, but it is unclear whether they were assisted by their union. Only once does Das Gupta say that the union was asked for help and was successful in having a complaint withdrawn.

CONCLUSION

Today's union leaders proudly proclaim their support for gender equality, and all major unions approach collective bargaining with this mindset. The mid-20th-century fixation on the needs of the male breadwinner no longer guides union decision-making, and action to advance women's rights is as likely to be framed by working women's experiences and aspirations as by the formal equality belief that women must be like men to have the economic opportunities and entitlements available to men. This profound shift in worldview is the accomplishment of three generations of feminist activists and the women and men who have called their leaders to account for the trade-offs made in negotiations or pushed their union to file grievances to advance their equality claims. The result is a more inclusive, gender-, race-, and sexuality-sensitive approach to collective bargaining that is securing women's right to dignity and respect on the job as well as improving their job opportunities and standard of living and helping resolve tensions between work and home.

This disruption of past practices was possible in large part because of changes in equality laws. In the span of a lifetime, Canadian law has moved from taking for granted employment practices that held women back simply because they were women to confirming the legitimacy of women's needs as women and as workers. Organized women were best positioned to capture the benefits of these changes. Union economic power, legal authority, and deep pockets made it possible for union women to solidify and expand their legal rights through collective bargaining and in so doing help make them available to nonunion women as well.

But this is not the whole story. Gender equality is unfinished business: progress has been slow and uneven, and obstacles remain. Turning the abstract principle of gender equality into rights on the job requires leadership, persistence, and a willingness to redefine "good union practice." At the local level, where bargaining priorities are set and decisions about grievances made, support for equity policies set by the union's national office can be diffuse, and the leadership must work within the politics of majority decision-making. Progress toward equality has been slow as well because the gender division of labour has been frozen in place by past practice and proposals for change that modify long-established seniority rights are highly controversial.

Unionism in Canada today struggles to represent all workers on their own terms. This strong commitment to social justice harkens back to the movement's more activist mid-20th-century roots, but with a contemporary focus on inclusion and diversity.

ACKNOWLEDGEMENT

Thank you to Sydney Chapados for her research assistance on this chapter.

KEY READINGS

Bentham, K. (2007). Labour's collective bargaining record on women's and family issues. In G. Hunt & D. Rayside (Eds.), *Equity, diversity, and Canadian labour* (pp. 101–129). Toronto: University of Toronto Press.

Forrest, A. (2009). Bargaining for equality: A path to union renewal. In J. Foley & P. Baker (Eds.), *Unions, equity, and the path to renewal* (pp. 97–118). Vancouver: UBC Press.

Haiven, J. (2007). Union response to pay equity: A cautionary tale. In G. Hunt & D. Rayside (Eds.), *Equity, diversity, and Canadian labour* (pp. 75–100). Toronto: University of Toronto Press.

Hunt, G., & Eaton, J. (2007). We are family: Labour responds to gay, lesbian, bisexual and transgender workers. In G. Hunt & D. Rayside (Eds.), *Equity, diversity, and Canadian labour* (pp. 130–155). Toronto: University of Toronto Press.

DISCUSSION QUESTIONS

1. What are some of the advantages of union membership for women?
2. Explain the difference between equal pay for equal work and equal pay for work of equal value/pay equity. Why is a pay equity approach better for women?
3. How does the grievance arbitration process help women achieve better terms and conditions of employment?

REFERENCES

Akyeampong, E. B. (1998). The rise of unionization among women. *Perspectives*. Retrieved from https://www150.statcan.gc.ca/n1/pub/75-001-x/1998004/4043-eng.pdf

Alberta (Solicitor General), 205 L.A.C. (4th) 32 (2001).

Arcila, A., Ferrer, A., & Schirle, T. (2017). Occupational segregation, skills, and the gender wage gap. Retrieved from http://www.payequity.gov.on.ca/en/DocsEN/Dr%20 Tammy%20Schirle_Gender-gap-final_report-2017-March24.pdf

Backhouse, C. (1999). *Colour-coded: A legal history of racism in Canada, 1900–1950*. Toronto: University of Toronto Press.

Bentham, K. (2007). Labour's collective bargaining record on women's and family issues. In G. Hunt & D. Rayside (Eds.), *Equity, diversity, and Canadian labour* (pp. 101–129). Toronto: University of Toronto Press.

Block, S., & Galabuzi, G.-E. (2011). *Canada's colour coded labour market: The gap for racialized workers*. Ottawa & Toronto: Canadian Centre for Policy Alternatives & the Wellesley Institute.

Bossen, M. (1975). *Sex discrimination in fringe benefits*. Ottawa: Advisory Council on the Status of Women.

Brand, D. (1994). *Bread out of stone*. Toronto: Coach House Press.

Briskin, L., & McDermott, P. (Eds.). (1993). *Women challenging unions: Feminism, democracy, and militancy*. Toronto: University of Toronto Press.

British Columbia (Public Service Employee Relations Commission) v. BCGSEU, [1999] 3 S.C.R. 3.

Canadian Labour Congress. (1968). *Canadian Labour Congress submission to the Royal Commission on the Status of Women*. Retrieved from http://riseupfeministarchive.ca/activism/organizations/canadian-labour-congress-clc/clc-1968-submission_to_royal_commission_status_of_women/

Canadian Labour Congress. (2018). Canada's union advantage. Retrieved from http://canadianlabour.ca/why-unions/women/canadas-union-advantage

Creese, G. (1999). *Contracting masculinity: Gender, class and race in a white-collar union, 1944–1994*. Toronto: Oxford University Press.

C.U.P.E. v. Wardair Inc., CarswellNat 888, CarswellNat 889, 76 di 103, 89 C.L.L.C.16,009 (1988).

Das Gupta, T. (1996). *Racism and paid work*. Toronto: Garamond Press.

Dominion Stores Ltd. (1976), 13 L.A.C. (2d) 433.

Dulude, L. (1995). *Seniority and employment equity for women*. Kingston, ON: IRC Press.

Foley, J. R., & Baker, P. L. (Eds.). (2009). *Unions, equity, and the path to renewal*. Vancouver & Toronto: UBC Press.

Forrest, A. (2007). Bargaining against the past: Fair pay, union practice, and the gender gap in pay. In G. Hunt and D. Rayside (Eds.), *Equity, diversity, and Canadian labour* (pp. 49–74). Toronto: University of Toronto Press.

Fortin, N., Green, D. A., Lemieux, T., Milligan, K., & Riddell, W. C. (2012). Canadian inequality: Recent developments and policy options. *Canadian Public Policy, 38*(2), 121–145.

Fudge, J. (1991). Gender issues in arbitration: An academic perspective. In W. Kaplan, J. Sack, & M. Gunderson (Eds.), *Labour arbitration yearbook, 1991* (pp. 119–131). Toronto: Butterworths-Lancaster House.

Guard, J. (1996). Fair play or fair pay: Gender relations, class consciousness and union solidarity in the Canadian UE (United Electrical, Radio and Machine Workers). *Labour/Le Travail, 37*, 149–177.

Gunderson, M. (1975). Male-female wage differentials and the impact of equal pay legislation. *Review of Economics and Statistics, 57*(4), 462–469.

Haiven, J. (2006). Zero tolerance—Can it work in a unionized environment? *Labour/Le Travail, 58*, 169–202.

Haiven, J. (2007). Union response to pay equity: A cautionary tale. In G. Hunt & D. Rayside (Eds.), *Equity, diversity, and Canadian labour* (pp. 75–100). Toronto: University of Toronto Press.

Harmatiuk v. Pasqual Hospital, 4 CHRR 239, D/1177–81 (1983).

Hart, S. (2012). Labour arbitration of co-worker sexual harassment cases in Canada. *Canadian Journal of Administrative Science, 29*(3), 268–279.

Hunt, G., & Eaton, J. (2007). We are family: Labour responds to gay, lesbian, bisexual and transgender workers. In G. Hunt & D. Rayside (Eds.), *Equity, diversity, and Canadian labour* (pp. 130–155). Toronto: University of Toronto Press.

Irish, D. (2016, May 28). Working While Black symposium in Halifax focuses on workplace racism. *CBC News*. Retrieved from https://www.cbc.ca/news/canada/nova-scotia/while-while-black-symposium-1.3605224

Jackson, A. (2005). *Work and labour in Canada: Critical issues*. Toronto: Canadian Scholars' Press.

Janzen v. Platy Enterprises Ltd. [1989] 1 SCR 1252.

Kainer, J. (1998). Pay equity and part-time work: An analysis of pay equity negotiations in Ontario supermarkets. *Canadian Woman Studies, 18*(1), 47–51.

Labour Canada Women's Bureau. (1985). *Maternity and child care leave in Canada*. Ottawa: Ministry of Labour.

Loblaw Groceterias Co. Ltd., 13 L.A.C. 96 (1962).

Luxton, M. (2001). Feminism as a class act: Working-class feminism and the women's movement in Canada. *Labour/Le Travail, 48*, 63–88.

Luxton, M., & Corman, J. (1991). Getting to work: The challenge of the Women Back into Stelco campaign. *Labour/Le Travail, 28*, 149–185.

MacDonald Hotel (1971), 23 L.A.C. 433.

Mills, S. (2011). The difficulty with diversity: White and aboriginal women workers' representations of diversity management in forest processing mills. *Labour/Le Travail, 67*, 45–67.

Mitchnik, M., & Etherington, B. (2012). *Labour arbitration in Canada* (2nd ed.). Toronto: Lancaster House.

Ontario Federation of Labour. (1968). *Ontario Federation of Labour submission to the Royal Commission on the Status of Women*. Retrieved from http://riseupfeministarchive.ca/activism/organizations/ontario-federation-of-labour/ofl-1968-submissionroyal commissionstatuswomen/

Organisation for Economic Co-operation and Development. (2018). Incidence of FTPT employment—common definition. Retrieved from https://stats.oecd.org/viewhtml.aspx?datasetcode=FTPTC_I&lang=en

Osprey Care Inc., 223 L.A.C. (4th), 274 (2012).

Ottawa Police Services Board v. Ottawa Police Assn., 159 L.A.C. (4th) 129 (2007).

Pay Equity Task Force. (2004). *Pay equity: A new approach to a fundamental right.* Ottawa: Department of Justice.

Pulkingham, J., & Van Der Gaag, T. (2004). Maternity/parental leave provisions in Canada. *Canadian Woman Studies, 23*(3), 116–125.

Quaker Oats Co., 11 L.A.C. 87 (1960).

Reitz, J. G., & Verma, A. (2004). Immigration, race, and labour: Unionization and wages in the Canadian labour market. *Industrial Relations, 43*(4), 835–854.

Report of the Royal Commission on the Status of Women in Canada. (1970). Ottawa: Information Canada.

Riverdale Hospital v. Ontario, 34 D.L.R. (3d) 289 (1973).

Sangster, J. (2011). Discipline and grieve: Gendering the Fordist accord. In *Transforming labour: Women and work in post-war Canada* (pp. 145–198). Toronto: University of Toronto Press.

Seputis, J. (2012, March 5). Toronto jail guard seeks workplace racism investigation. *CBC News.* Retrieved from https://www.cbc.ca/news/canada/toronto/toronto-jail-guard-seeks-workplace-racism-investigation-1.1129238

Sheppard, C. (1984). Affirmative action in times of recession: The dilemma of seniority-based layoffs. *University of Toronto Faculty Law Review, 42,* 1–25.

Soni-Sinha, U., & Yates, C. (2013). "Dirty work?" Gender, race and the union in industrial cleaning. *Gender, Work and Organization, 20*(6), 737–751.

Statistics Canada. (2016). Long term trends in unionization. Retrieved from http://www.statcan.gc.ca/pub/75-006-x/2013001/article/11878-eng.htm#a4

Sugiman, P. (1994). *Labour's dilemma: The gender politics of auto workers in Canada, 1937–1979.* Toronto: University of Toronto Press.

Tillotson, S. (1991). Human rights law as prism: Organizations, union and Ontario's Female Employees Fair Remuneration Act, 1951. *Canadian Historical Review, 72*(4), 532–557.

Townson, M. (1975). Organizing women workers. *Labour Gazette, 75*(6), 349–353.

Uppal, S. (2011). *Unionization 2011.* Statistics Canada, Catalogue no. 75–001–X, Perspectives on labour and income. Ottawa: Statistics Canada.

Waterloo (Regional Municipality) (1978), 20 L.A.C. (2d) 77.

White, J. (1990). *Mail & female: Women and the Canadian Union of Postal Workers.* Toronto: Thompson Educational Publishing.

White, J. (1993). *Sisters and solidarity: Women and unions in Canada.* Toronto: Thompson Educational Publishing.

Woodsworth, S. (1967). *Maternity protection for women workers in Canada.* Ottawa: Department of Labour, Women's Bureau.

Working While Black in Nova Scotia. (2018). Retrieved from https://workingwhileblackns.com/

Zimmer, L. (1987). How women reshape the prison guard role. *Gender and Society, 1*(4), 415–431.

CHAPTER 3

Women's Occupational Health and Safety

Katherine Lippel and Stephanie Premji

INTRODUCTION

The study of occupational health and safety looks at working conditions and the effects of those conditions on the health of workers. More specifically, it deals with the prevention of illness and injury at work, compensation for disability attributable to work, and issues relating to the reintegration of workers after work-related injury or disease. It is important to understand women's occupational health and safety because women make up almost half of the Canadian workforce and the majority of Canadian women spend a significant proportion of their lives doing paid work as well as unpaid work required by their social reproduction roles (caregiving, domestic work). Yet it is our experience that researchers who focus on women's health tend to ignore the fact that they are workers, and work and working conditions are often forgotten in literature on gender and health or women's health (see, for example, Hankivsky, 2012). Parallel to this, those interested in occupational health, be they scientists, regulators, or workplace actors (employers and unions), have also tended to forget that women make up a large proportion of the workforce. This is particularly true in the case of racialized immigrant women, who experience some of the poorest working conditions and related health outcomes relative to other workers, but whose issues and priorities are largely missing from research, policy framing, and public debates on employment in Canada.

A primary reason why it is wrong to be blind to gender when examining occupational health and safety is that men and women do different jobs, sometimes even within the same job titles (Armstrong & Messing, 2014; Messing, 1998). For example, among factory workers, male cutters were found to generally use machines whereas female cutters tended to use scissors (Premji, Lippel, & Messing, 2008). When men and women perform the same tasks they may still be exposed to different risks. In nontraditional jobs, women may perform the same tasks as men, but they may be the subject of violence and harassment (Legault, 2001) and provided with personal protective equipment designed for men's bodies. As Karen Messing (1998) has documented in her seminal work on women's occupational health, the hazards of paid work traditionally done by women, who are disproportionately in fields such as teaching and nursing, tend to be less visible than those to which men are exposed in typically male-dominated professions such as construction, mining, and trucking. Women often work in caring professions involving emotional labour, and the constraints of that work are often invisible to regulators and the workers themselves. The hazards to which racialized immigrant women are exposed are even less visible as they are more likely to work in "back of the house" jobs that either hide them from the public or carry an expectation of invisibility, such as cleaning (Messing, 2014). The tasks that women perform as caregivers, cleaners, teachers, and nurses are often viewed as an extension of unpaid work in the household and, as such, their work is undervalued because it is perceived to come naturally to women and often presumed to be light. Lifting 50 pounds of bricks is perceived as heavy work. Lifting a 50-pound child seems natural, doesn't seem to be work at all, and is certainly not seen as comparable to heavy work such as that done by bricklayers.

When women become ill, it is important for medical practitioners to question them about the paid work they do, yet historically (Dembe, 1996), and even today, the medical profession may be unaware of or uninterested in the working conditions of women (Lippel, 2003). This lack of awareness or interest may be particularly salient in the case of racialized immigrant women because of assumptions about labour market activities based on factors such as gender, culture, religion, and age, for example, assumptions that racialized immigrant women are not working or that they are working in light jobs. Recognition of the link between women's work and their health problems is important for diagnosis and treatment and for the determination of causality, which has implications for prevention and compensation. It is equally important for workplace parties and regulators to recognize the hazards of women's work so they can be prevented, and, if they become ill, so women can receive just compensation when disabled because of their work.

This chapter relies on an intersectional framework (Hankivsky, 2012). Intersectionality, which comes from the work of African American feminist scholars (Crenshaw, 1989), rejects a focus on any one category of analysis such as gender, racialized status, or social class. Instead, it favours the examination of different aspects of social identity in interaction, while linking microlevel dynamics to broader power relations. In the context of health research, Hankivsky (2012) has argued that a primary focus on gender and sex can undermine our understanding of the complexities of experiences of different types of women. Indeed, women are not a monolithic group, and differences among women are often as significant as between men and women. At the same time, within particular groups there exist considerable gender differences. For example, in reporting on research on temporary foreign workers and regulatory effectiveness of occupational health and safety protections, scholars have discussed the importance of being aware of layers of vulnerability (Sargeant & Tucker, 2009), with gender as one of several variables that can increase or decrease that vulnerability. In the same vein, research on racialized inequalities in occupational health has found that in some cases, inequalities were more evident or more pronounced among women (Premji & Lewchuk, 2014). A study in Spain found that social class was an important determinant of health for workers of both genders, but pathways varied, since "among men, part of the association between social class positions and poor health can be accounted for [by] psychosocial and physical working conditions and job insecurity. Among women the association between the worker, … class positions and health is substantially explained by working conditions, material well being at home and amount of household labour" (Borrell, Muntaner, Benach, & Artazcoz, 2004, p. 1869). Gender, class, migration, and **racialization**, as well as other factors such as religion, culture, age, sexual orientation, and geography, can therefore intersect in various ways to create highly uneven patterns of work and health.

Racialized immigrant women are overrepresented at the very bottom of the occupational ladder in low-paid, high-risk, and precarious jobs that are highly racialized and feminized (Noack & Vosko, 2011). Their labour market experiences are also characterized by underemployment, informal employment, intermittent or chronic unemployment, unpaid work (e.g., volunteering), and, in some cases, time- and resource-intensive skills training and job searching in an attempt to improve their situation (Access Alliance, 2014). Many racialized immigrant women work in factories, cleaning, or low-prestige service-sector jobs (for example, as personal support workers) where they face musculoskeletal and psychosocial risks and health problems, among others (Premji & Shakya, 2017). Their difficult working conditions are rooted in complex labour market and social barriers to decent employment, such as the lack of recognition of foreign credentials, discrimination by employers, and religious and cultural gendered role expectations (Premji et al., 2014). Government and settlement agency policies and programs can also serve to stream racialized immigrant women into low-paid and high-risk jobs. An example is the Quebec government–sponsored Petites Mains (Little Hands) sewing machine operator training program for low-income racialized immigrant women: sewing is a racialized and feminized occupation that involves highly repetitive work and low pay. Repetitive work can lead to musculoskeletal problems such as tendonitis, and pay may be based on productivity, such as piecework, which provides incentives to work intensively (Premji, Lippel, & Messing, 2008). These barriers are persistent and, in many cases, racialized immigrant women face cumulative long-term exposure to poor working conditions (Premji et al., 2014). In addition, their social and economic position means that they often lack the agency and support structures, such as unions, to address their conditions.

In this chapter we will first document the importance of retaining an intersectional lens when studying occupational exposures and their consequences for women's health and safety. We will then turn to women's right to compensation under workers' compensation legislation to see how the trivialization of women's work may lead to discrimination and denial of benefits, even though regulators and decision-makers may be unaware that the premises on which they rely are vehicles of discrimination. We start with a review of some of the common risks and health problems found in women's jobs and how these may be experienced differently by different groups of women.

INTERSECTIONAL ANALYSIS AS A KEY TO EFFECTIVE PREVENTION

Women's paid work and its associated hazards are often ignored by scientists such as epidemiologists and medical doctors, and science determines regulatory attention in many cases. If a substance such as asbestos is shown to be dangerous to workers' health, there is a greater chance that regulators will limit exposures and, in some cases, ban the use of the product; however, if there is little research, it is unlikely they will turn their attention to the product.

For example, research on occupational cancer has been shown to focus on jobs done by men, and many studies fail to include women—even, in some cases, women working in those jobs. For example, a woman who worked in a uranium mine told us she had been excluded from the studies documenting the health consequences of radon exposure in the mine where she worked, as the researchers wanted to study a homogeneous population. Our knowledge about occupational causes of cancers affecting women is much scantier than about cancers affecting men, a trend that was first noted in the early 1990s and continues to this day (Hohenadel, Raj, Demers, Hoar Zahm, & Blair, 2015; Hoar Zahm, Pottern, Lewis, Ward, & White, 1994). While scholars have attempted to document this type of **systemic discrimination** by which women's cancers are made to be invisible (Paiva, 2016), noting in particular that workers from racialized minorities (Hoar Zahm et al., 1994) and immigrants (Paiva, 2012) are particularly invisible, there is still little research on occupational cancers affecting women, a problem made worse by the fact that there is less and less research on occupational causes of cancer affecting workers in general (Raj, Hohenadel, Demers, Zahm, & Blair, 2014). Sometimes, because they have been little studied, women's work-related health problems are erroneously attributed to genetic, hormonal, or psychological causes or even to imagination. For example, women's symptoms of organic solvent exposure have been wrongly attributed to "hysteria" (Brabant, Mergler, & Messing, 1990).

Because traditional women's work looks less dangerous, there are fewer studies on the effects of that work, but when researchers focus on women's jobs they find there are significant risk factors to which workers are exposed (Messing, 1998). Women's, particularly racialized immigrant women's, work in factories often involves very highly repetitive motions, be it in food production, microelectronics, or textile production, so that while the work appears to be light, the cumulative effect of manipulating the weight of each processed object multiplied by the high number of repetitions is an important risk factor for a variety of musculoskeletal disorders such as tendonitis, epicondylitis, or carpal tunnel syndrome (Vézina, Tierney, & Messing, 1992; Lippel, 2003). The same is true of work involving prolonged standing, which takes its toll on the health of retail sales clerks and cashiers in supermarkets, but which is perceived to be banal by clients, judges, and policy-makers.

Health care is a dangerous occupation because workers are exposed to a variety of hazards: biological hazards such as exposure to infectious diseases;

ergonomic hazards that arise when lifting patients without adequate equipment; chemical hazards associated with the administration of chemotherapy; physical hazards related to exposure to radiation; and hazards associated with working with the public. Health-care workers, including nurses, nurse's aides, and personal support workers in long-term care (Banerjee et al., 2012) are particularly vulnerable to occupational violence, including various forms of assault committed by patients and their families (Lippel, 2018). In 2017 the Ontario Ministry of Labour reported that the health-care sector represented 11.7% of the labour market while 56% of lost-time injuries due to workplace violence occurred among registered nurses (Ontario Ministry of Labour, 2017). Racialized and linguistic-minority women are overrepresented in lower-ranking, front-line nursing professions, where there is a disproportionate risk of violence, as they were in the Banerjee et al. (2012) study. For example, visible minorities made up 15% of the labour force but 21% of nurse's aides in Canada. At the same time, they were underrepresented among managers (9%) and head nurses (8%), positions with authority to address problematic conditions (Premji & Etowa, 2014).

The same working conditions may be experienced differently by different groups of women and may be added to other sources of strain to negatively impact health. For example, the experience of underemployment, which is much more common among immigrant women than Canadian-born women (Galarneau & Morissette, 2009), has been linked to negative health impacts (Premji & Shakya, 2017) and to an increased risk of work injury (Premji & Smith, 2013). The juggling of work activities with skills training, job searching, and volunteering, and with a heavy household and childcare workload (amplified in the postmigration context of social isolation and in the absence of economic resources) can similarly increase workers' total health burden (Premji & Shakya, 2017). Long and difficult commutes by residents of low-income neighbourhoods largely devoid of good employment opportunities can add to the physical and mental strain associated with their employment and other activities (Premji, 2017). Furthermore, social marginalization increases vulnerability to expressions of racism and sexism as well as to harassment and exploitation, for example in the form of excessive expectations (de Castro, Fujishiro, Sweitzer, & Oliva, 2006). Understanding issues of importance to women's occupational health therefore requires an understanding of the experiences of diverse groups of women. Effective prevention of occupational injury and disease requires knowledge and acknowledgement of the specificities of women's working conditions and an understanding of disparities in workplace exposures to hazards.

INTERSECTIONAL ANALYSIS AS A KEY
TO EFFECTIVE WORKERS' COMPENSATION

Workers' compensation is one of the earliest social security systems in Canada, dating back to the beginning of the 20th century. It provides health care, rehabilitation benefits, and salary replacements for workers injured or disabled on the job. In a country like Canada, with little state support for those unable to work because of injury or illness, access to workers' compensation is particularly important as it is one of the few programs that provides income support that is proportional to a worker's preinjury earnings (Lippel, 2012).

Compensation for work-related disability is often more difficult to access for problems frequently affecting women as opposed to the usual claims filed by men. Musculoskeletal disorders and psychological injuries are among the health problems most often associated with women's work, while men are more likely to be exposed to violent accidents causing more visible physical injuries. First, workers are less likely to claim compensation for gradual-onset injuries (such as musculoskeletal injuries that evolve slowly over time) than for traumatic work accidents. In a representative sample of Quebec workers, 80% of workers who had lost time from work because of musculoskeletal problems that they attributed solely to work did not claim compensation (Stock et al., 2014), while 33.5% of those who suffered injury through a traumatic event (such as a fall, being hit by an object, or being involved in a motor vehicle accident) at work failed to report their injuries to the compensation board (Vézina et al., 2011). Among racialized immigrant women, lack of information about workers' compensation and fear of reporting because of low income, insecure status, and lack of proficiency in the majority language, which can be sources of exploitation by employers, contribute to underreporting (Premji, Messing, & Lippel, 2008). Accordingly, factors related to labour market and workplace dynamics can combine with the challenges associated with the establishment of work-relatedness for occupational diseases to minimize reporting of musculoskeletal disorders by women—particularly racialized immigrant women—employed in repetitive work. Given that costs of compensation drive prevention strategies by regulators, these patterns of underreporting disproportionately eclipse negative health consequences of women's jobs (Cox & Lippel, 2008).

Additionally, musculoskeletal disorders and psychological problems are often met with skepticism by regulators and decision-makers and are often contested by employers. Musculoskeletal disorders are among the most frequently compensated injuries in Canada, yet they are also among the claims that are the most likely to be denied or contested because they are invisible injuries in many cases, affecting muscles and tendons, causing incapacitating pain that cannot be perceived on an x-ray. Australian studies documented the difficulties and prejudice that women encountered when trying to access workers' compensation benefits in that country (Reid, Ewan, & Lowy, 1991).

In Quebec, several musculoskeletal disorders are presumed by law to be related to exposure to repetitive work, including tendonitis, bursitis, and tenosynovitis. However, research has shown the process to access compensation for those disorders to be highly litigious, and one study (Lippel, 2003) found that claims by women were disproportionately rejected by the appeal tribunal, in many cases because women's work, while being highly repetitive, was perceived to be light and therefore unlikely to be a cause of disability. The same study found that when medical doctors participated in the decision-making as advisors to the tribunal, women's success rates declined. Although there was no explicit discriminatory discourse, this statistical association led to the conclusion that when decision-making is dominated by reasoning of physicians, it is less likely that compensation will be granted, particularly when the work being done has not been extensively studied, a situation disproportionately affecting women.

Lippel's 2003 study examined decisions rendered by the workers' compensation appeal tribunal between 1994 and 1996 to measure the effect of a major decision rendered in 1993 that had denied benefits to women with tendonitis doing highly repetitive work, including coding postal codes, which involved on average 7,920 keystrokes per hour at Canada Post. In a previous study (Lippel, Messing, Stock, & Vézina, 1999), ergonomists, a physician, and a legal scholar joined together to try to understand that 1993 decision. They found that the judgment denying benefits relied heavily on epidemiological studies that did not fit well with the parameters of women's work and that the legal decision-maker had applied requirements of scientific certainty that health science professionals require, even though the law only requires that the evidence of causation of an illness by work be more probable than the evidence supporting the denial of causation. The decision involving the Canada Post workers led to a decade of decisions that raised the bar for compensation for all workers, a practice that disproportionately affected women, including a large number of racialized immigrant women, whose repetitive work involved a high number of gestures but less forceful individual movements.

The series of studies on musculoskeletal disorders and workers' compensation was conducted in partnership with three Quebec trade union federations, represented by members of their health and safety committees and women's committees. This partnership, l'Invisible qui fait mal (the invisible that hurts), facilitated dissemination of our results (Lippel, 2003) not only to scientific audiences but also to decision-makers and policy-makers in workers' compensation, and to worker representatives in the unions. Several years later Lippel (2009) repeated the study published in 2003 by looking at decisions rendered by the same appeal tribunal in 2006 and found there were no longer statistically significant differences in the success rates of men and women suffering from musculoskeletal disorders who filed workers' compensation claims, a finding that suggests that the situation improved over time.

Similar methods have been used to examine access to workers' compensation for mental health problems such as depression related to work. Lippel's first study (1999) comparing men's and women's claims in appeals for mental health diagnoses found that women's claims were disproportionately denied by the appeal tribunal. We then looked at appeal decisions in Quebec rendered between 1986 and 1994. After examining the medical evidence described by decision-makers and the factual situations they were relying on to make their decisions, we concluded that decision-makers had trivialized the stressful nature of women's work while acknowledging the stressful nature of men's work, even though many of the factual situations were analogous. We also found that decision-makers relied heavily on personal issues in women's lives to deny claims, while not mentioning personal issues of the men who filed claims.

This study was repeated to examine decisions rendered between 1998 and 2002 by the same tribunal, and again for decisions rendered in 2007 and 2008 (Lippel, 2017). No significant differences were found in success rates of men and women in these subsequent studies and, as was the case with our studies on compensation for musculoskeletal disorders described above, we conclude that the partnership with unions facilitated sensitization of decision-makers and union representatives to the importance of avoiding gender bias in the compensation process.

Despite these advances, studies have shown that the hazards in women's work continue to be understudied (Hohenadel et al., 2015), underestimated (Paiva, 2016), or misunderstood, as exemplified by a study (Premji, Lippel, & Messing, 2008) on Quebec workers' compensation appeal decisions involving piecework that found that employers and the tribunal lacked understanding of the complex reality of piecework as lived by the workers, a lack of understanding in many cases amplified by language barriers.

Recent regulatory reforms in Ontario relating to compensation for mental injuries attributable to workplace stress provide another illustration of the need to remain vigilant with regard to gender equality. Quebec has never excluded chronic stress from the definition of compensable injury, unlike several other Canadian provinces, including Ontario (Lippel & Sikka, 2010). Because the majority of claims for mental health problems related to chronic stress are submitted by women (Commission des normes, de l'équité, de la santé et de la sécurité du travail, 2016), an exclusion of this type of claim from the purview of the law disproportionately affects women workers. In 2017 Ontario revised that exclusion (Stronger, Healthier Ontario Act, 2017), although the changes and related policy suggest that access to compensation for mental health problems attributable to chronic stress will be more difficult than access to compensation for other health problems, allowing for different evidentiary thresholds for different illnesses, a proviso that could again adversely affect women.

As previously noted, violence against nurses is a particularly acute problem in Ontario, as admitted by the Ontario Ministry of Labour (2017). Thus, there is a certain irony in the fact that another recent regulatory reform in Ontario, in 2016, recognized post-traumatic stress disorder for first responders in its list of scheduled diseases presumed to be work-related but did not include nurses in the list of professions benefiting from the presumption. The occupations listed were all stereotypically male, including firefighters, ambulance service managers, paramedics, police officers, and prison guards (An Act to Amend the Workplace Safety and Insurance Act, 2016). Nurses were finally included in the presumption in 2018 (Plan for Care and Opportunity Act, 2018).

In 2018 violence in the workplace was on the agenda of the International Labour Conference, where there were discussions to adopt an international convention on the issue. There is evidence that LGBTQ workers are particularly vulnerable to occupational violence (Ferfolja, 2010; Rabelo & Cortina, 2014; Sangganjanavanich & Cavzos, 2010), and Canada, among other countries, sought to promote better protections for LGBTQ workers (International Labour Conference, 2018). Although much of the proposed convention was adopted, the provisions mentioning LGBTQ workers were not, as some delegations were adamantly opposed to their mention in the convention and the recommendation (International Labour Conference, 2018). This example illustrates the challenges of promoting inclusive regulatory protections in international venues such as the International Labour Conference.

At times lack of recognition by the workers' compensation legislation itself can negatively impact certain groups of women more than others. In Quebec domestic workers employed by individuals in private homes are excluded from the definition of *worker* under the legislation that addresses compensation and rehabilitation for occupational injuries and illnesses in that province. This means that domestic workers are not eligible for workers' compensation unless they pay their own premiums, as individuals who employ domestic workers are not obliged to pay workers' compensation premiums. This contrasts with the situation of all other workers in Quebec, who are automatically covered without paying premiums themselves. In 2008 the Commission des droits de la personne et des droits de la jeunesse (CDPDJ [Commission for Human and Youth Rights]) ruled that the exclusion of domestic workers was discriminatory on the triple bases of sex, social class, and ethnicity, as the work is largely done by low-income, racialized women. Despite this ruling, in 2018 domestic workers remain excluded from workers' compensation legislation in the province despite a long-standing campaign by community organizations and unions.

Thus far we have talked about challenges to equitable access to workers' compensation. We now turn briefly to the application of compensation rules when compensation coverage is accepted. One issue of importance is the right to support for returning to work after an injury, in particular the right to vocational rehabilitation. If a worker is unable to return to preinjury employment because of a permanent impairment resulting from her injury, she has the right, in most provinces, to support from the workers' compensation board to get help in returning to the labour market. Women often occupy jobs that are underpaid in relation to the skills they require. Workers who are immigrants, both men and women, are often obliged to take jobs for which they are overqualified. In both cases, the pay they earn does not reflect their true earning capacity. Workers' compensation provides benefits based on earnings at the time of the injury and provides rehabilitation sufficient to enable workers to attain the same earning capacity. When workers are underpaid at the time of their injury, they are less likely to access a robust rehabilitation program because their qualifications allow them, at least theoretically, to earn the same low salary they were earning before their injury. These compensation mechanisms leave women and immigrant workers of both sexes with insufficient support to return to meaningful employment that allows them to use their skills. For example, a plumber and a childcare worker both obtained college certificates in their professions. If each is injured at work and becomes unable to continue in their chosen profession, the plumber, who has a higher salary than the childcare worker, will be more likely to receive retraining, while the undervalued childcare worker will be considered able to earn the low preinjury pay she received from her work with children by occupying other low-wage but less interesting jobs (Cox & Lippel, 2008).

In summary, workers' compensation provides benefits to those who are injured or become ill because of their work, but the way systems are designed or applied allows for lesser protections for women in some circumstances because of the nature of the work they do, the nature of the injuries they suffer from, or the undervalued work they do at the time of injury (Cox & Lippel, 2008). The same is true of other categories of workers, for example, recent immigrants who are employed in jobs for which they are overqualified.

CONCLUSION

While this chapter shows that many challenges persist for obtaining equal treatment of men and women in occupational health and safety and workers' compensation, the news is not all bad. Partnerships between researchers and civil society, including unions, in the case of l'Invisible qui fait mal, have been shown to provide better conditions for ensuring that the right research questions are asked and that the research results have an impact. Policies by funding bodies such as the Canadian Institute for Health Research's policy on the integration of gender and sex in research designs when appropriate have helped push forward a better integration of gender issues in occupational health research. Interdisciplinary research bringing together health scientists, social scientists, and policy specialists promotes more effective change by providing evidence to decision-makers in a language they can understand. However, there remains work to be done, particularly in bringing to light the work and health issues of racialized immigrant women, a shift that requires their involvement in knowledge and policy development. The impact of this invisibility is significant because a lack of visibility results in a lack of recognition and compensation, and therefore a lack of incentive for employers to address the health problems in women's jobs. As the occupational health problems of women—particularly marginalized women—continue to be invisible in mainstream research and policy discussions, it is important to bring into focus how structural inequalities intersect in complex and cumulative ways to shape everyday experiences of work and health.

KEY READINGS

Armstrong, P., & Messing, K. (2014). Taking gender into account in occupational health research: Continuing tensions. *Policy and Practice in Health and Safety*, *12*(1), 3–16.

Cox, R., & Lippel, K. (2008). Falling through the legal cracks: The pitfalls of using workers' compensation data as indicators of work-related injuries and illnesses. *Policy and Practice in Health and Safety*, *6*(2), 9–30.

Messing, K. (1998). *One-eyed science: Occupational health and women workers*. Philadelphia: Temple University Press.

Premji, S., & Shakya, Y. (2017). Pathways between under/unemployment and health among racialized immigrant women in Toronto. *Ethnicity and Health, 22*(1), 17–35.

DISCUSSION QUESTIONS

1. Discuss three things that need to be considered to provide better protection of women's health and safety at work.
2. Give two examples of ways in which workers' compensation legislation can fail to provide adequate support for women who are injured or made ill by their work.
3. Discuss how intersectionality can help us understand women's work and health experiences.

REFERENCES

Access Alliance Multicultural Health and Community Services. (2014). *Like wonder women, goddesses, and robots: How immigrant women are impacted by and respond to precarious employment*. Toronto: Author.

An Act to Amend the Workplace Safety and Insurance Act, 1997 and the Ministry of Labour Act with Respect to Posttraumatic Stress Disorder, SO c. 4, 2016, 14(2).

Armstrong, P., & Messing, K. (2014). Taking gender into account in occupational health research: Continuing tensions. *Policy and Practice in Health and Safety, 12*(1), 3–16.

Banerjee, A., Daly, T., Armstrong, P., Szebehely, M., Armstrong, H., & Lafrance, S. (2012). Structural violence in long-term, residential care for older people: Comparing Canada and Scandinavia. *Social Science and Medicine, 74*(3), 39–398.

Borrell, C., Muntaner, C., Benach, J., & Artazcoz, L. (2004). Social class and self-reported health status among men and women: What is the role of work organisation, household material standards and household labour? *Social Science and Medicine, 58*(10), 1869–1887.

Brabant, C., Mergler, D., & Messing, K. (1990). Va te faire soigner, ton usine est malade: La place de l'hystérie de masse dans la problématique de la santé des femmes au travail. *Sante Mentale au Québec, 15*(1), 181–204.

Commission des normes, de l'équité, de la santé et de la sécurité du travail. (2016). *Statistiques sur les lésions attribuables au stress en milieu de travail (2011–2014)*. Retrieved from http://www.cnesst.gouv.qc.ca/Publications/300/Pages/DC_300_321.aspx

Cox, R., & Lippel, K. (2008). Falling through the legal cracks: The pitfalls of using workers' compensation data as indicators of work-related injuries and illnesses. *Policy and Practice in Health and Safety, 6*(2), 9–30.

Crenshaw, K. (1989). Demarginalizing the intersection of race and sex: A black feminist critique of antidiscrimination doctrine, feminist theory and antiracist politics. *University of Chicago Legal Forum*, *139*, 139–167.

de Castro, A. B., Fujishiro, K., Sweitzer, E., & Oliva, J. (2006). How immigrant workers experience workplace problems: A qualitative study. *Archives of Environmental and Occupational Health*, *61*(6), 249–258.

Dembe, A. E. (1996). *Occupation and disease. How social factors affect the conception of work-related disorders.* New Haven, CT: Yale University Press.

Ferfolja, T. (2010). Lesbian teachers, harassment and the workplace. *Teaching and Teacher Education*, *26*(3), 408–413.

Galarneau, D., & Morissette, R. (2009). Immigrants' education and required job skills. *Perspectives on Labour and Income*, *9*(12), 5–18.

Hankivsky, O. (2012). Women's health, men's health, and gender and health: Implications of intersectionality. *Social Science and Medicine*, *74*(11), 1712–1720.

Hanley, J., Premji, S., Messing, K., & Lippel, K. (2010). Action research for the health and safety of domestic workers in Montreal: Using numbers to tell stories and effect change. *New Solutions*, *20*(4), 421–439.

Hoar Zahm, S. H., Pottern, L. M., Lewis, D. R., Ward, M. H., & White, D. W. (1994). Inclusion of women and minorities in occupational cancer epidemiologic research. *Journal of Occupational Medicine*, *36*(8), s842–s847.

Hohenadel, K., Raj, P., Demers, P. A., Hoar Zahm, S., & Blair, A. (2015). The inclusion of women in studies of occupational cancer: A review of the epidemiologic literature from 1991–2009. *American Journal of Industrial Medicine*, *58*(3), 276–281.

International Labour Conference. (2018, June 8). Fifth item on the agenda: Violence and harassment against women and men in the world of work. 107th Session, Geneva.

Legault, M.-J. (2001). Violence auprès des femmes dans les secteurs d'emploi non traditionnellement féminins et indemnisation. *PISTES*, *3*(1).

Lippel, K. (1999). Workers' compensation and stress: Gender and access to compensation. *International Journal of Law and Psychiatry*, *22*(1), 79–89.

Lippel, K. (2003). Compensation for musculoskeletal disorders in Quebec: Systemic discrimination against women workers? *International Journal of Health Services*, *33*(2), 253–281.

Lippel, K. (2009). Le droit québécois et les troubles musculo-squelettiques: Règles relatives à l'indemnisation et à la prévention. *Pistes*, *11*(2). Retrieved from https://journals .openedition.org/pistes/2381

Lippel, K. (2012). Preserving workers' dignity in workers' compensation systems: An international perspective. *American Journal of Industrial Medicine*, *55*(6), 519–536.

Lippel, K. (2017). Workers' compensation for work-related mental health problems: An overview of Quebec law. In L. Lerouge (Ed.), *Psychosocial risks in labor and social security law* (pp. 291–304). Cham, Switzerland: Springer.

Lippel, K. (2018). Conceptualising violence at work through a gender lens: Regulation and strategies for prevention and redress. *University of Oxford Human Rights Hub Journal*, *1*(1), 142–166.

Lippel, K., Messing, K., Stock, S., & Vézina, N. (1999). La preuve de la causalité et l'indemnisation des lésions attribuables au travail répétitif: Rencontre des sciences de la santé et du droit. *Recueil annuel de Windsor d'accès à la justice/Windsor Yearbook of Access to Justice*, *17*, 35–85.

Lippel, K., & Sikka, A. (2010). Access to workers' compensation benefits and other legal protections for work-related mental health problems: A Canadian overview. *Canadian Journal of Public Health*, *101*(S.1), 16–22.

Messing, K. (1998). One-eyed science: Occupational health and women workers. Philadelphia: Temple University Press.

Messing, K. (2014). *Pain and prejudice*. Toronto: Between the Lines.

Noack, A. M., & Vosko, L. F. (2011). *Precarious jobs in Ontario: Mapping dimensions of labour market insecurity by workers' social location and context*. Toronto: Law Commission of Ontario.

Ontario Ministry of Labour. (2017). *Preventing workplace violence in the health care sector*. Retrieved from https://www.ontario.ca/page/preventing-workplace-violence-health-care-sector#section-8

Paiva, M. (2012). Des femmes invisibles. *Plein droit*, *2*(93), 21–24. doi:10.3917/pld.093.0021

Paiva, M. (2016). *De l'invisibilité des cancers d'origine professionnelle à l'invisibilisation des risques cancérogènes dans le travail des femmes*. Doctoral dissertation, University of Paris, France.

Plan for Care and Opportunity Act (Budget Measures), S.O. 2018, c. 8, Schedule 37.

Premji, S. (2017). Precarious employment and difficult daily commutes. *Relations Industrielles/ Industrial Relations*, *72*(1), 77–98.

Premji, S., & Etowa, J. B. (2014). Workforce utilization of visible and linguistic minorities in Canadian nursing. *Journal of Nursing Management*, *22*(1), 80–88.

Premji, S., & Lewchuk, W. (2014). Racialized and gendered disparities in health and safety among Chinese and white workers in Toronto. *Ethnicity and Health*, *19*(5), 512–528.

Premji, S., Lippel, K., & Messing, K. (2008). "We work by the second!" Piecework remuneration and occupational health and safety from an ethnicity- and gender-sensitive perspective. *Pistes*, *10*(1). Retrieved from https://journals.openedition.org/pistes/2193

Premji, S., Messing, K., & Lippel, K. (2008). Broken English, broken bones? Mechanisms linking language proficiency and occupational health in a Montreal garment factory. *International Journal of Health Services*, *38*(1), 1–19.

Premji, S., & Shakya, Y. (2017). Pathways between under/unemployment and health among racialized immigrant women in Toronto. *Ethnicity and Health*, *22*(1), 17–35.

Premji, S., Shakya, Y., Spasevski, M., Merolli, J., Athar, S., & Precarious Employment Core Research Group. (2014). Precarious work experiences of racialized immigrant women in Toronto: A community-based study. *Just Labour*, *22*, 122–143.

Premji, S., & Smith, P. (2013). Education-to-job mismatch and the risk of work injury. *Injury Prevention*, *19*(2), 106–111.

Rabelo, V., & Cortina, L. (2014). Two sides of the same coin: Gender harassment and heterosexist harassment in LGBQ work lives. *Law and Human Behavior*, *38*(4), 738–391.

Raj, P., Hohenadel, K., Demers, P. A., Zahm, S. H., & Blair, A. (2014). Recent trends in published occupational cancer epidemiology research: Results from a comprehensive review of the literature. *American Journal of Industrial Medicine*, *57*(3), 259–264.

Reid, J., Ewan, C., & Lowy, E. (1991). Pilgrimage of pain: The illness experiences of women with repetition strain injury and the search for credibility. *Social Science and Medicine*, *32*(5), 601–612.

Sangganjanavanich, V., & Cavzos, J. (2010). Workplace aggression: Toward social justice and advocacy in counselling for transgender individuals. *Journal of LGBT Issues in Counselling*, *4*(3), 187–201.

Sargeant, M., & Tucker, E. (2009). Layers of vulnerability in occupational safety and health for migrant workers: Case studies from Canada and the UK. *Policy and Practice in Health and Safety*, *7*(2), 51–73.

Statistics Canada. (2017). *The surge of women in the workforce*. Retrieved from http://www.statcan.gc.ca/pub/11-630-x/11-630-x2015009-eng.htm

Stock, S., Nicolakakis, N., Raïq, H., Messing, K., Lippel, K., & Turcot, A. (2014). Underreporting work absences for nontraumatic work-related musculoskeletal disorders to workers' compensation: Results of a 2007–2008 survey of the Québec working population. *American Journal of Public Health*, *104*(3), e94–e101.

Stronger, Healthier Ontario Act (Budget Measures), S.O. 2017, c. 8, schedule 33.

Vézina, M., Cloutier, E., Stock, S., Lippel, K., Fortin, É., Delisle, A., … Prud'homme, P. (2011). Québec survey on working and employment conditions and occupational health and safety (EQCOTESST): Summary (RR707). Montreal: Institut de recherche Robert-Sauvé en santé et en sécurité du travail. Retrieved from https://www.irsst.qc.ca/media/documents/PubIRSST/RR-707.pdf

Vézina, N., Tierney, D., & Messing, K. (1992). When is light work heavy? Components of the physical workload of sewing machine operators which may lead to health problems. *Applied Ergonomics*, *23*(4), 268–276.

CHAPTER 4

Unemployed and Underemployed Women in Canada

Leslie Nichols

INTRODUCTION

As of October 2018 approximately 1.14 million Canadians were unemployed, an unemployment rate of 5.7% (Statistics Canada, 2018e). **Underemployment** means working less than full-time or working at a job that is below a person's level of skills, education, or experience and cannot fulfill economic needs. In 2018 3.5 million Canadians worked part-time (Statistics Canada, 2018d). Underemployment is connected to lower wages and job satisfaction, and poorer physical and psychological health (Verbruggen, van Emmerick, Van Gils, Meng, & de Grip, 2015). A history of precarious employment (part-time, temporary work) can make it difficult to access employment insurance benefits during periods of unemployment.

Unemployment and underemployment can have harsh impacts on financial stability, physical and mental health, and the overall well-being of individuals and families. People in certain social categories suffer greater hardship as a result of unemployment and underemployment because of their more tenuous connection to the labour market, marginalization, and weaker social supports to sustain them during a life crisis. Those include women, racialized people, Indigenous people, older and younger workers, low-income individuals, and people with disabilities. People who have more than one of these fundamental traits or social conditions are at even greater disadvantage as their rate of unemployment and underemployment is higher and they have fewer resources for coping during periods of insufficient income. This chapter will examine how unemployment and underemployment impact Canadian women and compare differences in the issues that men and women face in relation to these experiences, with an emphasis on women across diverse vulnerable social groups and how those social categories intersect. By understanding how women in diverse circumstances experience unemployment and underemployment, policy-makers can better tailor policies to support the lived reality of working in the current labour market and women's equality in the workforce.

In June 2018 the unemployment rate for women 25 and over was 5%, and for men it was 5.2% (Statistics Canada, 2018c). Overall, women's unemployment rate tends to be lower than men's, in part due to the types of jobs that women are employed in. More men have left the labour force in recent years as jobs in fields such as manufacturing and construction suffered more downsizing during the recession that began in 2008 than jobs in fields such as education and health care, in which more women are employed. Thus, the employment rate may mask employment issues that impact women more than men, including underemployment and access to financial benefits when they are unemployed.

Women's unemployment and underemployment have been strongly affected by the dominance of neoliberal social and economic policies since the 1980s. A prime example of the hardship that neoliberal policies have caused is Canada's unemployment insurance program. The Unemployment Insurance Act was introduced in 1940 to provide financial support to unemployed soldiers returning from World War II and help them rejoin the labour market. Unemployment Insurance (UI) was a central component of the Canadian welfare state. Over the years UI underwent a series of transformations marked by both expansion and restriction of benefits. In 1996 the program was renamed **Employment Insurance** (EI) to reflect the shift toward the neoliberal philosophy.

The new EI policy instituted in 1996 changed the concept of who deserved financial support during unemployment and the amount of support they received. Access to EI benefits was made more difficult by increasing the hours of previous employment required for eligibility (Nichols, 2016b). This change especially impacted people who did not have full-time long-term jobs, particularly women and the marginalized groups mentioned above. Thus, the new policy favoured members of the workforce who were most likely to hold full-time jobs, while penalizing and further marginalizing those who were most in need of support to survive periods of unemployment and return to the workforce.

UNEMPLOYMENT AND UNDEREMPLOYMENT: THE CORE DATA

The official unemployment rate in Canada has held steady between about 6% and 8.5% over the past decade, with the highest rate occurring during the 2008 recession. But simple unemployment rate statistics cannot fully capture the employment situation of Canadian workers. The unemployment rate only considers people who are part of the labour force, defined narrowly as those who are working or actively looking for work. This definition does not include people who have stopped looking for work due to a lack of available jobs (called **"discouraged workers"**), women who have left the labour market because they can't afford childcare while working, older people who retired early because they were unable to find work, and so on. Many of these individuals are alienated from the workforce not by choice but by economic and social conditions. If these willing workers were included in the definition of the labour force, the unemployment rate might be considerably higher. Moreover, the unemployment rate calculates the number of unemployed people at the specific moment of the survey, leaving out those who were unemployed at other times during the year. Thus, there may be a significant difference between the government's official unemployment rate and the "lived" rate experienced by Canadians. Shields, Silver, and Wilson (2006, p. 107) found that including people who had been unemployed at some point during the preceding year more than doubled the official Canadian unemployment rate during the period from 1993 to 2001; at that time, the official unemployment rate was 8.7%, while the more accurate rate was 19.9%.

Statistics Canada also tallies unemployment among discouraged searchers; workers who are waiting to be recalled to their jobs, waiting for replies from employers, or waiting to begin working at a distant future date; and involuntary part-time workers. When those workers are added to the official unemployment rate of 6.1% for July 2018, the rate rises to 8.9% (Statistics Canada, 2018i).

Unemployment in Canada has been connected to global economic trends over the last 10 years. Following the 2008 recession, the average duration of an individual's unemployment in Canada increased from about 15 weeks to about 21 weeks (table 4.1). In July 2018, the rate of unemployment lasting one year or more was 0.5%, and the rate for three months or more was 1.8% (Statistics Canada, 2018i).

Table 4.1: Duration of Unemployment in Canada, 2007–2017

Year	Duration of unemployment (weeks)
2007/2008	15.3
2008/2009	14.9
2009/2010	18.4
2010/2011	20.4
2011/2012	21.1
2012/2013	20.6
2013/2014	21.1
2014/2015	20.6
2015/2016	19.8
2016/2017	20.3

Source: Adapted from Employment and Social Development Canada, 2018.

IMPACTS OF UNEMPLOYMENT AND UNDEREMPLOYMENT

Financial Impacts

Household financial security is essential for the well-being of workers and their families. Even with full-time employment, certain groups of people—including those with less education, single individuals, and renters—are at higher risk of financial insecurity in the form of excessive debt, physical and mental health issues (which have a direct impact on income), and lack of access to basic necessities (Chawla & Uppla, 2012, p. 3). Unemployed and underemployed people are at even greater risk. Once an individual becomes unemployed, lack of financial resources may interfere with efforts to return to the labour market, for example, to cover the cost of transportation, childcare, and clothing for interviews.

Workers who have accumulated the required work hours may be eligible for EI if they lose their job, but the amount of their EI benefit may be insufficient for survival as it amounts to only 55% of one's previous salary (Employment and Social Development Canada [ESDC], 2018). Starting in January

2018 the maximum EI weekly benefit was $547, but the average payout during 2016/2017 was only $447 ($1,788 per month; ESDC, 2018). By contrast, the 2018 cost of living for a family of four in a three-bedroom apartment outside the city centre was about $5,426 a month in Halifax, $4,875 in Montreal, $7,442 in Toronto, $4,823 in Winnipeg, and $6,579 in Vancouver, according to the Numbeo database. Those figures do not include the cost of childcare, health services, or income taxes. Clearly, Canadians cannot survive on 55% of their salary. Moreover, according to the *Globe and Mail* (Canadian Press, May 15, 2018), one-quarter of Canadians have almost no savings set aside for emergencies like loss of a job, and 56% have saved less than $10,000, which would only cover two to three months of living expenses.

Workers who are involuntarily employed part-time earn considerably less than full-time workers. In 2018 the average hourly wage for a part-time female worker was $19.73 compared to $26.70 for a full-time female worker (Statistics Canada, 2019). When part-time workers lose their jobs, they may find that they have not accumulated enough hours to qualify for EI, compounding their financial vulnerability.

Health Impacts

Although the 1984 Canada Health Act established universal health care, it does not cover all needed health services and related items, including prescription drugs, dental care, eye glasses, optometry, and long-term care. There are also limitations on mental health services and medical specialists. Thus, Canadians cover about 30% of their overall health-care needs through private insurance or employee benefits. Private health insurance costs an average of $1,800 per person per year. Those who lack private insurance pay out of pocket for services not covered by federal health insurance. Unemployed or underemployed workers may experience difficulties accessing needed medical services and medications. They may have lost their extended health-care benefits from their previous employer or, if they are underemployed, they may not have an extended plan that includes drugs and other medical care that is available to full-time workers as an added job benefit. They may not be able to afford transportation or childcare to go to medical appointments.

The stresses of unemployment and underemployment have a direct harmful impact on physical and mental health. These stresses can exacerbate preexisting health issues at a time when the individual's access to treatment has been reduced, interfering with self-care and attempts to return to work.

As people lose control of their work and finances their sense of self-agency and hope for the future decline. They often experience depression and anxiety and may turn to unhealthy coping mechanisms such as drugs and alcohol. These issues can lead to additional physical health problems, setting up a cycle of un-employment or underemployment, diminishing health, and reduced likelihood of returning to the labour force (Nichols, 2014).

Deskilling and Underemployment

Many workers who face underemployment also experience **deskilling**. Deskilling is a strategy used by employers to reduce their costs by refusing to recognize workers' education and work experience and either placing them in work that is below their level of skill or paying them a wage that is below their skills. Deskilling makes it difficult for qualified workers to find adequate employ-ment and obtain promotions. Man (2004) reports in her study of highly skilled Chinese immigrant women in Canada that they were deskilled into insecure and part-time positions, if not unemployed, due to Canada's immigration and settlement policies that devalue the skills of immigrant women. Similarly, young women workers are often deskilled in the labour market due to negative stereo-types about their potential to contribute to the workplace (Tyyskä, 2014).

GENDER DIFFERENCES IN UNEMPLOYMENT AND UNDEREMPLOYMENT

Hours Worked and Salary

There is a normative belief in our society that all adults are workers and that they all have a similar life cycle with respect to the labour market (Nichols, 2013). There are two problems with this belief. First, it does not take into account the many life events that may cause people to leave the labour market tempor-arily or permanently. Second, it ignores the important roles that people have beyond their work that consume their time, as citizens, community members, parents, and so on. Women, specifically, are expected to play a central role in the home, and indeed their work as mothers and homemakers is essential to society (Cooke & Gazso, 2009; Nichols, 2013; Pupo & Duffy, 2003).

Canadian women spent 3.9 hours a day on unpaid household tasks in 2015 and 3.9 hours on paid work, while men spent 5.2 hours on paid work and 2.4 hours on unpaid work (Moyser & Burlock, 2018). Calculated over one week, women spend 27.3 hours on unpaid labour, while men spend 16.8 hours—a difference of over 10 hours. In the course of one year, this difference adds up to more than two months of 8-hour days. These statistics reveal a gendered arrangement of household work that enhances men's socioeconomic status while leaving women financially dependent on their male partner. This in turn increases women's vulnerability in the event of a divorce and, in some cases, traps them in domestic violence.

The data suggest that women are slightly less likely to be unemployed than men, but it is important to understand the type of work that women do, and how much they earn. In 2014 Canadian women earned 88 cents to each dollar earned by men ($25.38 an hour for women compared to $28.92 for men; Moyser, 2017b). This salary difference can be attributed in part to women's overrepresentation in part-time work. In 2015 more than three times as many women (18.9%) were working part-time as men (5.5%; Moyser, 2017b). A similar trend is seen with full-time work: in 2014 women employed full-time earned 74% of men's salaries—$52,500 compared to $70,700 (Moyser, 2017b). Women's lower work hours and overrepresentation in part-time work have significant repercussions for both unemployment statistics and employment insurance benefits when they become unemployed.

Men were more impacted than women by the 2008 global recession. In 2009, 7% of women and 9.4% of men were unemployed (Ferrao, 2010), possibly because women were overrepresented in areas that saw growth, such as health care, social assistance, educational services, insurance, and real estate, while industries dominated by men, such as construction, manufacturing, and primary industries, experienced shrinkage during the downturn (Statistics Canada, 2015, 2016). But much of the difference in the unemployment rates for men and women may be explained by the increase in part-time jobs, in which women are overrepresented.

Freedom to Choose Whether and How Much to Work

One reason for women's lower work hours and salary is the number of hours they spend doing unpaid domestic labour, sometimes referred to as women's "second shift" (Hochschild & Machung, 1989). As the number of women in the workforce increased after World War II, it was hoped that men would take on their share of the household tasks. But, in fact, that has not happened (Hochschild & Machung, 1989). While women's work hours have increased over the last five decades, they still do most of the labour of caring for the home and family (Blossfeld & Drobnic, 2001; Breen & Cooke, 2005; Gershuny, 2000). Thus, the most common reason cited by women for their part-time employment is their responsibility for childcare (Moyser, 2017b).

This gendered partition of family duties is still being reinforced by traditional social expectations of women (Burda, Hamermesh, & Weil, 2007), such that women may feel pressured to contribute disproportionately to caring for their families compared to their spouses or domestic partners. Full-time work may not always be a choice for many of them.

Government policies and programs such as EI are based on an assumption that men and women are equally free to choose their labour market participation, but in fact the decision to work, at what type of job, and the number of work hours per week are conditioned by a number of personal and social factors that limit choice (Little, 2004; Teghtsoonian, 1996). This underlying assumption about women's freedom to choose their work participation does not acknowledge social discourses that define women as caregivers of their children, spouse, and elders and responsible for domestic work. The choice to work is also conditioned by social class. Some women might prefer to not work in order to care for their children but cannot afford to not work. Middle- and upper-class women have more freedom to choose whether to work and how much (Little, 2004).

A key resource that frees women to work is access to adequate and affordable childcare, but childcare is becoming increasingly unaffordable for low-income women in some areas as the federal government does not impose cost controls on daycare facilities and does not provide sufficient numbers of subsidized childcare spaces. The gender employment gap is greater in metropolitan areas and provinces with high daycare fees, indicating that in those areas women are staying home to care for their children because they can't afford daycare. Thus, in Montreal, where daycare cost $168 a month per child in 2017, 6.4% more men are employed than women. In Toronto, where daycare costs as much as $1,758 a month, 12.6% more men are employed than women, indicating that women in Toronto are staying home to care for their children because of the high cost of daycare (MacDonald & Friendly, 2017; Moyser, 2017b).

The ability to choose whether and how much to work is further complicated for single mothers, who make up one-quarter of low-wage workers. It is more difficult for them to move to higher-paid jobs because they have difficulty paying for childcare and they must shoulder all of the childcare and household work (Evans, 2009). Their financial security is also compromised by fathers who neglect to pay full child support (Tyyskä, 2014). In March 2012, 45% of Canadian fathers were at least two months behind in their child support payments (Kelly, 2013). In spite of these challenges, and out of necessity, 72% of lone mothers and 75.8% of coupled mothers worked in 2015 (Moyser, 2017b).

Table 4.2: Reasons for Involuntary Part-Time Work in Canada, 2015

	%	
	Women	**Men**
Part-time employment, all reasons	18.9	5.5
All involuntary reasons	32.8	47.0
Business conditions (downturn or increased costs)	23.3	35.0
Could not find full-time work	9.4	12.0

Source: Adapted from Moyser, 2017b.

Working involuntarily at part-time rather than full-time work is much more common for men than for women (table 4.2). In 2015, 47% of men were employed part time involuntarily, compared to 32.8% of women (Moyser, 2017b). This difference is due in part to women voluntarily choosing part-time work due to the demands of their unpaid household labour.

Health Impacts of Unemployment and Underemployment on Women

In addition to the general health impacts of unemployment and underemployment mentioned above, the impacts on women are compounded by their roles as caregivers and homemakers. Due to social conditioning, many women ensure that others are taken care of before meeting their own needs for health care, nutrition, and mental health support (Nichols, 2016b). Since many women are employed part-time, they may either not have any extended health-care benefits through their job or they may lose those benefits when they become unemployed, leaving them without coverage for medications. Again, they may prioritize paying for their children's health-care and medication needs over their own. The cost of childcare can also make it difficult for women to attend medical appointments, particularly if they are single mothers (Nichols, 2016b).

Retraining for Better Employment

Unemployment and underemployment may indicate a need for individuals to learn new skills that are in demand in the labour market and that will lead to steady full-time jobs. Retraining may consist of completing secondary or post-secondary academic degrees or training for specific trades and professions.

The federal and provincial governments have instituted policies and programs that encourage retraining for unemployed and underemployed people (Government of Canada, 2009), such as Second Career in Ontario, Alberta Works, and Skills Development in Nova Scotia. Eligible participants include workers who have been laid off who are receiving EI benefits. The programs are designed specifically for in-demand industries such as health care, dental care, computer and information systems, food services, tourism, and education.

Women who are caring for children may find it difficult to participate in or pay for retraining. While Second Career, for example, offers childcare, unemployed women who opt for retraining in a field not covered by this program or who desire to undertake university-level studies do not have access to paid childcare. Second Career offers a low basic living allowance of $410 a week ($1,640 a month), which the above cost-of-living figures show is not enough to take care of a family while attending retraining (Government of Ontario, 2018). Thus, some women may be forced to take on survival jobs rather than job retraining to make ends meet. Finally, some women may prioritize their children's education rather than their own in terms of their investment of time and money (Nichols, 2016b).

THE IMPACT OF EMPLOYMENT INSURANCE POLICIES ON WOMEN

The harsh conditions of the Great Depression in the 1930s encouraged a political shift toward Keynesian economics in Canada. Keynesianism, named for British economist John Maynard Keynes, was designed to reconcile the needs of workers and employers through the creation of a series of social protections for workers, including market regulation, ensuring adequate wages, and advancement of the industry through a stable and loyal workforce (Harvey, 2005). One of the key mechanisms that was introduced to deal with an unemployment rate of 19.3% was UI (Gower, 1992). The main goals of the policy were to provide financial assistance to unemployed workers and help them find suitable employment. Initially claimants required 12 to 20 weeks of work, depending on the region where they lived, with a minimum of 15 hours a week to qualify for UI benefits. The policy listed 40 acceptable reasons for leaving a job, such as workplace discrimination, childbirth, harassment, and moving due to a spouse's career. There was a two-week waiting period prior to receiving benefits, the amount of which was determined by earnings and total hours worked during the previous year (Townson & Hayes, 2007).

After over a decade of increasing neoliberal restrictions imposed on the welfare state, in 1996 UI was replaced by EI. This new approach to unemployed worker supports was designed to encourage people to work and to remain at their jobs. The most significant change in the new policy was an increase in the number of hours required to receive benefits. Depending on the region, unemployed workers now require 420 to 700 hours of work over the previous 12 months. This means that at the high end of the hours requirement, workers must accumulate 100 days at 35 hours per week, which is double the previous UI requirement (Townson & Hayes, 2007).

The unspoken underlying bias of the EI policy is that leaving the workforce to have and raise children is a woman's individual choice, when in fact reproduction and childcare are essential for society and for the economy (for regeneration of the working population) and have long been treated as women's obligation. Women's role in social reproduction affects whether and how much they work and how unemployment impacts them (Nichols, 2016b). Ultimately, women who reduce their work hours in order to take on the burden of social reproduction or unpaid domestic labour have difficulty accessing EI benefits because they cannot meet the minimum hours requirement.

Not surprisingly, more men than women receive EI benefits. In 2016/2017, 806,660 men received EI, compared to 514,470 women. This was a 10% decrease from the previous year for men and a 3.7% decrease for women. Men's weekly benefits are also higher than women's. In 2016/2017 men received an average of $474 per week, while women received $412 (ESDC, 2018), reflecting the wage gap between men and women and the gendered division of household labour: when women do more than half of household tasks they may have less time for paid work outside the home, resulting in lower EI benefits.

THE IMPACT OF INTERSECTING SOCIAL CONDITIONS ON WOMEN'S UNEMPLOYMENT AND UNDEREMPLOYMENT

Unemployment is not a uniform experience for women. Rather, some women experience more hardship during their unemployment due to the intersection of two or more fundamental traits and social conditions. An intersectional lens helps to better understand the varied unemployment experiences of individual women and groups of women.

Low-Income Women

Poverty is a significant issue in Canada, but there is no universally accepted method for defining poverty numerically (Fleras, 2017). *Absolute poverty* means a chronic lack of life necessities such as food, shelter, and clothing, while *relative poverty* is a measure of poverty in specific years, places, and levels of development. In Canada three measures are used to determine low income (Citizens for Public Justice, 2013):

1. *Low income cut-off* (LICO): The after-tax point at which a household spends 63.6% or more of its income on food, clothing, and shelter. This is the oldest and most commonly used definition of poverty.
2. *Low income measure* (LIM): 50% of the adjusted global median household income.
3. *Market Basket Measure* (MBM): The level at which a household does not have enough money for life necessities, taking into account local conditions.

The existence of three different definitions of poverty can lead to confusion over how to measure and improve poverty in Canada. An advantage of the LIM is that it provides a measure of the level of poverty in Canada compared to other countries.

It is estimated that one in seven Canadians (4.8 million people) are living in poverty (Fleras, 2017); 53.4% are women. People who live in poverty tend to be children, those in female-headed and lone-parent households and families headed by persons with disabilities, young adults between 18 and 24 years old, and unattached people, especially elderly women (Fleras, 2017). In fact, 1.9 million women live on a low income (Canadian Women's Foundation, 2018). There is a growing segment of working poor: families in poverty despite having at least one working person in the household, which includes 44% of Canadian households that are in poverty (Citizens for Public Justice, 2013). Single mothers are especially impacted as 30.4% are raising their children in poverty (Canadian Women's Foundation, 2018). Single mothers are twice as likely to find themselves seeking housing at emergency shelters as two-parent households (Canadian Women's Foundation, 2018).

The official low-income cut-off point (poverty line) in Canada varies by region due to the difference in the cost of living in urban and rural areas. For a family of four living in a city with a population of 500,000 or more in 2017, the cut-off was $39,701 after taxes. For the same family living in a rural area, the cut-off was $25,970. For a single person the urban poverty line was $20,998 and the rural poverty line was $13,735 (Statistics Canada, 2018g). Approximately 4.8 million Canadians lived in households below the low-income cut-off. Out of this total, 53.3% were women (Statistics Canada, 2018m).

The risk of poverty for women who are precariously employed is compounded when they lose their jobs, especially when they don't qualify for EI benefits due to insufficient work hours. They sometimes find that they lack the financial resources to participate in retraining, whether to pay for tuition and textbooks or for childcare. Taken together, these circumstances may prevent them from returning to work. Thus, paradoxically, a sufficient level of financial resources is needed simply to re-enter the labour market (Nichols, 2016a).

Racialized and Immigrant Women

The word *racialized* refers to a process by which a white majority population places racial meanings—usually limiting—on nonwhite groups. In Canadian government vocabulary, racialized individuals are also referred to as **visible minorities**, meaning "persons, other than Aboriginal peoples, who are non-Caucasian in race or non-white in colour" (ESDC, 2013). The term *visible minority* has been criticized by scholars and social justice advocates, who prefer the term "racialized" (City for All Women Initiative, 2016). The proportion of racialized women has grown in recent decades (table 4.3).

Racialized communities in Canada have a high rate of labour market attachment (Block & Galabuzi, 2011). In 2016, 67.4% of racialized women between

Table 4.3: Percentage of Racialized Canadian Women, 1981–2031

Year	%
1981	5
1986	6
1991	9
1996	11
2001	14
2006	16
2011	19
2016	23
2021	25 (projected)
2026	28 (projected)
2031	31 (projected)

Source: Adapted from Hudon, 2016.

Table 4.4: Unemployment Rate (%) of Canadians 25–64 Years Old, 2016

	All Canadians		Canadian-born		Immigrants	
	Women	Men	Women	Men	Women	Men
Racialized	8.2	6.9	6.3	7.1	8.4	6.8
Nonracialized	5.2	6.9	5.1	7.1	6.0	5.6

Source: Adapted from Statistics Canada, 2018f.

the ages of 25 and 64 and 80.5% of racialized men worked. This was very similar to the employment rate of nonracialized women and men (72.9% and 79% respectively; Statistics Canada, 2018f).

In Canada today, race and immigration are deeply connected. In 2016, 70% of racialized individuals were born outside Canada (Statistics Canada, 2017). Most new immigrants come to Canada from the Global South, with the top ethnicities being South Asian, Chinese, and Black (Statistics Canada, 2017). The population of immigrant women and girls has increased over the years, currently accounting for 66.7% of all immigrants (Hudon, 2016).

Immigrant status compounds workforce inequality for both racialized and nonracialized women, adding a third layer of complexity to women's lived realities (Hudon, 2016). Table 4.4 shows that racialized women have the highest unemployment rate compared to nonracialized women and men, pointing to the connection between immigrant status and race in the Canadian labour market.

The unemployment rate also varies among racialized women from different countries and regions (table 4.5). For example, Arab women immigrants are 14.8% more likely to be unemployed than Canadian-born Arab women, demonstrating the intersecting impacts of racialization and immigration status.

Racialized women and first-generation women immigrants have a higher chance of experiencing low-wage work than the average population. Table 4.6 shows that 20.3% of first-generation Canadian racialized women are low-wage earners, compared to 11% of nonracialized women of all generations (Statistics Canada, 2018j). Their low wages prevent them from accumulating savings to bridge periods of unemployment and to supplement their limited EI benefits. Poverty among racialized groups in Canada continues to grow even as their postsecondary education increases (ESDC, 2013).

Since racialized Canadians and immigrants are more likely to be unemployed or to work part-time, they face more difficulty accessing EI benefits.

Table 4.5: Women's Unemployment Rate (%) by Race and Ethnicity, Ages 25–64, 2016

	Total	Canadian	Immigrants
Racialized total	8.2	6.3	8.4
South Asian	9.8	6.5	10.2
Chinese	6.8	4.5	7.0
Black	10.1	8.5	10.3
Filipino	4.0	5.0	4.0
Latin American	8.7	7.4	8.5
Arab	14.2	7.4	14.8
Southeast Asian	7.0	5.2	7.2
West Asian	12.0	7.1	12.0
Korean	7.3	4.6	7.1
Japanese	4.9	3.6	5.2
Other race	8.0	7.7	8.1
Multiple racialized group	7.1	6.4	7.2

Source: Adapted from Statistics Canada, 2018f.

Table 4.6: Percentage of Low-Wage Canadians by Gender, Immigration Generation, and Racialized Status, Ages 25–54, 2016

	Women		Men	
Generation	Racialized	Nonracialized	Racialized	Nonracialized
All	18.8	11.0	17.6	9.6
1st	20.3	13.8	19.4	13.3
2nd	9.4	9.0	8.4	8.3
3rd or more	17.6	11.0	13.0	9.4

Note: "Low-wage" is based on the LIM-AT (50% of the median adjusted after-tax income).
Source: Statistics Canada, 2018j.

Approximately 27% of recent immigrants have fewer than the required insurable hours for EI (Vosko, 2011).

Notably, unemployment places additional stressors on immigrant women's mental health, compounded by social isolation (Rashid, Gregory, Kazemipur, & Scruby, 2013). Older immigrant women are particularly vulnerable to financial and social hardship during unemployment, especially if they lose a long-term job (Ng, 2011).

Indigenous Women

Indigenous women experience substantial hardships in the labour market. Lamb's (2015) study on Indigenous populations living off-reserve, based on the Canadian Labour Force Survey from 2007 to 2012, found that they were significantly impacted by the 2008 recession. Indigenous people in Canada experience lower employment and higher unemployment than non-Indigenous people (table 4.7; Lamb, 2015). Indigenous women's work situation is made more complex by their traditional role in the household performing unpaid labour (similar to non-Indigenous women), their high fertility rate, and high prominence of single parenthood (Lamb, 2015). The 2017 Aboriginal Peoples Survey reported that 43% of off-reserve Indigenous women and 47% of men were employed (Statistics Canada, 2018h).

According to an analysis by Moyser (2017a), Indigenous women experience a slightly larger gender gap in employment due to traditional gender norms, especially around childcare. More non-Indigenous women are employed in the labour market, and they have a lower unemployment rate than Indigenous women (table 4.8).

Table 4.7: Employment and Unemployment Rates of Core Working-Age Indigenous and Non-Indigenous People, 2007, 2010, and 2015

Year	Employment %		Unemployment %	
	Indigenous	Non-Indigenous	Indigenous	Non-Indigenous
2007	69.9	82.5	8.9	5.0
2010	65.8	80.9	12.1	6.8
2015	67.5	81.8	11.0	5.7

Note: Data for table 4.7 is for Indigenous people living off-reserve in the 10 provinces, which covered 78% of Indigenous people in 2011.
Source: Moyser, 2017a.

Table 4.8: Employment and Unemployment Rates of Core Working-Age Indigenous and Non-Indigenous Women, 2007–2015

	Employment %		Unemployment %	
Year	Indigenous	Non-Indigenous	Indigenous	Non-Indigenous
2007	64.6	78.5	8.7	4.7
2008	64.7	78.3	9.2	4.7
2009	65.2	77.4	10.3	6.0
2010	62.4	77.5	11.1	6.3
2011	64.1	77.6	9.6	5.9
2012	65.2	78.1	10.5	5.6
2013	65.8	78.5	9.1	5.5
2014	66.1	77.8	9.4	5.4
2015	63.2	78.0	10.9	5.3

Note: Data for table 4.7 is for Indigenous people living off-reserve in the 10 provinces, which covered 78% of Indigenous people in 2011.
Source: Moyser, 2017a.

The three most common job areas for Indigenous women are retail work, health care, and education (Statistics Canada, 2018b)—all sectors characterized by precarious low-wage work. Retail work often offers little chance for advancement. More research is needed on underemployment and unemployment of Indigenous women in Canada and their paid and unpaid work in the home and on and off reserves.

Young Women

Statistics Canada defines youth as 15 to 24 years of age; however, many scholars, organizations, and governments extend this age bracket to age 35. The youth category overlaps with childhood and adolescence, making the distinctions between them ambiguous (Tyyskä, 2014). Young people's work experience is complicated by their place in the life cycle. Often, they are still dependent on their parents while completing their education (Tyyskä, 2014). The long duration of postsecondary education and training delays their entry into full-time employment, and many young people must contend with low-paying, part-time, or temporary jobs.

The youth employment rate in Canada for men and women combined has remained fairly steady in recent decades at approximately 56% (Statistics Canada,

2015, 2018d), with young women gaining slightly on their male counterparts during that period. The unemployment rate also favours young women slightly. In 2015, 11.3% of young women compared to 15% of young men were unemployed (Moyser, 2017b). This may be the result of young women being overrepresented in industries with greater concentrations of youth, such as the service, childcare, and personal care industries, while men are also less likely to pursue postsecondary education, which may leave them with fewer employment opportunities.

In 2015, 65.1% of young women were enrolled in postsecondary education, compared to 58.2% of men. Among young people who did not attend postsecondary education, 61.1% of men compared to 44.8% of women were unemployed in 2015 (Moyser, 2017b). Young women also tend to enrol in more traditionally female fields such as nursing, social work, and the humanities and social sciences (Krahn, Lowe, & Hughes, 2008). These postsecondary programs often lead women into lower-paying jobs and precarious white-collar employment in the service sector.

Older Women

Most Canadian government organizations define older workers as over the age of 55. This is an important category as in the last decade more Canadians over the age of 55 have been engaged in work, with 36% of people over 55 working in June 2018 (Statistics Canada, 2018c). By 2036, 25% of the labour force is expected to be 55 or over (Statistics Canada, 2018a). In June 2018, 31.4% of women and 41% of men 55 years and older were working (Statistics Canada, 2018c). Thus, both men and women are working longer. A recent Statistics Canada report by Paula Arriagada (2018) noted that work is a significant portion of seniors' day as women work 5.7 hours and men 6.6 hours in paid work. More women 65 and older work in part-time positions (92.2%) compared to women 15 to 64 years old (73.5%). Their preference for part-time work may be related to health limitations or family responsibilities (Hudon & Milan, 2016). In 2015 women over 65 earned a median wage of $16,670 compared to $21,377 for men of the same age, reflecting older women's greater part-time employment (Statistics Canada, 2018b).

Older women's periods of unemployment last longer compared to the key working-age bracket (25 to 54 years of age). The unemployment rate of older men and women has hovered between about 4% and 6% over the years (Moyser, 2017b).

Older women workers experience difficulties when they lose employment due to employers' beliefs that they are less productive and too expensive and have outdated skills. Fournier, Zimmermann, Masdonati, and Gauthier's (2018) study on the experiences of older Canadian workers over an 18-month period found that women made up a large portion of workers who dealt with downgrading and feeling undervalued in the labour market.

Women with Disabilities

Turcotte (2014) notes that Statistics Canada defines disabled workers as individuals who are "limited in their daily activities because of a physical or mental disability, but participate actively in the labour market and often hold jobs that match their qualifications" (p. 2). Depending on the metric applied to determine the severity of the disability, approximately 13.7% of the Canadian adult population is disabled (Statistics Canada, 2013). Those with a higher degree of disability tend to be less engaged in work.

Women are more likely than men to be disabled and to be unemployed (Burlock, 2017). In 2011 the Council of Canadians with Disabilities reported that 8.7% of women (compared to 8.4% of men) with mild or moderate disabilities and 21% of women (compared to 11.8% of men) with severe disabilities were unemployed (Burlock, 2017). In 2014 disabled women tended to earn less than $50,000 a year, while disabled men tended to earn over $60,000 (Canadian Feminist Alliance for International Action & DisAbled Women's Action Network, 2017). In 2014, 23% of disabled women lived in poverty (Canadian Women's Foundation, 2018). Galer (2018) reports that disabled women have a higher rate of unemployment and poverty than disabled men. In 2011 the Council of Canadians with Disabilities characterized them as an "underutilized resource" for the labour market. Women with disabilities tend to work in nonstandard employment such as contract, part-time, temporary, or hidden labour. This leads them to be excluded from EI benefits. Further, disability often relegates people to unpaid volunteer work and involuntary part-time work.

Related to their high unemployment rate, it is not surprising that women with disabilities in the core working-age group (25 to 54) report that their life satisfaction is affected by stress related to their work, health, and finances (Stienstra, 2010). Thus, there is a connection between women's disability, employment status, and socioeconomic status.

CONCLUSION

Unemployment and underemployment can have a profound impact on women's financial and social well-being, their physical and mental health, the well-being of their families, and their attempts to establish autonomy and independence. An extended period of unemployment or underemployment can have a negative impact on their future efforts to find better-paid, secure, full-time jobs, thus increasing their risk of long-term poverty.

Women's experience of unemployment and underemployment is complex, but it becomes even more so when their diverse traits and social conditions, such as race, immigrant status, low income, disability, and age, are taken into account. An intersectional analysis that includes all of these important factors yields a better understanding of women's real lived experiences of work and avoids generalizations that arise from focusing on a single factor, such as race or gender. Currently our understanding of women's experiences of unemployment and underemployment is hampered by a lack of data on the diverse social groups to which women belong and how these traits and conditions interact. More research is needed in this area.

Women's inequality in the labour market, leading to underemployment and unemployment, is linked in part to our lack of acknowledgement as a society of women's essential role in social reproduction (Nichols, 2014). While more women work today than 50 years ago, there has been no significant change in how society conceives of their role in raising children and caring for the household. Women carry a double burden of many unpaid hours of household labour in addition to their paid work outside the home, which impacts the type of work they do, their work hours, and their salary. These two roles are not optional for women or for society: the supply of new workers must be constantly replenished through reproduction in order to sustain the economy, while stagnating wages and a rising cost of living mean that women must contribute to family finances as men's wages are often insufficient to support the family.

Yet public policies related to employment and unemployment are not framed around women's double roles as mothers and workers; in fact, they penalize women for circumstances that are the direct outcome of their essential role in reproduction. In order to fulfill their socially mandated functions as mothers and workers, and pending a more equal gendered division of labour, women require supports such as childcare, job training, health care, and employment insurance. Policy reform is needed in all of these areas to equalize the responsibilities and opportunities of men and women in the labour market and the impacts of unemployment and underemployment. Policy reform would take into account women's necessary absences from the labour market to give birth and raise children and ensure that their basic financial needs are met during these periods through equitable EI benefits. Flexible social policies would be adjusted to the multiple needs of individual women, rather than based on a male model of full-time secure employment applied indiscriminately to all workers.

There has been ongoing attention in Canada to creating affordable childcare. In 2017 the government of Ontario announced a commitment to creating affordable childcare (Monsebraaten, 2017). This echoes the platform introduced in the 2015 federal election by the New Democratic Party, which called for a childcare fee of $15 a day, with 60% of the amount covered by the federal government and 40% covered by the provinces (Milligan, 2014). This proposal has its roots in Quebec's childcare program, which costs between $8.05 and $22.15 a day, with subsidies for low-wage earners. Quebec's program has been shown to increase employment opportunities for young mothers (Milligan, 2014). These programs illustrate the importance of actively engaging in policy analysis and activism both from within and outside the political arena to bring about policy changes to lessen hardship for women who are unemployed and underemployed.

KEY READINGS

Nichols, L. (2016). Motherhood and unemployment: Intersectional experiences from Toronto and Halifax. *Canadian Review of Social Policy*, 76, 1–24.

Pupo, N., & Duffy, A. (2003). Caught in the net: The impact of changes to Canadian employment insurance legislation on part-time workers. *Social Policy and Society*, 2(1), 1–11.

Shields, J., Silver, S., & Wilson, S. (2006). Assessing employment risk: Dimensions in the measurement of unemployment. *Socialist Studies*, 2(2), 105–112.

DISCUSSION QUESTIONS

1. What factors contribute to underemployment becoming a major concern for Canadian women?
2. Which policy do you think would improve unemployed and underemployed women's situation more: the proposed universal childcare program in Ontario and nationally, or the free tuition program in Ontario?
3. What other policies should be introduced to better support unemployed and underemployed women in Canada?

REFERENCES

Arriagada, P. (2018). A day in the life: How do older Canadians spend their time? Ottawa: Statistics Canada. Retrieved from https://www150.statcan.gc.ca/n1/pub/75-006-x/2018001/article/54947-eng.htm

Block, S., & Galabuzi, G. (2011). *Canada's colour coded labour market: The gap for racialized workers.* Ottawa & Toronto: Canadian Centre for Policy Alternatives & the Wellesley Institute.

Blossfeld, H.-P., & Drobnic, S. (2001). *A cross-national comparative approach to couples' careers.* Oxford, UK: Oxford University Press.

Breen, R., & Cooke, L. P. (2005). The persistence of the gendered division of domestic labour. *European Sociological Review, 21*(1), 4–57.

Burda, M., Hamermesh, D. S., and Weil, P. (2007). Total work, gender, and social norms. NBER Working Paper No. 13000. Cambridge, MA: National Bureau of Economic Research. Retrieved from www.nber.org/papers/w13000.pdf?new_window=1

Burlock, A. (2017). Women with disabilities. Ottawa: Statistics Canada. Retrieved from https://www150.statcan.gc.ca/n1/pub/89-503-x/2015001/article/14695-eng.htm

Canadian Feminist Alliance for International Action & DisAbled Women's Action Network. (2017, February). *Women with disabilities in Canada: Report to the Committee on the Rights of Persons with Disabilities on the occasion of the committee's initial review of Canada.* Retrievedfromhttp://fafia-afai.org/wp-content/uploads/2017/02/FAFIA_DAWN_CRPD 2017.pdf

Canadian Press. (2018, May 5). More than half of Canadians have less than $10,000 set aside for emergencies: BMO. *Globe and Mail.* Retrieved from https://www.theglobeandmail .com/globe-investor/personal-finance/household-finances/more-than-half-of-canadians-have-less-than-10000-set-aside-for-emergencies-bmo/article26172527/

Canadian Women's Foundation. (2018). *Fact sheet: Women and poverty in Canada.* Retrieved from https://www.canadianwomen.org/wp-content/uploads/2018/09/Fact-Sheet-WOMEN-POVERTY-September-2018.pdf

Chawla, R. K., & Uppla, S. (2012). *Household debt in Canada.* Ottawa: Statistics Canada. Retrieved from www.statcan.gc.ca/pub/75-001-x/2012002/article/11636-eng.pdf

Citizens for Public Justice. (2013). *Poverty trends highlights: Canada 2013.* Retrieved from http://cpj.ca/sites/default/files/docs/Poverty-Trends-Highlights-2013.pdf

City for All Women Initiative. (2016). *Racialized people: Equity and inclusion snapshot.* Ottawa: Author. Retrieved from http://www.cawi-ivtf.org/sites/default/files/racialized_people_snapshot_en_2016_final_acc.pdf

Cooke, M., & Gazso, A. (2009). Taking a life course perspective on social assistance use in Canada: A different approach. *Canadian Journal of Sociology, 34*(2), 349–372.

Council of Canadians with Disabilities. (2011). Annual report: 2010–2011. Retrieved from http://www.ccdonline.ca/en/about/board/annualreports/2011

Employment and Social Development Canada. (2013). Snapshot of racialized poverty in Canada. Retrieved from www.esdc.gc.ca/eng/communities/reports/poverty_profile/snapshot.shtml

Employment and Social Development Canada. (2018). Employment Insurance Monitoring and Assessment Report for the fiscal year beginning April 1, 2016 and ending March 31, 2017. Retrieved from https://www.canada.ca/en/employment-social-development/programs/ei/ei-list/reports/monitoring2017.html

Evans, P. M. (2009). Lone mothers, workfare and precarious employment: Time for a Canadian basic income? *International Social Security Review, 62*(1), 45–63.

Ferrao, V. (2010). *Paid work: Women in Canada; A gender-based statistical report.* Ottawa: Statistics Canada, Social and Aboriginal Statistics Division. Retrieved from https://www150.statcan.gc.ca/n1/en/pub/89-503-x/2010001/article/11387-eng.pdf?st=ksc1uVN9

Fleras, A. (2017). *Inequality matters: Diversity and exclusion in Canada.* Don Mills, ON: Oxford University Press.

Fournier, G., Zimmermann, H., Masdonati, J., & Gauthier, C. (2018). Job loss in a group of older Canadian workers: Challenges in the sustainable labour market reintegration process. *Sustainability, 10*(7), 2245.

Galer, D. (2018). *Working towards equity: Disability rights, activism, and employment in the late twentieth-century Canada.* Toronto: University of Toronto Press.

Gershuny, J. (2000). *Changing times: Work and leisure in postindustrial society.* Oxford, UK: Oxford University Press.

Government of Canada. (2009). *Canada's economic action plan: A second report to Canadians.* Ottawa: Author.

Government of Ontario. (2017, March 29). Free tuition for hundreds of thousands of Ontario students. Retrieved from https://news.ontario.ca/opo/en/2017/03/free-tuition-for-hundreds-of-thousands-of-ontario-students.html

Government of Ontario. (2018). Second career. Retrieved from https://www.ontario.ca/page/second-career

Gower, D. (1992). A note on Canadian unemployment since 1921. *Perspectives on Labour and Income, 4*(3). Retrieved from https://www150.statcan.gc.ca/n1/en/pub/75-001-x/1992003/87-eng.pdf?st=ODepA4Gd

Harvey, D. (2005). *A brief history of neoliberalism.* Oxford, UK: Oxford University Press.

Hochschild, A. R., & Machung, A. (1989). *The second shift: Working parents and the revolution at home.* New York: Viking Penguin.

Hudon, T. (2016). Visible minority women. In *Women in Canada: A gender-based statistical report.* Ottawa: Statistics Canada. Retrieved from www.statcan.gc.ca/pub/89-503-x/2015001/article/14315-eng.htm

Hudon, T., & Milan, A. (2016). Senior women. In *Women in Canada: A gender-based statistical report.* Ottawa: Statistics Canada. Retrieved from https://www150.statcan.gc.ca/n1/pub/89-503-x/2015001/article/14316-eng.htm

Kelly, M. B. (2013). Payment patterns of child and spousal support. *Juristat.* Statistics Canada, Catalogue no. 85-002-X. Ottawa: Statistics Canada. Retrieved from www .statcan.gc.ca/pub/85-002-x/2013001/article/11780-eng.pdf

Krahn, H. J., Lowe, G. S., & Hughes, K. D. (2007). *Work, industry and Canadian society* (5th ed.). Toronto: Nelson Education.

Lamb, D. (2015). The economic impact of the great recession on Aboriginal people living off-reserve in Canada. *Relations industrielles, 70*(3), 457–485.

Little, M. H. (2004). *If I had a hammer: Retraining that really works.* Vancouver: University of British Columbia Press.

MacDonald, D., & Friendly, M. (2017, December). *Time out: Child care fees in Canada 2017.* Ottawa: Canadian Centre for Policy Alternatives. Retrieved from https://www .policyalternatives.ca/sites/default/files/uploads/publications/National%20Office/ 2017/12/Time%20Out.pdf

Man, G. (2004). Gender, work and migration: Deskilling Chinese immigrant women in Canada. *Women's Studies International Forum, 27*(2), 135–148.

Milligan, K. (2014, October 15). What can we learn from Quebec's child care experience? *Maclean's.* Retrieved from www.macleans.ca/economy/economicanalysis/what-can-we-learn-from-quebecs-child-care-experience/

Monsebraaten, L. (2017, June 6). Ontario commits to universally accessible child care. *Toronto Star.* Retrieved from www.thestar.com/news/queenspark/2017/06/06/ontario-commits-to-universally-accessible-child-care.html

Moyser, M. (2017a). Aboriginal people living off-reserve and the labour market: Estimates from the Labour Force Survey, 2007–2015. Ottawa: Statistics Canada. Retrieved from https://www150.statcan.gc.ca/n1/pub/71-588-x/71-588-x2017001-eng.htm

Moyser, M. (2017b). Women and paid work. In *Women in Canada: A gender-based statistical report.* Ottawa: Statistics Canada. Retrieved from www.statcan.gc.ca/pub/89-503-x/2015001/article/14694-eng.htm

Moyser, M., & Burlock, A. (2018). Time use: Total work burden, unpaid work, and leisure. In *Women in Canada: A gender-based statistical report.* Ottawa: Statistics Canada. Retrieved from https://www150.statcan.gc.ca/n1/pub/89-503-x/2015001/article/54931-eng.htm

Ng, W. (2011). A case study of the inequalities faced by disadvantaged, foreign-born, older workers in Canada. Toronto: Centre for Labour Management Relations. Retrieved from www.ryerson.ca/content/dam/clmr/Publications/Executive%20Summaries/Executive %20Summary%20-%20%22An%20Immigrant%20All%20Over%20Again%3 F%22%20The%20Inequalities%20Faced%20by%20Disadvantaged%2C%20Foreign-Born%2C%20Older%20Workers%20in%20Canada.pdf

Nichols, L. J. (2013). Analyzing policy frames for unemployed workers' supports within Canada. *AG: International Journal of Gender Studies, 2*(3), 219–245.

Nichols, L. (2014). *Unemployed women in neo-liberal Canada: An intersectional analysis of social well-being.* Unpublished dissertation, Ryerson University, Toronto.

Nichols, L. (2016a). Lived experiences of unemployed women in Toronto and Halifax, Canada, who were previously precariously employed. *Alternate Routes, 27,* 162–186.

Nichols, L. (2016b). Motherhood and unemployment: Intersectional experiences from Toronto and Halifax. *Canadian Review of Social Policy, 76,* 1–24.

Pupo, N., & Duffy, A. (2003). Caught in the net: The impact of changes to Canadian Employment Insurance legislation on part-time workers. *Social Policy and Society, 2* (1), 1–11.

Rashid, R., Gregory, D., Kazemipur, A., & Scruby, L. (2013). Immigration journey: A holistic exploration of pre- and post-migration life stories in a sample of Canadian immigrant women. *International Journal of Migration, Health and Social Care, 9*(4), 189–202.

Shields, J., Silver, S., & Wilson, S. (2006). Assessing employment risk: Dimensions in the measurement of unemployment. *Socialist Studies, 2*(2), 105–112.

Statistics Canada. (2013). Disability in Canada: Initial findings from the Canadian Survey on Disability. Retrieved from https://www150.statcan.gc.ca/n1/pub/89-654-x/89-654-x2013002-eng.htm

Statistics Canada. (2015). Employment rates, by age. Retrieved from https://www150.statcan.gc.ca/n1/pub/71-222-x/2008001/sectionb/b-emp-age-eng.htm

Statistics Canada. (2016). Employment by industry and sex. Retrieved from www.statcan.gc.ca/tables-tableaux/sum-som/l01/cst01/labor10a-eng.htm

Statistics Canada. (2017). Immigration and ethnocultural diversity: Key results from the 2016 census. Retrieved from https://www150.statcan.gc.ca/n1/daily-quotidien/171025/dq171025b-eng.htm?indid=14428-1&indgeo=0

Statistics Canada. (2018a). Characteristics related to the age structure of the Canadian labour force in 2017 and 2036. Retrieved from https://www150.statcan.gc.ca/n1/pub/89-28-0001/2018001/article/00005/age-eng.htm

Statistics Canada. (2018b). Industry—North American industry classification system (NAICS) 2012 (425), employment income statistics (3), highest certificate, diploma or degree (7), aboriginal identity (9), work activity during the reference year (4), age (5a) and sex (3) for the population aged 15 years and over who worked in 2015 and reported employment income in 2015, in private households of Canada, provinces and territories and census metropolitan areas, 2016 census—25% sample data. Retrieved from https://www12.statcan.gc.ca/census-recensement/2016/dp-pd/dt-td/Rp-eng.cfm?LANG=E&APATH=3&DETAIL=0&DIM=0&FL=A&FREE=0&GC=0&GID=0&GK=0&GRP=1&PID=112128&PRID=10&PTYPE=109445&S=0&SHOWALL=0&SUB=0&Temporal=2017&THEME=122&VID=0&VNAMEE=&VNAMEF=

Statistics Canada. (2018c). Table 1: Labour force characteristics by age group and sex, seasonally adjusted. Retrieved from https://www150.statcan.gc.ca/n1/daily-quotidien/180706/t001a-eng.htm

Statistics Canada. (2018d). Labour force characteristics by sex and detailed age group, annual. Retrieved from https://www150.statcan.gc.ca/t1/tbl1/en/tv.action?pid=1410001801&pickMembers%5B0%5D=1.1&pickMembers%5B1%5D=2.10

Statistics Canada. (2018e). Labour force characteristics by province, monthly, seasonally adjusted (Newfoundland and Labrador, Prince Edward Island, Nova Scotia, New Brunswick). Retrieved from www.statcan.gc.ca/tables-tableaux/sum-som/l01/cst01/lfss01a-eng.htm

Statistics Canada. (2018f). Labour force status (8), visible minority (15), immigrant status and period of immigration (11), highest certificate, diploma or degree (7), age (13a) and sex (3) for the population aged 15 years and over in private households of Canada, provinces and territories, census metropolitan areas and census agglomerations, 2016 census—25% sample data. Retrieved from https://www12.statcan.gc.ca/census-recensement/2016/dp-pd/dt-td/Rp-eng.cfm?TABID=2&LANG=E&APATH=3&DETAIL=0&DIM=0&FL=A&FREE=0&GC=0&GK=0&GRP=1&PID=110692&PRID=10&PTYPE=109445&S=0&SHOWALL=0&SUB=0&Temporal=2017&THEME=124&VID=0&VNAMEE=&VNAMEF=

Statistics Canada. (2018g). Low income cut-offs (LICOs) before and after tax by community and family size in 2016 constant dollars. Retrieved from www5.statcan.gc.ca/cansim/a05?lang=eng&id=2060092

Statistics Canada. (2018h). Off-reserve First Nations people entering the labour force: Findings from the 2017 Aboriginal Peoples Survey. Retrieved from https://www150.statcan.gc.ca/n1/pub/11-627-m/11-627-m2018045-eng.htm

Statistics Canada. (2018i). Supplementary unemployment rates, monthly, unadjusted for seasonality. Retrieved from www5.statcan.gc.ca/cansim/a26?lang=eng&id=2820085

Statistics Canada. (2018j). Visible minority (15), individual low-income status (6), low-income indicators (4), generation status (4), age (6) and sex (3) for the population in private households of Canada, provinces and territories, census metropolitan areas and census agglomerations, 2016 census—25% sample data. Retrieved from https://www12.statcan.gc.ca/census-recensement/2016/dp-pd/dt-td/Rp-eng.cfm?LANG=E&APATH=3&DETAIL=0&DIM=0&FL=A&FREE=0&GC=0&GID=0&GK=0&GRP=1&PID=110563&PRID=10&PTYPE=109445&S=0&SHOWALL=0&SUB=999&Temporal=2016,2017&THEME=119&VID=0&VNAMEE=&VNAMEF=

Statistics Canada. (2019). Employee wages by industry, annual. Retrieved from https://www150.statcan.gc.ca/t1/tbl1/en/tv.action?pid=1410006401&pickMembers%5B0%5

D=1.1&pickMembers%5B1%5D=2.2&pickMembers%5B2%5D=3.3&pickMember s%5B3%5D=5.3&pickMembers%5B4%5D=6.1

Stienstra, D. (June 2010). Fact sheet: Women and restructuring in Canada. Ottawa: CRIAW. Retrieved from http://www.criaw-icref.ca/sites/criaw/files/Women_and_ Restructuring_Factsheet_June_2010.pdf

Teghtsoonian, K. (1996). Promises, promises: "Choices for women" in Canadian and American child care policy debates. *Feminist Studies, 22*(1), 118–146.

Townson, M., & Hayes, K. (2007). *Women and the Employment Insurance Program.* Toronto: Canadian Centre for Policy Alternatives.

Turcotte, M. (2014). Persons with disabilities and employment. *Insights on Canadian so-ciety.* Ottawa: Statistics Canada. Retrieved from https://www150.statcan.gc.ca/n1/en/ pub/75-006-x/2014001/article/14115-eng.pdf?st=QC0f4Ebt

Tyyskä, V. (2014). *Long and winding road: Adolescents and youth in Canada today* (3rd ed.). Toronto: Canadian Scholars' Press.

Verbruggen. M., van Emmerick, H., Van Gils, A., Meng, C., & de Grip, A. (2015). Does early-career underemployment impact future career success? A path dependency per-spective. *Journal of Vocational Behaviour, 90,* 101–110.

Vosko, L. (2011). The challenge of expanding EI coverage: Charting exclusions and partial exclusions on the bases of gender, immigration status, age and place of residence and exploring avenues for inclusive policy redesign. Toronto: Mowat Centre for Policy In-novation, University of Toronto School of Public Policy and Governance. Retrieved from https://mowatcentre.ca/wp-content/uploads/publications/23_the_challenge.pdf

CHAPTER 5

Immigrant Women's Work: Paid and Unpaid Labour in the Neoliberal Economy

Leslie Nichols, Vappu Tyyskä, and Pramila Aggarwal

Canada's immigrant population continues to grow. In the 2016 census immigrants made up 21.9% of the population; that number is expected to rise to 28.2% by 2036 (Statistics Canada, 2017). Women make up 52.4% of the current immigrant population in Canada, compared to 47.6% men (Statistics Canada, 2018a). The predominance of female immigrants in Canada is consistent with the gender pattern worldwide, especially since the beginning of the Syrian refugee crisis (UNICEF, 2018). Internationally, women make up 48% of all migrants (United Nations, 2017). The main cities that attract Canadian immigrant women are Toronto, Montreal, and Vancouver, with the remainder spread across other parts of the country (Statistics Canada, 2017). A unique feature of the Canadian population profile is that one out of three of the 22.3% who are racialized are new immigrants (Statistics Canada, 2017). Currently the majority of immigrants come from South Asia along with the Philippines and China (Statistics Canada, 2017).

In 2018, 59.9% of Canadian immigrants were employed and 6.1% were unemployed (Statistics Canada, 2018b). Immigrant women were employed at a rate of 54.5%, compared to 65.8% of men (Statistics Canada, 2018b). The unemployment rate was 6.4% for women and 5.7% for men (Statistics Canada, 2018b). Thus, more immigrant men than women are part of the labour force, whether employed or searching for work.

Many studies have found that immigrant women tend to work in survival forms of employment with low wages, little guarantee of regular employment, few benefits, and little job security (Nichols, 2018; Premji & Shakya, 2017; Premji, Shakya, Spasevski, Merolli, & Athar, 2014). Immigrant women often accept survival jobs to support the family while their husbands search for employment or become accredited in their profession in Canada. Immigrant women often experience underemployment and unemployment as well as difficulties finding work due to deskilling, rejection of their foreign credentials by potential employers, discrimination, language barriers, lack of access to professional services such as job networks and workshops, and their immigration status (Premji & Shakya, 2017; Premji et al., 2014). Almost half of immigrant women work in sales, service, business, finance, and administration (Hudon, 2015), pointing to a lack of support for immigrant women in science, technology, engineering, and mathematics (STEM) careers (Muzaffar, 2017).

Immigrant women's ability to improve their employment situation with full-time work or searching for better-paid work is compromised by the expectation that they will do all or most of household labour, resulting in time poverty (Nichols, Etemadi, & Tyyskä, 2018). At the same time, social supports for settlement and employment have been cut back during the neoliberal era (Nichols, 2016; Nichols et al., 2018).

This chapter explores immigrant women's experience of paid and unpaid work through an intersectional lens, considering how they are impacted by their race, immigration status, migration stream, low socioeconomic status, age, and racialized status. The chapter begins with an understanding of how the concept of *immigrant women* has been socially constructed since Canada's colonial history, followed by an account of the connections between wage work and the family life of immigrant women.

THE SOCIAL CONSTRUCTION OF IMMIGRANT WOMEN

How immigrant women are viewed by the society around them has a major impact on their integration into the labour force and their success there. Limiting stereotypes of Canadian immigrant women have been entrenched from the creation of the nation-state to the current immigration policy. In Canada's founding years, British women were considered the ideal "mothers of the nation" (Folson, 2004; Guo, 2009) to help expand the country: "The nation was the home and the home was the women; all were best British" (Roberts, 1979, p. 201). Through this ideology, immigrant and racialized women were othered. Over time, the term *immigrant woman* came to include any woman who did not fit the image of the ideal British lady, making any racialized woman appear to be an immigrant woman (Nichols & Tyyskä, 2015).

This ideal of white British women formed the basis of Canada's early immigration policy as racialized non-British women were denied entry in an effort to keep Canada white (Folson, 2004). While Chinese men were recruited to build the first transcontinental railroad in the 1880s, their wives were not allowed to accompany them (Das Gupta, 2000). South Asian women were denied entry into Canada in the early 20th century due to fears that they would set up families and increase the nonwhite population (Dua, 2004).

Othering of immigrants—the practice of excluding people by labelling them as outsiders to a dominant social group—continued well into the time when women were allowed to migrate to Canada and work here. For the first part of the 20th century immigration policy favoured British and Finnish domestic workers (Das Gupta, 2000) because they fit the stereotype of the Canadian woman. In the second half of the 20th century, the immigration system allowed Caribbean women to enter Canada as domestic workers, but they were not granted permanent residency like their white precursors. In 1981 the policy was changed to allow these domestic workers to apply for permanent status after two years of employment. The implication that they were less desirable than other immigrants was clear.

The view of immigrant women as less desirable continues to impact them today across a wide range of employment fields as they experience discrimination and racism in their job search (Nichols, 2018), as well as exploitation on the job due to their immigrant status and cultural background.

THE IMPACT OF NEOLIBERALISM ON IMMIGRANT WOMEN

Neoliberalism—the "hands-off" policy characterized by a reduced role for government in regulating the economy and employment and declining support for citizens' social and economic needs that has been in force across the West since the 1980s—has had profound impacts for all workers. Scott-Marshall (2007, p. 22) cites these impacts of neoliberalism:

1. Deskilling: the elimination of skilled jobs by hiring unskilled workers or using technology
2. Decreased full-time jobs

3. Wage stagnation
4. An increase in precarious employment (part-time, temporary jobs)
5. Fewer promotion opportunities
6. An increase in overtime hours so that employers can hire fewer employees

Immigrant women confront those issues associated with neoliberalism and others as well. Under neoliberalism, funding for immigrant settlement services such as job and language training and assistance finding housing and employment has been reduced. In 2010 the national budget for Citizenship and Immigration Canada for immigrant settlement services was cut by $53 million (Ontario Council of Agencies Serving Immigrants [OCASI], n.d.). The OCASI 2016 report on the impact of settlement services funding cuts noted that from 2014/2015 to 2015/2016, 47 agencies or 69% reported funding cuts, with one organization suffering the largest cut of $640,000. The lost funding resulted in employee layoffs, salary cuts by way of reduced hours, and intensified worker stress due to increased workload (OCASI, 2016). Those who lost their employment were most frequently full-time employees working as program or support staff, who are an essential resource for immigrants through their settlement period. These cuts reflect a pervasive view of immigrants as a burden on the Canadian state and its resources, even though it is also widely acknowledged that immigrants are essential to growing the Canadian economy.

Funding for settlement services has changed from ethno-specific organizations to large multi-ethnic organizations, which are more successful in competing for funds from shrinking sources, leaving smaller agencies struggling to find funding and to meet the needs of specific immigrant populations (Ku, 2011). Mohsinni (2017) examined the case of a small ethno-specific agency in Toronto called the Afghan Women's Organization, whose mission is to support refugees and women. She found that many immigrant women prefer gender-specific programming, including language classes, due to their greater comfort with other women and with being served by an agency that supports their specific cultural and language needs. This agency receives 90% of its funding from the federal government. As funding has been reduced while the demand for services has simultaneously increased, agencies like the Afghan Women's Organization have experienced financial strain.

Settlement agencies are important for economic integration of newcomers because they provide immigrants with cultural knowledge, contacts with the local community, and instruction in job-hunting strategies. Agencies' success at achieving this is compromised by lack of funding, the short duration of services, and a focus on women's domestic duties rather than job skills in settlement programs, which has the effect of channelling them into cheap precarious labour. In these ways, inadequate settlement programs may reinforce the devaluation of immigrant women's skills (Creese & Wiebe, 2012).

Thus, neoliberalism has negatively impacted immigrant women's employment opportunities through both direct impacts on the labour market and a reduction of the support systems they need to obtain better employment in a challenging labour market.

GENDER AND IMMIGRATION CATEGORIES

In the 1960s Canada finally ended its policy of designating immigrants as desirable according to their country, religion, and other traits—which inevitably included race, even if that was not acknowledged—and adopted a new system that aimed to identify immigrants who had skills that would benefit the Canadian economy. The need for skilled workers has become increasingly urgent as the Canadian population ages and the birth rate declines. In 1967 a point system was instituted to evaluate immigrants' economic potential based on factors such as their education, work experience, and language skills. While this system appears well reasoned on the surface, the mechanisms of the policy continue the tradition of viewing some immigrants, namely men, as more desirable than others.

In the economic immigration class, one spouse is designated as the primary applicant and the other spouse and children are admitted as dependents. In the majority of cases, the husband is the primary applicant. This aspect of the immigration policy has important repercussions, because only the skills of the primary applicant are evaluated, reflecting a belief that only men will make a significant contribution to the Canadian economy. Women are considered on par with children, implying that they have no more economic value than children. In fact the government is wholly unaware of what immigrant women might bring to the economy beyond their roles as wives and mothers, because no effort is made to inquire about their skills.

Entering Canada as dependents has long-term impacts on immigrant women's daily life and their labour market experience. Canadian immigration policy repeats and reinforces traditional gender biases at work in this country and in many immigrant countries of origin, whereby men work and women perform unpaid household labour. Thus, it is not surprising that dependent applicants do not succeed in improving their employment status over time (Banerjee & Phan, 2015).

One explanation for this is that because the husband's economic progress is prioritized, the wife will take on survival employment to support the family while the husband does the "more important" work of attending school or job training programs or searching for professional employment. If he is successful in that, the wife may reduce her work hours or leave the labour market altogether.

When men are favoured during the immigration process, the message to women and men is that women's work is less important than their husband's. In a time of escalating refugee migration to Canada, as has occurred during the Syrian civil war, settlement resources become severely strained, limiting the support available to immigrant women to improve their economic prospects. If immigration policy were changed to evaluate the skills of both male and female applicants in the economic class, without dividing them into primary and secondary applicants, the government would be better able to assess the support needs of all applicants.

DESKILLING AND PRECARIOUS EMPLOYMENT

A major hardship for immigrants is employers' rejection of the education and experience that they acquired in their home country due to a belief that their foreign credentials and knowledge are not on par with Canadian standards. This reinforces the perception that immigrants are different (othering) and contributes to exploitation in the labour market.

In Canada there are five organizations that evaluate foreign credentials based on "level and type of learning; duration of study program; status of issuing institutions; the education system of the country concerned; and authenticity, currency, relevance, trustworthiness, and transferability of credential" (Guo, 2009, p. 42). Guo found that these organizations assess immigrants' credentials inconsistently and that even when immigrants present verified credentials, this does not necessarily lead to employment or licensing in their profession.

While deskilling can happen to any immigrant, Guo (2009) writes that "the category of immigrant women has served to commodify these workers, reinforcing their class position in providing cheap, docile labour to their employers under the watchful eyes of the state and under exploitive conditions that are often permeated with racism and sexism" (p. 44). Deskilling is a greater risk for immigrant women because their education and credentials are not as valued as men's to begin with. Moreover, not all immigrant women are treated in the same way. Those from countries that are considered more advanced, such as Britain, the United States, New Zealand, and Australia, and those with financial resources are able to regain their previous professional status in Canada (Guo, 2009). Others face deskilling due to their country of origin, gender, and race, continuing the pattern of devaluing them that begins during their application for immigration (Man, 2004).

When educated immigrants migrate en masse, it creates a "brain drain" that impacts the economy and society of the home country. Ironically, these same immigrants are then relegated to deskilled jobs in Canada for which they are overqualified. Deskilling forces many immigrant women into precarious part-time or temporary jobs (Man, 2004) with low wages and limited or no benefits, few chances for advancement, and a lack of government oversight of working conditions (PEPSO, 2018). Close to half of recent women immigrants are precariously employed (Noack & Vosko, 2011).

Immigrant women suffer broadly from low-wage employment. On average Canadian women face a 30% gender wage gap, increasing to 39% for immigrant women (Faraday, 2017). The gender wage gap varies by country of origin as in some countries cultural norms dictate that women are not educated and work only in the home (Frank & Huo, 2015).

EXPLOITATION ON THE JOB

Many scholars have found evidence that immigrant women are exploited in the labour market (Nichols, 2018; Nichols & Tyyskä, 2015; Premji et al., 2014). Their exploitation is related to both their precarious employment and discrimination. Gottfried et al. (2016) studied East Toronto immigrants and reported that difficulties with language comprehension can lead to exploitation when employers use immigrants' lack of English comprehension to violate employment laws, such as by denying employees breaks and vacation pay. They found that exploitation often pushes immigrants into the underground or shadow economy, where cash payments for wages are difficult or impossible to track, making employees ineligible for some government programs, such as Employment Insurance. Aktar, Topkara-Sarsu, and Dyson's 2013 study on the shadow economy in the east end of Toronto found that 38% of immigrants faced bullying or harassment in the workplace.

Many scholars and think tanks have reported on the failure of employers to comply with employment standards for newcomers (Aktar et al., 2013; Gottfried et al., 2016). Studies have documented the lack of compliance specifically in the case of immigrant women (Dlamini, Anucha, & Wolfe, 2012; Nichols, 2018). Employers use immigrants' lack of awareness of their employee rights to exploit workers (Gottfried et al., 2016). Similarly Aktar, Topkara-Sarsu, and Dyson (2013) reported key statistics from their study of 453 newcomer households in the east end of Toronto. They found that 41% experienced violations of employment standards and that knowledge of employment standards was poor: 48% did not know how many days of vacation they deserved, 34% did not know that injured workers were entitled to benefits, and 16% did not know the minimum wage. More than half of study participants said that they would not report health and safety violations due to potential impacts on their employment.

In a study of newcomer women in the Greater Toronto Area (Nichols, 2018), 7 out of 30 participants were not aware of any drawbacks of being paid under the table. They believed, as their employer told them, that they would earn more with unreported cash payments. They did not understand that failing to report their wages to the government meant that they were ineligible for supports such as Employment Insurance (see also Nichols, 2016). Dlamini, Anucha, and Wolfe (2012) explored employment violations against immigrant women in Windsor, Ontario. They found that the overwhelming majority of immigrant women (35 out of 37) would not report unfair labour practices due to fear of being fired.

DOMESTIC WORKERS

Immigrant women have a long history of migrating to Canada as domestic workers, beginning with British and Finnish domestics who were granted permanent residency in the early 1900s. From World War II to the 1970s Caribbean women came to Canada under the Caribbean Domestic Scheme. They could apply for landed status (now called permanent residency) after one year of live-in domestic work. From 1973 to 1981 a new program, the Temporary Authorization Program, was instituted to recruit Filipino women, who were granted temporary status and no citizenship. From 1981 to 1992, under the Foreign Domestic Movement Program, Filipino women could apply for permanent residency after two years of domestic work. From 1992 to 2014 the program was opened to other countries under the same regulations and renamed the Live-in Caregiver Program (LCP; Hsiung & Nichol, 2010).

There has been a sustained need for domestic childcare workers in Canada due to the lack of a universal childcare program. Canadians have long relied on women from the Global South to care for their children, most recently under the government-run Caregiver Program (Salami, 2016). In 2014 there were 16,238 permitted immigrant caregivers (Citizenship and Immigration Canada, 2014).

Immigrant women serving as caregivers experience labour exploitation such as being forced to work overtime without pay and being on-call around the clock, seven days a week. When they complete their domestic contract they experience further inequality in the Canadian labour market as a result of "stigmatization, having to take costly educational upgrading courses while simultaneously working in 'survival jobs,' and having to be their families' sole breadwinner" (Tungohan et al., 2015, p. 87). In order to be eligible for permanent residency, care workers in the LCP were required to live and work in their employer's home for 24 months over a four-year period, leaving women vulnerable to violations of their privacy and their person and exploitive working conditions. This population of domestic workers consisted of younger women, as the program requirements included an age restriction of 18 to 40 years old. Prokopenko and Hou (2018) report that 86.9% of live-in caregivers become permanent residents, while 12.6% leave Canada within 10 years of their arrival. Following the acknowledgement of abuse and exploitation by employers and recruiters in the LCP, the most recent Caregiver Program, which expired in November 2018, was divided into two streams, one for workers who cared for adults and one for childcare workers (Salami, 2016). The program allowed caregivers to live in or out of their employers' home and to work in health-care institutions like long-term care facilities.

Domestic work in Canada is highly racialized (Hsiung & Nichol, 2010). Caribbean women first entered Canada under immigration policies such as the 1910 Caribbean Domestic Scheme and the 1955 Household Service Workers Scheme. Entry in other categories was very limited due to the perception that Caribbean women "were or would become single parents and likely welfare recipients" (James, 2009, p. 95). While these domestic worker schemes have since been eliminated, their legacy has been the construction of Caribbean immigrant women as low-skilled domestic workers. As James (2009) writes, "Despite more than a quarter century since [the] elimination [of these programs], many African-Caribbean Canadian women continue to work as caregivers and unskilled employees" (p. 96) regardless of how much education they have.

The **global care chain** provides a theoretical explanation of domestic worker migration (Salami & Nelson, 2014). Fudge (2011) defines global care chains as "transnational networks that are formed for the purpose of maintaining daily life. These networks comprise households that transfer their caregiving tasks across borders" (p. 240). Female domestic workers are extracted from the South by the North in an unequal distribution of wealth and racial equality (Salami & Nelson, 2014). For example, Filipino women enter Canada through the Caregiver Program to take care of Canadian families, but they still must financially support their families back in the Philippines and find others to care for their own children, from whom they are separated for long periods before being able to reunite with them.

UNPAID HOUSEHOLD LABOUR AND TIME POVERTY

Immigrant women's economic prospects are greatly impacted by having to do "double shifts," working at paid jobs and also performing many hours a week of unpaid household labour. Native-born Canadian women labour under similar conditions, performing more household labour than their husbands even when both are employed (Nichols et al., 2018). But immigrant women sometimes deal with stronger cultural gender norms as well as extra demands imposed by their family structure.

Immigrant families are often modelled on the multigenerational extended family rather than the Western nuclear family. An immigrant household may house multiple families and generations in the same dwelling, with a strong presence of grandparents and in-laws. Although a larger household may mean that more adults are available to care for children, that advantage is sometimes offset by the cultural expectation that women will care for their husband, in-laws, parents, and grandparents, all while working part-time or full-time. This results in **time poverty** (Nichols et al., 2018)—a lack of time for self-care, education, social activities, and leisure in addition to performing required tasks. In a 2018 study (Nichols et al., 2018) in the Toronto area, Pakistani immigrant women reported doing 21 to 28 hours a week of unpaid household labour, compared to 14 hours a week for native-born Canadian women, even though they spent less time on childcare than native Canadian women. Much of their time at home was spent caring for in-laws and preparing elaborate Pakistani meals.

Time poverty is not only about lack of leisure for immigrant women. When unpaid household labour becomes excessive, these women are unable to improve their job prospects through education and training programs or the time-consuming task of job hunting. Like all women, they then risk becoming dependent on male earners and trapped in unsafe relationships (Nichols & Tyyskä, 2015).

Grandmothers are a case of two-way exploitation. As mentioned, immigrant women may be required by cultural norms to care for grandparents; however, some grandmothers are brought to Canada by their families who are established here for the specific purpose of providing unpaid childcare for their grandchildren (Nichols, 2016). Aggarwal and Das Gupta (2013) studied Sikh Punjabi grandmothers in Toronto who were sponsored by their adult children. They found that these women "effectively [became] unpaid 'live-in caregivers' for their families who cannot afford daycare fees" (p. 81). The fact that immigrant Pakistani women report doing fewer childcare hours than native-born Canadian women (Nichols, 2018) points to the shifting of this task to grandmothers, who are under the same cultural pressures to supply this labour as their daughters and daughters-in-law despite their advanced age. The outcome in both cases is that immigrant men have more time than women for major life activities and economic advancement.

This situation highlights difficult issues surrounding, on the one hand, respect for cultural norms of other countries and, on the other hand, Canadian values of freedom and equality for women. Yet native-born Canadian women struggle with a similar disconnect between values, laws, and family practices as they try to balance their desire for the satisfaction and economic independence that come from meaningful work against continuing gender practices that reinforce their inequality in the workplace and in the home.

CONCLUSION

For immigrants, work is essential for survival in their new host country. While both immigrant men and women's work experience in Canada is impacted by restrictive Canadian immigration policies emphasizing **social capital**, women are uniquely disadvantaged by immigration policies. The majority of immigrant women migrate to Canada as dependents, and their status and employment success are commonly dependent on their male partner. The immigration point system has the effect of dividing men and women into "primary" and "dependent" categories and works against socioeconomic equality for immigrant women. As a result, their preexisting professional status may be downgraded or hidden, and they often take on low-wage survival forms of employment in addition to their unpaid household labour.

While a large percentage of Canadian women struggle with reactionary social attitudes around their roles in the home and the workplace that are slow to change despite gender equality laws, immigrant women bear added burdens related to deskilling, rejection of their previous training and experience, race, religion, language, culture, and family structure that trap them in low-wage jobs and make them vulnerable to exploitation by employers. The predominance of neoliberal social and economic policies in Canada, as in other countries of the Global North, opens a large precarious space in the labour market that is often filled by immigrant women. The immigrant woman's individual ambition and effort may not be sufficient to overcome these obstacles in a system designed to benefit the traditional individual and corporate holders of wealth and power.

KEY READINGS

Fudge, J. (2011). Global care chains, employment agencies, and the conundrum of jurisdiction: Decent work for domestic workers in Canada. *Canadian Journal of Women and the Law, 23*(1), 235–264.

Hudon, T. (2015). Immigrant women. In *Women in Canada: A gender-based statistical report* (7th ed.). Retrieved from http://www.statcan.gc.ca/pub/89-03x/2015001/article/14217-eng.htm

Nichols, L. (2018). Newcomer women's experience of immigration and precarious work in Toronto. *Women's Health and Urban Life, 14*(1), 7–30.

DISCUSSION QUESTIONS

1. Why is it important that we reflect on the work of older women and grandmothers in a discussion about racialized and immigrant women workers?

2. How has usage of the term *immigrant woman* changed in the last few decades in Canada? What led to these changes?

3. How do race and culture impact immigrant women's work experience?

4. With respect to work, how should we deal with conflicts between the aspirations and rights of Canadian women and gender norms in other countries? Do you think Canada should accommodate gender norms of other countries that impact immigrant women's work, or should we encourage immigrants to adopt Canadian norms?

REFERENCES

Aggarwal, P., & Das Gupta, T. (2013). Conversations with Sikh Punjabi grandmothers in Toronto. *South Asian Diaspora, 5*(1), 77–90.

Aktar, N., Topkara-Sarsu, S., & Dyson, D. (2013). *Shadow economies: Economic survival strategies of Toronto immigrant communities.* Toronto: Wellesley Institute. Retrieved from http://www.wellesleyinstitute.com/wp-content/uploads/2013/10/Shadow-Economies-FINAL.pdf

Banerjee, R., & Phan, M. B. (2015). Do tied movers get tied down? The occupational displacement of dependent applicant immigrants in Canada. *Journal of International Migration and Integration, 16*(2), 333–353. doi:10.1007/s12134-014-0341-9

Citizenship and Immigration Canada. (2014). Canada facts and figures: Immigration overview; Temporary residents. Ottawa: Author. Retrieved from http://www.cic.gc.ca/english/pdf/2014-Facts-Figures-Temporary.pdf

Creese, G., & Wiebe, B. (2012). "Survival employment": Gender and deskilling among African immigrants in Canada. *International Migration, 50*(5), 56–76.

Das Gupta, T. (2000). Families of Native peoples, immigrants and people of colour. In B. Crow & L. Gotell (Eds.), *Open boundaries: A Canadian women's studies reader* (pp. 215–230). Toronto: Prentice Hall Canada.

Dlamini, N., Anucha, U., & Wolfe, B. (2012). Negotiated positions: Immigrant women's views and experiences of employment in Canada. *Affilia: Journal of Women and Social Work, 27*(4), 420–434.

Dua, E. (2004). "The Hindu woman's question": Canadian nation building and the social construction of gender for South Asian-Canadian women. In A. Calliste & G. J. Sefa Dei (Eds.), *Anti-racist feminism: Critical race and gender studies* (pp. 55–72). Halifax: Fernwood.

Faraday, F. (2017, September 14). Closing the gender pay gap: Canada's pay gap means women effectively work for free the rest of the year. *Canadian Women's Foundation*. Retrieved from https://www.canadianwomen.org/blog/closing-gender-pay-gap-canadas-pay-gap-means-women-effectively-work-free-rest-year/

Folson, R. B. (2004). Representation of the immigrant. In R. B. Folson (Ed.), *Calculated kindness: Global restructuring, immigration and settlement in Canada* (pp. 21–32). Halifax: Fernwood.

Frank, K., & Hou, F. (2015). Source-country female labour force participation and the wages of immigrant women in Canada. Ottawa: Statistics Canada. Retrieved from https://www150.statcan.gc.ca/n1/pub/11f0019m/11f0019m2015365-eng.htm

Fudge, J. (2011). Global care chains, employment agencies, and the conundrum of jurisdiction: Decent work for domestic workers in Canada. *Canadian Journal of Women and the Law, 23*(1), 235–264.

Gottfried, K., Shields, J., Akter, N., Dyson, D., Topkara-Sarsu, S., Egeh, H., & Guerra, S. (2016). Paving their way and earning their pay: Economic survival experiences of immigrants in East Toronto. *Alternate Routes, 27,* 137–161.

Guo, S. (2009). Difference, deficiency, and devaluation: Tracing the roots of non-recognition of foreign credentials for immigrant professionals in Canada. *Canadian Journal for the Study of Adult Education, 22*(2), 37–52.

Hsiung, P., & Nichol, K. (2010). Policies on and experiences of foreign domestic workers in Canada. *Sociology Compass, 4*(9), 766–778. doi:10.1111/j.1751-9020.2010.00320.x

Hudon, T. (2015). Immigrant women. In *Women in Canada: A gender-based statistical report* (7th ed.). Retrieved from http://www.statcan.gc.ca/pub/89-503-x/2015001/article/14217-eng.htm

James, C. E. (2009). African-Caribbean Canadians working "harder" to attain their immigrant dreams: Context, strategies, and consequences. *Wadabagei: A Journal of the Caribbean and its Diasporas, 12*(1), 92–108.

Ku, J. (2011). Ethnic activism and multicultural politics in immigrant settlement in Toronto, Canada. *Social Identities, 17*(2), 271–289.

Man, G. (2004). Gender, work and migration: Deskilling Chinese immigrant women in Canada. *Women's Studies International Forum, 27*, 135–148.

Mohsinni, A. (2017). *The impact of government funding cuts on ethno-specific settlement services in Ontario: The case of Afghan Association of Ontario and the Afghan Women's Organization.* Unpublished master's thesis, Ryerson University, Toronto.

Muzaffar, S. (2017, November 1). Bait-and-switch of Canadian dream: The compounding hurdles faced by highly skilled immigrant women in STEM sectors. *Canadian Centre for Policy Alternatives.* Retrieved from https://www.policyalternatives.ca/publications/monitor/bait-and-switch-canadian-dream

Nichols, L. J. (2016). Motherhood and unemployment: Intersectional experiences from Toronto and Halifax. *Canadian Review of Social Policy, 76*, 1–24.

Nichols, L. (2018). Newcomer women's experience of immigration and precarious work in Toronto. *Women's Health and Urban Life, 14*(1), 7–30.

Nichols, L. J., Etemadi, T., & Tyyskä, V. (2018). Time poverty of Pakistani immigrant women in Toronto. *South Asian Diaspora, 10*(1), 31–44.

Nichols, L., & Tyyskä, V. (2015). Immigrant women in Canada and the United States. In J. Shields & H. Bauder (Eds.), *Immigrant experiences in North America: Understanding settlement and integration* (pp. 248–272). Toronto: Canadian Scholars' Press.

Noack, A., & Vosko, L. (2011). *Precarious jobs in Ontario: Mapping dimensions of labour market insecurity by workers' social location and context.* Toronto: Law Commission of Ontario. Retrieved from https://www.lco-cdo.org/wp-content/uploads/2012/01/vulnerable-workers-call-for-papers-noack-vosko.pdf

Ontario Council of Agencies Serving Immigrants. (n.d.). Federal budget 2011 may have future cuts to immigrant settlement. Retrieved from http://www.ocasi.org/federal-budget-2011-may-have-future-cuts-immigrant-settlement

Ontario Council of Agencies Serving Immigrants. (2016, November). *Telling our stories from the frontline: Adverse institutional impacts of cuts to immigrant settlement funding in Ontario.* Toronto: Author. Retrieved from http://www.ocasi.org/sites/default/files/telling-our-stories-from-the-frontline_1.pdf

PEPSO. (2018). Getting left behind: Who gained and who didn't in an improving labour market. Hamilton, ON: Author. Retrieved from https://pepso.ca/documents/pepso-glb-final-lores_2018-06-18_r4-for-website.pdf

Premji, S., & Shakya, Y. (2017). Pathways between under/unemployment and health among racialized immigrant women in Toronto. *Ethnicity and Health, 22*(1), 17–35.

Premji, S., Shakya, Y., Spasevski, M., Merolli, J., & Athar, S. (2014). Precarious work experiences of racialized immigrant women in Toronto: A community-based study. *Just Labour, 22*, 122–143.

Prokopenko, E., & Hou, F. (2018). How temporary were Canada's temporary foreign workers? Ottawa: Statistics Canada. Retrieved from https://www150.statcan.gc.ca/n1/pub/11f0019m/11f0019m2018402-eng.htm

Roberts, B. (1979). "A work of empire": Canadian reformers and British female immigration. In L. Kealey (Ed.), *A not unreasonable claim: Women and reform in Canada, 1880s–1920s* (pp. 185–201). Toronto: Women's Press.

Salami, B. (2016). Migrant nurses and federal caregiver programs in Canada: Migration and health human resources paradox. *Canadian Journal of Nursing Research, 48*(2), 35–40.

Salami, B., & Nelson, S. (2014). The downward occupational mobility of internationally educated nurses to domestic workers. *Nursing Inquiry, 21*(2), 153–161. doi:10.1111/nin.12029

Scott-Marshall, H. (2007). Work-related insecurity in the new economy: Evaluating the consequences for health. In H. Prechel (Ed.), *Politics and neoliberalism: Structure, process and outcome* (pp. 21–60). Oxford, UK: Elsevier.

Statistics Canada. (2017, October 25). Immigrant and ethnocultural diversity: Key results from the 2016 census. Retrieved from http://www.statcan.gc.ca/daily-quotidien/171025/dq171025b-eng.htm

Statistics Canada. (2018a). Immigration status and period of immigration, 2016 counts, female, age (total), Canada, provinces and territories, 2016 census—25% sample data. Retrieved from https://www12.statcan.gc.ca/census-recensement/2016/dp-pd/hlt-fst/imm/Table.cfm?Lang=E&T=11&Geo=00&SP=1&view=1&age=4&sex=3

Statistics Canada. (2018b). Labour force characteristics of immigrants by country of birth, annual. Retrieved from https://www150.statcan.gc.ca/t1/tbl1/en/tv.action?pid=1410008901

Tungohan, E., Banerjee, R., Chu, W., Cleto, P., de Leon, C., Garcia, M., … & Sorio, C. (2015). After the Live-in Caregiver Program: Filipina caregivers' experiences of graduated and uneven citizenship. *Canadian Ethnic Studies, 47*(1), 87–105.

UNICEF. (2018). Syrian refugees and other affected populations in Turkey, Lebanon, Jordan, Iraq and Egypt. Retrieved from https://www.unicef.org/appeals/syrianrefugees.html

United Nations. (2017). *International migration report.* New York: UN Department of Economic and Social Affairs. Retrieved from http://www.un.org/en/development/desa/population/migration/publications/migrationreport/docs/MigrationReport2017_Highlights.pdf

CHAPTER 6

"Not Just a Job": Disability, Work, and Gender

Esther Ignagni

In thinking about disabled women in relation to work, this chapter assumes a critical Disability Studies framework. In this framework disability is not understood as an individual problem in need of solution. Disability Studies takes up disability as a sociopolitical and sociocultural phenomenon, something that is co-constructed in relationships. It is an interdisciplinary field of scholarship that originates from the disability rights movement, aspires to disability justice work, and animates disability community. Disability Studies interrogates the values we give to bodies and minds and how we constitute what are livable lives. Disability Studies scholars think through how we make meaning of people, human rights issues, and social justice issues together with queer theory, critical race theory, antiracism, postcolonial thought, and feminism. In this work we understand disability as desirable, agentive, generative, creative, and a site of critique, solidarity, and belonging.

This chapter uses the term *disability* in full recognition that it fails to capture the heterogeneity and complexity of disability experience. In its more than 40-year history, Disability Studies has variegated and proliferated our understandings and articulations of body-mind differences. To attempt to repeatedly list those insights and identities would be to fail, since the list is necessarily fluid and mutable. Therefore, this chapter uses *disability* to capture the scholarship, activism, and art of disabled, mad, neurodiverse, deaf, spoonie, sick, debilitated women, people, communities, and movements. Similarly, this chapter's use of the term *disabled*, as in *disabled women*, is an intentional turning away from officially sanctioned "person-first" language, as in *a person with a disability*, in a desire to draw attention to the conditions of disablement imposed through our social, cultural, and political organization on women who live with body-mind differences (Crow, 1996; Titchkosky, 2003).

Defining disability is a complex, evolving, and often controversial process. In Canada there is no single official definition of disability. Following its ratification of the UN Convention on the Rights of Persons with Disabilities in 2010, Canada has largely assumed the World Health Organization's framing of disability as a phenomenon that reflects an interaction between features of a person's body and mind and features of the society in which they live. This definition acknowledges a person's impairment or body-mind difference with respect to function, while accounting for social oppression confronted in unaccommodating, inaccessible, and actively exclusionary environments. These physical and social barriers make it difficult, if not impossible, for those living with body-mind difference to function and thrive (Mingus, 2011; Shakespeare, 2013).

The complexity of disability definitions is intensified by the array of possible body-mind differences. Impairment can be "congenital, acquired, temporary, life-long, episodic, static or progressive" (Human Resources and Skills Development Canada [HRSDC], 2013, p. 4). As noted in the Federal Reference Guide on Disability (HRSDC, 2013), impairments are typically understood as varying in severity, roughly referencing the degree to which body-mind difference impacts one's activities of daily living either through the way impairment influences function or through the ways that differences in function and appearance are excluded as a result of barriers in the physical and social environment or are actively discriminated against (World Health Organization, 2011). Therefore, assessments of severity and disability itself are attenuated by the degree to which sociopolitical and sociocultural contexts are accommodating, accessible, and welcoming of body-mind difference. As such, disability definitions have and continue to evolve, extending past dominant medical definitions.

THEORETICAL ORIENTATIONS

Disability Studies has encompassed critical scholarship from its inception in the 1970s. Like academic feminism, Disability Studies as a form of academic scholarship arose from both the desire for social change and the disability activist movements fighting for that change (Goodley, 2014; Linton, 1998). Its emergence was largely situated in the disability rights movement of the time, centred on the desire of disabled people to play an active role in the labour market, to lead and to aspire within public spheres, and to have control over their own bodies. Like feminist theory, Disability Studies began as a school of interdisciplinary academic thought, diverging from existing disciplinary approaches that took disabled people themselves as objects of study, housed mainly in the medical and rehabilitation fields. Central to its scholarship was the radical viewpoint that rather than our individual bodies being the problematic, it is the social, cultural, and political organization of our work, education, leisure, and intimate lives that must be the site of analysis and transformation (Goodley, 2014; Oliver & Bochel, 1991). This social model of disability served as a practical tool of analysis to identify how normative social organizations failed to accommodate a diversity of embodiments.

The social model analysis also acted as a corrective to the dominant and enduring conceptions of disability as an individual tragedy due to genetic or environmental insult or injury. Disability is conventionally and discursively considered to be associated with pain and suffering and thereby incompatible with health, well-being, and flourishing. The problems generally attached to disability, ranging from discomfort and distress to poverty and social isolation, are routinely understood as a consequence of individual impairment—physical, sensory, cognitive, or affective deficiency or defect. This focus on the physical body of the individual disabled person means that disabled people's concerns are typically defined as medical issues and by extension best addressed through medical authority in the forms of treatment, rehabilitation, and, whenever possible, cure. From this perspective, a disabled woman's struggles in securing and maintaining paid employment would be located in her inherent, individual, and therefore personal, corporeal anomaly, deficiency, or defect.

The social model analysis, by contrast, redirects attention to examining disabling barriers that disabled women might encounter in the labour market—for example, how training, hiring, daily work arrangements, work sites, opportunities for advancement, or work-related benefits are enmeshed within ableist systems of power and privilege and the ways in which our social and physical environments are organized to exclude certain types of people with impairments. Thus, it supports the recasting of disability as a condition that is socially created through policies, legislation, administrative processes, built environments, and tacit social and symbolic assumptions rather than a purely medical condition.

The early project of Disability Studies was to document this exclusion by drawing attention to the barriers confronted by disabled people to paid work entry and participation. An early text, *Disabling Barriers, Enabling Environments*

(Swain, Finkelstein, French, & Oliver, 1993), brought together activist and scholarly analyses of the social creation of disablement through the economic and social organization of wage labour, including accounts of the segregation of young adults in daycare centres, rendering them unavailable for paid work; the economic basis of disabled people's dependency on the social care industry; the role of technology in limiting and enhancing employment participation; and the unique forms of labour force discrimination faced by deaf, blind, and learning disabled people. Much of the early scholarship was rooted in a historical materialist analysis that ties the creation of disability to the spread of industrial capitalism with its new individuated work regimes, ethos, and disciplines. This analysis pivoted on the contention that the absence of disabled people from the industrial labour market dictates their wider social exclusion (Abberley, 2002). One line of thought connected citizenship and exclusion from paid work; citizenship is linked with being an active economic agent through participation in the paid labour force. In turn, those excluded from work face a denial of political and social rights that depend in part on the capacity to leverage market resources and fashion oneself into both a good worker and a consumer. Moreover, medical authority, with its prevailing logic of cure and care, legitimated disabled people's exclusion from the labour market by reinforcing bodily standards and ambitions—productive, tireless, adaptable, efficient—that aligned with work characterizations in capitalist industrial societies in terms of paid work and profit maximization (Graby, 2015; Stone, 1986). Taken further, disability became useful as a state justification for excluding women, immigrants, racialized people, and others from the material rewards of capitalist economies and other forms or economic and social participation. As Doug Baynton (2013) notes, larger discourses of inherent pathology (e.g., impaired cognition, physical weakness or frailty, physical deficits) served to clarify and justify the domination and marginalization of certain undesirable groups.

HISTORY OF DISABLED WORKERS

The relationship between work and disability in Canada is shadowed by the legacy of institutionalization. In her historical analysis of the Michener Centre, a residential facility for people with intellectual disabilities in Alberta, Claudia Malacrida (2015) traces the intertwining practices of institutionalization and disabled Canadians' relationship to work. Michener, like other residential facilities across Canada and other Western countries, was initially established to provide intensive education to those deemed feeble-minded, an umbrella term that encompassed not only disabled people but certain immigrants, Indigenous people, criminals, poor people, and women who challenged gender codes (Stubblefield, 2007).

In practice, these institutions addressed a number of economic and moral preoccupations of Western nations in the late 19th and early 20th centuries, including eugenicist efforts to segregate those deemed genetically inferior to prevent their free movement in the larger community and potential weakening of the young Canadian nation's population (McLaren, 1990). Coupled with these moral fears were concerns that the feeble-minded were not able to make a productive contribution to society through participation in the capitalist economy. Dubbed "training schools," institutions initially held the promise of educating and habilitating residents with the goal of returning them to community life, but, as Malacrida notes, entry to these facilities was a "life-sentence," with residents eventually transferring to adult institutions where they would live until their deaths.

Despite their failure to provide promised vocational training, institutions brought disabled people's work lives into relief. In a historical analysis of institutionalization in Canada, Nick Clarke (2006) notes that the average age of residents in some British Columbia residential institutions was approximately 55 years. This relatively older demographic suggests market demands for unskilled or semiskilled workers, particularly in the West's natural resource industries. Labour market demands of the time that pivoted on physical labour accommodated workers who were labelled as developmentally or intellectually disabled. However, once these workers could no longer perform the work, or as labour market demands shifted with emerging mechanical advances, they were quickly absorbed into institutions. Similarly, rates of institutionalization of young developmentally disabled people were much lower in rural areas where formalized intelligence testing was not universal and systematic (Strong-Boag, 2007) and where the agricultural economy could sustain workers who were unable to meet these constructed standards. A gender analysis of this extra-institutional work remains to be done, but it is possible that some disabled women were able to avoid institutionalization through domestic, agricultural, or even sex work.

In addition to work in the mainstream economy, there is a growing documentation of forced unpaid labour of disabled people not only in segregated settings such as residential care and training facilities, but also in sheltered workshops and jails (Galer, 2018; Reaume, 2000; Seth, Slark, Boulanger, & Dolmage, 2015). Cure, care, and even punishment legitimated resident and inmate labour, but vocational training was generally touted as a therapeutic intervention, designed to habilitate people deemed feeble-minded and recuperate "wasted human po-tential." In practice vocational and occupational instruction served as a cover for economic exploitation (Malacrida, 2015). Analysis to determine the economic contribution of this labour is currently underway, but it is largely understood that unpaid, compulsory patient labour sustained the institutions themselves and contributed to their surrounding communities.

Institutional labour was markedly gendered, with institutionalized women performing feminized tasks. Records from the recently closed Huronia Regional Centre in Orillia, Ontario, indicate that female residents cooked, provided care for fragile members of the facility, sewed and repaired resident uniforms, and did the laundry. Institutionalized women's labour involved emotional effort given its imbrication with intimate life. For example, archival records document how female survivors were charged with crafting coffin liners for Huronia's resi-dents and administrators, work that was simultaneously highly skilled, physi-cally straining, and emotionally laden (Collins, 2017). Disability historian Susan Schweik (personal communication, 2015) also gestures to the intimate nature of exploitative labour in her recent research documenting the unpaid childcare pro-vided by institutionalized women to children born within the institution, often including their own. Institutional administrators discovered that infants thrived when female residents offered nurturance and care, raising robust and healthy toddlers who were highly desirable for prospective adoptive parents. In a cruel twist, these same women often lost custody of their own children, ostensibly due to their presumed incapacity to parent and their institutionalized status.

FEMINIST CRITIQUE

Disabled women have, to a limited extent, enjoyed the gains achieved by the feminist movement with respect to workforce participation. Historically, femi-nist struggles have sought to transform the relationship between state and gender. In terms of women's work lives, feminist struggles began in the late 19th century with the introduction of labour legislation and safe workplaces (Brown, 1992). In the 20th century feminist interventions expanded to equal opportunity, equal pay, pay equity, and labour legislation concerns with maternity. These endeav-ours continue today as movement efforts recalibrate on broader social policies supporting **gender parity** in the workplace, such as struggles for public daycare, daycare subsidies, and family leave policies (Brodie, 1995; Brown, 1992).

Few comprehensive gendered analyses of disabled women's work in and beyond institutional settings exist, although some are underway. The elision of the history of disabled women's labour contribution in segregated and institutionalized settings is an extension of the elision of gendered labour in general.

In his review of historical analyses of work, Reaume (2018) attempts to extract a gendered account of disabled workers. He notes how disabled male veterans were historically prioritized in Canadian approaches to paid employment and disability. Disabled women, naturalized as tied to the domestic sphere of home and family on the basis of their sex, were largely understood as having no claim to paid labour. Reaume does locate some exceptions to this view, including a Dictaphone training program for blind women and a government business-loan program enabling disabled women to set up music training enterprises. But when disabled women were involved in paid labour, their role was limited. For example, work responsibilities in Canada's sheltered workshops for people labelled with intellectual impairments were divided along gender lines (Galer, 2018). Women's workplace injuries were played down, understood as minimally disrupting their lives. Reaume (2018) also cites other historians' findings that women who have been injured on the job have found their work more devalued compared to men, as reflected in compensation claims (likely based on a wage system that pays women less than men).

Early Disability Studies scholarship, particularly social model analyses, has not given much room for understanding the unique experiences of disabled people or for appreciating the way that society is organized to exclude, for example, racialized disabled people or disabled women in specific ways. More recently, there have been some attempts to assume an intersectionality theoretical approach, but the complexity of disability experience has been more practically illuminated through the use of feminist, critical race, and postcolonialist thought.

Feminist disability scholars have lauded sociopolitical framings of disability and the social model analysis in particular, citing that it has saved lives (Crow, 1996; Morris, 1991; Thomas, 1999, 2007) by replacing devalued and limited received narratives of disability difference with politicized and empowered understanding of disabled women's lives. This reframing has offered disabled people a sense of hope and fostered a resistance to conditions of disablement. However, these same scholars have critiqued its masculinist assumptions and its sidelining of gendered concerns. These critiques target how the social model creates a false distinction between the natural body and the cultural world of oppression (Shildrick, 2015) and overlooks the relevance of disability representations in shaping ableist cultures (Hall, 2011) and its failure to account for the psycho-emotional effects of disability exclusion, such as internalizing negative messages about disability (Reeve, 2006). As such, feminist disability scholars have mobilized a range of feminist theories to better understand how the intersection of disability and gender relations influences the experience and context of disabled women.

Following the tradition of feminist Disability Studies we turn to reflecting on the gendered forms of disablement experienced by disabled women in securing and maintaining work, tracing the broader experiences of disabled people in relationship to work and drawing out existing or potential gendered analyses.

EXCLUSION FROM THE WORKFORCE

Disabled Canadians' relationship to work remains precarious, marginalized, and a source of marked social exclusion. The 2012 Canadian Survey on Disability (CSD) noted that nearly 2.1 million women or 14.9% of women aged 15 years or older reported living with one or more disabilities that impacted their activities of daily living (Burlock, 2017). In the 2012 National Household Survey, just over 2.1 million people aged 25 to 64, or 11% of Canadians, reported living with some form of physical, mental, or sensory impairment.[1] To account for the diversity in impairment, a severity score was developed. The score accounted for the number of impairment types, the degree of the functional impact of the impairment, and the frequency of activity limitation. Accordingly, the survey reported lower levels of employment participation among both women and men with more severe or moderate impairments. While some disabled people may not be able to participate in the labour force because of the intensity and number of their impairments, a lack of adequate accommodations and resources supporting employment also contributes to labour force exclusion (Shier, Graham, & Jones, 2009; Turcotte, 2014).

The unemployment rate among disabled Canadians 25 to 64 years old was 11% in 2011, compared with 6% for those who did not report living with an impairment (Turcotte, 2014). Turcotte (2014) suggests that the participation rate—"the percentage of the population employed or seeking employment"— was 55% for disabled persons (p. 3), almost 30 points lower than their non-disabled counterparts. This gap decreases when employment is adjusted for age, Indigenous identity, education, and gender—all social conditions that tend to affect the employment rate. The adjusted employment rate stands at 68% for disabled persons, compared to 80% for the nondisabled population (Turcotte, 2014).

Disabled women are less likely to hold professional or managerial positions and to work full-time all year, and they earn less than their non-disabled counterparts (e.g., an average $3,500/year less for professional positions; Burlock, 2017;

Turcotte, 2014). Only when disabled people are able to secure a university education do these differences begin to decrease (Turcotte, 2014).

While there are negligible differences between disabled women and men with respect to educational attainment, disabled women fare poorly compared to nondisabled men and women. According to the 2011 Canadian Survey on Disability, 18.3% of disabled women aged 25 to 54 reported that they had no certificate, diploma, or degree, significantly more than the 8.3% of nondisabled women in that age group who had not obtained a certificate, diploma, or degree (Burlock, 2017). Severity of impairment also influenced level of education: in this core working-age group, 21.9% of those with severe and very severe impairments had no education credential, versus 14.6% of those with moderate impairments (Burlock, 2017). The same CDS data also indicated that disabled women were half as likely to have obtained a bachelor's degree or higher compared with nondisabled women (15.7% versus 30.7%, respectively). Across all findings, women with severe and very severe impairments were less likely to have received a certificate, diploma, or degree, and obtained bachelor's degrees or higher at lower rates than their counterparts with mild or moderate impairments (10.5% versus 21%, respectively; Burlock, 2017).

The combination of gender and disability deepens the marginalization of disabled women in relation to paid work (Fawcett, 2000; Turcotte, 2014). Disabled women are slightly overrepresented among disabled Canadians: the proportion of disabled men and women is roughly equal from ages 15 to 29, but the proportion of women 30 years and older who report impairments is roughly 2% higher than men (Burlock, 2017). While gender analyses of disabled people's relationship to the workforce are limited, older analyses based on Human Resources and Skills Development Canada data indicate that gender intensifies the disadvantage experienced by disabled people in relation to work. In recent analyses of disabled women and barriers to employment in Canada, disabled women are more likely than others to be unemployed, to live in poverty, to be precariously employed, to experience workplace ableism (discrimination against disabled people), and to encounter a range of practical barriers to work, such as a lack of transportation, childcare, or attendant care.

Once employed, disabled women, like their male counterparts, face barriers in the form of horizontal segregation (Abberley, 2002). Disabled people tend to be sequestered into particular occupations, such as customer service and sales, within certain sectors, such as banking for those with postsecondary education or physical trades and goods and services for people with certain forms of cognitive or learning differences (Fredeen, Martin, Birch, & Wafer, 2012;

Turcotte, 2014). This funnelling of disabled people into specific labour sectors has implications for some disabled women. They are less likely to be managers in professional occupations and are almost entirely absent in the physical trades and goods sector.

Further, disabled workers tend to miss opportunities for career advancement or mobility. They are passed over for promotion or not considered for managerial positions at one extreme, or limited to part-time contractual work at the other (Dossa, 2009; Roulstone & Williams, 2014). In her narrative analysis of racialized disabled women, Parin Dossa (2009) gives an example of a disabled woman caught in part-time, front-line social services work that required her to work evenings and weekends. She felt unable to resist these working conditions for fear of losing her employment. In that setting, the employee was often mistaken for a client rather than a worker, a misconception that works against career advancement. In other instances, disabled workers may experience the "glass partition effect," whereby they remain in a single occupation for prolonged periods, sometimes extending to their entire career. While ostensibly voluntary, these occupational containments mean that disabled people miss out on opportunities for learning, increased earning power, enhanced benefits and pensions, fulfillment of career aspirations, and the opportunity to occupy positions of authority and leadership (Roulstone & Williams, 2014). In their study of disabled white-collar workers, Roulstone & Williams (2014) found that workers were hesitant to leave positions in which they had already secured accommodations and invested in shifting the normative culture of their workplace. They expressed anxiety about entering new positions with unknown demands and inherent disabling barriers, leaving them with the double burden of learning the ropes while simultaneously contending with an exclusionary work arrangement. Although Roulstone and Williams do not offer a gender analysis, we can speculate that disabled women would also be concerned with gendered issues related to parental leave, family leave, or other caregiving matters. The lower earning power and prolonged job stagnation also are factors that lead to earlier retirement, potentially putting older disabled women at increased risk of poverty (Abberley, 2002; Crawford, 2013). However understandable individual disabled workers' career immobility may be, notions of disabled workers as inflexible, cautious, and not as capable of taking on new and enhanced tasks—notions at odds with the contemporary neoliberal work ethos—are reinforced, rendering disabled women's work lives more precarious.

The implication of this neoliberal ethos for disabled women is illuminated by recent data demonstrating that disabled employees take fewer sick and personal days and show high job commitment (Fredeen et al., 2012). While such findings make the business case to hire more disabled workers, they also gesture to the ableist pressures that disabled people may experience at work. Disabled workers' idealized performance may belie fears of being perceived as inefficient, unproductive, or an otherwise undesirable employee. Disabled women may find such rigorous job performance standards impossible to meet given the demands of their domestic labour, or they may forego domestic responsibilities in an effort to retain employment. The latter strategy places them in an acutely difficult position since their domestic labour, particularly as parents, often comes under formal and informal scrutiny and assessment (Clarke & McKay, 2014; Ignagni & Fudge Schormans, 2016). Moreover, such tensions may leave disabled women without protective social networks to buffer labour market fluctuations along with everyday and workplace ableism and other forms of discrimination, and the economic precarity that accompanies being single and living alone.

Poverty is another disabling barrier with gendered implications in relation to work. Disabled people constitute about 40% of those who live at or below the low-income cut-off, with those who are also sole parents, older, and living alone at particular risk (Burlock, 2017; Crawford, 2013; Wall, 2017). According to a report based on the 2014 Longitudinal and International Study of Adults, 23.1% of disabled women have low after-tax incomes, compared to 9.3% of nondisabled working-age women (Wall, 2017). Another analysis, based on the 2009 Survey of Labour and Income Dynamics, reports that disabled women 15 years and older who are at or below the low-income cut-off receive a greater percentage of their income through government transfers as opposed to private market sources compared both to disabled poor men and nondisabled poor women (Crawford, 2013). This report also notes that as poor disabled women grow older, specifically 54 to 64 years, they earn a greater share of their income through non-government-supported employment compared to their poor nondisabled female counterparts (Crawford, 2013). Disabled women 15 years and older who lived alone reported the lowest household income on average, $25,690, compared to $34,000 for their nondisabled female counterparts (Burlock, 2017). Disabled women's overrepresentation among poor Canadians speaks in part to their weaker attachment to the labour market—a situation that is exacerbated by the intersection of disability and poverty. Working inevitably carries expenses related to transportation, childcare, clothing, and conveniently located housing, as well as the costs of accommodations within the work site that may not have been anticipated and addressed by employers. For disabled women, accessible transportation, childcare, and housing may not be readily available or affordable

(Dumais, Prohet, Ducharme, Archambault, & Ménard-Dunn, 2015). Disabled women who cannot secure or pay for these resources may not be able to consider employment.

Canadian government assistance for disabled women has been described as "patchy" and complex (Prince, 2016a). It is enmeshed in a network of programs and policies located across a range of government sectors, contingent on specific impairments or impairment origin, means tested, tied to employment and programmatic obligations, and distributed through all levels of government (Prince, 2009, 2016b). The resources that might mitigate disabled women's income insecurity or assist them with entering and remaining in the workforce are buried within bureaucratic systems. This hit-or-miss character of government assistance disadvantages disabled women, who may lack the expertise, ability, time, energy, and financial resources to navigate it.

A second major disabling barrier to work has been inaccessible workplaces or lack of accommodations. Although most statistical analyses suggest that disabled people do not report lack of accommodations as a reason for unemployment or lack of labour market participation, qualitative research has indicated otherwise. Certain female-dominated occupations, such as those in social services or health care, may involve body-based expectations like driving or physical movement or be housed in older, inaccessible facilities (Chouinard, 2010; Dossa, 2009). Requests for accommodation may also be met with hesitation or poorly understood by employers and coworkers (Deveau, 2011). Significantly, employers disclose fears around the cost of providing accommodations; however, as the 2012 Federal Panel Report on hiring disabled people in the business sector indicated, accommodation costs are quite low (Fredeen et al., 2012).

The practical complexity of disabled women's work and family lives points to additional needs for accommodations. As mentioned above, in order to pursue employment, disabled women may require accessible transportation, housing, and childcare, as well as nurturance and personal support within their homes. Disabled women, particularly those who are parenting alone, must synchronize multiple, often partially accessible, systems (Prilleltensky, 2003). For example, a woman may find that she must work within personal support workers, time constraints to help her and her children prepare for their day. She must schedule a paratransit pick-up to transport her child to school or daycare and then take her to her workplace—a trip that could last up to two hours in large urban centres. This type of scheduling work both structures and disrupts the hectic morning routine experienced by many Canadian families. There are many places where things go wrong and become delayed, with potential impacts on a woman's work performance. Disabled women need workplaces that embrace a generous conception of accommodation and are able to understand the contingency and contradictions of blending gendered domestic and paid employment labours.

A third area of disablement relates to attitudinal barriers within the workplace. Disabled people have described experiences of workplace discrimination ranging from taunting, relegation to tokenistic positions, assumptions of incapacity or weakness, patronizing and unsolicited offers of assistance, and use of ableist language of suffering or confinement (Dossa, 2009; Shier et al., 2009). Ableist discrimination dovetails with its sexist forms. For example, assumptions of fragility, dependency, and incapacity may open disabled women to unwanted physical touch in the guise of assistance, or a reinforcement of feminized exclusions from specific work tasks. While some discrimination is clearly hostile, most forms may emerge from a lack of knowledge about and experience with disability. On the surface, it might seem that this sort of discrimination could be easily addressed through education and training for employers and coworkers to dispel myths and to guide universal design in work practices (Fredeen et al., 2012). However, other forms of attitudinal discrimination may be tacit, embedded within the work arrangements themselves. Commentators such as Prince (2009, 2016a), Shier et al. (2009), Chouinard (2010), and others have contended that neoliberal economies and state restructuring have led to the intensification and rationalization of workplaces, potentially giving rise to a form of neoliberal ableism or "able nationalism" that deepens the impact of austerity on disabled people (Mitchell & Snyder, 2015). Few explorations of workplace ableisms are gendered; however, there are clear gender implications when disabled women attempt to leverage the human rights system to challenge their disablement.

Despite the Canadian Human Rights Act and the provincial rights codes to seek redress, disabled women are particularly marginalized because the time and energy required to pursue human rights claims is difficult to balance with the added domestic and accessibility labour they perform. Disabled women have fewer material resources to manage these competing labours or to secure legal counsel, especially in light of severe cuts to funding of resources to support human rights claims over the last 15 years. At the same time, legal redress remains situated in the market, with fines, settlements, and compensation largely expressed in dollar amounts, rather than structural change. This tendency toward market-based solutions forces disabled women to understand and make claims to their value in terms of wages or out-of-pocket expenses. Yet the impact of discrimination on their minds and bodies and to their unpaid social reproduction work (that is, the impact on self-care, leisure time with family, or the emotional labour of supporting attendant workers) cannot be so easily monetized (Malhotra, 2014; Russell, 1998). Finally, our human rights system is organized around a single-issue complaint process, meaning that disabled women, like racialized, poor, queer, or immigrant women, cannot make claims that reflect the intersecting systems of power and privilege that give rise to their experience of discrimination. When their complaints do lead to human rights victories, such as that of Donna Jodhan (*Canada [Attorney-General] v. Jodhan*, 2012), gender issues are erased from the larger labour force benefit. Jodhan, a blind woman, was unable to complete an online application for a job with the federal government because the electronic process was inaccessible for her. When she complained, she was instructed to complete a print application or seek assistance. Unable to find an accessible solution, Jodhan sought a declaration under section 18.1 of the Federal Courts Act that the "standards implemented by the federal government for providing visually impaired Canadians with access to government information and service on the Internet" and their implementation denied her equal access to government information and services. The case rested on the claim that this failure violated section 15.1 of the Canadian Charter of Rights and Freedoms. The Federal Court of Appeal found that Jodhan had been "denied equal access to, and equal benefit from, government information and services provided online to the public on the Internet and that this constitutes discrimination on the basis of her physical disability." The appeal court noted that blind people had not been reasonably accommodated through alternate information channels. Alternatives such as phone or mail did not constitute substantively equal treatment. Online information accessibility provided substantive equality, since, like a ramp, it provided visually impaired people with dignified and independent access to information. While the case is clearly one of disability access, given that federal civil service positions are dominated by female employees, we could speculate about gendered components to Jodhan's case that were not raised. For example, disabled women may be more viewed as more dependent, more likely to rely on others, and inherently suited to accept assistance. This problematic interplay of sexist and ableist assumptions may have tacitly subdued any government concerns about inaccessible online job postings and applications.

EXPANDING THE SCOPE OF DISABLED WOMEN'S WORK

A second way that feminist disability scholars have contributed to the understanding of disabled women's relationship to work has been to examine social reproduction. Early Disability Studies and the social model analysis in particular were consistent with masculinist theorizing: the so-called private realm of home and family was held to be rightless and as such not taken into account as a site of disablement nor as a site where ableism could flourish (Brown, 1992). Feminist political theorists helped challenge the notion of women's social reproduction labour performed in family and other intimate spheres as "natural and prepolitical" (Brodie, 1995; Brown, 1992, p. 17). These analyses have pointed to shifting historical and cultural constructions of women's ostensibly natural suitability and capacity for social reproduction work and the taken-for-granted ways that this work supports capitalism. The work that disabled women have done in families and other intimate spaces was not initially taken as political by disability rights activists. Until recently this has left disabled women to assert their contributions to the larger society and to identify the disabling barriers they encounter in these endeavours. In what follows we introduce two forms of non-normative social reproduction work: care work and body work. Unlike our earlier discussion about disablement related to the workforce, these examples draw on disabled women's embodied labours to enflesh the masculinist and macho project of Disability Studies.

One of the major projects of feminist disability analysis has been to rethink the relationship between care and disability. Early disability activists promoted independent living (IL), a model and philosophy of personal support run by and for people with (primarily) physical impairments to assist with activities of daily living.

The IL model arose from the challenges that disabled people confronted in accessing personal support workers outside institutional settings (DeJong, 1979; Morris, 2001; Yoshida, Willi, Parker, & Locker, 2006). It also reflected the early disability activist regard for care as an anathema, as holding disabled people in asymmetrical power relationships in which they were viewed as dependent and a burden on their nondisabled caregivers. These critiques tapped into dominant discourses of disability as leading to the intensification of another's labour, a drain on public resources, and devoid of agency and autonomy (Morris, 2001). In response, the IL model redefined care as help, obtained through a network of paid formal personal support workers under the disabled person's control and direction. While this model has been revised and more robustly funded in Canada in the 2000s, it gestures to the work of everyday living that is integral to disabled life. Disabled feminists, with their greater attention to the material body and embodiment, have noted that personal support entails the administrative labour of hiring and firing, scheduling, assigning work tasks, and offering care instruction (Kelly, 2011, 2013; Morris, 2001). Layered onto these administrative activities is the work of maintaining collegial relationships among personal assistants and with oneself and managing the emotional dynamic, particularly during intimate interactions (Hande & Kelly, 2015; Liddiard, 2014). This blend of administrative and emotional labours is not only crucial to sustaining the smooth realization of the IL model, but also another area of invisible labour performed by disabled people.

Another focus of feminist disability analysis with respect to work is the labour involved in living with body-mind difference. A key critique leveraged at the social model and sociopolitical disablement analyses is their neglect of the experience of impairment and the psychic and emotional work of moving through ableist cultures (Mingus, 2011; Shildrick, 2015; Thomas, 1999; Wendell, 2001). Carol Thomas (1999, 2007) introduced the concept of *impairment effects*, an element of the biosocial impaired body. Thomas (1999) contends that embodied difference inevitably leads to different ways of interaction with our environments and cultures. Each interaction opens up the potential for ableist encounter: over and over again we witness normative moments in which our presence as a disabled person was not anticipated or desired. Disabled female scholars have written about how impairment effects enter their work lives, creating situations of discomfort, uncertainty, and outright discrimination that must be managed. Assessing the shifting demands of access and accommodation, disclosing hidden impairments, using humour to defuse coworker discomfort, creatively reworking inaccessible environments, or pointing out ableist assumptions in one's sphere of work—all of these entail a blend of emotional, creative, and administrative knowledge and labour that facilitates the disabled person's work and may have positive consequences for nondisabled workers.

WORK AS CONTAINMENT

The opening sections of this chapter pointed to the exploitation of disabled women's labour in the context of institutions. Today, access to work for disabled people is increasingly tied to certain forms of contemporary unwalled institutionalization. The deinstitutionalization policies and practices of the 1980s in many parts of Canada and the Global North have given way to forms of transinstitutionalization: the containment of disabled and other marginalized people through smaller-scale, community-based residential settings such as group homes and through a web of state policies that monitor, regulate, and punish disabled people through the promise of meagre material security and limited freedom of movement (Ben-Moshe, Chapman, & Carey, 2014; Hayley, personal communication, 2017).

Over the past two decades, Canada, along with the United States, advanced industrial countries in the European Union, Australia, and New Zealand, has adopted strategies to reduce social benefits and welfare expenditures and to increase incentives to work. Neoliberal discourses about economic efficiency and "crippling," expensive, and unsustainable social service programming (McRuer, 2010) have been deployed to defend austerity measures. As a result, income security programs, for example, have been restructured to be increasingly tied to work obligations (Grover & Soldatic, 2013; Prince, 2016b). In their efforts to increase labour market participation contemporary welfare programs have "emphasized financial incentives, active job searching and participation in labour market programmes" (Shier et al., 2009, p. 64).

Disabled women seem to have ambivalent experiences related to participation in government assistance for work programs. Some find the information offered in the programs generally helpful and instructive (Campolieti, Gunderson, & Smith, 2014). Others have indicated that supported employment arrangements offer a safe place to connect with other disabled employees and are experienced as more understanding and accepting of non-normative ways of working (Butcher & Wilton, 2008). In her Canadian online survey conducted in the late 2000s with 80 disabled women around their experience of employment assistance, Chouinard (2010) found that more than half of her sample would not have been able to earn a living wage without such programs. While positive in one regard, this does provide insight into how disabled women are ultimately contained by these programs, since failure to participate would have serious material consequences. In addition, within the work setting, Chouinard's participants encountered many of the same barriers that disabled people encounter in any employment setting, including lack of accommodations and ableist employer and coworker attitudes.

Crucially, disabled women found that they experienced a unique form of discrimination. Programs that offered a wage subsidy to employers created a "revolving door of employment" in which job opportunities would end as soon as the government portion of the wage lapsed. Chouinard (2010) notes that disabled women characterized this transient and contingent commitment to disabled workers and avoidance of paying out of pocket as a form of employer abuse.

POSTWORK FUTURES

Over the past decade, a strengthening postwork discourse has been emerging along with the disability justice movement. The analysis builds on several emerging lines of critique of the early privileging of labour and historical materialist roots of the movement itself. Feminist disabled activist Sunny Taylor (2004) argued that our value as humans should not be determined by our capacity to maximize profit, but by our contributions to culture in its most generous formulations. Art, mutual care, activism, and other forms of conviviality contribute to the fabric of our shared world and our value beyond monetization. While her essay does not engage with gender explicitly, her affirming alternatives to labour force participation might be associated with more feminized activities that are conventionally the purview of women's lives. She urges disabled people to set aside "nonworking guilt" in appreciation of their own inherent value.

Taylor's work dovetails with the acknowledgement that the centralizing of work in the disability movement has led to the marginalization of those who cannot work, particularly those whose impairments preclude them from participating in the waged labour force (Kittay, 2011; Shakespeare, 2013). If access to work is the route to citizenship, then where are the opportunities for those with complex impairments to claim belonging and contribution? Taken further, postwork approaches such as Taylor's have the potential to challenge dividing practices in neoliberal economies whereby those at the lower-wage and less-skilled ends of the labour market will never be viewed as efficient workers or optimal citizens (Graby, 2015; Malhotra, 2014). Assuming an attentiveness to gender, postwork approaches may also illuminate practices contributing to gender divisions. For example, structural barriers limiting disabled women's capacity to secure labour opportunities open to disabled men (e.g., day labour, physical labour), due either to the nature of the work or to sexist assumptions about who is best suited to perform particular jobs, only deepen gender divisions with respect to poverty and reliance on social assistance.

Postwork analyses also challenge the primacy of work as a means to health and well-being. Abberley (2002) suggests that work and health are tied together in contradictory arguments that inadvertently promote ableist framings of human value and contribution. Health becomes synonymous with the capacity to work, which is affirmed as positive. By extension, states of distress and illness are seen as incompatible with work, always undesirable, and open for remedy. This poses specific problems for women, who must contend with enduring sexist assumptions that female embodiments are inherently fragile, limited, leaky, unpredictable, and deficient (Shildrick, 2015; Wendell, 2001). These ableist logics have formed the foundation for the exclusion of women from the public sphere, including equal paid work opportunities. Unfortunately, mainstream feminist response has been to promote women's capacity and fortitude, without challenging the ableism driving their social containment or questioning the valorization of work itself (Baynton, 2013).

Graby (2015) also notes how the emphasis on work has been co-opted by the neoliberal state to create a range of individualized interventions directed at disabled people to distinguish them from able workers, while simultaneously clawing back universally available state resources. As with other marginalized groups, these programs ultimately divide disabled people into those who can be capacitated into future workers desired under neoliberal conditions and others who are left to wither (Fritsch, 2015). Even those who do work attract ableist assessments, since without adequate accommodation in neoliberal work environments, they will never be viewed as efficient workers (Malhotra, 2014). Given the difficulties faced by Canadian disabled women, particularly those deemed to be more severely disabled, to secure the resources of capacitation, such as public transit, childcare, adequate housing, or workplace accommodations (Burlock, 2017), we can see that disabled women may be particularly vulnerable to the debilitating effects of employment (stress, overwork, fatigue). This raises important questions about the apparent benefits that work delivers to disabled women's well-being and the degree to which work only deepens gender and other social divisions.

Scholars such as Graby (2015) and Malhotra (2014) have promoted the decommodification of labour, pushing for a new socioeconomic order in which social services and supports are treated as universal rights rather than conditioned on an individual's ability to earn wages. Universal state interventions such as a guaranteed annual income and universal daycare would ensure a living wage for disabled people whether or not they participate in the workforce. Malhotra (2014) argues that this is "more relevant in the post-2008 economic crash environment, in which the stock market recovery has not translated into a significant number of new jobs for the working" (p. 44). Such interventions, while always reliant on women's social reproduction labour, may also hold promise for disabled women. Since the poorest disabled women rely on social benefits for income, including child benefits, and their caregiving labour is often unrecognized by disability and feminist advocates alike and poorly compensated by the state, disabled women are positioned to benefit most from such postwork interventions.

A postwork perspective avoids a wage labour system that promotes (competitive) divisions among disabled people. Returning to Sunny Taylor's (2004) vision, a postwork perspective acknowledges the value of living the relational interdependence that emerges from embodied and enminded differences.

CONCLUSION

This chapter has introduced some of the main concerns faced by disabled women in relation to work, drawing from insights from critical Disability Studies and feminist approaches. Feminist analyses have not adequately addressed disability, and early Disability Studies commentators overlooked gender differences, resulting in persistent gender-based concerns in current knowledge about disability and work. Disabling barriers to work include accommodations, ableist attitudes and assumptions, and poverty, all of which are experienced differently by disabled women.

While Canada's human rights legislation has been used to secure the equality of disabled Canadians with respect to transportation, education, access to services, and many other spheres, the specific concerns of disabled women, particularly at the intersection of ableism and sexism, may require focused legal intervention and innovation. Both legal and policy efforts need to be directed to uncover, document, and address how explicit and casual ableism contour disabled women's work lives and intersect with assumptions about indigeneity, race, class, migration, and gender and sexual identity. Emerging disability justice approaches that emphasize intersectional understandings of disability and access (Mingus, 2011) may direct us to consider how access to work and accessibility at work shift with structural changes such as changes in Canadian immigration policy or the Truth and Reconciliation Commission report. Focusing on the former, we might ask, how does disabled newcomer women's exclusion from work render them uniquely vulnerable to violence or isolation? Or, are these women contributing to underground economies, and what are these economies and what working conditions do they offer? As an extension to intersectional analyses, we need more information about the work lives of disabled women in remote, northern, rural, and even suburban parts of Canada, where distance, weather, and dated infrastructure make access to work acutely difficult.

Knowledge about disabled women's everyday work lives must be expanded and detailed. Experiences of disabled women across different sectors would be helpful, particularly beyond the retail and service sectors in which disabled women appear to more readily secure employment. How do women with physical impairments fare in nursing or other health-care professions? How do the higher rates of workplace injuries in this sector shape the way disability is perceived, and what are the consequences of reporting injuries or illness for returning to work for injured health-care workers, how patients are regarded, and so on? Similarly, how do workers with histories of psychiatric diagnosis and intervention fare in female-dominated professions such as social work, where women's mental health concerns are both a target of practice intervention and a source of surveillance around professional conduct? The experiences of women with invisible and contested body-mind differences such as pain or episodic illnesses are also important for understanding the relationship between work and disability and how neoliberal workplaces respond to the unique and dynamic needs of any worker.

Relational and phenomenological scholarship within Disability Studies may be helpful in directing inquiry into the embodied experiences of different forms of labour for disabled women. Disability rights advocacy and activism have invested much energy in getting disabled workers in the workplace door and securing appropriate accommodations for them, achieving legal, policy, and employment gains for disabled women. However, once employed, disabled women may experience an array of unanticipated demands. Reflecting on these demands may inform practical strategies toward the moving horizon of workplace accessibility, since complete and final access is not possible given the dynamic conditions of work. Perhaps more significantly, reflecting on disability, women, and work can surface and challenge the normative and intensifying demands of productivity, performance, and pace that characterize all work lives.

Work is an important source of identity and belonging, facilitates community participation, and enables people to survive and thrive. As such, disabled women's exclusion and marginalized participation in all forms of work remains a key focus of activism and advocacy. Along with calls for inclusion, we must value the interdependence, flexibility, rest, and self-care that characterize all forms of disabled women's endeavours for the way these transform the human relationship to work.

NOTE

1. This figure is slightly lower than other national reports, such as the 2006 Participation Activity Limitation Survey, which indicated that 14.7% of Canadian children and adults live with an impairment (HRSDC, 2013), or the Canadian Survey on Disability, in which 13.7% of Canadians self-identified as living with an impairment in 2012 (Wall, 2017).

KEY READINGS

Dossa, P. (2009). *Racialized bodies, disabling worlds: Storied lives of immigrant Muslim women.* Toronto: University of Toronto Press.

Liddiard, K. (2014). The work of disabled identities in intimate relationships. *Disability and Society, 29*(1), 115–128.

Ryan, S., & Runswick-Cole, K. (2008). Repositioning mothers: Mothers, disabled children and disability studies. *Disability and Society, 23*(3), 199–210.

Stone, S. D., Crooks, V. A., & Owen, M. (Eds.). (2014). *Working bodies: Chronic illness in the Canadian workplace.* Montreal: McGill-Queen's Press.

DISCUSSION QUESTIONS

1. How does disability impact gender expectations that limit nondisabled women's participation in the paid labour force?

2. Discuss how disabled women have had ambivalent relations with care work, positioned as contributing to the caring labours of others, while their own caring work is erased or systemically precluded. What opportunities for coalition building and joint activism might be possible between formal caregivers like personal support coworkers (who are predominantly women) and disabled women?

3. Disabled women have been largely neglected in terms of their social reproduction work as partners and parents. Instead, feminist attention has been on the work that mothers of disabled children perform. How can these two perspectives at the nexus of gender and disability be seen to work in tandem? How might the struggles of disabled women and mothers of disabled children be mutually enhanced?

REFERENCES

Abberley, P. (2002). Work, disability, disabled people and European social theory. In C. Barnes, M. Oliver, & L. Barton (Eds.), *Disability studies today* (pp. 61–79). Oxford, UK: Polity Press.

Baynton, D. (2013). Disability and the justification of inequality in American history. In L. Davis (Ed.), *The disability studies reader* (3rd ed.) (pp. 15–31). London: Routledge.

Ben Moshe, L., Chapman, C., & Carey, A. (2014). *Disability incarcerated: Imprisonment and disability in the United States and Canada.* New York: Palgrave MacMillan.

Brodie, J. (1995). *Politics on the margins: Restructuring and the Canadian women's movement.* Toronto: Fernwood.

Brown, W. (1992). Finding the man in the state. *Feminist Studies, 18*(1), 7–34.

Burlock, A. (2017). Women with disabilities. In *Women in Canada: A gender-based statistical report*. Ottawa: Government of Canada.

Butcher, S., & Wilton, R. (2008). Stuck in transition? Exploring the spaces of employment training for youth with intellectual disability. *Geoforum*, *39*(2), 1079–1092.

Campolieti, M., Gunderson, M. K., & Smith, J. A. (2014). The effect of vocational rehabilitation on the employment outcomes of disability insurance beneficiaries: New evidence from Canada. *IZA Journal of Labor Policy*, *3*(1), 10.

Canada (Attorney-General) v. Jodhan. Federal Court of Appeal 161 (2012).

Chouinard, V. (2010). Women with disabilities' experiences of government employment assistance in Canada. *Disability and Rehabilitation*, *32*(2), 148–158.

Clarke, H., & McKay, S. (2014). Disability, partnership and parenting. *Disability and Society*, *29*(4), 543–555.

Clarke, N. (2006). Opening closed doors and breaching high walls: Some approaches for studying intellectual disability in Canadian history. *Histoire Sociale/Social History*, *39*(78), 467–485.

Collins, K. (2017). *A stitch in time: Mourning the unnamed*. Master's thesis, York University, Toronto. Retrieved from https://yorkspace.library.yorku.ca/xmlui/handle/10315/33914

Crawford, C. (2013). *Looking into poverty: Income sources of poor people with disabilities in Canada*. Toronto: Institute for Research and Development on Inclusion and Society.

Crow, L. (1996). *Including all of our lives: Renewing the social model of disability*. In C. Barnes & G. Mercer (Eds.), *The disability divide: Illness and disability* (pp. 55–72). Leeds, UK: Disability Press.

DeJong, G. (1979). *The movement for independent living: Origins, ideology, and implications for disability research*. Ann Arbor: University of Michigan, University Center for International Rehabilitation.

Deveau, J. L. (2011). Workplace accommodation and audit-based evaluation process for compliance with the Employment Equity Act: Inclusionary practices that exclude—an institutional ethnography. *Canadian Journal of Sociology*, *36*(3), 151–172.

Dossa, P. (2009). *Racialized bodies, disabling worlds: Storied lives of immigrant Muslim women*. Toronto: University of Toronto Press.

Dumais, L., Prohet, A., Ducharme, M., Archambault, L., & Ménard-Dunn, M. (2015, March). Review of extra costs linked to disability. *Council of Canadians with Disabilities*. Retrieved from http://www.ccdonline.ca/en/socialpolicy/poverty-citizenship/income-security-reform/extra-costs-linked-to-disability

Fawcett, G. (2000). *Bringing down the barriers: The labour market and women with disabilities in Ontario*. Ottawa: Canadian Council on Social Development.

Fredeen, K. J., Martin, K., Birch, G., & Wafer, M. (2012). *Rethinking disability in the private sector: Report from the panel on labour market opportunities for persons with disabilities*.

Retrieved from http://digitalcommons.ilr.cornell.edu/cgi/viewcontent.cgi?article=156 4&context=gladnetcollect

Fritsch, K. (2015). Desiring disability differently: Neoliberalism, heterotopic imagination and intracorporeal reconfigurations. *Foucault Studies, 19*, 43–66.

Galer, D. (2018). *Working towards equity: Disability rights, activism, and employment in late twentieth-century Canada.* Toronto: University of Toronto Press.

Goodley, D. (2014). *Dis/ability studies: Theorising disablism and ableism.* London: Routledge.

Graby, S. (2015). Access to work or liberation from work? Disabled people, autonomy, and postwork politics. *Canadian Journal of Disability Studies, 4*(2), 132–161.

Grover, C., & Soldatic, K. (2013). Neoliberal restructuring, disabled people and social (in) security in Australia and Britain. *Scandinavian Journal of Disability Research, 15*(3), 216–232.

Hall, K. Q. (Ed.). (2011). *Feminist disability studies.* Bloomington: Indiana University Press.

Hande, M. J., & Kelly, C. (2015). Organizing survival and resistance in austere times: Shifting disability activism and care politics in Ontario, Canada. *Disability and Society, 30*(7), 961–975.

Human Resources and Skills Development Canada. (2013). *Federal disability reference guide.* Catalogue no. ISSD-091-06-13E. Ottawa: Government of Canada.

Ignagni, E., & Fudge Schormans, A. (2016). Reimagining parenting possibilities: The experience of people labeled with intellectual and developmental disabilities. *International Journal of Birth and Parenting Education, 3*(1), 9–12.

Kelly, C. (2011). Making "care" accessible: Personal assistance for disabled people and the politics of language. *Critical Social Policy, 31*(4), 562–582.

Kelly, C. (2013). Building bridges with accessible care: Disability studies, feminist care scholarship, and beyond. *Hypatia, 28*(4), 784–800.

Kittay, E. F. (2011). The ethics of care, dependency and disability. *Ratio Juris, 24*(1), 49–58.

Liddiard, K. (2014). The work of disabled identities in intimate relationships. *Disability and Society, 29*(1), 115–128.

Linton, S. (1998). *Claiming disability: Knowledge and identity.* New York: NYU Press.

Malacrida, C. (2015). *A special hell: Institutional life in Alberta's eugenic years.* Toronto: University of Toronto Press.

Malhotra, R. (2014). Beyond wage labor: The politics of disablement. *Tikkun, 29*(4), 43–44.

McLaren, A. (1990). *Our own master race: Eugenics in Canada, 1885–1945.* Toronto: McClelland & Stewart.

McRuer, R. (2010). Disability nationalism in crip times. *Journal of Literary and Cultural Disability Studies, 4*(2), 163–178. doi:10.3828/jlcds.2010.13

Mingus, M. (2011, February 12). Changing the framework. *Leaving Evidence.* Retrieved from https://leavingevidence.wordpress.com/2011/02/12/changing-the-framework-disability-justice/

Mitchell, D. T., & Snyder, S. L. (2015). *The biopolitics of disability: Neoliberalism, ablenationalism, and peripheral embodiment.* Ann Arbor: University of Michigan Press.

Morris, J. (1991). *Pride against prejudice: Transforming attitudes to disability.* Philadelphia: New Society.

Morris, J. (2001). Impairment and disability: Constructing an ethics of care that promotes human rights. *Hypatia, 16*(4), 1–16.

Oliver, M., & Bochel, H. M. (1991). The politics of disablement. *International Journal of Rehabilitation Research, 14*(2), 185.

Prilleltensky, O. (2003). A ramp to motherhood: The experiences of mothers with physical disabilities. *Sexuality and Disability, 21*(1), 21–47.

Prince, M. J. (2009). *Absent citizens: Disability politics and policy in Canada.* Toronto: University of Toronto Press.

Prince, M. (2016a, August). *Inclusive employment for Canadians with disabilities.* IRPP study no. 60. Montreal: Institute for Research on Public Policy.

Prince, M. (2016b). *Struggling for social citizenship.* Montreal: McGill-Queen's University Press.

Reaume, G. (2000). *Remembrance of patients past: Patient life at the Toronto Hospital for the Insane, 1870–1940.* Toronto: University of Toronto Press.

Reaume, G. (2018). Gender and the value of work in Canadian disability history. In R. Malhotra & B. Isitt (Eds.), *Disabling barriers: Social movements, disability history and the law* (pp. 42–63). Toronto: University of Toronto Press.

Reeve, D. (2006). Towards a psychology of disability: The emotional effects of living in a disabling society. In D. Goodley & R. Lawthom (Eds.), *Disability and psychology: Critical introductions and reflections* (pp. 94–107). Houndsmills, UK: Palgrave Macmillan.

Roulstone, A., & Williams, J. (2014). Being disabled, being a manager: "Glass partitions" and conditional identities in the contemporary workplace. *Disability and Society, 29*(1), 16–29.

Russell, M. (1998). *Beyond ramps: Disability at the end of the social contract: A warning from an uppity crip.* Monroe, ME: Common Courage Press.

Seth, P., Slark, M., Boulanger, J., & Dolmage, L. (2015). Survivors and sisters talk about the Huronia class action lawsuit, control, and the kind of support we want. *Journal on Developmental Disabilities, 21*(2), 60–68.

Shakespeare, T. (2013). The social model of disability. In L. J. Davis (Ed.), *The disability studies reader* (3rd ed.) (pp. 197–204). London: Routledge.

Shier, M., Graham, J. R., & Jones, M. E. (2009). Barriers to employment as experienced by disabled people: A qualitative analysis in Calgary and Regina, Canada. *Disability and Society, 24*(1), 63–75.

Shildrick, M. (2015). *Leaky bodies and boundaries: Feminism, postmodernism and (bio)ethics.* New York: Routledge.

Stone, D. A. (1986). *The disabled state.* Philadelphia: Temple University Press.

Strong-Boag, V. (2007). "Children of adversity": Disabilities and child welfare in Canada from the nineteenth to the twenty-first century. *Journal of Family History, 32*(4), 413–432.

Stubblefield, A. (2007). "Beyond the pale": Tainted whiteness, cognitive disability, and eugenic sterilization. *Hypatia, 22*(2), 162–181.

Swain, J., Finkelstein, V., French, S., & Oliver, M. (1993). *Disabling barriers: Enabling environments.* London: Sage.

Taylor, S. (2004). The right not to work: Power and disability. *Monthly Review, 55*(10), 30–31.

Thomas, C. (1999). *Female forms: Experiencing and understanding disability.* London: McGraw-Hill Education.

Thomas, C. (2007). *Sociologies of disability and illness: Contested ideas in disability studies and medical sociology.* London: Palgrave Macmillan.

Titchkosky, T. (2003). Disability, self, and society. Toronto: University of Toronto Press.

Turcotte, M. (2014, December 3). *Persons with disabilities and employment.* Ottawa: Statistics Canada. Retrieved from http://www.statcan.gc.ca/pub/75-006-x/2014001/article/14115-eng.pdf

Wall, K. (2017, August 11). Low income among persons with a disability in Canada. *The Daily.* Retrieved from https://www150.statcan.gc.ca/n1/pub/75-006-x/2017001/article/54854-eng.htm

Wendell, S. (2001). Unhealthy disabled: Treating chronic illnesses as disabilities. *Hypatia, 16*(4), 17–33.

World Health Organization. (2011). *World report on disability.* Geneva: WHO Library Cataloguing-in-Publication Data.

Yoshida, K. Willi, V., Parker, I., & Locker, D. (2006). The emergence of self-managed attendant services in Ontario. In M. A. McColl & L. Jongbloed (Eds.), *Disability and social policy in Canada* (pp. 315–336). Toronto: Captus Press.

CHAPTER 7

Young Women: Navigating the Education-Employment Divide

Leslie Nichols

Youth is a critical life phase during which people are maturing physically, emotionally, and socially; finishing their education; having their first paid work experiences; making long-term career plans; and founding a family. Subtle and explicit messages about women's place in society, the family, and the workforce are strongly reinforced during this transitional period from childhood to adulthood, influencing young women's decisions about their education, work, and motherhood. Decisions that young people make often have a long-term impact on their life course, including the social and economic status that they achieve. But individual decisions are only one component that determines socioeconomic outcomes for young women: existing social norms and stereotypes, politically motivated economic policies, social expectations of mothers, and sexism and sexual harassment in the workplace play equally important roles. Those factors become more powerful and controlling for young women in intersecting social categories such as race, ethnicity, and immigrant status. This chapter will investigate the many social factors outside young women's individual agency that contribute to their success or failure in the workforce.

HOW OLD ARE YOUNG WOMEN?

We begin our understanding of young women's work with a definition of the term *young women*, which is not as simple as it may seem. *Youth* refers to the phase of life following childhood through the first phase of adulthood (Tyyskä, 2014). It is more difficult to specify an age range for this group. The United Nations (UN; 2017) describes youth as "a more fluid category than a fixed age-group." The UN defines youth as 15 to 24 years old, but it also recognizes various age ranges for youth used by member states and organizations, such as the African Youth Charter, which establishes the age range as 15 to 35 years old (UN, 2017). The age range of the youth category has been extended in recent years because young people are spending more years in school compared to the past, which delays key signifiers of adulthood like forming families and leaving their parents' home (UN, 2017).

Some authors (Kainer, 2015; Moyser, 2017) prefer to limit the youth category to ages 15 to 24 to distinguish them from the core working-age group of 25 to 54 years old, viewed by some economists as the main labour force that supports the economy and the **gross domestic product (GDP,** the value of goods and services produced by a country). In this view, young workers are engaged in their education and working casually and thus are not fully productive workers. But many young workers are in fact working full-time and making a significant contribution to the economy. Thus, this chapter will consider the broader age group of 15 to 34.

DEMOGRAPHICS AND EMPLOYMENT PATTERNS OF YOUNG WORKING WOMEN

There are about 9 million Canadians in the 15 to 34 age group, distributed approximately equally across four age subgroups and between males and females (table 7.1). The large size of this population underscores the importance of understanding its employment dynamics.

Table 7.1: Age and Gender Distribution of Canadian Youth, 2016

	Age, % in each group			
	15 to 19	**20 to 24**	**25 to 29**	**30 to 34**
Both genders	23	25	26	26
Females	48.7	51	50	49.3
Males	51.3	49	50	50.7

Note: Statistics Canada records data only for "female" or "male" genders. It does not account for transgender, intersex, or other gender categories.
Source: Adapted from Statistics Canada, 2018c.

Young women make up a significant group of Canadian workers, with distinctive characteristics, needs, and challenges. More than half (57.2%) of women between the ages of 15 and 24 were employed in 2015 (Moyser, 2017), about equal to the number of young men. The diversity of young women is consistent with the general changing **demographics** of Canada as the population is becoming more diverse. In the 2016 census (Statistics Canada, 2018a, 2018g, 2018m), 27.5% of women ages 15 to 34 self-reported as racialized, 6% were Indigenous, 6% were newcomers (resided in Canada less than five years), and 18.6% were immigrants (resided in Canada for any period of time). The number of young racialized women is especially significant as there was an increase of 14% of youth (male and female) in this category from 1996 to 2016 (Statistics Canada, 2018i). Young women's changing demographics impact where they work, at what age they begin working, and cultural expectations of their gender roles. In addition, due to demographic changes in society, specifically an increase in the elderly population, some young women may feel pressure to care for parents or grandparents while attempting to finish their eduction, begin a career, and have children.

Three conclusions can be drawn about youth employment from the data in table 7.2: more young women work part-time, more young men work full-time, and more young men are unemployed or underemployed. Between 1976 and 1978, 76% of young men and 58% of young women worked full-time (Statistics Canada, 2018b). Since then full-time employment has risen for young women and declined for young men. The data point to different paths for males and females. Young women are more likely to pursue postsecondary education, work part-time by choice, and delay becoming mothers because of the time commitment that motherhood requires compared to men's lesser participation in

Table 7.2: Employment Patterns of Canadian Youth

	%	
	Males	Females
15–34 years old; worked part-time in 2016	26.9	40.2
15–34 years old; worked full-time in 2016	74.1	59.8
15–24 years old; unemployed in 2016	17.0	14.1
15–24 years old; involuntarily employed part-time in 2015	20.4	18.7

Source: Statistics Canada, 2018a, c, d, h, i, k, m, n; Moyser, 2017.

parenting. Because more young women are in school, they are less likely to be working full-time.

Young men's higher unemployment rate may be due to young women's greater willingness to accept low-wage service jobs as a step toward better employment. Similar to global labour trends reported by the International Labour Organization in 2016, young Canadian women workers are highly concentrated in health care, education, retail trades, the hospitality industry (hotels, motels), social services, office and administrative jobs, cleaning, and food services (International Labour Organization, 2016; Moyser, 2017; Statistics Canada, 2018f). While some positions in health care (doctors, nurses) and education (teachers) are skilled jobs with higher wages, many of the other jobs that young women are employed in are menial low-wage work.

Many young people must work while attending school. In November 2018 this was the case for 45.4% of female students and 37% of male students (part-time and full-time) between the ages of 15 and 29 years old (Statistics Canada, 2018l), again reflecting young women's high employment in service jobs. From this data a picture emerges of young women facing triple burdens of school, work, and planning for motherhood.

THE IMPACT OF NEOLIBERALISM ON YOUNG WORKING WOMEN

The neoliberal policy paradigm has had a significant impact on young women workers in Canada. In force since the 1980s, neoliberalism is a "laissez-faire" (hands-off) approach to policy-making that involves a limited role for the state, particularly with respect to labour and the economy, while also reducing supports for citizens' social and economic needs. Neoliberal policies have resulted in a loss of permanent full-time jobs, sluggish wages, limited opportunities for advancement, and increased required overtime work (Scott-Marshall, 2007). The oldest young workers were born at the beginning of the neoliberal era, meaning that their parents were impacted by these changes. Loughlin and Barling's (2001) study of young worker's work values, behaviours, and attitudes found that many youth saw their parents or guardians "downsized" or fired from their jobs, leaving youth with feelings of betrayal and distrust toward authority.

Consistent with the trend toward involuntary nonstandard employment that grew out of neoliberalism, 18.7% of young women workers are involuntarily employed at part-time jobs, meaning they are working fewer hours than they would like due to economic slack or because they can't find full-time work (Moyser, 2017).

At the same time, there has been a loss of paid entry-level positions, which have been replaced by often unpaid work-integrated-learning (**WIL**) positions such as co-ops, practicums, and internships (Langille, 2015). The quality and pay status of WIL positions then influence the career path and wages of young workers after graduation as young women find themselves in lower-paid non-technical jobs.

The decline in jobs associated with neoliberalism and **globalization** (business practices designed to increase profits by buying, selling, and manufacturing goods and marketing services internationally rather than only locally) has led to increased migration of people to other regions of their home country or to other countries in search of adequate employment (Martin & Jackson, 2008; Nichols & Tyyskä, 2015). This migration has had a significant impact on young women as they attempt to combine paid work and the unpaid household labour that is expected of them. When males with families leave home to work in other cities or provinces, women remain at home to care for the household, compromising their ability to work outside the home and weakening family and community structure, as Martin and Jackson (2008) found of young women residing in Newfoundland and Labrador communities with high out-migration.

Under neoliberalism unions have declined as corporate profits are prioritized over worker well-being, leaving workers vulnerable to loss of job security. Like many workers in the neoliberal era, young women have experienced challenges when they have attempted to organize into unions to improve their working conditions. In her study of Canadian women organizers, Kainer (2015) found that "the hegemonic masculine values of individualism, competition, risk-taking, and total commitment to the paid job embedded in the union organizing culture—combined with their age—deepened and reinforced systemic inequalities for young women organizers" (p. 123), pointing to their dual forms of gender and age oppression.

NEGATIVE PERCEPTIONS OF YOUNG WOMEN, DESKILLING, AND EXPLOITATION

Deskilling refers to the failure of employers to acknowledge workers' credentials, skills, and experience, so that they are placed in work below their ability level, assigned job titles that don't reflect the level of work they do, or paid below the level of their work and skills. Often deskilling is a result of employers' biases around factors such as age, race, gender, or culture that are unrelated to the work performed. Deskilling and not paying equitable wages benefit employers while preventing workers from progressing to better positions.

Deskilling impacts young workers when they are perceived in a negative light as lacking skills and experience, not fully developed mentally, and lacking full capability to analyze actions and conditions that could lead to injury or other harm on the job. Art Deane (2012), a safety manager at Human Development Consultants, a commercial enterprise that provides on-the-job technical training in organizations on several continents, notes that youth are seen as "young, new, and inexperienced workers." The firm reports that 50% of injuries suffered by young workers occur within their first six months on the job and 20% happen during the first month. It attributes this high rate of injuries to insufficient workplace safety programs geared to the young worker population, including a focus on critical thinking. Taking a different view, the 2012 report of the Ontario Federation of Labour characterizes youth workers as diverse, urban, cultured, smart, and educated. This report states that young workers tend to work in the same positions as senior colleagues but with less security and fewer benefits.

The socioeconomic demotion of youth especially applies to young women, who often work in low-wage and low-skilled employment in the retail or restaurant industries. Some employers stereotype them as still living under their parents' roof and thus not needing a living wage, an attitude that goes back to the early 19th-century male-breadwinner model of work as the preserve of men supporting families. Unions contribute to maintaining youth in low-wage employment by prioritizing high wages for older male workers on the pretext that young workers are not supporting a family (Khosla, 2014). Acker (1990) found that restaurants tended to hire and distribute workers based on gendered stereotypes throughout the workplace. Hall (1993) observed that this gendered division in the workplace was based on biased views of women's work: the work that women do in restaurants is seen as an extension of their unpaid household labour and their natural abilities and skills. In this view, a waitress cares for her patrons like a mother would care for her children. Thus, most of the work that young women do is deemed to be innate and to not require skills.

Because the work that young women do is viewed as low skilled, these jobs tend to be precarious in nature (Hughes & Tadic, 1998; Khosla, 2014). Examples of precarious employment include part-time work, day labour (whereby workers are hired for a single day), temporary work, and contract work. In her study on working women in the Greater Toronto Area, Khosla (2014) reported that young women were frustrated by their inability to move out of the cycle of precarious work in spite of their education and skills.

In an attempt to find more stable work, young women workers frequently take on WIL internships during their postsecondary education. However, as de Peuter, Cohen, and Brophy (2015) report, women are often hired for unpaid WIL positions rather than for entry-level positions that would lead to longer-term commitment and mentoring on the part of the employer. While WIL positions can offer an opportunity to acquire useful job skills, this is less often the case for young women than for young men (Turcotte, Nichols, & Philipps, 2016). Therefore, young women are often pulled into unpaid WIL positions that do not lead to any meaningful skills or later offers of employment from the WIL employer. In fact these positions can lead to a cycle of precarious employment as young women leave their postsecondary education (Langille, 2015) less prepared for the job market than their fellow male students who were employed in paid positions in technology, business, trades, and other lucrative fields.

BALANCING FAMILY AND WORK

The age span of young women workers coincides with the period of bearing and raising children. Fertility begins to decline at age 30, with a steeper decline at 35 (Bretherick, Fairbrother, Avila, Harbord, & Robinson, 2010). This means that for many young women, work comes into conflict with their desire to have a family—and with the State's need for young women to produce new workers to sustain the economy. Maternity leave has existed in Canada since the liberalization of unemployment insurance in 1971, paying benefits equal to 55% of previous insurable salary for 52 weeks or 33% for 61 weeks in all of Canada expect Quebec (where the program is more generous at 75% of previous salary). However, the coverage is inadequate in terms of both duration and benefits (Government of Canada, 2017; Nichols, 2012).

Family gender norms may place significant pressures on young women in their education and future work. This includes different treatment of sons and daughters, whereby parents may encourage and pay for postsecondary education for their sons but not their daughters, reinforcing "gender-typed career and family-related choices" (Tyyskä, 2014, p. 106) and the notion that young women should prepare for marriage and a family rather than a career.

While the Canadian Employment Insurance Special Benefits program for expectant mothers and new parents of either gender provides some benefits for young women who decide to have a family, young mothers who want to work or attend school must confront the difficulty of finding affordable childcare. The only province that has low-cost childcare is Quebec, where the fee began at $5 a day in 1997, increased to $7 a day in 2004, and in 2018 stood at $8.05 to $22.15 depending on family income (Fortin, 2018; Government of Quebec, 2017;

McKenzie, 2014). MacDonald and Friendly (2017) analyzed childcare fees in Canadian cities during 2017. They found that infant daycare fees ranged widely, from $168 a month in Montreal to $651 in Winnipeg and $1,758 in Toronto. What is most significant about the Quebec fees is that the same fee is charged for all children regardless of age. In the rest of Canada, daycare is considerably more expensive for infants up to 18 months (MacDonald & Friendly, 2017), illustrating the overall significance of this policy for young mothers' engagement with the labour market (McKenzie, 2014).

Fortin (2018) indicates that Quebec's universal childcare program has allowed more women to combine raising children with paid work outside the home. He notes that in 2016, 85% of Quebec women between the ages of 20 and 44 worked, compared to 80% in the rest of Canada. Between 1997 and 2016 employment of young mothers with children up to five years old in Quebec increased by 16% (from 64% to 80%), compared to a 4% increase (from 67% to 71%) in the rest of Canada. This increase in young women's employment is estimated to have contributed an additional 12% or $250 billion to the Canadian economy since 1976 (Tencer, 2018).

Women frequently cite the lack of affordable childcare as their reason for working part-time rather than full-time (Moyser, 2017). The 2015 General Social Survey on time use in Canada (Houle, Turcotte, & Wendt, 2017) found that mothers do more household work than men, regardless of their employment status; young mothers spend more time on childcare even if they work; and the younger the child is, the more time a mother spends on childcare. These findings underline the difficulties that young women have with combining childcare and paid work.

STREAMING YOUNG WOMEN INTO FEMINIZED EDUCATION PROGRAMS AND CAREERS

Young women have been entering higher education in high numbers. In 2016, 40.7% of young women between the ages of 25 and 34 held a bachelor's degree or higher (Statistics Canada, 2017b). For the first time ever, young women made up nearly half (48.5%) of doctoral degree holders (Statistics Canada, 2018e). However, due to socialization in childhood and enduring stereotyped gender roles, there is a clear gendered division in the fields of study and work chosen by young people. Young women are overrepresented in "pink collar" or BHASE (business, humanities, health, arts, social science, and education) fields, including nursing, education, the humanities, social sciences, and social work (Tyyskä, 2014).

Table 7.3: Percentage of Bachelor's Degree Holders Ages 25–34 Employed in Profession Close to Education Field, by Gender, 2016

Fields of Study	Women	Men
STEM (science, technology, engineering, and math)		
All STEM fields	30.5	59.6
Science and science technology	16.1	26.3
Math, computer, and information sciences	40.6	66.5
Engineering	69.1	73
BHASE (business, humanities, health, arts, social science, and education)		
Nursing	95.4	93.1
Education and teaching	87.3	79.8

Source: Statistics Canada, 2017a.

Young men are more likely to enter STEM (science, technology, engineering, and math) fields.

Education researchers refer to a "pipeline" that leads students through their STEM studies to a STEM career, with the risk of losing women and minority students who "leak" out of the pipeline due to social and cultural pressures. They may fail to finish their education or change to a non-STEM major or career (table 7.3).

Among the women who held trade certificates in 2013, most were in traditionally female professions such as hairstyling (90%), early childhood education (94%), and computer user-support technicians (54%; Ferguson, 2016). In 2013 women accounted for 39% of graduates with a STEM university degree (Hango, 2013), but in 2014, only 22% of STEM professionals were women (Shendruk, 2015). Thus, although young women may enter and graduate from STEM programs, many of them do not continue on to a STEM career. This could be due to traditional gender roles that direct young women into caring labour, or hostility toward women in STEM programs (Shendruk, 2015; Tyyskä, 2014). Female professionals in STEM careers also earn lower salaries (table 7.4), illustrating a gender wage gap in these fields (Statistics Canada, 2017c).

Women's traditional jobs are ascribed low social status (Tyyskä, 2014). Charles (2002) characterizes these jobs as "low pay … boring, low grade, low status, involv[ing] subservience, and … jobs that men would not want to do. They are associated with 'feminine' qualities of caring, being good with people,

Table 7.4: Average Wages of Canadian Women and Men 25–34 Years Old in STEM and BHASE Careers, 2015

Profession	Women	Men
STEM	$59,490	$72,443
BHASE	$53,345	$58,488

Source: Statistics Canada, 2017c.

and dexterity" (p. 31). This means that the careers that young women are encouraged to be employed in are set up to be devalued, which then influences young mothers to opt to stay out of the labour market to care for children.

DIFFICULTIES COMBINING EDUCATION AND WORK

More young women than men work while studying, whether part-time during the school year or full-time during the summer (Tyyskä, 2014). Thus, combining school and work is a greater challenge for young women.

Recalling that high school students as young as 15 are part of the workforce, it must be acknowledged that they face stresses similar to older workers. The "work" that high school students do in school resembles the household labour that women perform: it is expected of them, it takes significant time, it is essential to society and the economy, and it is unpaid. In fact, adolescents spend just as much time in school, doing homework, and doing paid work as people in the core working-age group of 25 to 54 years old spend on paid and unpaid work—about 53 hours per week (Marshall, 2007; Moyser & Burlock, 2018).

Young student workers must negotiate the trade-off between working and studying, which can have an impact on their final educational attainment (Neyt, Omey, Verhaest, & Baert, 2017). Students frequently blame arriving late to class, absences, late or uncompleted assignments, and low test scores on employment (DeSimone, 2008). Tannock (2001) found that working more than 20 hours a week impacts adolescents' education. The 2002 Youth in Transitions Survey, conducted by Statistics Canada and Human Resources and Skills Development Canada (Statistics Canada, 2002), found that as hours of employment increased, the performance of 15-year-olds declined in reading, math, and science. Working more than 20 hours a week also increases the chance of wandering attention in class, which is correlated with lower academic performance (Monahan, Lee, & Steinberg, 2011). Substance abuse and deviant behaviour also increase as work hours increase (Monahan et al., 2011).

SEXUAL HARASSMENT

With the Me Too and Time's Up movements that began in October 2017, acknowledgement of the prevalence of sexual harassment in the workplace, particularly against women, is growing (Zacharek, Dockterman, & Edwards, 2017). Beginning with American actor Rose McGowan, many young women have made public their stories of being sexually harassed while attempting to break into the entertainment industry. The Canadian Labour Code defines *sexual harassment* as "any conduct, comment, gesture, or contact of a sexual nature that is likely to cause offence or humiliation to any employee; or that might, on reasonable grounds, be perceived by that employee as placing a condition of a sexual nature on employment or on any opportunity for training or promotion" (Government of Canada, 2017). Examples of sexual harassment in the workplace include inappropriate touching, sexually suggestive comments, and displaying degrading photos of women. Sexual harassment is rooted in gender inequality, where the victim is perceived as having less power than the perpetrator.

According to Statistics Canada (2018j), *sexual assault* "encompasses a wide range of criminal acts in the Criminal Code of Canada. Such conduct ranges from unwanted sexual touching to sexual violence resulting in serious physical injury or disfigurement to the victim." The sexual assault rate for young Canadians between 15 and 24 years old is 18 times higher than for women over age 55 (Canadian Women's Foundation, 2016). The majority (82%) of victims under the age of 18 are female (Canadian Women's Foundation, 2016). Clearly, both age and gender put young women at increased risk of sexual assault. A further concern is that sexual assault on young women is correlated with substance abuse and academic issues such as dropping out, transferring to another college or university, and lower grades (Senn et al., 2017).

Both sexual harassment and sexual assault impact young women on the job. In 2018 the Angus Reid Institute, a Canadian research organization, conducted a survey of 2,004 Canadians that confirmed the high prevalence of workplace sexual harassment. More than half of the women surveyed reported having been subjected to sexual harassment on the job at some point in their working lives and most women said they took precautions to avoid it, such as avoiding coworkers who made them feel uncomfortable or dressing conservatively. The longer they spent in the workplace, the more likely they were to be victims of sexual harassment. In the 18 to 34 age group, 42% of women said they had experienced sexual harassment and 20% had experienced nonconsensual sexual touching. Comparing younger and older women, the study found that "younger women are more likely to have been harassed within the last year while older women's experiences mostly occurred six or more years ago," pointing to the increased vulnerability of young women on the job. The study concluded from the statistics that "work environments that tolerate or foster harassment also foster abuse."

A disconcerting finding of the Angus Reid survey was that a sizeable number of young men in the 18 to 34 age group believe that specific sexual behaviours, such as expressing sexual interest in a coworker and making comments about female coworkers' bodies, are acceptable in the workplace. In contrast, significantly fewer young women agreed that those behaviours are acceptable.

In the Angus Reid study close to three-quarters of women who experienced sexual harassment or nonconsensual sexual touching on the job did not report it to their employer. If they did report it, the majority of the women felt that their employer failed to take concrete action on the matter or was nonresponsive and dismissive. In a previous study in 2014, the Angus Reid Institute investigated why so many women don't report these incidents at work and identified 10 reasons:

1. Preferred to deal with it on their own
2. Felt the issue was too minor
3. Didn't think the employer would respond well
4. Embarrassed by what occurred
5. Not sure it constituted harassment
6. Afraid of losing their job
7. Afraid it would hurt their career
8. Thought no one would believe them
9. Wanted to avoid talking about it
10. Afraid to come forward

Those explanations can be characterized by themes of shame, fear of retaliation, self-doubt, and feeling outpowered by males. In that sense, the women in the Angus Reid study have much in common with the women in the entertainment industry who began the Me Too movement. They reported fearing that if they had come out with their stories earlier, their careers would have suffered (Dockterman, 2017). And, in fact, many women involved in the Me Too movement have reported that their male pepetrators did take retaliatory action to harm their careers. Thus, young women's fears that lead them to not report sexual harassment and assault in the workplace may be well-founded. In addition to the predictable lack of helpful response from their employer, they are at a point in their working lives where they are more likely to be in junior positions with less authority and can ill afford to jeopardize their positions.

The failure of employers to take action against sexual harassment and assault reflects the pervasiveness of norms that cast women as always sexually available and policy gaps in employment standards, the Criminal Code, and organizations that need to be rectified to ensure nontolerance of these acts against women.

CONCLUSION

Although many young workers experience difficulties in the labour market due to negative perceptions of them, young women deal with additional burdens related to **patriarchy**, ageism, combining work and school, balancing work with planning for their future family, and sexual assault and harassment in the workplace. They receive inadequate support for entering STEM educational programs and careers and are instead streamed into low-wage, low-skilled service jobs. Devaluation of their abilities begins in high school and postsecondary institutions, where they are placed in WIL programs that do not provide them with skills that will lead to good jobs. The prevalence of internships for young women in unpaid, low-skilled work has increased under neoliberal economic policies.

The pattern of undertraining and underemployment that beings at a critical time in their education contributes to long-term disadvantges in their working lives. These disadvantages are compounded by factors such as race, ethnicity, and immigrant status. From ages 15 to 34, a long period of 19 years, young women are finishing their education and becoming established in their careers. This age group also includes the years of bearing and raising children. For young women, the transition to adulthood and making a place for themselves in the workforce is about much more than getting a good education and choosing the right career. It is equally about grappling with long-standing social norms that predefine their abilities, their potential, whether they deserve an equal place in the workforce with equal pay, and the expectations of them as wives and mothers performing unpaid household labour. While much is demanded of young women, social supports such as affordable daycare that would allow them to work full-time while raising children are lacking.

KEY READINGS

Fortin, P. (2018). Quebec's childcare program at 20: How it has done, and what the rest of Canada can learn. *Inroads: A Journal of Opinion, 42*, 52–64.

Kainer, J. (2015). Intersectionality at work: Young women organizers' participation in labour youth programs in Canada. *Resources for Feminist Research*, 34(3/4), 102–132.

Langille, A. (2015). Lost in transition: The regulation of unpaid labour during the school-to-labour market transition in Ontario. *E-journal of International and Comparative Labour Studies*, 4(1), 1–24.

DISCUSSION QUESTIONS

1. What type of assistance do young women need in order to prepare for well-paid jobs? Have you or young women you know had the needed support in high school, college, and university?

2. What types of obstacles have you or young women you know experienced in obtaining an education that will lead to a good job? What about obstacles in searching for work or while on the job?

3. Have you witnessed or heard about incidents of sexual harassment or assault at your educational institution or your workplace? What was this experience like for the victim? What was the outcome of the incident?

4. In your own life as a student and worker, what factors make your situation easier or more complicated? Think about things like your gender, age, race, culture, language, income, and geographic location.

5. What can be done to change attitudes toward young women workers and how they are treated? What needs to change?

REFERENCES

Acker, J. (1990). Hierarchies, jobs, bodies: A theory of gendered organizations. *Gender and Society*, 4(2), 139–158.

Angus Reid Institute. (2014, December 5). Three-in-ten Canadians say they've been sexually harassed at work, but very few have reported this to their employers. Retrieved from http://angusreid.org/sexual-harassment/

Angus Reid Institute. (2018, February 9). #Metoo: Moment or movement? Retrieved from http://angusreid.org/me-too/

Bretherick, K. L., Fairbrother, N., Avila, L., Harbord, S. H. A., & Robinson, W. P. (2010). Fertility and aging: Do reproductive-aged Canadian women know what they need to know? *Fertility and Sterility*, 93(7), 2162–2168.

Canadian Women's Foundation. (2016). *Facts about sexual assault and harassment.* Retrieved from https://www.canadianwomen.org/wp-content/uploads/2017/09/Facts-About-Sexual-Assault-and-Harassment.pdf

Charles, N. (2002). *Gender in modern Britain*. New York: Oxford University Press.

Deane, A. (2012). *Some Canadian workplace injury and fatality facts*. Edmonton: Human Development Consultants. Retrieved from http://www.safethink.ca/resources/pdf/Canadian%20Workplace%20Injury%20and%20Fatality%20Facts.pdf

de Peuter, G., Cohen, N., & Brophy, E. (2015). Interrogating internships: Unpaid work, creative industries, and higher education. *TripleC*, *13*(2), 329–335.

DeSimone, J. S. (2008, May). The impact of employment during school on college student academic performance. National Bureau of Economic Research Working Paper no. 14006. Retrieved from http://www.nber.org/papers/w14006

Dockterman, E. (2017, December 6). Rose McGowan: "They really f--ed with the wrong person." *Time*. Retrieved from http://time.com/5049676/rose-mcgowan-interview-transcript-person-of-the-year-2017/

Ferguson, S. J. (2016). Women and education: Qualifications, skills, and technology. Ottawa: Statistics Canada. Retrieved from https://www150.statcan.gc.ca/n1/pub/89-503-x/2015001/article/14640-eng.htm

Fortin, P. (2018). Quebec's childcare program at 20: How it has done, and what the rest of Canada can learn. *Inroads: A Journal of Opinion*, *42*, 52–64.

Government of Canada. (2017). Sexual harassment. Retrieved from https://www.canada.ca/en/employment-social-development/services/labour-standards/reports/sexual-harassment.html

Government of Quebec. (2017). Daily daycare costs: Determine the net daily cost of your childcare expenses. Retrieved from http://www.budget.finances.gouv.qc.ca/budget/outils/garde_en.asp

Hall, E. (1993). Smiling, deferring, and flirting: Doing gender by giving "good service." *Work and Occupations*, *20*(4), 452–471.

Hango, D. (2013). Gender differences in science, technology, engineering, mathematics, and computer science (STEM) programs at university. Ottawa: Statistics Canada. Retrieved from https://www150.statcan.gc.ca/n1/pub/75-006-x/2013001/article/11874-eng.htm

Houle, P., Turcotte, M., & Wendt, M. (2017). Changes in parents' participation in domestic tasks and care for children from 1986 to 2015. Ottawa: Statistics Canada. Retrieved from https://www150.statcan.gc.ca/n1/pub/89-652-x/89-652-x2017001-eng.htm

Hughes, K., & Tadic, V. (1998). "Something to deal with": Customer sexual harassment and women's retail service work in Canada. *Women, Gender and Organizations*, *5*(4), 207–219.

International Labour Organization. (2016). *Women at work: Trends 2016*. Geneva: Author. Retrieved from http://www.ilo.org/wcmsp5/groups/public/---dgreports/---dcomm/---publ/documents/publication/wcms_457317.pdf

Kainer, J. (2015). Intersectionality at work: Young women organizers' participation in labour youth programs in Canada. *Resources for Feminist Research*, 34(3/4), 102–132.

Khosla, P. (2014). *Working women, working poor.* Toronto: Women and Work Research Group (Unifor). Retrieved from https://pepso.ca/documents/working-women-working-poor-2014.pdf

Langille, A. (2015). Lost in transition: The regulation of unpaid labour during the school-to-labour market transition in Ontario. *E-journal of International and Comparative Labour Studies*, 4(1), 1–24.

Loughlin, C., & Barling, J. (2001). Young workers' work values, attitudes, and behaviours. *Journal of Occupational and Organizational Psychology*, 74(4), 543–558.

MacDonald, D., & Friendly, M. (2017, December). *Time out: Child care fees in Canada 2017.* Ottawa: Canadian Centre for Policy Alternatives. Retrieved from https://www.policyalternatives.ca/sites/default/files/uploads/publications/National%20Office/2017/12/Time%20Out.pdf

Marshall, K. (2007, May). The busy lives of teens. *The Daily*, 8(5). Retrieved from https://www150.statcan.gc.ca/n1/pub/75-001-x/10507/9635-eng.htm

Martin, D., & Jackson, L. (2008). Young women in Coastal Newfoundland and Labrador talk about their social relationships and health. *Newfoundland and Labrador*, 23(1), 61–77.

McKenzie, D. (2014). A long history of failure: Feeling the effects of Canada's childcare policy. *Canadian Journal of Law and Society*, 29(3), 397–412.

Monahan, K. C., Lee, J. M., & Steinberg, L. (2011). Revisiting the impact of part-time work on adolescent adjustment: Distinguishing between selection and socialization using propensity score matching. *Child Development*, 82(1), 96–112.

Moyser, M. (2017). Women and paid work. In *Women in Canada: A gender-based statistical report.* Ottawa: Statistics Canada. Retrieved from https://www150.statcan.gc.ca/n1/pub/89-503-x/2015001/article/14694-eng.htm

Moyser, M., & Burlock, A. (2018). Time use: Total work burden, unpaid work, and leisure. In *Women in Canada: A gender-based statistical report.* Ottawa: Statistics Canada. Retrieved from https://www150.statcan.gc.ca/n1/pub/89-503-x/2015001/article/54931-eng.htm

Neyt, B., Omey, E., Verhaest, D., & Baert, S. (2017, September). Does student work really affect educational outcomes? A review of the literature. IZA DP No. 11023. Bonn, Germany: IZA Institute of Labor Economics. Retrieved from https://www.iza.org/publications/dp/11023

Nichols, L. (2012). Alliance building to create change: The women's movement and the 1982 CUPW Strike. *Just Labour: A Canadian Journal of Work and Society*, 19, 59–72.

Nichols, L., & Tyyskä, V. (2015). Immigrant women in Canada and the United States. In J. Shields & H. Bauder (Eds.), *Immigrant experiences in North America: Understanding settlement and integration* (pp. 248–272). Toronto: Canadian Scholars' Press.

Ontario Federation of Labour. (2012). Pulling up the ladder: Austerity's impact on the next generation. Toronto: Workers Under 30 Committee. Retrieved from http://ofl.ca/wp-content/uploads/2012.11.09-Report-PullingUptheLadder-Web.pdf

Scott-Marshall, H. (2007). Work-related insecurity in the new economy: Evaluating the consequences for health. In H. Prechel (Ed.), *Politics and neoliberalism: Structure, process and outcome* (pp. 21–60). Oxford: Elsevier.

Senn, C. Y., Eliasziw, M., Hobden, K. L., Newby-Clark, I. R., Barata, P. C., Radtke, H. L., & Thurston, W. E. (2017). Secondary and 2-year outcomes of sexual assault resistance program for university women. *Psychology of Women Quarterly, 41*(2), 147–162.

Shendruk, A. (2015, June 18). Gender inequality in the sciences? It's still very present in Canada. *Maclean's*. Retrieved from https://www.macleans.ca/society/science/gender-inequality-in-the-sciences-its-still-very-present-in-canada/

Statistics Canada. (2002, January 23). Youth in transition survey. *The Daily*. Retrieved from https://www150.statcan.gc.ca/n1/daily-quotidien/020123/dq020123a-eng.htm

Statistics Canada. (2017a, November 29). Are young bachelor's degree holders finding jobs that match their studies? *Census in Brief*. Retrieved from https://www12.statcan.gc.ca/census-recensement/2016/as-sa/98-200-x/2016025/98-200-x2016025-eng.cfm?wbdisable=true

Statistics Canada. (2017b). Education in Canada: Key results from the 2016 census. *The Daily*. Retrieved from https://www150.statcan.gc.ca/n1/daily-quotidien/171129/dq171129a-eng.htm

Statistics Canada. (2017c). Is field of study a factor in the earnings of young bachelor's degree holders? *Census in Brief*. Retrieved from https://www12.statcan.gc.ca/census-recensement/2016/as-sa/98-200-x/2016023/98-200-x2016023-eng.cfm

Statistics Canada. (2018a). Aboriginal population profile, 2016 census. Retrieved from https://www12.statcan.gc.ca/census-recensement/2016/dp-pd/abpopprof/details/page.cfm?Lang=E&Geo1=PR&Code1=01&Data=Count&SearchText=Canada&SearchType=Begins&B1=All&C1=All&SEX_ID=3&AGE_ID=7&RESGEO_ID=1

Statistics Canada. (2018b). Canadian youth and full-time work: A slower transition. Retrieved from https://www150.statcan.gc.ca/n1/pub/11-630-x/11-630-x2017004-eng.htm

Statistics Canada. (2018c). Census profile, 2016 census. Retrieved from http://www12.statcan.gc.ca/census-recensement/2016/dp-pd/prof/details/Page.cfm?Lang=E&Geo1=PR&Code1=01&Geo2=&Code2=&Data=Count&SearchText=Canada&SearchType=Begins&SearchPR=01&B1=All&GeoLevel=PR&GeoCode=01

Statistics Canada. (2018d). Employment income groups (18), occupation—national occupational classification (NOC) 2016 (13A), work activity during the reference year (9), age (9) and sex (3) for the population aged 15 years and over in private households of Canada, provinces and territories and census metropolitan areas, 2016 census—25% sample data. Retrieved from https://www12.statcan.gc.ca/census-recensement/2016/dp-pd/dt-td/Rp-eng.cfm?LANG=E&APATH=7&DETAIL=0&DIM=0&FL=W&FREE=0&GC=0&GID=0&GK=0&GRP=1&PID=111865&PRID=10&PTYPE=109445&S=0&SHOWALL=0&SUB=0&Temporal=2016,2017&THEME=0&VID=0&VNAMEE=Work%20activity%20during%20the%20reference%20year%20%2889%29&VNAMEF=Travail%20pendant%20l%27ann%C3%A9e%20de%20r%C3%A9f%C3%A9rence%20%2889%29

Statistics Canada. (2018e). Highest certificate, diploma or degree (15), major field of study—classification of instructional programs (cip) 2016 (14), school attendance (3), age (13a) and sex (3) for the population aged 15 years and over in private households of Canada, provinces and territories, census divisions and census subdivisions, 2016 census—25% sample data. Retrieved from www12.statcan.gc.ca/census-recensement/2016/dp-pd/dt-td/Rp-eng.cfm?APATH=3&DETAIL=0&DIM=0&FL=A&FREE=0&GC=0&GID=0&GK=0&GRP=1&LANG=E&PID=110634&PRID=10&PTYPE=109445&S=0&SHOWALL=0&SUB=0&THEME=123&Temporal=2016&VID=0&VNAMEE=&VNAMEF=

Statistics Canada. (2018f). Immigration and ethnocultural diversity in Canada. *National Household Survey 2011*. Retrieved from http://www12.statcan.gc.ca/nhs-enm/2011/as-sa/99-010-x/99-010-x2011001-eng.pdf

Statistics Canada. (2018g). Immigration status and period of immigration, 2016 counts, female, age (total), Canada, provinces and territories, 2016 census—25% sample data. Retrieved from https://www12.statcan.gc.ca/census-recensement/2016/dp-pd/hlt-fst/imm/Table.cfm?Lang=E&T=11&Geo=00&SP=1&view=1&age=4&sex=3

Statistics Canada. (2018h). Labour force status (8), highest certificate, diploma or degree (15), age (12a) and sex (3) for the population aged 15 years and over in private households of Canada, provinces and territories, census divisions and census subdivisions, 2016 census—25% sample data. Retrieved from https://www12.statcan.gc.ca/census-recensement/2016/dp-pd/dt-td/Rp-eng.cfm?TABID=2&LANG=E&APATH=3&DETAIL=0&DIM=0&FL=A&FREE=0&GC=0&GK=0&GRP=1&PID=112134&PRID=10&PTYPE=109445&S=0&SHOWALL=0&SUB=0&Temporal=2017&THEME=123&VID=0&VNAMEE=&VNAMEF=

Statistics Canada. (2018i, February 7). A portrait of Canadian youth. Retrieved from https://www150.statcan.gc.ca/n1/pub/11-631-x/11-631-x2018001-eng.htm

Statistics Canada. (2018j). Survey description. Retrieved from https://www150.statcan
.gc.ca/n1/pub/85-002-x/2018001/article/54893/06-eng.htm

Statistics Canada. (2018k). Unemployment by type of work sought and search method, annual (x 1,000). Retrieved from https://www150.statcan.gc.ca/t1/tbl1/en/tv.action?pid=
1410005901&pickMembers%5B0%5D=1.1&pickMembers%5B1%5D=3.3&pickMe
mbers%5B2%5D=4.2

Statistics Canada. (2018l). Unemployment rate, participation rate, and employment rate by
type of student during school months, monthly, unadjusted for seasonality. Retrieved
from https://www150.statcan.gc.ca/t1/tbl1/en/tv.action?pid=1410002101&pickMemb
ers%5B0%5D=1.1&pickMembers%5B1%5D=4.2&pickMembers%5B2%5D=5.1

Statistics Canada. (2018m). Visible minority (total—population by visible minority), both
sexes, age (total), Canada, provinces and territories, 2016 census—25% sample data.
Retrieved from https://www12.statcan.gc.ca/census-recensement/2016/dp-pd/hlt-fst/
imm/Table.cfm?Lang=E&T=41&Geo=00&SP=1&vismin=1&age=1&sex=1

Statistics Canada. (2018n). Work activity during the reference year by selected age groups
(15 to 24), male, total—highest certificate, diploma or degree, 2015 counts, Canada,
provinces and territories, 2016 census—25% sample data. Retrieved from https://
www12.statcan.gc.ca/census-recensement/2016/dp-pd/hlt-fst/lab-tra/Table.cfm?Lang
=E&T=11&Geo=00&SP=1&view=1&age=2&sex=2&education=1

Tannock, S. (2001). *Youth at work: The unionized fast-food and grocery workplace.* Philadelphia:
Temple University Press.

Tencer, D. (2018, March 3). Look how much smaller Canada's economy would be without
women. *Huffington Post.* Retrieved from https://www.huffingtonpost.ca/2018/03/08/
women-workforce-canada_a_23380416/

Turcotte, J. F., Nichols, L., & Philipps, L. (2016). Maximizing opportunity, mitigating risk:
Aligning law, policy and practice to strengthen work-integrated learning in Ontario.
Toronto: Higher Education Quality Council of Ontario. Retrieved from http://www
.heqco.ca/SiteCollectionDocuments/Maximizing-Opportunity-Mitigating-Risk.pdf

Tyyskä, V. (2014). *Youth and society: The long and winding road* (3rd ed.). Toronto: Canadian
Scholars' Press.

United Nations. (2017). What do we mean by "youth"? *UNESCO.* Retrieved from http://
www.unesco.org/new/en/social-and-human-sciences/themes/youth/youth-definition/

Zacharek, S., Dockterman, E., & Edwards, H. S. (2017, December 18). The silence breakers.
Time. Retrieved from http://time.com/time-person-of-the-year-2017-silence-breakers/

CHAPTER 8

Childcare: Working in Early Childhood Education and Care in Canada

Susan Prentice

INTRODUCTION

Childcare is a crucial step in a paradoxical gendered loop: mothers often need to hire other women to do some of the childcare work that the mothers previously did for free. Mothers who use childcare, of course, continue to have primary responsibility for their own children, but they replace some of their care by paying others to do it. This is, in fact, the way the Canadian tax system has seen childcare since 1972. A family that has childcare expenses may deduct some of the childcare costs at tax time. However, only the lowest-earning adult may claim the Child Care Expense Deduction (Revenue Canada, 2017), and only up to a certain amount, regardless of how much the childcare bill really was. Since women almost always earn less than men, the tax system institutionalizes the gendered loop without actually solving the problem of childcare access.

Childcare services support all parents in a household: mothers, fathers, and same-sex partners chief among them. But in practice, childcare services have stronger impacts on mothers than fathers. For example, just 9.4% of the parents who take a paid parental leave in Canada are fathers, even though all parents are eligible (Statistics Canada, 2015). More mothers modify their paid work to accommodate their children than do fathers. Some scholars choose gender-neutral language and others use sex-specific language to discuss the current reality.

This chapter primarily opts for the latter and generally refers to mothers while recognizing that fathers and same-sex parents are also affected.[1]

The vast majority of Canadian mothers are in the paid labour force: 71% of mothers of children aged 0 to 2 and 77% of mothers children aged 3 to 5 work, and employment rates for mothers of school-aged children are even higher (Friendly et al., 2018, p. 166). Mothers who wish to enter paid labour, who train or study, or who need time to contribute to community life require childcare services such as childcare centres, family home childcare, nannies, and baby-sitters. When these services are regulated and licensed to meet provincial standards, they are considered part of the early childhood education and care (ECEC) or childcare system. When mothers use ECEC, virtually all of the people who provide them with care are other women. Childcare work is thus doubly important to feminist studies of women and work: women as mothers need care, and women as childcare staff provide the care.

While ECEC settings are crucial environments for children's growth and development, they are also work environments for adult caregivers. The quality of early ECEC services is intimately linked to the qualifications of the caregivers (UNICEF, 2008). There is a research consensus that quality "depends above all else on the ability of the caregiver to build relationships with children, and to help provide a secure, consistent, sensitive, stimulating, and rewarding environment" (UNICEF, 2008, p. 6). In case there's any doubt, the American National Research Council confirms that the workforce is the "critical component of quality" in childcare settings (UNICEF, 2008, p. 23).

There is virtually no other paid work in Canada that is more female-dominated than childcare. An astonishing 96% to 98% of Canadian childcare providers are women (Halfon, 2014). In childcare centres and licensed family childcare homes and as nannies, women dominate the childcare field. Sometimes they have specialized early childhood education (ECE) training through community college or university degrees; often they are untrained. All of them earn low wages. While researchers have long identified a general tendency to underappreciate and inadequately pay traditionally feminized skills, childcare work is particularly devalued. When advocates first brought daycare-worker pay to public attention, they used parking lot attendants and zookeepers as their comparators, pointing out how little value or respect was accorded to childcare work (Cook, Corr, & Breitkreuz, 2017; Schom-Moffat, 1984). Childcare educators were dismissed as simply "nice ladies who love children" (Stonehouse, 1989, p. 61) or women with "pleasant dispositions and limited abilities" (Taggart, 2011, cited in Cook et al., 2017, p. 57).

This chapter first offers a brief overview of social reproduction theory and Canada's social policy architecture to sketch out the landscape for childcare.

It then provides a description of Canada's ECEC workforce, looking at staff employed in childcare centres and in regulated family homes as well as nannies employed through federal immigration programs. Since 1997, Quebec has had a very different approach to family and childcare policy, and so childcare work in Quebec warrants its own discussion. Finally, the chapter considers what ECEC advocates, trade unions, women's groups, and equity-seeking organizations are doing to try to remedy the poor pay and working conditions of childcare staff.

CHILDCARE: SOCIAL REPRODUCTION AND SOCIAL POLICY IN CANADA

In order for people to go to work, they need to be fed, clothed, rested, and restored, on both a daily and a generational basis. Social scientists call this work of caring for people **social reproduction**. Social reproduction occurs in private households as unpaid domestic work, and it generally falls to women in their roles as mothers, wives, and daughters. It takes skill, attention, and labour to create and recreate people and to support their ability to be productive. Without women's social reproduction work, the economy would quickly grind to a halt. This is why historian Stephanie Coontz (1988) has explained that the family is a "major intersection between personal choice and social compulsion" (p. 2).

Nevertheless, economists have largely ignored social reproduction due to its association with the private sphere, which is assumed to be a sphere of consumption and not of production. Social reproduction is not seen as something that concerns the world of politics and economics. As the brilliant feminist economist Nancy Folbre (2001) once quipped, economists have tended to assume that "God, nature, the family and 'Super Mom'—or some combination thereof— would automatically provide whatever care was needed" (p. 1). However, contemporary political, economic, and social changes mean that both the quantity and the quality of care are under increasing pressure as more people need care and more people provide care. Scholars have called this the "care crisis," and it is finally forcing questions of social reproduction onto the political stage in Canada and around the world.

Historically, some caring tasks that were formerly performed by the family have successfully become public: first education and then health care were socialized in the early and mid-20th century in Canada. More recently, care for the elderly and people with disabilities have become important new social services. The reasons why households might need social services are explained primarily by economics. Today's job market often requires people to work shifts and irregular hours and to manage job precarity. Many jobs are insecure and pay just minimum wage. In Canada, about 6 in 10 minimum-wage earners are women and one-third of them are members of racialized communities. The share of racialized employees earning minimum wage is 47% higher than for the total population ($15 Fairness, 2017). Intersectional theory reminds us that analysis and advocacy must be very attentive to the ways that gender, class, race, ability, sexuality, and other identities are woven together (Crenshaw, 1991).

Childcare in Canada is not a public service, in the classic sense of the term. Children and parents have no right to childcare services. Governments almost never own and operate childcare facilities. Childcare isn't a service that the state provides or guarantees for its citizens, unlike education or health care. Childcare workers aren't public employees, unlike schoolteachers. Instead, childcare services are delivered by the not-for-profit voluntary sector and the commercial market. While about 70% of Canada's regulated childcare spaces are not-for-profit, about 30% are commercial—and commercial owners tend to lobby for lower quality standards (Friendly et al., 2018, p. 171). Unlike education or health, childcare remains a private family responsibility, just as it was decades ago. This state persists despite the fact that "developmental scientists, economists, and business and labour leaders have widely recognized the importance of early care and education in shaping children's development, promoting the health of families, and building a strong economy" (Whitebook, McLean, & Austin, 2016, p. 1). The role of government in childcare is largely restricted to provincial regulations and licensing of services, coordinating the finances of fee subsidies to low-income families, and organizing some reimbursement of childcare costs through the federal income tax system.

One of the most important demographic changes in Canada has been the massive entry of women into the paid labour force since the 1970s. In Canada today, the vast majority of mothers are employed. Even when their children are very young, over 70% of Canadian mothers nationwide have a paid job. By the time their children are school-aged, more than 80% of mothers work for pay (Friendly et al., 2018). Moreover, even when mothers are not in the paid labour force, they may be students or community volunteers who need childcare. Parents often want their children to benefit from early learning and childcare services, quite independent of their job status. Canada's social policy has not kept pace with these social changes and the growing desire for childcare services, and national family policy is weak.

The decade of Conservative rule under Prime Minister Stephen Harper (2006–2015) made family policy much worse (Bezanson, 2017). The numbers make it clear just how much Canada's social policy lags behind contemporary needs. Canada has 4.9 million children aged 0 to 12 years, but there are just 1.35 million regulated childcare spaces in centres and family homes (Friendly et al., 2018). This means that there is a licensed space for slightly more than one in four Canadian children. In the absence of regulated care, families turn to a range of other options, mainly the unregulated grey market of baby-sitting, augmented by friends and family, and sometimes private nannies for the most affluent.

Childcare is a market-based service in Canada and parent fees are the main revenue for a childcare facility (Friendly & Prentice, 2009). The cost of childcare varies by the age of children: infants need more staff than school-age children, and so infant care costs more than toddler or school-age care. The costs can be staggering and vary significantly across the country. Toronto has the highest fees for infants ($1,758 a month) and toddlers ($1,354 a month; Macdonald & Friendly, 2017). Prices are lower in other cities: parents in Winnipeg, for example, pay just under $651/month for infant care (MacDonald & Friendly, 2017). The most affordable care is found in Quebec, where parents pay just $8.25 per day (about $255 per month) per child, regardless of the age of their children. Outside Quebec each province has some kind of partial fee subsidy to assist some low-income families who use regulated care. Nevertheless, fee subsidies are not a sign that childcare is a public service, since subsidies never cover the full cost of care and they quickly end if parent income rises.

Staff wages make up at least 80% of a nonprofit childcare centre's budget (but can be less in commercial centres, where owners are trying to squeeze out profits by keeping labour costs low). The dilemma is that in order for childcare staff to be paid more,[2] parent fees must generally go up. Only two provinces, Quebec and Manitoba, have a province-wide system of flat fees; everywhere else, fees are set by the boards of directors of nonprofit childcare centres or by owners of commercial centres. This is a key element of the policy architecture that causes so many problems for the childcare workforce.

CANADA'S CHILDCARE WORKFORCE: CHILDCARE CENTRES AND FAMILY HOMES

Children are cared for in Canada's licensed childcare centres and regulated family homes by approximately 200,000 early childhood educators and assistants. In the unlicensed sector there are an uncertain number of paid baby-sitters, nannies, and parents' helpers (estimated at 70,000 or more), in addition to care provided for free by family and friends (Child Care Human Resources Sector Council [CCHRSC], 2009, p. 2).[3]

To call the childcare sector "female dominated" is an understatement. Almost all childcare centre staff are women. In Canada, this pattern dates back to the very earliest studies of what was then called "daycare" (Schom-Moffat, 1984). The absence of men in childcare is an international phenomenon. In the UK, just 2% of early childhood educators are men (Men in Child Care, 2017). Even in Sweden, with its remarkably well-developed and much-admired childcare system, just 2.5% of carers are men (Flising, 2005). In Australia, the figure jumps a bit: 5.6% of the national ECEC workforce is male (Simos, 2013). In the US, the childcare workforce is "almost exclusively female" (Whitebook et al., 2016, p. 6).

Wages for ECEs are much lower than those of other teaching jobs. This finding holds true across most countries. In the US, childcare workers are in the second-lowest percentile of annual earnings for all occupations (Whitebook et al., 2016). Researchers in the US bluntly point out that childcare wages are unlivable. Nearly half of all US childcare workers qualify for some kind of welfare program, such as Medicaid (subsidized health care) or food stamps. In Australia, childcare educators earn about half of the average national wage, and just one-third of what their counterparts in schools earn (Big Steps, 2017). In contrast, in Scandinavian countries, a bachelor's degree is needed to work as an ECE teacher, staff earn good pay, and their job has high status (Organisation for Economic Co-operation and Development [OECD], 2012).

In Canada, childcare wages are well below the national average. This trend is long-standing. In 2010, centre-based childcare educators earned an average of $25,100 and home-based providers earned an average of $10,925 (Halfon, 2014). This represents about 54% of the average wage for all occupations (Flanagan, Beach, & Varmuza, 2013, p. 18). Wages are better for childcare staff with specialized training: in 2012, educators with no postsecondary ECE qualifications earned an average of $13 per hour compared to $16.88 for an ECE certificate or diploma and $17.20 for an ECE-related university degree (Flanagan et al., 2013, p. 19). The low pay of childcare workers is compounded by the fact that they rarely have pensions and long-term disability or other workplace benefits. These realities are very troubling, since the ability of staff to provide high-quality care and education is influenced by their working conditions, including salary and benefits.

Childcare staff earn low wages despite quite high levels of education—contrary to popular myths that early childhood education is unskilled work that anyone can do. In the US, a majority (53%) of centre-based and 30% percent of home-based childcare staff report having college degrees. Almost one-third hold a BA or graduate or professional degree (National Survey of Early Care and Education [NSECE], 2013, p. 4). Canada shows an even stronger pattern of higher education: 77% of ECE workers have a postsecondary credential (a one-year certificate, two-year diploma, or three- or four-year university degree), compared to 58% of the total workforce in Canada (CCHRSC, 2009, p. 4). No province requires all childcare staff to have postsecondary ECE training.

There is a striking and demoralizing lack of return on childcare training. One comprehensive US study (Whitebook et al., 2016) found that for early educators who have invested in their education, "often at tremendous cost to themselves and their families," middle-class earnings remain out of reach. As the researchers point out, "a bachelor's degree in early childhood education occupies the dubious distinction of the college major with the lowest projected lifetime earnings" (p. 15). They conclude that the current system of preparing, supporting, and rewarding early educators in the US remains "ineffective, inefficient, and inequitable" (p. 15). Canadian data are not available, but are likely very similar given the documented correlation between higher education and low wages for Canadian ECE workers.

Besides being women and poorly paid, what else is known about the demographics of Canada's childcare educators? On average, childcare educators are young, relative to all occupations (Flanagan et al., 2013). Their median age in 2012 was 38 years—an increase, however, from earlier surveys. We have less reliable data on other demographics. Research shows that most educators are Canadian born; about 15% are born outside Canada and are now Canadian citizens; and less than 5% are permanent residents on work visas (Flanagan et al., 2013, p. 9). Studies show that 5.4% of Canada's childcare educators are members of racialized communities, and about 4% are First Nations, Inuit, or Métis. More than four in five childcare staff speak English as their first language, 5.7% speak French, and 12.4% speak a first language other than French or English (Flanagan et al., 2013, p. 9).

The state of Canadian data about the childcare workforce is troubling. Research on these workers was collected by the Child Care Human Resources Sector Council, which was defunded by the Conservative federal government in 2013. This arms-length organization was the only group to specifically study the childcare labour force, and since it was shut down, data gathering has not continued. Even when the council was operational, it did not report current or historic data on race or ethnicity in the childcare sector, unlike in the US, where such data are tracked. This means that we cannot make evidence-based claims about stratification in the Canadian early childhood workforce by race, ethnicity, or language. American data show that 63% of centre staff and licensed home providers are white, 16 to 17% are African American, 14 to 16% are Hispanic, and 5 to 6% are of other races and ethnicities (Whitebook et al., 2016, p. 8.) In Australia, researchers have found that one-third of family home care providers are migrant women (Cook et al., 2017), but there is no family home care data for Canada.

The absence of data makes it impossible to know how intersectionality operates in Canadian childcare. Many civil society organizations have called for Canada to do a better job of data collection and analysis, but governments have yet to act (Cleveland, Colley, Friendly, & Lero, 2003; Torjman, 2017). In June 2017, when Federal Minister of Families, Children, and Social Development Jean-Yves Duclos announced a new multi-year early-learning and childcare plan, he lamented that "data around early learning and child care in Canada is both scarce and of poor quality" (Radwanski, 2017), yet it is unclear if the government will actually remedy the knowledge gap. We know very little about children in childcare settings either—and particularly little about Indigenous children, who are the most disadvantaged youngsters in Canada (Brittain & Blackstock, 2015).

While we may imagine that working with young children is easy, the reality is quite different: "Long hours of work and high level of responsibility for the care and safety of small children create heavy workloads that can be, and often are, overwhelming" (Halfon, 2014, p. 9). Despite this, most childcare educators love their jobs. Surveys find that over 80% of educators report very high job satisfaction and few report frustration with their job (Flanagan et al., 2013, p. 24). Almost all (94% to 97%) agree with the statement that their work is important (Flanagan et al., 2013, p. 24).

Despite their outstanding levels of job satisfaction, childcare educators leave the field at a high rate. One national survey found that 25% of program staff are currently looking for a new job and plan to leave the regulated childcare sector within three years (Flanagan et al., 2013, p. 26). Most who exit cite low wages: "Across all national surveys, low wages have been consistently identified as the primary reason for leaving the field" (Halfon, 2014, p. 10). In Canada, 25% of childcare staff work at a second job—a damning indictment of poor pay (Flanagan et al., 2013, p. 9). Childcare is a kind of revolving door: many will train and enter the field, but a big share will leave fairly quickly, even though they have loved their work. Many leave to work in the school system, where their training and experience are valued and where wages and benefits are better.

Family home childcare providers are particularly vulnerable to this revolving door; studies show that most regulated homes are open for four years or less (Kershaw, Forer, & Goelman, 2005). Family home childcare is "precarious," according to one study (Cox, 2005), and the days are exceptionally long, averaging 56 hours per week, for wages that are even lower than those of centre-based staff (Doherty, Lero, Goelman, Tougas, & LaGrange, 2000). Family home providers juggle multiple and often conflicting roles: "mother to her own children who are usually present, paid care provider for other people's children, provider of support to child care families, and business owner/operator" (Doherty et al., 2000, p. 14). The challenges of providing early childhood care and education are complex in regulated homes. As a result, turnover in family home care is even higher than in centres.

Retention is a major issue in both childcare centres and regulated homes. Many educators with ECE experience and training look for better-paying sectors in which to care for children. As the sad joke goes: "Question: Why did the childcare worker cross the road? Answer: To find a job in a kindergarten classroom." Educators very often find work in schools as educational assistants, in recreation programs, and in other children's settings. Childcare centre directors find it hard to recruit new staff to fill empty positions. As a result, childcare centres often cannot meet the regulatory requirements for trained staff. In Manitoba, for example, regulations stipulate that two-thirds of staff in childcare centres must hold ECE credentials. Due to labour market shortages, however, about 30% of Manitoba's centres have an exemption to their license because they cannot attract and retain enough trained educators (Prentice, 2016).

The quality of early childhood care is directly linked to the adult workforce. International comparative studies have found that job satisfaction and retention—and therefore the quality of ECEC—can be improved by high staff-child ratios and low group size, competitive wages and benefits, reasonable schedule and workload, low staff turnover, a good physical environment, and a competent and supportive manager (OECD, 2012). These conditions are hard to meet and sustain in Canada's patchwork of childcare services. The problem, as Marcy Whitebook (2013) explains, is that tackling childcare workforce issues like low pay and low status "challenges basic assumptions in our society about the importance of caregiving work, the role of mothers of young children in the workforce, the role of government in the delivery of childcare services, and the capacity of the private marketplace to address the broader public welfare" (p. 6). In the end, it is very hard to argue that being a childcare educator is a good job. As Kimberly Morgan (2005) bluntly claims, there is a "junk job" quality to childcare: despite the fact that the work is intrinsically rewarding as well as socially valuable and important, childcare workers do worthy work for unlivable wages.

ALTERNATIVES TO THE CHILDCARE CRISIS: NANNIES

Affluent families that need childcare have an option that is out of financial reach for most households: they can hire a private nanny, very often someone who lives in their home. The federal government has long had a policy of supporting nannies, through a range of different programs going back to the 1950s. The best-known, established in 1992, was the **Live-in Caregiver Program (LICP)**, succeeded in 2014 by the Caring for Children Pathway Program, part of the Temporary Foreign Workers Program. On the one hand, because nanny care is neither regulated nor licensed, it cannot be considered part of the ECEC system. On the other hand, because it is a formal federal program through which Canada organizes social reproduction, it plays an important role in the landscape of caring for children.

The LICP allowed a family to hire a foreign national nanny who was required to work for and live with the family for two years. After two years, the nanny could apply for permanent residence, although this provision ended in 2014. The LICP was thus for many years a route to Canadian citizenship for women from the Global South. Mothers would regularly leave their own young children in their home countries to work as care providers for affluent families in Canada.

Feminist critics raised many problems with the LICP (Arat-Koc, 1989; Bakan & Stasiulus, 1997; Rosen, Baustad, & Edwards, 2017). First, they were shocked at the federal requirement that nannies had to live with the family they worked for and could not change employers. This was, they observed, a clear example of 20th-century servitude that put some women at serious risk of sexual and physical abuse. Why, they asked, were women required to live with their employers when other, mainly male, migrants were not subject to the same restriction? Second, they pointed to the contradictions of the global care chain, in which affluent and primarily white women could displace their care needs through the exploitation of racialized immigrants, who then had to rely on their own kin and social networks to care for the children they left behind. Third, many raised ethical questions about the morality of the "nanny solution," arguing it was evidence of a very incomplete and unfinished feminist struggle, pitting powerful and powerless women against each other (Tronto, 2002). "The grim truth," explains Audrey Macklin (1994), "is that some women's access to the high-paying, high-status professions is facilitated through the revival of semi-indentured servitude. Put another way, one woman is exercising class and citizenship privilege to buy her way out of sex oppression" (p. 34). The federal successor program to the LICP eliminated the requirement that nannies live in their employers' homes, but it also ended the automatic right to apply for permanent residency after two years—giving with one hand while taking back with the other.

Migrant workers' rights groups fought to fix the inequities and inherently exploitative features of the LICP and are currently fighting its successor program. Importing migrant labour to solve the childcare needs of class-privileged women appeals to governments for a number of reasons. Most importantly, nanny programs reflect the federal government's preference for and reliance on the private family and the market to care for young children. Nannies are a cheap form of childcare who solve much of the childcare problem for highly privileged parents without the government incurring the expense of a national childcare system. As Elizabeth Adamson (2017) has explained, the use of foreign domestic workers "appeased both conservatives and liberals alike, as it maintained a status quo of private home-based care ... with minimum public investment" (p. 200). Many critics and advocates have pointed out that the nanny problem can never be remedied without an effective national childcare program.

QUEBEC'S INNOVATIONS

When it comes to children, mothers, and childcare staff, the best place in Canada is Quebec. In 1997 Quebec launched an ambitious social policy innovation, creating a system of widely available and very low cost regulated childcare. For many years, childcare in Quebec cost just $5 per day, although the daily fee went up to $8.05 per day in 2017 and $8.25 per day in 2019 and there is widespread provincial concern that fees might rise again (CBC, 2018). Quebec has a distinctive approach to making childcare widely available and affordable, and its childcare staff earn the best wages in the country. The province has virtually solved the gap between supply and demand: there is essentially enough childcare to serve all the families that want or need it. Today in most urban centres there is a regulated space for six in ten children in a system of more than 240,000 spaces (Government of Quebec, 2015). Quebec has a roughly equal supply of not-for-profit childcare, commercial childcare centres, and licensed family homes. The high and rapidly growing share of for-profit childcare has raised concerns, and Quebec advocates are grappling with the issue.

Quebec currently spends over $2.3 billion a year on childcare (still less than the 1% of GDP recommended by the OECD), and this has enabled the province to support a large network of centres and regulated homes. As in the rest of Canada, 98% of childcare staff are women. Their wages, however, are the best in Canada: in 2012, Quebec's educators earned an average of $19.13 per hour, which was about $4 higher than the Canadian average for childcare staff. Directors of Quebec childcare centres did even better, earning $32.64 per hour, compared to just $22 per hour for directors in the rest of Canada (Flanagan et al., 2013, p. 16).

Economist Pierre Fortin and his team have calculated that universal access to low-fee childcare in Quebec induced nearly 70,000 more mothers to hold jobs than if no such program had existed—an increase of 3.8% in women's employment (Fortin, Godbout, & St-Cerny, 2012). What's more, the family poverty rate fell by over 40%, and Fortin and others attribute this poverty drop directly to the provincial childcare program. Quebec's domestic income (GDP) was higher by about 1.7% ($5 billion) as a result of the childcare policy, which grew the economy as more women worked and thus paid taxes. Based on the cascade of positive economic effects from the universal childcare program, Fortin's team concluded that the program is profitable for both the provincial and federal governments, which also reap some benefits from the increased taxes of newly working mothers. The economists are at pains to point out that the childcare system does much better than just pay for itself. Quebec's net expenditure generates a favourable budgetary impact. Thus, Fortin and team conclude that "the programme is extremely popular with young families of all incomes and is definitely here to stay" (Fortin & St-Cerny, 2012, p. 3). Quebec's example shows that social reproduction needs can successfully be dealt with by social policy, and that good childcare systems for children, families, and care providers can be built if governments make them a priority.

CHANGING CHILDCARE WORK: SOCIAL MOVEMENTS

What are social movements and activists doing to tackle the childcare crisis, which denies worthy wages to early childhood educators? The answer is complex, as different groups try different strategies. Ivy Bourgeault and Patricia Khokher (2006) studied wage-improvement campaigns in nursing, midwifery, and childcare to understand how female-dominated sectors have tried to increase their pay. They found that increasing entry-to-practice credentials, organizing and unionizing, seeking pay equity, and fighting for public funding have been the main strategies. They report that the greatest successes for nurses and midwives came when these strategies were used in combination, yet gains for childcare staff have been much slower than for other female-dominated professions.

A paradox of pay equity campaigns is that they require a male comparator group. Since childcare is so female dominated, male comparators don't exist, and so the childcare workforce has not been able to use pay equity mechanisms.

Many childcare professional associations have sought to raise the educational credentials of staff. In Quebec, for example, the lead provincial organization, the Association québécoise des centres de la petite enfance (Quebec Association of Child Care Centers [AQCPE], 2017) has called for all staff, in centres and well as in regulated homes, to have specialized ECE postsecondary education. In Ontario, the College of Early Childhood Educators has made the job category a protected title, meaning that only people registered with the college can call themselves early childhood educators (in the same way that only people registered with the Ontario College of Architects can legally call themselves architects). In Alberta, an accreditation system has been set up to ensure high quality care and professional recognition. Despite these efforts, increasing entry-to-practice requirements, or "credentialism," has had scant effect on wages.

A more effective strategy has been to unionize. Although many people associate unions with industrial jobs, collective bargaining occurs in all work settings. In Canada, about 20% of childcare educators are unionized (Flanagan et al., 2013, p. 19). In 2012, in unionized centres, the average wage of educators was $20.11 per hour compared to $15.50 for nonunionized staff. Moreover, a higher percentage of unionized educators have pensions or Registered Retirement Savings Plans and other benefits. This pattern has also been found in the US. Although just 10% of US childcare workers are unionized (nearly halved since the early 1980s), their average 2012 wage was US$17.39 per hour, compared to $11 for nonunionized educators (Whitebook et al., 2016, p. 13). Unions have long understood that childcare staff are exploited. As the Canadian Union of Public Employees explained, "Through their low wages, child care providers continue to subsidize a grossly under-funded service—in an area of work which is demanding and strenuous, as well as essential economically and socially for the well being of families" (cited in Bourgeault & Khokher, 2006, p. 420).

The most promising strategy for raising wages seems to rest with public policy change. As a result, the childcare advocacy movement calls for a universally accessible, publicly funded childcare system. Advocates have made connections between scarce spaces, high fees, and weak subsidies, and low wages for childcare staff, explaining that this "three-legged stool" is persistently vulnerable under the current social policy architecture. Only a full-scale social commitment to making childcare an essential public service for 21st-century families will generate the Canada-wide changes that are needed. Advocates work to lobby the federal government and change national policy through the Child Care Advocacy Association of Canada, and many provinces have provincial advocacy chapters or coalitions that focus on provincial policy as well.

CONCLUSION

This chapter has argued that redressing the conditions of childcare work is essential for women as mothers and caregivers. After all, it is impossible to build and sustain quality childcare programs without a professional workforce that earns fair wages for this important work.

When childcare services are a patchwork of centres and regulated homes owned and operated by commercial businesses, or not-for-profit volunteers, neither children nor staff have the experiences they need and deserve. In the absence of public funding and universal access, low-paid staff supply the cheap labour that sustains private operations. Policy changes are required for Canada's childcare staff to have decent wages for their worthy work. When this happens, it will be a sign that governments are stepping up to accept more responsibility for social reproduction.

Done right, childcare services have far-reaching and positive social effects, as the Quebec example shows. Where services remain inadequate, exploitative options like nanny care and unregulated baby-sitters will persist. Silke Staab (2015) of UN Women argues that there is a triple dividend from good childcare: well-designed investments in ECEC services can have "major economic and social pay-offs for families, individuals and societies at large by: (1) facilitating women's labour force participation, (2) enhancing children's capabilities and (3) creating decent jobs in the paid care sector." These gains can more fairly distribute the work of social reproduction and ensure that the needs of childcare staff, mothers, and children are met.

NOTES

1. We can look forward to the day when men's rates of employment are as changed by the arrival of children as women's, when Canada collects as much data on working fathers as it does on working mothers, when there are as many lone-father-led households as lone-mother households, and when fathers take as much parental leave as mothers do. At that point, we can switch to fully gender-neutral language.

2. In this chapter *early childhood educator* or *ECE* refers to a staff person who has specialized postsecondary education in early childhood education, through a certificate, diploma, or degree. *Childcare staff* and *worker* refer to all employees in the regulated childcare sector.

3. The broader ECEC workforce also includes kindergarten teachers (about 33,000) as well as teachers' assistants working in elementary schools (approximately 8,000), but since they work in the public education system they are not included in this discussion.

KEY READINGS

Bezanson, K. (2017). Mad men social policy: Families, social reproduction and child care in a conservative Canada. In R. Langford, S. Prentice, & P. Albanese (Eds.), *Caring for children: Social movements and public policy in Canada* (pp. 19–36). Vancouver: University of British Columbia Press.

Bourgeault, I. L., & Khokher, P. (2006). Making a better living from caregiving: Comparing strategies to improve wages for care providers. *Canadian Review of Sociology and Anthropology, 43*(4), 405–425.

Folbre, N. (2001). *The invisible heart: Economics and family values.* New York: New Press.

Friendly, M., & Prentice, S. (2009). *About Canada: Childcare.* Halifax: Fernwood.

DISCUSSION QUESTIONS

1. Almost all Canadian childcare advocates call for a system of publicly owned or not-for-profit childcare services. Others believe that for-profit services could help meet childcare needs. What are the benefits and risks of public and not-for-profit childcare services, particularly with respect to childcare staff? What are the benefits and risks of commercial childcare services?

2. The federal government has recently expanded parental leave to 18 months, in large part because Canada has very little infant childcare. Discuss the strengths and weaknesses of this strategy. Would you want to take an 18-month leave from your job after the birth or adoption of a child? Why or why not? Which parents are more likely to take a longer leave, and why?

3. Some critics of childcare services think that children should stay home with their parents until they start school, and so children should not be enrolled in childcare services. How would you discuss the issue of working mothers with a person who held this point of view? What arguments are likely to change their point of view?

4. What are some of the reasons why so few men are early childhood educators? What arguments would you use if were trying to encourage men to consider a career in early childhood education? How successful do you think such a campaign would be?

5. What are the main reasons why more mothers than fathers stay home with their children? Do you think these factors are likely to change or stay the same over the next 10 years? Why or why not?

6. Explore the childcare needs of racialized, immigrant, or Indigenous families. Would these families benefit from a universally accessible, publicly funded childcare system? In what ways are their needs distinct?

7. This chapter has argued that Quebec is a leader in childcare provision. What reasons explain why Quebec's policy is so different from the rest of Canada? What lessons can the federal government and other provinces draw from Quebec's experience?

REFERENCES

$15 Fairness. (2017). Fight for $15 and fairness: Fact sheet. Retrieved from http://15andfairness.org/the-facts/

Adamson, E. (2017). Crossing boundaries: In-home childcare and migration. In R. Langford, S. Prentice, & P. Albanese (Eds.), *Caring for children: Social movements and public policy in Canada* (pp. 186–207). Vancouver: University of British Columbia Press.

Arat-Koc, S. (1989). In the privacy of our own home: Foreign domestic workers as solution to the crisis of the domestic sphere in Canada. *Studies in Political Economy, 28*, 33–58.

Association québéçoise des centres de la petite enfance. (2017). *Déclaration sur l'éducation à la petite enfance: Pour la reconnaissance du droit de tous les enfants à des services éducatifs de qualité dès la naissance.* Retrieved from https://www.aqcpe.com/content/uploads/2017/05/declaration-sommet-sur-leducation-a-la-petite-enfance.pdf

Bakan, A., & Stasiulus, D. (1997). *Not one of the family: Foreign domestic workers in Canada.* Toronto: University of Toronto Press.

Bezanson, K. (2017). Mad men social policy: Families, social reproduction and child care in a conservative Canada. In R. Langford, S. Prentice, & P. Albanese (Eds.), *Caring for children: Social movements and public policy in Canada* (pp. 19–36). Vancouver: University of British Columbia Press.

Big Steps. (2017). Big steps: Value our future. Retrieved from http://www.bigsteps.org.au/

Bourgeault, I. L., & Khokher, P. (2006). Making a better living from caregiving: Comparing strategies to improve wages for care providers. *Canadian Review of Sociology and Anthropology, 43*(4), 405–425.

Brittain, M., & Blackstock, C. (2015). *First Nations child poverty: A literature review and analysis*. Ottawa: First Nations Children's Action Research and Education Services, First Nations Child and Family Caring Society of Canada.

CBC. (2018, January 1). Fee increases and tax breaks: What Quebecers will pay in 2018. Retrieved from https://www.cbc.ca/news/canada/montreal/quebec-fees-january-2018-what-to-expect-1.4468457

Child Care Human Resources Sector Council. (2009). *A portrait of Canada's early childhood education and care workforce*. Ottawa: Author. Retrieved from http://www.ccsc-cssge.ca/sites/default/files/uploads/Projects-Pubs-Docs/1.1portraitbrochure_e.pdf

Cleveland, G., Colley, S., Friendly, M., & Lero, D. (2003). *The state of data on early childhood education and care in Canada*. Toronto: Childcare Resource and Research Unit, University of Toronto.

Cook, K., Corr, L., & Breitkreuz, R. (2017). The framing of Australian childcare policy problems and their solution. *Critical Social Policy, 37*(1), 42–63. doi:10.1177/0261018316653952

Coontz, S. (1988). *The social origins of private life: A history of American families 1600–1900*. London: Verso.

Cox, R. (2005). *Making family child care work: Strategies for improving the working conditions of family childcare providers*. Ottawa: Status of Women Canada. Retrieved from http://ccsc-cssge.ca/sites/default/files/uploads/Projects-Pubs-Docs/MakingChildCareWork.pdf

Crenshaw, K. (1991). Mapping the margins: Intersectionality, identity politics, and violence against women of color. *Stanford Law Review, 43*(6), 1241–1299.

Doherty, G., Lero, D., Goelman, H., Tougas, J., & LaGrange, A. (2000). *You bet I care! Caring and learning environments: Quality in regulated family child care across Canada*. Guelph, ON: Centre for Families, Work and Well-Being, University of Guelph.

Flanagan, K., Beach, J., & Varmuza, P. (2013). *You bet we still care: A survey of centre-based early childhood education and care in Canada. Highlights report*. Ottawa: Child Care Human Resources Sector Council. Retrieved from http://www.ccsc-cssge.ca/sites/default/files/uploads/Projects-Pubs-Docs/EN%20Pub%20Chart/YouBetSurveyReport_Final.pdf

Flising, B. (2005, September). *A few remarks on men in child care and gender aspects in Sweden*. Paper presented at the Men in Child Care Conference, London. Retrieved from http://www.meninchildcare.co.uk/MiC-05-Sweden.pdf

Folbre, N. (2001). *The invisible heart: Economics and family values*. New York: New Press.

Fortin, P., Godbout, L., & St-Cerny, S. (2012). *Impact of Quebec's universal low-fee childcare program on female labour force participation, domestic income, and government budgets: Working paper*. Retrieved from https://www.oise.utoronto.ca/atkinson/UserFiles/File/News/Fortin-Godbout-St_Cerny_eng.pdf

Fortin, P., & St-Cerny, S. (2012). Lessons from Quebec's universal low-fee child-care programme. *Juncture: IPPR*. Retrieved from https://www.ippr.org/juncture/lessons-from-quebecs-universal-low-fee-childcare-programme

Friendly, M., Larsen, E., Feltham, L., Grady, B., Forer, B., & Jones, M. (2018). *Early childhood education and care in Canada 2016*. Toronto: Childcare Resource and Research Unit. Retrieved from http://childcarecanada.org/publications/ecec-canada/early-childhood-education-and-care-canada-2016

Friendly, M., & Prentice, S. (2009). *About Canada: Childcare*. Halifax: Fernwood.

Government of Quebec. (2015). *Situation des centres de la petite enfance, des garderies et de la garde en milieu familial au Québec en 2013: Analyse des rapports d'activités 2012—2013 soumis par les divisions des entreprises de services de garde éducatifs à l'enfance*. Retrieved from https://www.mfa.gouv.qc.ca/fr/publication/Documents/Situation_des_CPE_et_des_garderies-2013.pdf

Halfon, S. (2014). *Canada's childcare workforce*. Toronto: Moving Child Care Forward. Retrieved from http://movingchildcareforward.ca/images/policybriefs/MCCF_canadas_childcare_workforce.pdf

Kershaw, P., Forer, B., & Goelman, H. (2005). Hidden fragility: Closure among child care services in BC. *Early Childhood Research Quarterly, 20*, 417–432.

Macdonald, D., & Klinger, T. (2015). *They go up so fast: 2015 child care fees in Canadian cities*. Ottawa: Canadian Centre for Policy Alternatives. Retrieved from https://www.policyalternatives.ca/publications/reports/they-go-so-fast

Macklin, A. (1994). On the outside looking in: Foreign domestic workers in Canada. In W. Giles & S. Arat-Koc (Eds.), *Maid in the market: Women's paid domestic labour* (pp. 13–39). Halifax: Fernwood.

Macdonald, D., & Friendly, M. (2017, December 12). *Time out: Child care fees in Canada 2017*. Ottawa: Canadian Centre for Policy Alternatives. Retrieved from https://www.policyalternatives.ca/timeout

Men in Child Care. (2017). Men in child care: Children need men too! Retrieved from http://www.meninchildcare.co.uk/

Morgan, K. (2005). The "production" of child care: How labor markets shape social policy and vice versa. *Social Politics: International Studies in Gender, State and Society, 12*(2), 243–263.

National Survey of Early Care and Education. (2013). *Number and characteristics of early care and education (ECE) teachers and caregivers: Initial findings from the National Survey of Early Care and Education (NSECE): OPRE Report #2013—38*. Washington, DC: Office of Planning, Research and Evaluation, Administration for Children and Families, US Department of Health and Human Services.

Organisation for Economic Co-operation and Development. (2012). *Starting strong III*. Paris: Author.

Prentice, S. (2016, December 22). How to really help Manitoba families: Build a universal childcare system. *Winnipeg Free Press.*

Radwanski, A. (2017, June 16). For Trudeau's Liberals, universal daycare is a distant dream. *Globe and Mail.*

Revenue Canada (2017). T778 Child care expenses deduction for 2017. Retrieved from https://www.canada.ca/content/dam/cra-arc/formspubs/pbg/t778/t778-17e.pdf

Rosen, R., Baustad, S., & Edwards, M. (2017). The crisis of social reproduction under global capitalism: Working-class women and children in the struggle for universal childcare. In R. Langford, S. Prentice, & P. Albanese (Eds.), *Caring for children: Social movements and public policy in Canada* (pp. 164–185). Vancouver: University of British Columbia Press.

Schom-Moffat, P. (1984). *The bottom-line: Wages and working conditions of workers in the formal day care market.* Ottawa: Status of Women Canada, Task Force on Child Care.

Simos, M. (2013). More men needed to work in childcare industry to balance female-dominated workforce. *Adelaide Now.* Retrieved from http://www.adelaidenow.com.au/news/south-australia/more-men-needed-to-work-in-childcare-industry-to-balance-female-dominated-workforce/news-story/178f7175b18cf32b089868c092a777fd

Staab, S. (2015). *Gender equality, child development and job creation: How to reap the "triple dividend" from early childhood education and care services.* Retrieved from http://www.unwomen.org/en/digital-library/publications/2015/12/gender-equality-child-development-job-creation

Statistics Canada. (2015, November 23). Employment Insurance coverage survey, 2014. *The Daily.* Retrieved from http://www.statcan.gc.ca/daily-quotidien/151123/dq151123b-eng.pdf

Stonehouse, A. (1989). Nice ladies who love children: The status of the early childhood professional in society. *Early Child Development and Care, 52*(1–4), 61–79.

Taggart, G. (2011). Don't we care? The ethics and emotional labour of early years professionalism. *Early Years, 31*(1), 85–95.

Torjman, S. (2017). *National child data strategy: Results of a feasibility study.* Ottawa: Caledon Institute of Social Policy.

Tronto, J. (2002). The "nanny" question in feminism. *Hypatia, 17*(2), 34–51.

UNICEF. (2008). *The child care transition: A league table of early childhood education and care in economically advanced countries.* Retrieved from https://www.unicef-irc.org/publications/507-the-child-care-transition-a-league-table-of-early-childhood-education-and-care-in.html

Whitebook, M. (2013). Preschool teaching at a crossroad. *Employment Research Newsletter, 20*(3), 4–6.

Whitebook, M., McLean, C., & Austin, L. (2016). *The early childhood workforce index: State of the early childhood workforce.* Berkeley: Center for the Study of Child Care Employment, University of California, Berkeley.

CHAPTER 9

Minoritized Faculty in Canada's Universities and Colleges: Gender, Power, and Academic Work

Sandra Acker and Linda Muzzin

INTRODUCTION

The teaching profession has long been regarded as an example of "women's work." While community college faculty share with elementary and secondary school-teachers a central commitment to teaching, university faculty conduct research as well. Given their past record of male domination, universities are not generally seen as sites of women's work, except at the support-staff level. Despite their history as trade schools, colleges employ proportionately more women faculty than universities do. In Canada, postsecondary education (PSE) is regulated by the provinces, and thus its organization varies from place to place. Institutions themselves can also take many forms. Some universities emphasize research more than others, and some community colleges have renamed themselves poly-technics or institutes of technology.[1] This chapter discusses faculty in all of these institutional types.

The central concern of the chapter is gender and women academics. But writing in a general way about "women" or "men" can risk *essentialism*—the tendency to see all members of a group as the same. There are always cross-cutting dimensions (intersections) to any identity. The term *intersectionality* refers to the way in which different attributes, such as gender, race, social class, or having a disability, operate together in any situation and how their impact can shift for a person over time (Valentine, 2007).

Much of what has been written about PSE ignores gender or simply compares women as a group with men as a group. Alternatively, it may feature the experiences of one group, such as white women, without attending to racial and ethnic variations. Writings on universities and colleges as organizations and on PSE policy often disregard equity issues.

It is important to think carefully about the terms used when talking and writing about improving social justice in PSE. For example, *equality of opportunity*, while a positive phrase, means giving everyone the same treatment, without acknowledging different starting points. The term **equity**, which means improving chances for differently situated groups to realize their potential, is preferable. Another popular idea is increasing *diversity*, which refers to including more people from varied backgrounds—for example, when recruiting university or college students. While diversity is certainly a worthy goal, it can also be used in a superficial way as a marketing tool to claim an institution is "diverse" in order to attract people of colour, but without necessarily following up to ensure that racism and discrimination are eradicated (Ahmed, 2009).

To simply call someone a minority or member of a minority group may imply that they lack something important. This chapter focuses instead on the process of **minoritization**—how social relationships that involve power imbalance are created among groups. In this context, minoritized groups include women, who make up half of the population but are minoritized as academics, as are faculty from racial, Indigenous, and sexual minorities and faculty with disabilities. Within PSE, disadvantage and oppression can take many forms. Like individual identities, these oppressions intersect and reinforce one another within the power relations of academic work.

In a discussion of intersectionality, Yuval-Davis (2006, p. 198) identifies four different locations where power is visible: (1) organizational (embedded in laws, agencies, organizations, and the family), (2) intersubjective (involving formal and informal relationships among people), (3) experiential (daily life feelings of inclusion, exclusion, and attitudes toward others), and (4) representational (expressed in images, symbols, media, and texts). Yuval-Davis's typology serves as an organizing guide for this chapter.

HOW ACADEMIC WORK IS ORGANIZED

Researchers and theorists from various disciplines have tried to describe and explain how and why universities and colleges remain stubbornly patriarchal institutions dominated by men, while at the same time espousing principles of equality, meritocracy, and freedom of expression. Even today, Britton (2017) writes, "Universities are gendered organizations nested within a gendered hierarchy. The highest prestige institutions, the highest paying disciplines, and the most influential positions are all male-dominated" (p. 5).

Individuals entering classic university careers in Canada first obtain a doctorate and then (possibly after a postdoctoral position or temporary university employment) secure tenure-track (permanent) assistant professor positions. Following a thorough review of their research, teaching, and institutional service some five or six years later, they usually achieve tenured positions with job security and the title of associate professor. Later they may be promoted to a full professorship. The classic college career is somewhat different. Traditionally, new college teachers move from a position in a workplace related to an area of training within the college (for example, nursing) to an instructor position that could become permanent after one or two years of satisfactory performance.

In recent years, in response to increased enrolment and insufficient funding in both universities and colleges, these classic patterns have been disrupted as academics are hired on short-term contracts without job security (Brownlee, 2015). These positions may be full- or part-time, and faculty are referred to variously as sessional, contract, adjunct, and contingent instructors.[2] The Canadian Association of University Teachers (CAUT; 2017b) estimates that almost a third of university professors in Canada fall into this category, and while it is difficult to obtain statistics for college faculty, in Ontario about 70% of this group are contingent (Colleges Ontario, 2014). Contingent academics may hold other jobs (for example, as a doctor or lawyer) and teach one or two classes, but most depend on this work for their livelihood and would prefer a full-time continuing position (CAUT, 2018b). Despite their precarious position in the academic labour market, they are often very well qualified. A recent survey of university and college contingent faculty showed that 49% had a doctorate, medical degree, or postdoctoral degree (CAUT, 2018b, p. 14).

Minoritized faculty are overrepresented in the contingent labour force. In 2015 women made up 38.2% of full-time permanent university faculty and 46.7% of full-time permanent college faculty; in contrast, they were 51% of "temporary full-time and temporary/permanent part-time faculty" (i.e., contingent) in universities and 61.3% in colleges (CAUT, 2017a). Statistics are not collected routinely on race, and even more rarely on race and gender together, so it is not known if there are more racially minoritized women in precarious academic work. However, 27% of the 2018 CAUT survey respondents self-identified as "other than white" (racialized), and 2% identified as Indigenous (2017a, p. 51).

The authors of the report draw on these figures and comparisons with census data to suggest that the contingent labour force has a greater share of minoritized faculty than the classic permanent one (2017a, p. 14).

Historically, Canadian universities and colleges had different missions, with the first colleges, founded in the 1960s, providing access to working-class, women, racialized, and Indigenous students, groups that were traditionally underrepresented in universities. Research was located largely in universities. However, several new trends blur the difference in institutional mandates. For example, a 2011 study found that about half of Ontario universities had introduced a "teaching stream" in which full-time academics were contracted to teach more classes and do little or no research (Vajoczki, Fenton, Menard, & Pollon, 2011, p. 18). As in the contingent pathway, this teaching stream was majority (60%) female (pp. 21–22). Another trend that blurs the institutional mandates of universities and colleges is the offering of bachelor's programs in some colleges that formerly only offered certificates and diplomas.

Minoritized individuals tend to be overrepresented in certain career paths within organizations, often those with less status and security. In Canadian society, women and men have historically been expected to follow different pathways in life, with men viewed as breadwinners and women as homemakers. Remnants of this pattern are embedded in the organization of academic work (Acker & Dillabough, 2007). One example is the uneven distribution of women (and men) in different subject fields. In 2016/2017, women comprised 65% of full-time university teachers in education, but only 20.6% of those in mathematics, computer sciences, and information sciences, and 15.5% of those in architecture, engineering, and related technologies (CAUT, 2018a, p. 3).

Women faculty also encounter issues related to social expectations that they will do the majority of the domestic work, elder care, and childcare at home. Combining a demanding professional career in academia with care responsibilities is frequently identified as a source of stress for women academics (Acker, Webber, & Smyth, 2016; Bonneville, 2016). Trying to be a good parent or elder caregiver and a good academic is a balancing act. Susan Brown (2011) recalls explaining to her five-year-old why she would be away at a conference and being met with the emphatic response, "The day you quit your job will be the best day of my life!" (p. 70). Among contingent faculty, the CAUT survey referred to above reported that 56% of respondents said that precarious employment had impacted their ability to have children or purchase a house (CAUT, 2018b, p. 23). Yet, as Ecklund and Lincoln (2016) argue, difficulties with work-family balance should not be seen as a personal dilemma or an issue only for women, but instead a consequence of harmful academic cultures that prize devotion to work over everything else.

Minoritized faculty at universities and colleges are also disadvantaged by the ways in which service to the institution is organized. Researchers in Canada and the United States find that women and racialized faculty are more likely to be asked to fill departmental and institutional service roles such as committee memberships, admissions, curriculum planning, and advising (Acker et al., 2016; Guarino & Borden, 2017). In a US study, Hirshfield and Joseph (2012) used the term "identity taxation" to describe the "extra burden of service, advising, and mentorship expectations" (p. 213) disproportionately expected of women professors and professors of colour. Their study drew on an intersectional analysis to highlight the subtleties of how identity taxation works for women faculty in different racialized groups.

In Canada, Monture-OKanee (1995, p. 19) wrote that as an Indigenous woman faculty member at a law school, the extra work required for being expert at both traditional law and the practices of her community doubled her intellectual workload, while service requests were extreme. A similar situation was found among women contingent college teachers in northern Canada who drive to reserves to teach and provide extensive counselling to their students beyond what is expected of faculty in other programs (Muzzin, Bachynskyj, Zankowicz, Vinci, & Meaghan, 2009). The extra layer of service is good for public relations, student success, and Indigenous communities, but may make it harder for individuals to accumulate the other achievements (such as publications) necessary for their subsequent career opportunities.

EXPLORING THE GAPS

Yuval-Davis's second location of power, the intersubjective, refers to interactions between individuals or groups. Thinking about interactions leads us to ask where minoritized and nonminoritized faculty are found (or absent) in universities and colleges. One approach is to look for statistical information on these points. The earlier discussion of contingent faculty featured these kinds of comparisons. Unfortunately, Canadian statistics that might give us robust answers about many relevant issues do not exist or are not publicly available. Some statistical data are available on "gender gaps" (comparisons of women and men; Baker, 2012), but these published statistics tend to regard "women" and "men" as homogeneous categories, ignoring any variation within a group rather than looking at subgroups whose experiences may not be the same as those of the majority.

In general, figures are lacking on faculty who are racially or sexually minoritized, in colleges rather than universities, and contingent rather than full-time. As a result, much of the discussion below concerns full-time women university faculty without intersectional nuances.

Gender Gaps Over Time

The first gender gap described here refers to comparisons of numbers of university women and men appointed and promoted and how the pattern has changed over time. In the late 19th and early 20th centuries, Canadian universities were not the complex organizations they are today. The 1901 census listed 47 women among 857 academics (Brandt, Black, Bourne, & Fahrni, 2011, p. 155). Marika Ainley (2012), who spent a lifetime writing women scientists back into the history of science, discovered that women holding roles such as temporary assistant lecturers and lab technicians were not necessarily included in official records. Moreover, she writes, "Canadian women had been socialized to be modest, so neither the majority of women scientists nor their relatives, friends, and colleagues sought to preserve their papers" (p. 18).

In the 1960s, with its many social and demographic changes, such as Quebec's Quiet Revolution and the women's movement, concern grew about many aspects of girls' and women's education. There was a major expansion of the numbers of universities and community colleges (called CEGEPs or Collèges d'enseignement général et professionnel in Quebec) at this time. But even in the mid-1960s, only about 10% of full-time university professors were women, mostly in education, nursing, household science, and arts (Robbins, Luxton, Eichler, & Descarries, 2008, p. 24). The situation was slightly different in community colleges, where vocational programs for female-dominated occupations in health and social services have had, from their inception, a majority of women instructors.

Given the desire for change, in 1970 a Royal Commission on the Status of Women considered pay equity, safeguarding Indigenous women's status upon marriage, and combatting violence against women. Advocacy groups of the day joined together to become influential coalitions that worked on issues of minoritization. In 1984 a Royal Commission on Equality in Employment, conducted by Justice Rosalie Abella, made recommendations that led to the Employment Equity Act and the Federal Contractors Program, both holding employers to standards and commitments to increase representation and improve treatment of four designated groups: women, members of visible minorities, Aboriginal peoples, and persons with disabilities.[3] The Federal Contractors Program had a major influence on the hiring of women academics as well as on their salaries.

Over this period, the gender gap in women's representation among university faculty began to close, if slowly. By 2016 women made up just under 40% of Canadian university academics (Statistics Canada, 2017). A greater presence does not necessarily mean the achievement of equity, as other gaps remain. The Expert Panel on Women in University Research (2012) concluded that (1) women's progress in Canadian universities is uneven by discipline and rank; (2) the higher the rank, the lower the percentage of women in comparison to men; (3) the Canadian profile resembles that of other economically advanced nations; and (4) the panel was hampered due to a paucity of Canadian data (pp. xv–xvi).

A few years earlier, Ornstein, Stewart, and Drakich (2007) did a statistical analysis of men's and women's university careers and confirmed that while time to tenure was slightly longer for women, the major difference overall was that women were promoted more slowly to full professor, the highest rank. Why do men's academic careers progress faster than women's? Ornstein et al. (2007) suggest that while most of the research trying to answer this question has explored family issues, their evidence points to the workplace. They conclude, "disciplines strongly influence careers. ... There is a continuum stretching from the 'hardest' sciences (natural science, engineering and mathematics), through the less hard sciences (medicine), the harder social sciences (law and criminology), [and] the softer social sciences (the humanities and fine arts), with practitioner-dominated disciplines such as journalism at the end. This continuum corresponds to disciplinary differences in the speed of promotion (shorter times in 'harder' areas) and to the relative position of women in disciplines (better in softer areas)" (p. 19). Their finding that women reach full professor status faster in disciplines where they are better represented, such as education, nursing, humanities, medicine, and fine arts, could be a consequence of women's presence being historically more accepted in these fields. It might also mean that when women are present to make promotion decisions, other women progress more rapidly.

Gender Gaps in Academic Leadership

There is numerical evidence of a second gender gap in appointments to prestigious positions such as Canada Research Chairs (CRCs) and other academic leadership roles. On the surface, the CRC program, introduced in 2000, was a positive, substantial federal government investment in academic research, creating several thousand high-prestige, research-oriented university professorships.

But in the first year of the program, only 11.5% of the "Tier 1" (senior) positions went to women (Forsyth, 2011, p. 180). One reason for this gender gap was an allocation mechanism that gave 80% of the funding to science and medicine, fields where male researchers predominate. In 2003 eight women academics brought a human rights complaint against the program. By 2008 they had settled out of court as the CRC program had agreed to set equity targets for each of the four groups designated by the 1984 Royal Commission on Equality in Employment. Since that time, there are more women CRCs and an Equity, Diversity, and Inclusion Action Plan has been put in place (Government of Canada, 2018). Institutions are now required to adopt such plans and reach their targets or risk losing their ability to hold CRC positions.

CRCs could be considered leaders in their universities as well as in their disciplinary fields as they are given the resources to gather many students and researchers under their wings. More often, leaders are understood to be those in formal hierarchical management positions, including department chairs, deans, vice-presidents, vice-provosts, provosts, and presidents. As of 2016, 30% of Canadian college presidents were women, compared to 20% of those heading universities (Tamburri, 2016; Wiart, 2016). Arguably a prestige hierarchy is visible here, with women more likely to lead lower-status institutions. There are also some indications that women in senior university administrative positions such as provost or president are at greater risk of termination or early departure (Cafley, 2015). Further, Lavigne (2016) found a pattern of nonreappointment for women deans and racialized deans.

Minoritized faculty aspiring to leadership positions are said to encounter a "second glass ceiling" or, once in place, a "glass cliff" (Peterson, 2016). The glass cliff metaphor refers to the practice of hiring minoritized individuals into especially difficult and turbulent situations where they have a greater chance of failure. The truncated or nonrenewed appointments reported by Cafley (2015) and Lavigne (2016) could be related to this glass cliff. Moreover, people outside the mainstream, that is, not white and male, will be more visible than others in senior roles, and consequently they risk receiving more scrutiny and critical commentary.

Gender Gaps in Country Comparisons

Beyond statistical data as described above, additional information on gaps comes from surveys: questionnaires distributed to (usually large) numbers of people. A cross-national survey of faculty called the Changing Academic Profession (CAP) study has provided comparative information on university faculty according to gender and age. The CAP study was coordinated by researchers in Germany, the United States, and Japan, with local teams in over 18 countries administering a survey to full-time academics in 2007 and 2008 (Metcalfe & Gonzales, 2013, p. 5). Of 12 countries compared on measures of job satisfaction, Canada had the highest scores (Bentley, Coates, Dobson, Goedegebuure, & Meek, 2013, p. 251). Despite this cheerful news, analysis of the gender gap in job satisfaction within the Canadian data showed that "a much larger share of males [than females] reported very high satisfaction" (31% versus 18%) and that women were more likely than men to agree or strongly agree that their job was a source of considerable personal strain (49% compared with 38%; Weinrib et al., 2013, pp. 91–92).

When Metcalfe and Gonzalez (2013) used the CAP data to look more closely at the situation of women and men faculty in Canada, the United States, and Mexico, they found that, on the one hand, across all three countries women were disadvantaged compared to men with respect to job stress, opportunities for academic collaboration, promotions, and family responsibilities. On the other hand, the patterns were complex and the size of the gender gap was not identical across countries. Their results suggest that generalizations about gender gaps should take into account national and cultural differences that could influence the findings.

Gender Gaps Found through Qualitative Research

In a survey like the CAP study, it is difficult to discern the reasons for some of the findings reported. In contrast to most quantitative (number-based) comparative studies, qualitative research centres personal stories or interviews with small numbers of faculty speaking or writing about their academic careers. While not easily generalizable, this type of research is better at helping us understand how different features of the environment interact and affect minoritized individuals and groups.

For example, qualitative studies can build on a quantitative finding, such as Ornstein et al.'s (2007) discovery that there are disciplinary differences in opportunities for women, discussed above. In a qualitative study of 40 university nursing faculty and administrators, Muzzin and Limoges (2008) conclude that despite the gains in status made by nursing faculty in recent decades, women researchers in this field are relatively disadvantaged in obtaining research funding for a variety of reasons. Their situation relates to the hospital- and college-based education obtained by the majority of nursing faculty over much of the last century, as compared to their male colleagues in, for example, medicine, many of whom have had university training in advanced research methods.

Qualitative studies also give indications of why women surveyed by the CAP project might report less satisfaction than their male counterparts do. As noted earlier, when women are interviewed they often discuss the difficulties of balancing care responsibilities with ever-increasing workloads (Bonneville, 2016) and the overload of service responsibilities that seem to be optional for male colleagues but expected of women (Acker et al., 2016). Some studies have identified health and mental health issues for women who try to excel in a stressful work climate (Mountz, 2016; Parizeau et al., 2016). Robbins (2012) lists a number of academic workplace culture factors, such as the devaluation of women's authority and competence, inflexible policies, insufficient mentoring, old boys' networks, and "macho" research climates in some fields. She also reminds us that wider social, political, and economic structures interact with academic conditions to sustain gender gaps (pp. 2–3).

Gaps beyond Gender

Some data are available on gaps for minoritized groups such as racialized and Indigenous faculty, although these figures are not usually shown for women and men separately. A 2018 CAUT publication, based mostly on 2016 census data, states that in 2016, racialized academics comprised 21% of university faculty and 15% of college instructors, while Indigenous academics made up 1.4% of all university professors and 3% of college instructors (2018a, p. 2). Of these four groups, only racialized university faculty appeared in a proportion similar to their representation in the labour force more generally.

Unfortunately, these figures do not show gender gaps within these comparisons. Moreover, categories such as "visible minority" (see note 3) or "racialized" may obscure different situations of subgroups divided by ethnicity or national origin. For example, among university faculty, the representation of South Asians is 5.1%, Chinese 5.7%, Black 2%, and Latin American 1.4% (CAUT, 2018b, p. 6).

As noted above, qualitative research helps us understand the experience of minoritization. There are examples of qualitative Canadian research conducted by Indigenous women professors and professors of colour (Henry et al., 2017a, b); stories of the experiences of women contingent faculty (Hannah, Paul, & Vethamany-Globus, 2002); and analyses of the experiences of academics who are sexual minorities (Lenskyj, 2005; Nielsen & Alderson, 2014). Surprisingly, only a few Canadian studies consider the impact of social class background on academics (Haney, 2015). Disability-informed research on the Canadian professoriate is also difficult to find but has been increasing (Waterfield, Beagan, & Weinberg, 2017).

METAPHORS OF THE ACADEMY AND THE EXPERIENCES OF MINORITIZED FACULTY

Yuval-Davis's third category is the experiential—how people think and feel in their everyday lives. Writers often reach for metaphors to dramatize the experience of inequality: minoritized academics climb the career "ladder," leak out of the "pipeline," or find their ambitions thwarted by a "glass ceiling" or a "glass cliff." Instead of the "ivory tower" (a metaphor for a university emphasizing its intellectual rather than practical focus), they may toil (along with many administrative staff members) in the "ivory basement" (Eveline, 2004). Positive metaphors are less in evidence: "breaking the glass ceiling" might be one example. A popular metaphor, coined in the United States by Hall and Sandler (1982), is the phrase "chilly climate," used to describe the unwelcoming atmosphere surrounding women in PSE. Full-time Canadian women academics naming themselves the Chilly Collective (1995) took up the metaphor in their book, *Breaking Anonymity.* Soon after, 50 women contingent faculty revealed their experiences, emphasizing that what was "chilly" for those in tenured positions was better than their own working conditions, which were described as a "tundra," a frozen, treeless landscape (Hannah et al., 2002).

A different set of metaphors appears in narratives by Canadian women academics minoritized by race or sexual orientation. They use images of space and colonialism such as "unsettling relations" (Bannerji, Carty, Dehli, Heald, & McKenna, 1991), "dangerous territories" (Roman & Eyre, 1997), and "seen but not heard" (Luther, Whitmore, & Moreau, 2003). More recently, a US article about proactive hiring of racialized minorities in community colleges used the "dangerous work" metaphor (Levin, Jackson-Boothby, Haberler, & Walker, 2015). These metaphors emphasize the traumatic impacts of racism, ableism, ageism, and **homophobia** intertwined with sexism in higher education and convey that faculty not in the white, male, able-bodied, heterosexual mainstream face a hostile environment. Associated with these situations is the metaphor of "lip service" when referring to, for example, the ubiquitous phrase in hiring advertisements, "We especially welcome applications from visible minorities" (Henry, 2015). Policies regarding racial equity are deemed to be inadequate and not fully implemented (Henry et al., 2017b; Henry & Tator, 2009).

The interface between instructor and student is a point where the climate can be tense. The US community college literature shows that the classroom may be a particular challenge for women who teach trades. Lester (2008) describes the experience of an African American welding instructor who often found herself not just the only woman among the faculty, but ridiculed by students in the classroom (p. 292). She eventually managed to turn this dynamic around by challenging her male students to weld better than her. We do not have a similar literature in Canada—indeed we have few Canadian studies of the experiences of college faculty at all, and what we have tends not to deal with gender.

Canadian research raises questions about bias in student responses to minoritized faculty and its impact on course evaluations. Eidinger (2017) notes that women instructors who are young or short have particular difficulty establishing authority and that they are told that they should "smile more" or be "more approachable and friendly." Bannerji (1995) also remarks on the impact of being short as well as a person of colour—"I am a non-white, five-foot-one woman" (p. 100)—in her moving discussion of the feelings that washed over her as she lectured about racism:

> While I am lecturing on "bodies" in history, in social organization of relations and spaces, constructed by the gaze of power, I am actually projecting my own body forward through my words. I am in/scribing rather than erasing it. First I must draw attention to it, focus this gaze, let it develop me into a construct. Then I take this construct, this "South Asian" woman and break it up piece by piece. … I am the teacher, my body is offered up to them to learn from, the room is an arena … [and] I am an actor in a theatre of cruelty. (pp. 101–102)

This phenomenon of embodiment and the desire for authenticity is important for LGBTQ (lesbian, gay, bisexual, transgender, and queer) professors, who must juggle a complicated set of considerations—for example, the size, level, and subject matter of the class and the type of surrounding community—when deciding whether to "come out" in the classroom (Nielsen & Alderson, 2014). Lenskyj (2005) described the "acute reaction somewhere in the pit of my stomach" (p. 159) that she experienced when a student in a graduate course on women and education "made a statement … that, while she was okay with gay men, she 'couldn't stand lesbians'" (p. 158). Lenskyj intervened immediately, revealing her identity as a lesbian and, in subsequent courses, came out in the first class so that students would understand her positioning.

KNOWLEDGE PRODUCTION BY MARGINALIZED FACULTY

Yuval-Davis's fourth category of power relations is termed *representation* (2006, p. 198). The meaning of the word here is broader than the everyday word, as used in the gender gap data above, where the concern was with whether women or people in some other category appeared or not (were represented) in segments of PSE. Yuval-Davis's usage links representation with discourses—sets of ideas that circulate at a particular point in history and may present as truths that make other competing ideas unthinkable. These ideas are found in images, symbols, media, and texts, as well as speeches and conversations. The questions raised by this second meaning of representation are somewhat different. For example, rather than counting numbers of black or Indigenous women professors, considering representation as discourse would lead to questioning how black feminist or Indigenous knowledges are constructed and valued in the academy. Another discourse that has become very powerful in the 21st century is that of neoliberalism, an economic discourse that challenges many traditional features of universities and colleges.

Minoritized Faculty Produce New Knowledges

In the 1970s and 1980s individual institutions and groups of women were investigating the experiences of the growing cadre of minoritized faculty, developing critiques of institutional shortcomings, and creating new scholarship and teaching initiatives, including women's studies programs and programs centring race, sexuality, and disability. A feminist genre of writing on and by minoritized academics began to appear.

More broadly, feminist texts promoting multiple ways of knowing the world have asked who produces what knowledges and for whom. To mention only a few from scores of well-known feminist scholars in Canada and the United States, Canadian historian of science Marika Ainley (2012) began writing women's history or "herstory," while networks of historians created resource materials for schoolteachers that were lacking at the time (Fine-Meyer, 2013). Sociologist Dorothy E. Smith (1987, 1990) built a large network within the women's movement and academia, producing a series of books about the standpoint of women and how dominant texts in disciplines such as sociology do not reflect women's lived experiences. In the United States, philosopher Sandra Harding (1998), also using standpoint theory, questions the global reach and dominance of hard science, while Patricia Hill Collins (1986, 1990), a foundational scholar of black feminist thought, builds on the idea that the "outsider within" (e.g., a minoritized academic) may have access to special insights. Legal scholar Kimberlé Crenshaw coined the term *intersectionality* in 1989 to help explain the oppression of African American women. Judith Butler (1999), another American philosopher, has also been important in Canada and worldwide through her writing on how gender is produced rather than simply assigned. In Canada, the past decade has thus far produced several strong edited volumes that critically consider the production of knowledge from a feminist standpoint (Brown, Perreault, Wallace, & Zwicker, 2011; Luxton & Mossman, 2012; Whittaker, 2015).

Following the lead of black and Indigenous scholars, many writers agree that the term *knowledge* should be replaced by *knowledges* to signal that knowledge is contested and different forms of knowledge are acceptable in different communities (Massaquoi & Wane, 2007). Marie Battiste (2013) and Verna St. Denis (St. Denis & Schick, 2003) link knowledge produced in universities to the colonial subjugation of Indigenous knowledges and call for a process of decolonization to reverse the harmful effects of a history of colonization. The report of the Truth and Reconciliation Commission of Canada (TRC; 2015)—established in 2008 to document the history of Indian residential schools—has stimulated a number of initiatives in PSE, including rethinking of curricula to better integrate Indigenous perspectives (Cote-Meek, 2017) and a reconceptualization of how research related to Indigenous Peoples might be conducted (McGregor, 2018). Joining these other influential theoretical perspectives is a focus on disability and how it plays out in the academy for both women and men. Scholars like Tanya Titchkosky (2011) and Bea Waterfield, Brenda Beagan, and Merlinda Weinberg (2017) have challenged us to think differently about disability in Canadian academic institutions and to re-examine the assumption that able-bodiedness is a desirable or required quality for academics.

Together, the work of scholars such as those named above has raised questions about the nature of knowledge and inspired feminist writing in the 21st century.

Writing about, Living in, and Resisting Neoliberalism

Much contemporary critical writing about the academy focuses on the discourse and practice of neoliberalism. According to Swarts (2013), neoliberalism was promoted by political leaders such as Margaret Thatcher in the UK and Ronald Reagan in the US, who rejected state economic intervention, public ownership, union involvement, full employment, and government commitments to equity and provision of social services in favour of international free trade and de-regulation in all areas of the economy. In academia these ideas were translated into *corporatization* (Reimer, 2004): the introduction of business principles into PSE governance, and the production of knowledge judged by its contribution to governmental economic goals. The trend toward hiring contingent rather than permanent faculty is an example of a business principle (saving money) being applied despite its negative consequences. Corporatization includes a discourse of new managerialism and audit logic, meaning that in the university, adminis-trators (managers) keep close watch on faculty productivity (reduced to numbers of students taught, publications, and external research grants) and encourage na-tional and global competition among institutions chasing reputation and ranking. While Canadian universities have not gone to the extremes of those in the UK and Australia in their push for relentless calibration and comparison (Davies & Bansel, 2010), many academics report being "uneasy" (Acker & Webber, 2016) as the pressures mount and academic work, aided by new technologies, spreads into all places and times of day, a feature sometimes thought to be particularly troubling for women (Mountz, 2016).

In the classrooms of the corporatized university, students become consumers who have consumer power. Webber (2008) writes about the disrespect shown by some students to women faculty teaching women's studies classes. Webber's analysis also shows the ways in which student course evaluations become a "dis-ciplinary tool of the new managerialism" (p. 49), discouraging the use of con-tentious and difficult course material, especially for contingent and untenured faculty, who need good evaluations to continue in their positions.

Newson and Polster (2010) have called for Canadian feminists to take action to define the university we wish to have rather than the one that corporatiza-tion forces upon us. Another recent effort to resist some of the negative effects of university corporatization is the slow professor movement, analogous to the slow food movement and built on the idea that academic life would be improved if the pace were less hectic. Reflective practice, working collaboratively, and caring for students and self as part of "slow scholarship"—all compatible with feminist principles—have been promoted by Berg and Seeber (2016) and Mountz et al. (2016).

In Canadian colleges, neoliberalism has meant a significant reduction in public funding, and this reduction limits their equity mission. Like universities, colleges have adapted to making up financial shortfalls by increasing tuition fees, advertising on campus, seeking funding from industry, and growing the flexible nonpermanent contingent workforce. For example, at some colleges, female-dominated programs such as early childhood education have been converted entirely to online formats (Muzzin & Meaghan, 2016) taught by contingent faculty. A consequence of this fragmented workforce is reduced ability of faculty unions to negotiate with PSE administrators and government regarding salaries and other benefits (Mackay, 2014) and a growing estrangement between faculty and administrators (Muzzin, 2016).

Muzzin and Meaghan (2014, 2016) present one of the few critical feminist analyses of neoliberalism in Canadian colleges. They found that in several rounds of neoliberal restructuring, in locations with small cadres of liberal arts teachers, some of the first casualties were literacy, labour studies, and women's studies programs—programs that do not fit the prevailing emphasis on vocational skills. However, faculty in female-dominated fields such as the 65 health professions taught in Canadian colleges, especially nursing, have been able to use their strong licensing boards and unions to maintain the quality and accreditation of their programs; faculty resist cuts by college administrators targeting large female-dominated programs in their attempts to deal with inadequate funding (McKnight & Muzzin, 2014).

Scholarly commentaries on neoliberalism in PSE almost always regard it as highly negative (Levin, Aliyeva, & Walker, 2016) and stress the untoward effects of attempts to make public institutions work as if they are businesses, when their purposes and ways of functioning are traditionally quite different. The challenge is to find ways to continue efforts to make these institutions more socially just, such as increasing the numerical representation of minoritized faculty and incorporating the alternative knowledges they bring, without such efforts being lost in the tide of neoliberalism that has swept across PSE.

CONCLUSION

A useful metaphor for considering change is that of a glass half full or half empty, suggesting that an ambiguous situation can be looked at in both optimistic and pessimistic ways. The optimistic half-full glass shows that since the 1984 Abella Royal Commission on Equality in Employment, minoritized faculty have arrived in the academy in greater numbers. Scholarship has transformed from the days when it centred on the achievements of white men. White women have arguably been the major beneficiaries of what Newson (2012) describes as marginalized faculty transforming PSE "from being a relatively enclosed, elitist and patriarchal institution to becoming more open, accessible and women-inclusive"

(p. 43), which is not to say that they no longer face discrimination and disadvantage. But based on theoretical work challenging white privilege and prejudicial ideas about heterosexuality and able-bodiedness, we can anticipate a continuing reconceptualization of what counts as knowledge, bringing into closer view those knowledges that have been marginalized until now.

Our half-empty glass shows that a gender gap still exists in (1) hiring into secure academic positions, (2) appointments to prestigious chairs and full professorships, (3) subject fields that are nontraditional for women, and (4) administrative leadership. Quantitative gender gap studies at times raise more questions than they answer. Why do so many women academics report so much stress? What are the comparable experiences and interactions of college faculty, so neglected by PSE scholars? How do women faculty minoritized by race, indigeneity, sexual orientation, or disability fare, since they are rarely visible in official statistics or survey data at this level of detail? How can we extend the list of minoritizing characteristics to include ethnicity, age, language, and possibly others?

Qualitative research shows that part of the story is that minoritized faculty experience a kind of identity taxation, or work not expected of nonminoritized faculty, such as women serving on departmental or institutional committees or racialized faculty mentoring racialized students. While identity taxation may contribute to a better climate in which women and other minoritized groups have more say in decision-making and contribute to their communities, it is nonetheless unfair, as well as troubling when unrecognized and unrewarded.

For some minoritized academics, especially those teaching embodied equity, the classroom can be an uncomfortable site. Chilly climates are still around. Proactive hiring of designated groups and equity policies too often stop at lip service rather than fully valuing the major contributions to colleges and universities that minoritized faculty make. Under neoliberalism, where contingent faculty have become an important sector of the workforce, faculty unions have diminished power to maintain existing gains in equity. Thus, our achievements are, like a glass, fragile. Canada still has a long way to go in documenting and addressing academic minoritization.

NOTES

1. In British Columbia, for example, five former community colleges are named *special purpose universities*, while three colleges are named *institutes*. Note that in the US *college* is often used as a synonym for *university*, whereas in Canada it is generally the

equivalent to the US *community college. College* in this chapter is used in the Canadian sense, meaning community college rather than university.

2. In the Canadian PSE literature, these positions are most often referred to as *contract* or *contingent. Adjunct* is used in some places but is mainly regarded as an American term. The term *contingent* is used here to be consistent with other Canadian scholarship.

3. These terms have undergone some challenges over the years. For example, many writers dislike *visible minority*, as it appears to regard many different subgroups as alike, as well as begging the question of who is determining what is "visible." Moreover, it obscures variations among groups that are not technically classified as visible minorities but are minoritized as members of various ethnic or nationality groups. *Indigenous* now usually replaces *Aboriginal*. How best to describe disability is also contentious (Titchkosky, 2011).

KEY READINGS

Brown, S. (2011). School/work, home/work: Academic mothering and the unfinished work of feminism. In S. Brown, J. Perreault, J.-A. Wallace, & H. Zwicker (Eds.), *Not drowning but waving: Women, feminism and the liberal arts* (pp. 67–85). Edmonton: University of Alberta Press.

Henry, A. (2015). "We especially welcome applications from members of visible minority groups": Reflections on race, gender and life at three universities. *Race, Ethnicity and Education, 18*(5), 589–610.

Hirshfield, L. A., & Joseph, T. D. (2012). "We need a woman, we need a black woman": Gender, race, and identity taxation in the academy. *Gender and Education, 24*(2), 213–227.

Lester, J. (2008). Performing gender in the workplace: Gender socialization, power, and identity among women faculty members. *Community College Review, 35*(4), 277–305.

Metcalfe, A. S., & Gonzalez, L. P. (2013). Underrepresentation of women in the academic profession: A comparative analysis of the North American region. *NASPA Journal about Women in Higher Education, 6*(1), 1–21.

Monture-OKanee, P. A. (1995). Introduction—Surviving the contradictions: Personal notes on academia. In the Chilly Collective (Eds.), *Breaking anonymity: The chilly climate for women faculty* (pp. 11–28). Waterloo, ON: Wilfrid Laurier University Press.

Muzzin, L., & Limoges, J. (2008). "A pretty incredible structural injustice": Contingent faculty in Canadian university nursing. In A. Wagner, S. Acker, & K. Mayuzumi (Eds.), *Whose university is it anyway? Power and privilege on gendered terrain* (pp. 157–172). Toronto: Sumach Press.

DISCUSSION QUESTIONS

1. Of Yuval-Davis's various sites at which power relations can be examined (organizational, intersubjective, experiential, representational), which have proved the richest for understanding intersectionality in academic work and why?

2. In your own education history can you think of instances when you were being minoritized and others when you felt privileged or advantaged? How might the ideas in this chapter explain these instances?

3. Verna St. Denis and Carol Schick (2003) teach their students to understand minoritization from an Indigenous perspective by writing their own story within a colonizing, patriarchal society. How might you frame your own history?

4. What do you understand the metaphor of a glass half empty or half full to mean? Can you think of examples relevant to your own schooling or teaching? Can you do the same with one or two of the other metaphors in the chapter, such as "chilly climate" or "glass cliff"? How useful (or how limited) are these metaphors in conveying a sense of what a situation is like?

5. What do you understand by the term *knowledge production*? Which of the feminist theorists discussed above are you most aware of and why? Can you name others who have influenced society who are not named in the chapter?

REFERENCES

Acker, S., & Dillabough, J.-A. (2007). Women "learning to labour" in the "male emporium": Exploring gendered work in teacher education. *Gender and Education, 19*(3), 297–316.

Acker, S., & Webber, M. (2016). Uneasy academic subjectivities in the contemporary Ontario university. In J. Smith, J. Rattray, T. Peseta, & D. Loads (Eds.), *Identity work in the contemporary university* (pp. 61–75). Rotterdam, Netherlands: Sense.

Acker, S., Webber, M., & Smyth, E. (2016). Continuity or change? Gender, family, and academic work for junior faculty in Ontario universities. *NASPA Journal about Women in Higher Education, 9*(1), 1–38.

Ahmed, S. (2009). Embodying diversity: Problems and paradoxes for black feminists. *Race, Ethnicity and Education, 12*(1), 41–52.

Ainley, M. G. (2012). *Creating complicated lives: Women and science at English-Canadian universities, 1880–1980.* Montreal & Kingston: McGill-Queen's University Press.

Baker, M. (2012). *Academic careers and the gender gap.* Vancouver: UBC Press.

Bannerji, H. (1995). *Thinking through: Essays on feminism, Marxism and anti-racism.* Toronto: Women's Press.

Bannerji, H., Carty, L., Dehli, K., Heald, S., & McKenna, K. (1991). *Unsettling relations: The university as a site of feminist struggles*. Toronto: Women's Press.

Battiste, M. (2013). *Decolonizing education*. Saskatoon: Purich Publishing.

Bentley, P., Coates, H., Dobson, I., Goedegebuure, L., & Meek, V. L. (2013). Academic job satisfaction from an international comparative perspective: Factors associated with satisfaction across 12 countries. In P. Bentley, H. Coates, I. Dobson, L. Goedegebuure, & V. L. Meek (Eds.), *Job satisfaction around the academic world* (pp. 239–262). Dordrecht, Netherlands: Springer.

Berg, M., & Seeber, B. K. (2016). *The slow professor: Changing the culture of speed in the academy*. Toronto: University of Toronto Press.

Bonneville, L. (2016). Women in academia: Stories of female university professors in a research-intensive Canadian university. *Higher Education Review, 48*(2), 71–97.

Brandt, G., Black, N., Bourne, P., & Fahrni, M. (2011). *Canadian women: A history* (3rd ed.). Toronto: Nelson.

Britton, D. M. (2017). Beyond the chilly climate: The salience of gender in women's academic careers. *Gender and Society, 31*(1), 5–27.

Brown, S. (2011). School/work, home/work: Academic mothering and the unfinished work of feminism. In S. Brown, J. Perreault, J.-A. Wallace, & H. Zwicker (Eds.), *Not drowning but waving: Women, feminism and the liberal arts* (pp. 67–85). Edmonton: University of Alberta Press.

Brown, S., Perreault, J., Wallace, J.-A., & Zwicker, H. (Eds.). (2011). *Not drowning but waving: Women, feminism and the liberal arts*. Edmonton: University of Alberta Press.

Brownlee, J. (2015*). Academia, Inc.: How corporatization is transforming Canadian universities*. Winnipeg: Fernwood.

Butler, J. (1999). *Gender trouble: Feminism and the subversion of identity*. New York: Routledge.

Cafley, J. (2015, September 8). Why have so many Canadian university presidencies failed? *University Affairs*. Retrieved from www.universityaffairs.ca/opinion/in-my-opinion/why-have-so-many-canadian-university-presidencies-failed/

Canadian Association of University Teachers. (2017a). Almanac of post-secondary education in Canada. Section 2: Academic Staff. Retrieved from https://www.caut.ca/resources/almanac/academic-staff

Canadian Association of University Teachers. (2017b, October). By the numbers/Contract academic staff in Canada. Retrieved from https://www.caut.ca/bulletin/2017/10/numbers-contract-academic-staff-canada

Canadian Association of University Teachers. (2018a, April 6). Employment and wage equity remain elusive for academics in Canada's universities and colleges. Retrieved from https://www.caut.ca/latest/2018/04/employment-and-wage-equity-remain-elusive-academics-canadas-universities-and-colleges

Canadian Association of University Teachers. (2018b). *Out of the shadows: Experiences of contract academic staff.* Ottawa: Author. Retrieved from https://www.caut.ca/sites/default/files/cas_report.pdf

Chilly Collective. (Eds.). (1995). *Breaking anonymity: The chilly climate for women faculty.* Waterloo, ON: Wilfrid Laurier University Press.

Colleges Ontario. (2014). *Environmental scan 2013: College resources.* Toronto: Author. Retrieved from www.collegesontario.org/research/2013_environmental_scan/CO_EnvScan_12_College_Resources_WEB.pdf

Collins, P. H. (1986). Learning from the outsider within: The sociological significance of black feminist thought. *Social Problems, 33*(6), 14–32.

Collins, P. H. (1990). *Black feminist thought: Knowledge, consciousness, and the politics of empowerment.* New York: Routledge.

Cote-Meek, S. (2017, February 16). Postsecondary education and reconciliation. Op-ed reprinted from *Policy Options* magazine by Universities Canada. Retrieved from https://www.univcan.ca/media-room/media-releases/postsecondary-education-reconciliation/

Crenshaw, K. (1989). Demarginalizing the intersection of race and sex: A black feminist critique of antidiscrimination doctrine, feminist theory and antiracist politics. *University of Chicago Legal Forum, 1*, Art. 8, 139–167.

Davies, B., & Bansel, P. (2010). Governmentality and academic work: Shaping the hearts and minds of academic workers. *Journal of Curriculum Theorizing, 26*(3), 5–20.

Ecklund, E. H., & Lincoln, A. E. (2016). *Failing families, failing science: Work-family conflict in academic science.* New York: New York University Press.

Eidinger, A. (2017, March 30). She's hot: Female sessional instructors, gender bias, and student evaluations. *ActiveHistory.ca.* Retrieved from http://activehistory.ca/2017/shes-hot-female-sessional-instructors-gender-bias-and-student-evaluations/

Eveline, J. (2004). *Ivory basement leadership: Power and invisibility in the changing university.* Crawley: University of Western Australia Press.

Expert Panel on Women in University Research. (2012). *Strengthening Canada's research capacity: The gender dimension.* Ottawa: Council of Canadian Academies.

Fine-Meyer, R. (2013). The Ontario Women's History Network: Linking teachers, scholars and history communities. In C. Carstairs & N. Janoviĉek (Eds.), *Feminist history in Canada: New essays on women, gender, work, and nation* (pp. 200–217). Vancouver: UBC Press.

Forsyth, L. (2011). Desperately seeking equity: Systemic discrimination and the Canada Research Chairs program. In S. Brown, J. Perreault, J.-A. Wallace, & H. Zwicker (Eds.), *Not drowning but waving: Women, feminism, and the liberal arts* (pp. 173–193). Edmonton: University of Alberta Press.

Government of Canada. (2018). Canada Research Chairs program equity, diversity and inclusion action plan. Retrieved from http://www.chairs-chaires.gc.ca/program-programme/equity-equite/action_plan-plan_action-eng.aspx

Guarino, C. M., & Borden, V. M. H. (2017). Faculty service loads and gender: Are women taking care of the academic family? *Research in Higher Education, 58*(6), 672–694.

Hall, R. M., & Sandler, B. R. (1982). The classroom climate: A chilly one for women? Washington, DC: Association of American Colleges.

Haney, T. (2015). Factory to faculty: Socioeconomic difference and the educational experience of university professors. *Canadian Review of Sociology, 52*(2), 160–186.

Hannah, E., Paul, L., & Vethamany–Globus, S. (Eds.). (2002). *Women in the Canadian academic tundra: Challenging the chill.* Montreal & Kingston: McGill-Queen's University Press.

Harding, S. (1998). *Is science multicultural? Postcolonialisms, feminisms, and epistemologies.* Bloomington: Indiana University Press.

Henry, A. (2015). "We especially welcome applications from members of visible minority groups": Reflections on race, gender and life at three universities. *Race, Ethnicity and Education, 18*(5), 589–610.

Henry, F., Dua, E., James, C., Kobayashi, A., Li, P., Ramos, H., & Smith, M. S. (2017a). *The equity myth: Racialization and indigeneity at Canadian universities.* Vancouver: UBC Press.

Henry, F., Dua, E., Kobayashi, A., James, C., Li, P., Ramos, H., & Smith, M. S. (2017b). Race, racialization and indigeneity in Canadian universities. *Race, Ethnicity and Education, 20*(3), 300–314.

Henry, F., & Tator, C. (Eds.). (2009). *Racism in the Canadian university: Demanding social justice, inclusion and equity.* Toronto: University of Toronto Press.

Hirshfield, L. A., & Joseph, T. D. (2012). "We need a woman, we need a black woman": Gender, race, and identity taxation in the academy. *Gender and Education, 24*(2), 213–227.

Lavigne, E. (2016, December 7). *Paths to the Canadian deanship: A study of Canadian universities' appointment announcements.* Paper presented at the Society for Research into Higher Education Annual Meeting, Newport, UK.

Lenskyj, H. (2005). *A lot to learn: Girls, women and education in the twentieth century.* Toronto: Women's Press.

Lester, J. (2008). Performing gender in the workplace. Gender socialization, power, and identity among women faculty members. *Community College Review, 35*(4), 277–305.

Levin, J., Alliyeva, A., & Walker, L. (2016). From community college to university: Institutionalization and neoliberalism in British Columbia and Alberta. *Canadian Journal of Higher Education, 46*(2), 165–180.

Levin, J., Jackson-Boothby, A., Haberler, Z., & Walker, L. (2015). "Dangerous work": Improving conditions for faculty of color in the community college. *Community College Journal of Research and Practice, 39,* 852–864.

Luther, R., Whitmore, E., & Moreau, B. (2003). *Seen but not heard: Aboriginal women and women of colour in the academy* (2nd ed.). Ottawa: Canadian Research Institute for the Advancement of Women.

Luxton, M., & Mossman, M. J. (Eds.). (2012). *Reconsidering knowledge: Feminism and the academy.* Halifax: Fernwood.

Mackay, K. (2014). *College faculty: Report on education in Ontario colleges.* Toronto: Ontario Public Services Employees Union.

Massaquoi, N., & Wane, N. N. (2007). *Theorizing empowerment: Canadian perspectives on black feminist thought.* Toronto: Inanna Press.

McGregor, D. (2018). From "decolonized" to reconciliation research in Canada: Drawing from Indigenous research paradigms. *ACME: An International Journal for Critical Geographers, 17*(3), 810–831.

McKnight, K., & Muzzin, L. (2014). "Academic freedom" or "bottom line": Public college healthcare professionals teaching in a global economy. *College Quarterly, 17*(1). Retrieved from www.collegequarterly.ca/2014-vol17-num01-winter/mcknight-muzzin.html

Metcalfe, A. S., & Gonzalez, L. P. (2013). Underrepresentation of women in the academic profession: A comparative analysis of the North American region. *NASPA Journal about Women in Higher Education, 6*(1), 1–21.

Monture-OKanee, P. A. (1995). Introduction. Surviving the contradictions: Personal notes on academia. In the Chilly Collective (Ed.), *Breaking anonymity: The chilly climate for women faculty* (pp. 11–28). Waterloo, ON: Wilfrid Laurier University Press.

Mountz, A. (2016). Women on the edge: Workplace stress at universities in North America. *Canadian Geographer, 60*(2), 205–218.

Mountz, A., Bonds, A., Mansfield, B., Loyd, J., Hyndman, J., Walton-Roberts, M., … Curren, W. (2016). For slow scholarship: A feminist politics of resistance through collective action in the neoliberal university. *ACME: An International E-Journal for Critical Geographies, 14*(4), 1235–1259.

Muzzin, L. (2016). Theorizing college governance across epistemic differences: Awareness contexts of college administrators and faculty. *Canadian Journal of Higher Education, 46*(3), 41–54.

Muzzin, L., Bachynskyj, A., Zankowicz, K., Vinci, A., & Meaghan, D. (2009, May 30). *"No time to think" and Aboriginal faculty in Canadian postsecondary institutions.* Paper presented at the Canadian Society for the Study of Higher Education Annual Meeting, Ottawa.

Muzzin, L., & Limoges, J. (2008). "A pretty incredible structural injustice": Contingent faculty in Canadian university nursing. In A. Wagner, S. Acker, & K. Mayuzumi (Eds.), *Whose university is it anyway? Power and privilege on gendered terrain* (pp. 157–172). Toronto: Sumach Press.

Muzzin, L., & Meaghan, D. (2014). Public colleges and democracy. *Innovation Journal: The Public Sector Innovation Journal, 19*(1), Art. 6.

Muzzin, L., & Meaghan, D. (2016). Addressing inequities in the college of the twenty-first century. In *Conference Proceedings, Higher Education in International Transformation Conference*. Oshawa, ON: University of Ontario Institute of Technology.

Newson, J. (2012). Academic feminism's entanglements with university corporatization. *Topia, 28,* 41–63.

Newson, J., & Polster, C. (Eds.). (2010). *Academic callings: The university we have had, now have, and could have.* Toronto: Canadian Scholars' Press.

Nielsen, E.-J., & Alderson, K. G. (2014). Lesbian and queer women professors disclosing in the classroom: An act of authenticity. *Counseling Psychologist, 42*(8), 1084–1107.

Ornstein, M., Stewart, P., & Drakich, J. (2007). Promotion at Canadian universities: The intersection of gender, discipline and institution. *Canadian Journal of Higher Education, 37*(3), 1–25.

Parizeau, K., Shillington, L., Hawkins, R., Sultana, F., Mountz, A., Mullings, B., & Peake, L. (2016). Breaking the silence: A feminist call to action. *Canadian Geographer, 60*(2), 192–204.

Peterson, H. (2016). Is managing academics "women's work"? Exploring the glass cliff in higher education management. *Educational Management Administration & Leadership, 44*(1), 112–127.

Reimer, M. (Ed.). (2004). *Inside Corporate U: Women in the academy speak out.* Toronto: Sumach Press.

Robbins, W. (2012). Critiquing Canada's research culture: Social, cultural, and political restraints on women's university careers. *Forum on Public Policy: A Journal of the Oxford Round Table.* Academic OneFile. Retrieved from http://link.galegroup.com.myaccess.library.utoronto.ca/apps/doc/A317588381/AONE?u=utoronto_main&sid=AONE&xid=f00840fb

Robbins, W., Luxton, M., Eichler, M., & Descarries, F. (2008). (Eds.). *Minds of our own: Inventing feminist scholarship and women's studies in Canada and Quebec, 1966–76.* Waterloo, ON: Wilfrid Laurier University Press.

Roman, L. G., & Eyre, L. (Eds.). (1997). *Dangerous territories: Struggles for difference and equality.* New York: Routledge.

Royal Commission on Equality in Employment. (1984). *Report.* Ottawa: Minister of Supply and Services Canada.

Royal Commission on the Status of Women in Canada. (1970). *Report.* Ottawa: Information Canada.

Smith, D. E. (1987). *The everyday world as problematic.* Toronto: University of Toronto Press.

Smith, D. E. (1990). *The conceptual practices of power: A feminist sociology of knowledge.* Toronto: University of Toronto Press.

St. Denis, V., & Schick, C. (2003). What makes anti-racist pedagogy in teacher education difficult? Three popular ideological assumptions. *Alberta Journal of Educational Research, 49*(1), 55–69.

Statistics Canada. (2017). Number and salaries of full-time teaching staff at Canadian universities, 2016/2017. Retrieved from www.statcan.gc.ca/daily-quotidien/170425/dq170425b-eng.htm

Swarts, J. (2013). *Constructing neoliberalism: Economic transformation in Anglo-American democracies.* Toronto: University of Toronto Press.

Tamburri, R. (2016, October 5). Women still struggle to make it to the top leadership posts in academe. *University Affairs.* Retrieved from https://www.universityaffairs.ca/features/feature-article/women-still-struggle-make-top-leadership-posts-academe/

Titchkosky, T. (2011). *The question of access: Disability, space, meaning.* Toronto: University of Toronto Press.

Truth and Reconciliation Commission of Canada. (2015). *Honouring the truth, reconciling for the future.* Final Report of the TRC. Retrieved from http://www.trc.ca/websites/trcinstitution/File/2015/Honouring_the_Truth_Reconciling_for_the_Future_July_23_2015.pdf

Vajoczki, S., Fenton, N., Menard, K., & Pollon, D. (2011). *Teaching-stream faculty in Ontario Universities.* Toronto: Higher Education Quality Council of Ontario.

Valentine, G. (2007). Theorizing and researching intersectionality: A challenge for feminist geography. *Professional Geographer, 59*(1), 10–21.

Waterfield, B., Beagan, B., & Weinberg, M. (2017). Disabled academics: A case study in Canadian universities. *Disability and Society, 33*(3), 327–348.

Webber, M. (2008). Miss Congeniality meets the new managerialism: Feminism, contingent labour, and the new university. *Canadian Journal of Higher Education, 38*(3), 37–56.

Weinrib, J., Jones, G., Metcalfe, A. S., Fisher, D., Gingras, Y., Rubenson, K., & Snee, I. (2013). Canadian university faculty perceptions of job satisfaction: "The future is not what it used to be." In P. Bentley, H. Coates, I. Dobson, L. Goedegebuure, & V. L. Meek (Eds.), *Job satisfaction around the academic world* (pp. 83–102). Dordrecht, Netherlands: Springer.

Whittaker, E. (Ed.). (2015). *Solitudes of the workplace: Women in universities.* Montreal & Kingston: McGill-Queen's University Press.

Wiart, N. (2016, November 28). Canadian colleges have more women at the helm than universities. *Maclean's Magazine.* Retrieved from www.macleans.ca/education/college/canadian-colleges-have-more-women-at-the-helm-than-universities

Yuval-Davis, N. (2006). Intersectionality and feminist politics. *European Journal of Women's Studies, 13*(3), 193–209.

CHAPTER 10

Black Women's Small Businesses as Historical Spaces of Resistance

Melanie Knight

> The vast majority of Black women in the United States know in girlhood that
> we will be workers.
>
> —hooks, *Sisters of the Yam: Black Women and Self-Recovery*

In her book *Sisters of the Yam: Black Women and Self-Recovery*, bell hooks (1993) recounts observing her mother working hard and raising seven children. Even as a stay-at-home mom, hooks's mother never allowed her six daughters to imagine they would not become working women. Although black women may know they will be workers from an early age and may, in fact, encounter that reality early in life, they no doubt also know that the labour market can be extremely hostile toward them. This chapter presents a brief history of black women's work in Canada and the United States from slavery to the present, focusing on the emergence and significance of entrepreneurship—self-employment, or employment as an independent contract worker—for black women. The chapter uses an **interlocking framework of oppression** in order to account for the experiences of black women and show their particular forms of oppression in the labour market and thereby their unique experiences with entrepreneurship. Entry into and participation in entrepreneurship are often linked to wage work and are therefore also contingent on the politics of that space. On the one hand, entrepreneurship enables people to supplement income and, on the other, to find creative independence and autonomy as workers. Black women have also used their independent status to define themselves as knowledgeable professional workers, a status otherwise denied to them. Entrepreneurship also enables people to cultivate and produce movements around social causes. Race, gender, and class have been and continue to be central organizing features in the capitalist industrial labour system. Black women's specific histories have contributed to entrepreneurship's particular appearance, function, and practice in the 21st century.

SLAVERY, IDEOLOGIES OF RACE AND GENDER, AND THE BLACK FEMALE WORKER

A study of black women and work in North America must surely begin with slavery. The plantation economy in the United States has been described as "a system within a capitalist mode of production" (Fox-Genovese, 1998, p. 55). Slave labour was essential to the economic growth of the colonial and 19th-century United States as "cotton and tobacco exports provided needed foreign exchange for the colonies and profits for investment, as well as high standards of living and wealth for slave owners and their descendants" (Amott & Matthaei, 1991, p. 142). Although slavery in Canada is often described as less harsh and pervasive than in the United States and the Caribbean, it was based on the same principle: the ownership of humans. The two largest groups of slaves in Canada, the Indigenous Pawnee and people of African origins, were predominantly used as servants by colonists, wealthy landowners, the military, and some clergy (Donovan, 1995; Elgersman, 1999). Many laws contributed to the decline of slavery in Canada before it was abolished in 1833. It was not uncommon before 1833 for free and enslaved blacks to live together in the same communities (Winks, 1997).

Black women were central to the successful functioning of this system, in both producing and replenishing labour. Sterling's (1984) book, *We Are Your Sisters: Black Women in the Nineteenth Century*, examines narratives of former slave women and their descendants. Slave women's lives, as reflected in the book, were entirely structured around labour. Sterling notes that "by the time she was ten years old, a slave girl was classified as a half-hand. At puberty she was doing the work of a woman, and woman's work was scarcely distinguishable from man's" (p. 13). This consisted of caring for children and elderly slaves as well as their mistresses and their children. For Jacqueline Jones (1985), however, these descriptions fail to capture the extent to which black women were exploited. She notes that "the definition of the slave women's work is problematic. If work is any activity that leads, either directly or indirectly, to the production of marketable goods, then slave women did nothing but work" (p. 14).

Slavery was organized, structured, and upheld through specific ideologies of race and gender. Jacqueline Jones (1985) describes slavery as a "microcosm" where "racial and patriarchal ideologies [were] wedded to the pursuit of profit" (p. 12). This "weddedness" is no more evident than in the status of black female slaves, who produced confusion for plantation owners. The difficulty for slave owners was reconciling between notions of "women *qua* 'equal' black workers and women *qua* 'unequal' reproducers" (Jones, 1985, p. 12). While the status of a slave was exclusively that of a worker, the status of woman—a term that denoted a white woman—was that of reproducer. Black female slaves disrupted this particular hierarchy and order of things. Slave owners quickly abandoned notions of female difference and fragility in the case of black women. Black women were made to perform a variety of duties, including those assigned to male slaves.

The plantation economy, although often imagined as insular and impenetrable, produced not only a specific race, gender, and class social order, but a social and economic fragmentation of black women's lives that required particular negotiations in order for them to survive. Their resistance against bondage manifested in different ways, including the poisoning of masters, infanticide of their own children, physical retaliation, and fleeing. Another dimension of resistance that is often neglected is participation in other kinds of work that enabled black women to transcend their inferior status (Jones, 1985), that is, small money-making ventures that served in part to disrupt the system. Entrepreneurship has served a particular purpose in black women's lives, less as an aberration and more as a means of survival and an integral part of their daily lives.

THE CREATION OF THE BLACK ENTREPRENEUR CLASS

Jacqueline Jones (1998) provides a more detailed overview of the different kinds of labour and economic infrastructures on Southern US plantations. Slave communities in the American South were not static, but included a mixture of labour activities performed by slaves and free workers. Even the largest plantations, Jones notes, "boasted complex local labour systems" (p. 193). She observes that while slave holders described the plantation system as binding slave and master as a loving family, what existed was a "tangible 'organic' Southern community at odds with the planters' mythical one" (p. 194). She adds that plantations resembled "proto-industrial, self-contained villages" (p. 195).

A bartering and selling system was evident on plantations. Slaves were occasionally given wages for working on Sunday, their day of rest. Harley, Wilson, and Logan (2002) give the example of Harriet Jacobs's mother baking pies to sell at the market in hopes of purchasing her children. Enslaved women also found work as laundresses. In addition to their work on the plantation, they did washing for two or three families to earn money. They would then purchase goods and products such as grain, food supplies, and fabric for their own families or make items that they would then sell. Urban slave women worked in "port cities, as marketers, often selling merchandise, such as fish and prepared foods from street carts or selling sex to supplement their incomes. Urban slave women and men also ran food and drink establishments supported by black patrons" (Harley, Wilson, & Logan, 2002, p. 2). Plantations fostered trade systems whereby black slaves took food and equipment from their masters and sold them to poor white men. According to Jacqueline Jones (1998) this internal slave economy (which included bartering and small business activity) changed the dynamic of the plantation economy. These various economical infrastructures enabled slaves to "carve out a sphere of autonomous behavior for themselves" (Jones, 1998, p. 198).

The early creation of the black entrepreneur class in Canada is more difficult to examine as there is considerably less research on this subject. During the late 18th century both black refugees fleeing American enslavement in wartime and black Loyalists who joined the British military in exchange for freedom settled in the Maritimes and in Ontario, lured by the promise of free land and the chance for a better life (Whitfield, 2005). In 1837 there were approximately 50 black families living in Toronto. The numbers increased during the 1840s and 1850s when black slaves fled from the United States. In Toronto itself there were approximately 1,200 blacks at that time (Hill, 1985). After the American Civil War many blacks returned to the United States. The decline of the black population in Canada was evident in the Maritimes as well as Ontario (Hill, 1985; Winks, 1997).

The Canadian 1784 census reveals that due to the scarcity of work, black Loyalist women in Nova Scotia made crafts that they sold at markets. It was work that "brought in money vital to the survival of the family" (Hamilton, 1994, p. 33). Black-owned businesses in Toronto during the 19th century included hotels, restaurants, dress shops, and livery stables. Contractors Jack Mosee and William Willis "undertook [in 1799] to open a road from Yonge Street, York, westward through 'the Pinery'" (Hill, 1985, p. 47). The first ice houses were started by two black entrepreneurs in the late 1840s (Hill, 1985).

During the mid- to late 19th century countries such as the United States, Britain, and Canada became more and more industrialized. Mass-production jobs became more desirable than crafts and agricultural work (Amott & Matthaei,

1991; Jones, 1998). From 1865 to 1890 many blacks in the Southern United States moved from rural to urban centres for greater freedom and better working conditions. Despite the move, Glenn (2002) notes, "the vast majority of urban black men and women were confined to low-paying, irregular, and low-status positions" (p. 106). Aside from limited employment opportunities in factories, black American women's main form of income came from domestic work (Aptheker, 1982; Dill, 1994; Leashore, 1984). These trends were also evident among blacks living in Canada (Brand, 1994, 1999; Calliste, 1991, 1993).

TWENTIETH-CENTURY CANADIAN IMMIGRATION POLICIES AND BLACK WOMEN'S WORK

Canadian immigration policies during the 20th century were clearly racist and predominantly sought to establish a white settler society (Jakubowski, 1997; Stasiulis, 1995). These policies outlined a hierarchy of desired immigrants that placed blacks in the third tier, as least desirable. The Canadian Immigration Act of 1910 prohibited entry to "any race deemed unsuited to the climate or requirements of Canada" (Walker, 1980, p. 94). Between 1896 and 1907 of the one and a half million immigrants who arrived in Canada, fewer than 1,000 were black (Walker, 1980). The desire to increase the white settler population was achieved by having a larger number of immigrant bureaus in London than in countries in the Global South, allocating land to white settlers, giving bonuses to officers who recruited immigrants from Britain, and paying for the cost of fares and settlement for white women domestics (Troper, 1993). Meanwhile, black settlers from Alabama were denied access to privileges such as land and settlement expenses that were granted to whites when they tried to settle in Western Canada; in fact they were told to return to the United States (Walker, 1980). The 1911 census reported 208 blacks living in Alberta and only 23 in Calgary (Palmer & Palmer, 1985).

Black women who were allowed entry into Canada came as domestic workers through the Domestic Scheme Program or as nurses. From 1922 to 1931, 74% of the 768 Caribbean blacks who immigrated to Canada came as domestic workers. The numbers were slightly lower between 1955 and 1961, with 44% of the 4,219 Caribbean immigrants being female domestics (Calliste, 1991, pp. 136, 141). It was not until 1967, when official changes to the immigration policy were made and a point system was introduced, that more blacks came to Canada. In 1961 there were 12,000 Caribbean-born immigrants in Canada; by 1981 the number was 200,000, and in the early 1990s the Caribbean community was estimated at 455,000 (Siemiatycki, Rees, Ng, & Rahi, 2001, p. 19). The large majority of Caribbean women who immigrated during the 1970s and 1980s worked as nurses. The Department of Citizenship and Immigration admitted nurses and nursing students under four categories, which streamlined black nurses into particular low-waged nursing positions. Canadian immigration officials justified restricting the entry of professional and skilled workers from the Caribbean on the grounds that Canadians were not accustomed to seeing black people in "positions which would place them on the same economic and social levels with their white neighbours" (Calliste, 1993, p. 90). This attitude reflected the stereotypical perception that blacks were better suited, even inherently suited, to service jobs or those that required heavy physical labour, rather than positions of authority.

Black Canadian women's relegation to domestic work and nursing and the formalization of this status by the Canadian government had other consequences for black communities, household structures, and patterns of family organization. The government of Canada required that women who immigrated from the Caribbean as domestics or nurses be single with no dependents. This policy was established to ensure that those who came were not burdens on the state. Children and extended family members could also complicate the live-in requirements of nannies and other domestic workers. This policy contributed to the creation of a greater proportion of black female-headed households in Canada. By the early 1980s there were 10 Caribbean women for every 8 men. For Jamaicans this number was 10 to 7 (Siemiatycki et al., 2001; Torczyner, 1997). Hill Collins (1998) views this predicament in the context of global capitalist development. She notes that research on "patterns of industrial development and on the accompanying structures of race and gender-segmented labour markets reveals important connections between the stage of capitalist development encountered by people and the household structures and patterns of family organization that emerge" (p. 28). Taking Mexican immigration during the 1980s as her example, she explains how factories on the Mexican side of the border that hired mainly women and not men forced Mexican men to travel alone to the United States to find work. The increase in female-headed households can be directly linked to industrial policies and the kinds of industries and jobs available in particular regions. In addition to recognizing the reasons for the emergence of female-headed households, it is also important to recognize the effects that this has on other aspects of women's lives, including their employment patterns.

During the early to mid-20th century employment was highly precarious for black Canadian women. Aside from nursing and domestic work, between 1920 and 1940 labour shortages gave some black women the opportunity to work in factories. Racist policies enforced by factory managers continued to position black women in the lower tier of factory work. Regardless of class status, education, income, or morals, the majority of black men and women were forced into low-status and low-pay positions (Sugiman, 2001). Racial solidarity among whites manifested in the denial of blacks' participation in unions (Das Gupta, 2007; B. W. Jones, 1984). Beverly W. Jones (1984) recounts the experiences of 15 black female tobacco workers in Durham, North Carolina, between 1908 and 1930. Black women were forced to take the dirtiest and more dangerous jobs, as stemmers, sorters, hangers, and pullers, positions that white women were rarely considered for. Extreme wage differentials between black and white women, Jones notes, "also forced many into the labour force at an early age. Black women thus worked for a longer part of their lives, and henceforth were more vulnerable to diseases and other health problems" (p. 446). White women would occupy the less hazardous and dangerous positions, positions deemed "suitable for ladies," all in the name of protecting white women's "racial honor" (Janiewski, 1987, p. 163).

The Great Depression of the 1930s in Canada proved to be a very trying time. Brand (1994) notes, "Depression or not, Black women had to work. Black families, urban and rural, could not survive strictly on the male wage. They survived on the wages of women working in service and men working as porters on the railroad and in general labour" (p. 174). The limited factory work that was open to black women in Canada during World War II once again steered them back to domestic work when the war ended. With such high levels of precariousness in the labour market, black women always found alterative means to survive.

BLACK FEMALE ENTREPRENEURSHIP FROM THE NINETEENTH CENTURY ONWARD

In an article about urban blacks in Alberta, Palmer and Palmer (1985) note that several of the 30 black families identified in Calgary in 1927 were entrepreneurs. This was also the case among blacks in Edmonton. Some ran pool halls, barbershops, cafés, a horse-drawn delivery service, a hotel, and boarding houses; some were seamstresses, junk dealers, and grocery and candy store owners. These Alberta communities, according to Palmer and Palmer, were somewhat distinct from one another. Blacks in Calgary primarily worked as porters, while those in Edmonton worked as tradesmen and construction and railway workers. The authors add that "the emergence of this class of Negro businessmen reflected a similar trend in northern American cities" (p. 10).

Boyd (2000) provides a more in-depth analysis and examines African American women's reliance on entrepreneurship during the Great Depression in the US. Providing board and lodging in private homes was common due to high rents, and at least one-third of black families in the urban North earned money in this manner. Black women played a leadership role in providing these services as well as being the "go-between" for blacks who were looking for work and shelter. Taking in boarders became "part of the informal family economy of Black communities" (Boyd, 2000, p. 651). Others were forced to work in their homes as hairdressers, dressmakers, seamstresses, or laundresses (Cooper, 2000) because they were denied access to education, professions, and certain types of work.

Bristow (1994) stated that "patterns revealed by the Canadian census data may underestimate Black women's work in earning income for the family" (p. 98). For example, the census often listed black women only under one occupation, such as "housewife." This practice omitted a great many additional activities that black families undertook. For one, many of the women listed as housewives had husbands who were listed as owning a business. The work that black women performed alongside their husbands went unnoticed. Mary Ann Shadd Cary, who settled in Sandwich, Ontario (now Windsor), in 1851, was listed in the 1861 census as an "editress," but she was also a teacher and a housewife. In addition, while census data listed black women only under one occupation, mainly as housewives, they advertised themselves as seamstresses in newspaper ads. Statistics leave many questions unanswered, such as whether the women worked alone and how much money they made from combined labour. Canadian census data did not report the fact that black women in Chatham, Ontario, were workers, mothers, and political activists. According to Bristow (1994), the ways in which black women built networks and formed a culture were also invisible in this official knowledge. For example, Mary Bibb (1820–1877), although often remembered as a teacher, was also a journalist, activist, and entrepreneur who fought for the rights of blacks in the United States and Canada (Cooper, 1994).

Bobb-Smith's (2003) analysis of Afro-Caribbean women's experiences in Canada provides another example of black women's simultaneous participation in two statuses of work. She refers to how policies in colonial and neocolonial times affected the migration of Caribbean men and women and produced an increasing number of female-headed households. She adds that "as a result, these policies … forced many less-educated Anglophone Caribbean women to empower themselves by becoming entrepreneurs in gender-segregated jobs such as domestic work, higglering [hawking], and wayside vending" (p. 135). She presents narratives of black women who remember their mothers selling products from the land, washing for rich people, selling pastries, and sewing. Many recount that they, their mothers, or their aunts held multiple jobs simultaneously throughout their lives. For Caribbean women, being "workers and, at times, earners is not a strange phenomenon" (Bobb-Smith, 2003, p. 135). Bobb-Smith differentiates here between a worker, one who works in wage work, and an earner, one who earns for oneself.

Black women's complex relationship with entrepreneurship in the 20th century provided them with greater levels of economic and social independence. However, participation in two statuses of work was also, no doubt, a greater burden for marginalized workers. Black women are seldom able to make a clean break from wage work. Alfred and Staton (1995) note that for some black women, work as entrepreneurs paid their way to better jobs.

Some research examines reasons why black women partake in entrepreneurship, knowing its perilousness. Being an entrepreneur or self-employed is an alluring status for black women precisely because of their histories of oppression. Aside from preventing them from attaining this autonomous sense of self, blacks' subordination under slavery solidified the status of nonslaves, in particular whites, as democratized, free, and able to self-govern (Glenn, 2002; Keizer, 2004). For example, during the post-emancipation period in the United States, "Southern planters could not reconcile themselves to the fact of emancipation; they believed that 'free black labor' was a contradiction in terms, that blacks would never work of their own free will" (Jones, 1985, p. 45). In addition to the greater feeling of independence and ability to supplement income that entrepreneurship offers, black women have also been attracted to entrepreneurship because it enables them to craft professional identities for themselves, based on respect and dignity otherwise denied to them. Harley (1997) cites Higginbotham's work on the professionalization of domestic servants, who could be defined as solo self-employed, as an example. The professionalization of domestic work conducted in homes included wearing a uniform, at the workers' insistence, or refusing to wash and clean on their hands and knees. This professionalization was largely possible as a result of black women's less restricted status as non-wage workers.

Black women used their status as entrepreneurs and business owners to bring attention to broader social issues that were important to the black community. Entrepreneurship allowed women to carve a platform to speak about black causes. Madame C. J. Walker was an entrepreneur from Louisiana who became one of the wealthiest women in America by manufacturing and marketing hair care products from the early 1900s to the height of her career in 1919, when she died suddenly. She is often described as a pioneer, philanthropist, and social activist. She began working as a washerwoman many years before developing her hair care products. When Booker T. Washington, one of Walker's strongest critics, claimed that her business did little to uplift the race, Walker replied that she provided more than "just hair care" (Gill, 2001, p. 173). In addition to hair care, she trained her employees to help black women with other household and social matters. Hair care was her way into the lives of black women of different class status. Once inside her clients' homes, Walker felt it safe and imperative to attend to black women's many needs. The home was central to her business success as well as her social and political agenda. In an article on African American female entrepreneurship and activism, Gill (2001) examines the political activism of beauty culturists such as hairdressers, salon owners, and beauty product manufacturers during the mid-20th century. She refers specifically to the establishments of these beauty culturists, or beauty activists, as she labels them, as political sites because of their engagement in social reform as members of women's clubs. The salons were also hotbeds for political manoeuvrings.

Shifting attention to a different group of black women entrepreneurs, scholars like Angela Davis, Sharon Harley, and Lynn Hudson attempt to shatter the foundation of the "canon of acceptable Black heroines" (Hudson, 2003, p. 1). Harley's (2002) article "'Working for Nothing but for a Living': Black Women in the Underground Economy" examines the lives of women before the 1950s who earned part of their income through various criminal activities in night clubs, dance halls, and jook joints (small establishments for eating, drinking, and dancing with live music or a jukebox). Most of these women also worked in private homes of whites as washerwomen during the day. Harley does not limit her analysis to women's business dealings but is interested in how their various activities transcended gender roles. The majority of women in the underground economy at that time were working class and were either bootleggers who sold whiskey or ran gambling schemes. All moved back and forth between the illegal and legal economy. For example, Odessa Madre became one of the most prominent black women in Washington, DC, in the 1930s and 1940s. Although Odessa graduated from an elite high school and could have worked as a secretary or a teacher, she chose a different form of employment. Starting as early as age 17, she became known as the queen of Washington's underworld, and at one point owned "an 'empire of joints' which sold everything from bootleg liquor to sex" (Harley, 2002, p. 53). The line drawn between legality and illegality in research on nontraditional black female business activities needs to be questioned. African American feminist legal scholar Regina Austin rejects the distinction between lawful and unlawful activity, claiming that it is socially constructed by an oppressive white society. We must contemplate how and why something is illegal and the methods of surveillance surrounding it.

Like Odessa, blues singers Ma Rainey, Bessie Smith, and Billie Holiday, who are described in Angela Davis's (1998) book *Blues Legacies and Black Feminism*, used their status and careers to express their social reality as well as political agenda. These women, although not officially described as entrepreneurs, challenged the politics of sexuality, gender norms, and women's role in the labour force both through their actions and in their lyrics. For example, Davis contends that "the representations of love and sexuality in women's blues often blatantly contradicted mainstream ideological assumptions regarding women and being in love. They also challenged the notion that women's 'place' was in the domestic sphere" (Davis, 1998, p. 11). Love "was not represented as an idealized realm to which unfulfilled dreams of happiness were relegated. The historical African American vision of individual sexual love linked it inextricably with possibilities of social freedom in the economic and political realms" (Davis, 1998, p. 10). Blues singers were often in positions that were in complete contradiction to the ideals of womanhood. They worked outside the home and occupied forms of employment that were contradictory to what was deemed desirable and suitable for women.

Mary Pleasant is another example of a black female entrepreneur in a non-traditional profession. Lynn Hudson (2003) narrates her life in *The Making of "Mammy Pleasant": A Black Entrepreneur in Nineteenth-Century San Francisco*. Mary Pleasant, a boarding house owner in the mid-19th century, achieved a great deal of financial success as an entrepreneur but struggled to challenge the many obstacles placed in her way. With very little formal education, Pleasant initially worked as a servant in white households since little else was available. Eventually, she was able to open her own boarding house. Her accumulated wealth generated much anxiety among the white majority. There was a great deal of suspicion around how she acquired her wealth and status—she was suspected of blackmailing customers or having cheated her way to wealth. Although a successful businesswoman, she was often portrayed as an oversexed black woman and often referred to as San Francisco's black madam and once as "the happy Black hooker" (Hudson, 2003, p. 60). The wealth that she acquired from her businesses enabled her to support the black nationalist cause. Pleasant used her earnings to purchase guns for a slave revolt as well as pay for attorneys to defend falsely accused blacks. The seductiveness of entrepreneurship for these women, however unrespectable, came from its ability to challenge hegemonic ideals of womanhood, family, sexuality, and women's place in society. To be considered entrepreneurial has not been an uncontested process for black women. Mary Pleasant's life exemplifies the contradictions that emerge when black women try to embody the entrepreneurial ideals and the status of entrepreneur.

THE PRESENT-DAY CONTEXT

Racialized entrepreneurs, and blacks in particular, are often described as being the least entrepreneurial immigrant group in Canada (Henry, 1993; Lo et al., 2001; Lo, Teixeira, & Truelove, 2002). Some researchers attribute low perform-ance in entrepreneurship to systemic racism, exemplified in blacks' difficulties in obtaining bank financing or their lack of experience in running family businesses (Henry, 1993; Lo et al., 2001; Scott, 1994; Teixeira, 2002; Uneke, 1996). Others ascribe blacks' lower rates of participation in entrepreneurship to the black com-munity not being a unified market—it is more a fragmented social structure than a coherent community. Blacks are also said to be constrained by fewer resources due to class and ethnicity (Lo et al., 2001). The existing research suggests that the businesses of racialized women entrepreneurs are comparatively smaller and less profitable than those owned by men (Anselm, 1994; Baxter & Raw, 1988; Lo, Teixeira, & Truelove, 2002; Mirchandani, 2002). Cultural factors, the invis-ibility of women in family businesses, and the small size of their businesses are cited as reasons. They also tend to be concentrated in the service sector of the economy (as hairdressers, cooks, daycare workers, nurses and personal aides, and educators).

How the notion of low participation is conceptualized and, more import-antly, what this claim implies warrant attention. Some critical scholars challenge the discourse of failure as it pertains to black business activity and the notion that blacks lack distinct cultural resources essential for business creation and success (see, for example, Basu & Werbner, 2001; Knight, 2004). Unlike other ethnic groups, blacks have not necessarily entered conventional business indus-tries like clothing and foods, but have formed "ethnic enclave economies in the music industry" that are "'visible' aurally rather than spatially" (Basu & Werbner, 2001, p. 241). The mental shift from enclave to economy requires a reconcep-tualization of the notion of ethnic entrepreneurship to focus more broadly on the *"organization* of ethnic industries" (p. 239, emphasis in original). Although it is undeniable that there are few black Canadian women entrepreneurs, we may be underestimating their presence.

To provide a few key government statistics, in 2011, 3% (about 234,000) of the Canadian labour force were black women and 3.1% were self-employed (approximately 7,600), compared to 10.4% for everyone else in the labour force (Statistics Canada, 2014). Over the years, my research has generated interesting demographic information that provides a bit more context to Canadian government statistics. Overall, black women entrepreneurs are highly educated (undergraduate degree or higher), more often between the ages of 26 and 40, and Canadian citizens, born in Canada or abroad. Similar to nonblack women, many are married or living with common-law partners and have children. In terms of business characteristics, three or four industries predominate: professional, technical, scientific, and finance; social and personal services; media, publishing, and entertainment; and culture, crafts, and recreation. One difference that I have noticed more recently is an increase in black women located in social and personal services and fewer in the professional category. This may be the result of sampling or labour market shifts. In addition to the use of personal assets and support from family, black women in more precarious forms of self-employment are still attached to wage work, complicating visibility and participation in entrepreneurship (Knight, 2014). Participation in wage work is largely due to women's need for greater financial security, networking opportunities, and resources. Those in wage work struggle to negotiate the demands of wage work and their small-business activities. Profitability is similar, with half of black women entrepreneurs listing their business as profitable. Over the years, more women seem to be interested in exporting goods.

Black women's decision to become self-employed is approached with caution and trepidation. They point to struggles with the precariousness of self-employment. They have limited access to traditional banks and seek mentors through informal networks. Membership in professional associations is out of their reach as these often have exorbitant fees. Community programs are helpful, but women often seek expert subject matter advice and knowledge on specific industry practices. Many want greater financial literacy and knowledge of up-to-date information and communication technology and social media tools. Community organizations are less able to provide women with information on how to conduct and assess research. For many women, data are either inaccessible or too convoluted to understand.

Black women participate in entrepreneurship for various reasons. Structural factors (push factors) that contribute to women's entry into entrepreneurship include the segmented labour market, in which racialized women are more likely to occupy low-wage, low-status jobs (Anthias & Lazaridis, 2000; Mirchandani et al., 2010). Other structural factors are workplace dissatisfaction, racial and gender discrimination, and the glass-ceiling effect (invisible barriers to advancement; Cheung, 2005, Mirchandani et al., 2011; Westwood & Bhachu, 1988). A pull factor that attracts black women to self-employment is the independent status of entrepreneurship, which frees them from the victimization and racism of wage work. Other rewards for participating in entrepreneurship include more economic and social flexibility, control over their destiny, a more positive outlook on life, and a feeling of nondependence on the system. As entrepreneurs, black women are also able to fashion themselves into respectable, professional, knowledgeable workers, an identity long denied to them (Knight, 2014).

Moving beyond push-pull factors, research on women's entrepreneurship, in particular that of racialized women, rarely examines the nuances—work habits, perceptions of them as businesswomen, competition, ways of innovating, practices of exportation, informal learning, and so on—of their actual work as entrepreneurs. One major barrier that is often not acknowledged in the literature is the specific negative perception of their abilities as racialized women. Black women constantly struggle with how their bodies are read and responded to. Racism in entrepreneurship is not simply a precondition of wage work or a result of discrimination by lending agencies, but an everyday occurrence for black women. The black skin acts as a trap or script that enforces black women's immobility as workers and their continued occupation in menial labour (Knight, 2011).

Other negotiations emerge among women with businesses in creative industries who use entrepreneurship as a way to redefine notions of blackness in Canada and create stronger political communities. The official hegemonic discourse of multiculturalism recounts a story of black history in Canada that is highly sanitized and, ultimately, commodified. An example is the narrative of Canada as a saviour to African Americans fleeing slavery through the underground railroad versus Canada's own history of slavery. With few options available to them, black women entrepreneurs are forced to operate within the space of multiculturalism. Participating in the program of multiculturalism entails, in part, participating in events that are usually limited to specific time periods (e.g., Black History Month). Others broaden this space by creating an alternative notion of blackness in Canada—blackness as both diasporic (external to Canada) and rooted historically in Canada (Knight, 2012).

Finally, the branding of a business in a competitive labour market is a challenging feat. In order to circumvent this challenge, women create transnational linkages with the US, the Caribbean, Europe, and countries in Africa.

They create global connections and source materials outside Canada that they then sell to a Canadian and global market. For example, one black woman with a clothing business purchases fabrics in Harlem and Ghana and creates clothing designs, which she then sells online to Canadian and international clients. Black women entrepreneurs gain experience in the global sector, which then helps raise their profile in Canada. Another woman, a journalist, took a freelance job in Nigeria for a year, where she reported on the entertainment scene. There is a mobility not only of capital but of labour. Women rely greatly on informal learning such as industry knowledge, business knowledge, and knowledge of self to craft their brand and use social media in strategic ways.

CONCLUSION

How do black Canadian women participate in entrepreneurship, and what does their participation tell us about how they are regulated? Simply pointing to the disparaging statistics or the selective history of some, or to blacks' potential to achieve or their inability to do so, provides little information on why the labour market is segmented along class, gender, and racial lines and how black women turn to entrepreneurship to negotiate the labour market economy. Race, gender, and class have been and continue to be central organizing features in the capitalist industrial labour system. Black Canadian women's experiences as entrepreneurs, both in terms of how they are drawn to entrepreneurship and their participation in it, have been informed by specific histories of slavery, indentured labour, and migration in Canada.

Contesting the notion that black women have little history as entrepreneurs, this chapter has shown a complex relationship between the black female worker and entrepreneurship. There is, in fact, a long history of entrepreneurship in black communities. It has been a constant in black women's lives. A theoretical framework of interlocking oppressions and a sociohistorical analysis of the simultaneous operation of race, class, and gender shows black women's distinct positions in the labour market. It is this distinct history that has informed black women's participation in entrepreneurship. Women's entrepreneurship is inextricably linked to their participation in wage work. Even though research often positions these two statuses of work as operating distinctly from one another, this distinction negates the level of precariousness that many workers are faced with, in particular racialized women. Second, a non-interlocking sociohistorical framework does not provide for the fluid ways in which workers shift and oscillate between economic infrastructures depending on need or desire. Despite entrepreneurship's contradictions and precarious nature, we must not underestimate the possibilities that it can provide to marginalized communities.

KEY READINGS

Bristow, P., Brand, D., Carty, L., Cooper, A. P., Hamilton, S., & Shadd, A. (1994). *"We're rooted here and they can't pull us up": Essays in African Canadian women's history*. Toronto: University of Toronto Press.

Chancy, M. J. A. (1997). *Searching for safe spaces: Afro-Caribbean women writers in exile*. Philadelphia: Temple University Press.

Hudson, L. (2003). *The making of "Mammy Pleasant": A black entrepreneur in nineteenth-century San Francisco*. Urbana: University of Illinois Press.

Knight, M. (2014). Race-ing, classing and gendering racialized women's participation in entrepreneurship. *Gender, Work and Organization, 23*(3). doi:10.1111/gwao.12060

DISCUSSION QUESTIONS

1. After reading this chapter, can you provide examples of diverse forms of black business activity (past or present)? Think about types of businesses, space of operation, the time period, and so on.

2. Why is it important to frame participation in entrepreneurship through a sociohistorical lens?

3. Why is black Canadian women's history of entrepreneurship rarely acknowledged in national narratives on entrepreneurship and innovation?

REFERENCES

Alfred, M., & Staton, P. (1995). *Black women in Canada: Past and present*. Toronto: Green Dragon Press.

Amott, T., & Matthaei, J. (1991). *Race, gender and work: A multi-cultural economic history of women in the United States*. Montreal: Black Rose Books.

Anselm, M. (1994). Innovation, constraints and success: The case of visible minority entrepreneurs. *Canadian Woman Studies/Les Cahiers de la Femme, 15*(1), 33–37.

Anthias, F., & Lazaridis, G. (Eds.). (2000). *Gender and migration in southern Europe: Women on the move*. New York: Berg.

Aptheker, B. (1982). *Woman's legacy: Essays on race, sex, and class in American history*. Amherst: University of Massachusetts Press.

Austin, R. (1992). The black community: Its lawbreakers and the politics of identification. *Southern California Law Review, 65*(4), 1769–1817.

Basu, D., & Werbner, P. (2001). Bootstrap capitalism and the culture industries: A critique of invidious comparisons in the study of ethnic entrepreneurship. *Ethnic and Racial Studies, 24*(2), 236–262.

Baxter, S., & Raw, G. (1988). Fast food, fettered work: Chinese women in the ethnic catering industry. In S. Westwood & P. Bhachu (Eds.), *Enterprising women* (pp. 58–76). New York: Routledge & Kegan Paul.

Bobb-Smith, Y. (2003). *I know who I am: A Caribbean woman's identity in Canada*. Toronto: Women's Press.

Boyd, R. L. (2000). Race, labour market disadvantage, and survivalist entrepreneurship: Black women in the urban North during the Great Depression. *Sociological Forum, 15*(4), 647–670.

Brand, D. (1994). "We weren't allowed to go into factory work until Hitler started the war": The 1920s to the 1940s. In P. Bristow, D. Brand, L. Carty, A. P. Cooper, S. Hamilton, & A. Shadd (Eds.), *"We're rooted here and they can't pull us up": Essays in African Canadian women's history* (pp. 171–191). Toronto: University of Toronto Press.

Brand, D. (1999). Black women and work: The impact of racially constructed gender roles on the sexual division of labour. In E. Dua & A. Robertson (Eds.), *Scratching the surface: Canadian anti-racist feminist thought* (pp. 83–96). Toronto: Women's Press.

Bristow, P. (1994). "Whatever you raise in the ground you can sell it in Chatham": Black women in Bruxton and Chatham, 1850–65. In P. Bristow, D. Brand, L. Carty, A. P. Cooper, S. Hamilton, & A. Shadd (Eds.), *"We're rooted here and they can't pull us up": Essays in African Canadian women's history* (pp. 69–142). Toronto: University of Toronto Press.

Calliste, A. (1991). Canada's immigration policy and domestics from the Caribbean: The second domestic scheme. In J. Vorst & Society of Socialist Studies (Eds.), *Race, class, gender: Bonds and barriers* (2nd ed., pp. 136–168). Toronto: Between the Lines.

Calliste, A. (1993). Women of exceptional merit: Immigration of Caribbean nurses to Canada. *Canadian Journal of Women and the Law, 6*(1), 85–102.

Cheung, L. (2005). *Racial status and employment outcomes*. Canadian Labour Congress Research Paper #34. Retrieved from www.canadianlabour.ca/updir/racialstatusEn.pdf

Cooper, A. P. (1994). Black women and work in nineteenth-century Canada West: Black woman teacher Mary Bibb. In P. Bristow, D. Brand, L. Carty, A. P. Cooper, S. Hamilton, & A. Shadd (Eds.), *"We're rooted here and they can't pull us up": Essays in African Canadian women's history* (pp. 143–170). Toronto: University of Toronto Press.

Cooper, A. (2000). Constructing black women's historical knowledge: Afua Cooper. *Atlantis, 25*(1), 39–50.

Das Gupta, T. (2007). Racism/anti-racism, precarious employment, and unions. In T. D. Gupta, C. E. James, R. C. A. Maaka, G.-E. Galabuzi, & C. Andersen (Eds.), *Race and racialization: Essential readings* (pp. 350–355). Toronto: Canadian Scholars' Press.

Davis, A. Y. (1998). *Blues legacies and black feminism: Gertrude Ma Rainey, Bessie Smith, and Billie Holiday.* New York: Vintage Books.

Dill, B. T. (1994). *Across the boundaries of race and class: An exploration of work and family among black female domestic servants.* New York: Garland.

Donovan, K. (1995). Slaves and their owners in Ile Royale, 1713–1760. *Acadiensis, 25*(1), 3–32.

Elgersman, M. G. (1999). *Unyielding spirits: Black women and slavery in early Canada and Jamaica.* New York: Garland.

Fox-Genovese, E. (1988). *Within the plantation household: Black and White women of the old south.* Chapel Hill: University of North Carolina Press.

Gill, T. M. (2001). "I had my own business ... so I didn't have to worry": Beauty salons, beauty culturists, and the politics of African-American female entrepreneurship. In P. Scranton (Ed.), *Beauty and business: Commerce, gender and culture in modern America* (pp. 169–194). New York: Routledge.

Glenn, E. N. (2002). *Unequal freedom: How race and gender shaped American citizenship and labour.* Cambridge, MA: Harvard University Press.

Hamilton, S. (1994). Naming names, naming ourselves: A survey of early black women in Nova Scotia. In P. Bristow, D. Brand, L. Carty, A. P. Cooper, S. Hamilton, & A. Shadd (Eds.), *"We're rooted here and they can't pull us up": Essays in African Canadian women's history* (pp. 13–40). Toronto: University of Toronto Press.

Harley, S. (1997). Speaking up: The politics of black women's labour history. In E. Higginbotham & M. Romero (Eds.), *Women and work: Exploring race, ethnicity and class* (pp. 28–51). Thousand Oaks, CA: Sage.

Harley, S. (2002). "Working for nothing but for a living": Black women in the underground economy. In S. Harley & the Black Women and Work Collective (Eds.), *Sister circle: Black women and work* (pp. 48–66). New Brunswick, NJ: Rutgers University Press.

Harley, S., Wilson, F. R., & Logan, S. W. (2002). Introduction: Historical overview of black women and work. In S. Harley & the Black Women and Work Collective (Eds.), *Sister circle: Black women and work* (pp. 1–10). New Brunswick, NJ: Rutgers University Press.

Henry, F. (1993). *A survey of black business in metropolitan Toronto.* Toronto: Multicultural and Race Relations Division of Metropolitan Toronto & Black Pages & Black Business and Professional Association.

Hill, D. G. (1985). Black history in early Toronto. Address delivered to Black History Conference, February 18, 1978. Archives of Ontario, reference code F 2130-7-0-6. Retrieved from http://www.archives.gov.on.ca/en/explore/online/dan_hill/papers/big_052_black-historyp11.aspx

Hill Collins, P. (1998). Intersections of race, class, gender and nation: Some implications for black family studies. *Journal of Comparative Family Studies, 29*(1), 27–36.

hooks, b. (1993). *Sisters of the yam: Black women and self-recovery.* Toronto: Between the Lines.

Hudson, L. (2003). *The making of "Mammy Pleasant": A Black entrepreneur in nineteenth-century San Francisco.* Urbana: University of Illinois Press.

Jakubowski, L. M. (1997). *Immigration and the legalization of racism.* Halifax: Fernwood.

Janiewski, D. (1987). Seeking "a new day and a new way": Black women and unions in the Southern tobacco industry. In C. Groneman & M. B. Norton (Eds.), *"To Toil the Livelong Day": America's Women at Work, 1780–1980* (pp. 161–178). Ithaca, NY: Cornell University Press.

Jones, B. W. (1984). Race, sex, and class: Black female tobacco workers in Durham, North Carolina, 1920–1940, and the development of female consciousness. *Feminist Studies, 10,* 444–450.

Jones, J. (1985). *Labour of love, labour of sorrow: Black women, work and the family from slavery to the present.* New York: Basic Books.

Jones, J. (1998). *American work: Four centuries of black and white labour.* New York: Norton.

Keizer, A. (2004). *Black subjects: Identity formation in the contemporary narrative of slavery.* Ithaca, NY: Cornell University Press.

Knight, M. (2004). Black Canadian self-employed women in the twenty-first century: A critical approach. *Canadian Woman Studies/Les Cahiers de la Femme, 23*(2), 104–110.

Knight, M. (2011). "Guess who's coming to dinner?": Negotiating visibility, encounters and racism in entrepreneurship. *Critical Race and Whiteness Studies Journal, 7*(2), 1–18.

Knight, M. (2012). For us by us (FUBU): The politicized space of black women's entrepreneurship in Canada. *Southern Journal of Canadian Studies, 5*(1–2), 162–183.

Knight, M. (2014). Race-ing, classing and gendering racialized women's participation in entrepreneurship. *Gender, Work and Organization, 23*(3). doi:10.1111/gwao.12060

Leashore, B. R. (1984). Black female workers: Live-in domestics in Detroit, Michigan, 1860–1880. *Phylon, 45*(2), 111–120.

Lo, L., Preston, V., Wang, S., Reil, K., Harvey, E., & Siu, B. (2001). *Immigrants' economic status in Toronto: Rethinking settlement and integration strategies.* Working paper no. 15. Toronto: Joint Centre of Excellence for Research on Immigration and Settlement.

Lo, L., Teixeira, C., & Truelove, M. (2002). *Cultural resources, ethnic strategies, and immigrant entrepreneurship: A comparative study of five immigrant groups in the Toronto CMA.* Working paper no. 21. Toronto: Joint Centre of Excellence for Research on Immigration and Settlement.

Mirchandani, K. (2002). A special kind of exclusion: Race, gender and self-employment. *Atlantis, 27*(1), 25–38.

Mirchandani, K., Ng, R., Coloma-Moya, N., Maitra, S., Rawlings, T., Shan, H., … Slade, B. (2011). The entrenchment of racial categories in precarious employment. In N. Pupo,

D. Glenday, & A. Duffy (Eds.), *The shifting landscape of work* (pp. 119–138). Toronto: Nelson Educational.

Mirchandani, K., Ng, R., Coloma-Moya, N., Maitra, S., Rawlings, T., Siddiqui, K., … Slade, B. (2010). Transitioning into contingent work: Immigrants' learning and resistance. In P. Sawchuk & A. Taylor (Eds.), *Challenging transitions in learning and work: Reflections on policy and practice* (pp. 231–242). Rotterdam: Sense.

Palmer, H., & Palmer, T. (Eds). (1985). *Peoples of Alberta*. Saskatoon: Western Producer Prairie Books.

Scott, J. (1994). Afro-Caribbean women entrepreneurs: Barriers to self-employment in Toronto. *Canadian Woman Studies/Les Cahiers de la Femme, 15*(1), 38–41.

Siemiatycki, M., Rees, T., Ng, R., & Rahi, K. (2001). *Integrating community diversity in Toronto: On whose terms?* Working paper no. 14. Toronto: Joint Centre for Excellence in Research on Immigration and Settlement.

Stasiulis, D. (1995). Deep diversity: Race and ethnicity in Canadian politics. In M. Whittington & G. Williams (Eds.), *Canadian politics in the 1990s* (4th ed., pp. 191–217). Toronto: Nelson Canada.

Statistics Canada. (2014). National household survey, 2011. Retrieved from http://www.odesi.ca

Sterling, D. (Ed.). (1984). *We are your sisters: Black women in the nineteenth century*. New York: Norton.

Sugiman, P. (2001). Privilege and oppression: The configuration of race, gender and class in Southern Ontario auto plants, 1939–1949. *Labour/Le travail, 47*, 83–113.

Teixeira, C. (2002). *Black entrepreneurship in Toronto*. Toronto: Black Pages.

Torczyner, J. L., in collaboration with Boxhill, W., James, C., & Mulder, C. (1997). *Diversity, mobility and change: The dynamics of black communities in Canada*. Montreal: McGill University, School of Social Work.

Troper, H. (1993). Canada's immigration policy since 1945. *International Journal Intercultural Relations, 48*(2), 255–281.

Uneke, O. (1996). Ethnicity and small-business ownership: Contracts between blacks and Chinese in Toronto. *Work, Employment and Society, 10*(3), 529–548.

Walker, J. W. St. G. (1980). *A history of blacks in Canada*. Ottawa: Minister of State Multiculturalism.

Westwood, S., & Bhachu, P. (1988). Introduction. In S. Westwood & P. Bhachu (Eds.), *Enterprising women* (pp. 1–20). London: Routledge.

Whitfield, H. A. (2005). *Canadian ethnography series: Vol. 2. From American slaves to Nova Scotian subjects: The case of the black refugees, 1813–1840*. Toronto: Pearson Prentice Hall.

Winks, R. W. (1997). *The blacks in Canada: A history*. Montreal: McGill-Queen's University Press.

CHAPTER 11

Black Women in Canadian University Sports

Danielle Gabay

INTRODUCTION

Black female student athletes have participated and excelled in Canadian universities for decades; however, the literature regarding black females' participation in postsecondary academics and athletics is scarce. A number of gifted and talented student athletes have attended Canadian institutions of higher education. Sylvia Sweeney (basketball), Molly Killingbeck (track and field), and Jillian Richardson (track and field) all attended Canadian universities in the 1970s and 1980s, setting numerous varsity and Canadian records and representing their respective universities on the world athletic stage. Although Canadian institutions have educated some notable black female athletes in addition to many other successful black females, scant research has been conducted on their experiences during their postsecondary education (Humber, 2004). While the names and athletic achievements of a few student athletes are known, little else is about these individuals or their professional development.

In Canadian universities, the student experience is widely embraced as an important factor in the delivery of education, as positive student experiences can lead to educational engagement and negative experiences to withdrawal (Danylchuk, 1995). In addition, Canadian universities agree that sport enhances the quality of student life on campus, since participants gain valuable educational and life lessons by pursuing athletic excellence. Furthermore, university athletics are considered beneficial to the university as a whole, as they generate revenue and help build the university's overall image and the university community gains pleasure from watching friends, family, and students compete (Danylchuk & MacLean, 2001).

Both scholarly attention and institutional efforts have been directed toward understanding and improving the student experience at Canadian universities. However, in the Canadian context, the focus on the student experience has emphasized the general undergraduate student population, with little attention to the experiences of specific student subgroups, such as black students, student athletes, or female student athletes of colour.

In spite of stated federal and provincial priorities to increase participation in sports (particularly for underrepresented groups), elevate the level of Canadian athletes, and promote equity in all social institutions (Sport Canada, 2012), there still remains a lack of direct focus on specific groups in the population. Given institutional and governmental priorities regarding the student experience and equity in sport participation (particularly with regard to high-level competition and sport leadership), it seems sensible for universities to develop programs, policies, initiatives, and research agendas that address the concerns and experiences of specific student populations. However, this becomes problematic when there is little to no research or documentation with which to work.

To date, research on Canadian student athletes has mainly focused on academic achievement (GPA, graduation rates; Chinn, 1991; Curtis & McTeer, 1990) and athletic and student identity development (Lally & Kerr, 2005; Miller & Kerr, 2003). Most studies have focused on single institutions. There have been few studies on the overall (athletic, academic, and social) postsecondary experience of student athletes in Canada and no systematic studies on student athletes across Canadian campuses. Research on women of colour in the Canadian context has generally focused on black women faculty and their challenges in the academy. There have been very few studies on black female students in Canadian higher education, and no empirical studies have taken the race or ethnicity of Canadian student athletes into account.

The available US-based literature regarding black women and athletics in higher education reveals a multitude of factors that may contribute to the challenges and negotiations that black women college athletes encounter. Researchers have found that they experience racism and discrimination from teammates, coaches, faculty, and staff (Bruening, Armstrong, & Pastore, 2005); limited access to social support (Suggs, 2001); negative stereotyping by peers and faculty (Engstrom & Sedlacek, 1991; Engstrom, Sedlacek, & McEwen, 1995); and negative stereotyping by the general public, reinforced by the mainstream media (Corbett & Johnson, 1993; Schell, 1999). Hyatt (2003) found that many black female student athletes have more difficulty transitioning into university because many are the first in their family to attend university and thus they may not receive adequate support. Black female athletes are overrepresented in revenue-generating sports such as basketball, track and field, and volleyball but under-represented in the general student population (Wilson, 2008). Universities invest more effort in recruiting black female athletes for their athletic abilities than for their academic abilities. These women lack role models and experience high vis-ibility (Person, Benson-Quaziena, & Rogers 2001). While the backdrop of the black female student athlete's experience in higher education appears to be dis-mal and fraught with challenges, researchers have also noted positive aspects of their athletic experience, such as financial assistance, being a role model, added motivation to work harder, and increased confidence and skills (Sellers, Kuper-minc, & Alphonse, 1997).

In response to the dearth of research in Canada, I conducted interviews with black female student athletes to explore their academic, athletic, and social experiences (Gabay, 2013). This national study targeted black female varsity-level student athletes competing in basketball, field hockey, ice hockey, rugby, soccer, track and field, and volleyball. The 32 participants were located in each of the four geographical regions designated by U Sports (the governing body for uni-versity sports in Canada) and were studying in various academic fields, includ-ing kinesiology, political science, history, psychology, accounting, sociology, and biochemistry. They ranged from 18 to 26 years old. The study used an inter-sectional framework to examine how race, gender, and athleticism intersect to shape black women's experience of work within a university sport context. Five themes emerged from the interviews: athletic work, academic work, commun-ity work, part-time work, and work in sport. This chapter relates the women's experiences in their own words to render a picture of their lives as students and as athletes, and to suggest implications for policy and practice surrounding the university experience and professional development from the participants' own perspectives.

INTERSECTIONALITY AND BLACK WOMEN UNIVERSITY ATHLETES

Intersectional theory is used to examine how various socially and culturally con-structed categories, such as race, gender, class, and other categories of identity, interact on numerous and often simultaneous levels in contributing to systematic social inequality (Crenshaw, 1991). Intersectionality suggests that traditional forms of oppression, such as those based on race/ethnicity, gender, religion, nationality, sexual orientation, class, or disability, are not experienced separately; instead, these various forms of discrimination intersect, producing a system of oppression. These social identities and associated discrimination ultimately shape individual and group experiences (Museus & Griffin, 2011).

Crenshaw (1991) wrote, "The intersection of racism and sexism factors into black women's lives in ways that cannot be captured wholly by looking at the race or gender dimensions of those experiences separately" (p. 1244). Intersectionality allows for the voices and realities of those at the margins of society to be brought to the forefront and for the identification of legitimate concerns among people at a particular intersection (Delgado, 2011). Athletes have multiple, fragmented, and conflicting identities (Lally & Kerr, 2005), and they navigate not only personal identities but also social and cultural identities. Intersectionality can be utilized to analyze how race, gender, athleticism, the student role, and work intersect to shape the university sport experience of black female student athletes, and to expose the complexities of this intersection, for which traditional theoretical models typically do not account.

U SPORTS GOVERNING BODY

U Sports, called Canadian Interuniversity Sport (CIS) until 2016, is the national governing body of university sport in Canada. The organization includes the majority of degree-granting universities in the country. The 56 member universities of U Sports are currently organized into four regional associations: (1) Atlantic University Sport (AUS), (2) Canada West Universities Athletic Association (CWUAA), (3) Ontario University Athletics (OUA), and (4) Réseau du sport étudiant du Québec/Quebec Student Sports Federation (RSEQ/QSSF; USPORTS 2018a, 2018b). Approximately 12,000 student athletes compete in the organization. Twenty-one national championships are held for 12 sports, including field hockey, rugby, soccer, cross-country, football, swimming, wrestling, volleyball, track and field, basketball, ice hockey, and curling.

Students entering U Sports institutions directly from high school are eligible to participate if they achieved a grade average of 60% or higher in high school. Once in university, to remain eligible they must take and pass three full courses or six half courses each year. They are allowed to compete for five years (2018c).

Under U Sports policies, financial assistance for athletes can include "scholarships, bursaries, prizes, leadership awards, merit awards, housing, and all other non-employment financial benefit received by an athlete from the institution" (USPORTS, 2018d, pp. 50–52). The value of scholarships is limited to tuition and compulsory fees. Athletic scholarships must be administered through the university, and their value and amount differ across institutions. In Canada, to receive an athletic scholarship at the beginning of the first year of university, a student must have a minimum entering grade average of 80% (USPORTS, 2018d, pp. 50–54).

ATHLETIC WORK

The majority of participants generally brought to light experiences with athletic training commitments; positions as role models; and athletic, gender, and racial stereotypes surrounding athletic participation. The narratives also depict the challenges experienced and the work adjustments the women had to make in order to sufficiently or successfully navigate their university experience.

All women in the study made reference to the pressures they faced as a result of their athletic training demands. About half of the participants felt they were successful in their roles as student athletes, whereas the other half felt they had not excelled in their sport as they thought they would. Many participants reported being unprepared to deal with the level and commitment of practice and competition level in university athletics.

One participant describes how she had to limit the time she spent on academics to fit in her athletic commitments: "[Due to my athletic commitments] I don't have as much time to focus on [academic] assignments. … So, I have a strict schedule that I need to stick to in order to get stuff done. Instead of being able to spend three hours on an assignment … I may only get to spend two hours because I have practice. Time, yes, I have to pay attention to time, which can get stressful."

Another participant described how she stressed over her athletic work: "Balancing academics and athletics can get stressful. If I were to have a test the next day that I had to study for, but I also had practice that night, I'd still have to go to practice. … It's your responsibility to organize your time and they expect you to be there. … I guess we put so much time into athletics and it can sometimes take away from school. And it can also add more stress. The stress can take away from the whole university experience." In the same way, another participant noted, "There are times when you just want to study and you don't want to go to practice. … There are times when it's almost too much to handle. It does become stressful, especially when midterms start. … As a student athlete, you can't expect to cram the night before. Other people can cram the night before because they don't have practice or a game. … So academics and sports are consuming."

Another participant found that even though she had been a student athlete in high school, she still found the athletic work to be challenging and time-consuming because university athletics were more competitive and required a higher level of commitment than high school athletics:

> It's a tough balance, even though I had been a student athlete in high school. Coming into [this city], it was really hard because the level of skill on this team and in this area was higher than it was [in high school]. … And now I'm in a huge varsity program. We have to be at practice at least 80% of the time or they will cut you [from the team]. You have to work twice as hard. So it's hard balancing school and practice, but if you're good with time management then you're okay, but I know a lot of people have a really hard time with it, even when they are years into the program.

For the women in the study, as for student athletes in general, balancing academics and athletics was a common challenge that resulted in several participants receiving lower grades than they were used to. When the athletic-academic balance became too challenging, some participants responded by changing their majors to areas of study that were more conducive to their athletic training schedule, such as kinesiology or recreation and leisure studies. This finding with regard to athletic work and time pressures did not appear to be unique to the black female student athlete experience, as studies on other racialized and non-racialized groups have generated similar results.

Athletic work also encompassed taking on the job of being a role model or peer mentor. These positions required the upper-year black women to support younger or first-year student athletes of colour in their transition into both the university and the athletic culture as well as providing emotional support. Their tasks included training together, tutoring in school work, providing a listening ear, assisting peers in finding financial resources, and assisting teammates with course selection and career exploration. Although almost all of the participants who spoke about being a role model discussed their satisfaction and willingness to be peer mentors, some noted that doing so was not a choice. Some women reported that often being the only black female on their team placed them in a position in which others perceived them as representing their entire race. At times they were also thrust into the position of role model for up-and-coming black female athletes. Sometimes they were required to mentor multiple younger athletes simultaneously. Whereas most generally had positive reflections on their role model status, some reflected on the burden that comes with being perceived as a role model, namely the added work and responsibility to maintain the public image and to represent their group in a positive light.

The continued existence of racial stereotypes was also evident in the athletic realm. The women in the study noted that the general expectation that they were athletically gifted and superior because of their race caused added pressure to perform. They noted that although they did not necessarily agree with these expectations, they did not want to let down their teammates or their racial group by not performing well athletically. Gender stereotypes also created challenges for participants. The women revealed that they had to contend with views and assumptions that they were less feminine or lesbian because they competed in certain sports (more often than not, basketball or rugby). As a result, a number of participants stated that they spent a significant amount of time attempting to disprove racial, gender, and sexuality stereotypes. One participant's comments about stereotypes exemplified a number of participants' experiences:

> You hear a lot of that at the track and at competition or just talking to people—that whole stereotype that black people are stronger and faster and whatnot. It is still very prevalent. ... They say things like, "Oh, the black girl is going to win." And when the black athlete doesn't win, people say, "What's going on?" Or when we're at a race, my friends will come to me and say, "I'm scared of so and so, or that black girl." So, people do make those assumptions. ... They assume an athlete's level of competitiveness is based on their race.

Similarly, one respondent stated that an expectation exists for black student athletes to be athletically superior and the stereotypes created a sense of anxiety around their athletic work: "Yes, I think people believe you're supposed to be faster or scoring all these goals [if you're black]. I had that [experience] in practice, where I was performing better than most people but I still got yelled at because I wasn't performing even higher. So I feel that even if I play better than all the girls on the team, I still have to be 10 times better to be taken seriously or to get playing time. Yes, I have to be a step higher than a varsity athlete."

Another participant expressed a similar view of expectations that tend to be more rigid for blacks than nonblacks due to stereotypes of black athleticism: "I guess there is an expectation. They always expect you to be super athletic or super fast, you know? They don't expect that from the white athletes. Okay, yeah, I'm flattered, but you know, not all of us are like that. ... They always expect you to fall into that stereotype of being super athletic." One woman discussed how the stereotypes are both athletically and academically bound:

> I feel like I constantly have to work to overcome the stereotype that "black people don't care about school" and "all black people are sprinters who can obviously run fast." No, I don't run fast because I'm black. I run fast because I train for it. I excel because I work hard for it. I feel like I'm always trying to work against the stereotypes, which gets frustrating. But if I can be a black female student athlete that's successful academically and athletically and show other people that they can do it, then why not?

Another woman described how the stereotypes and, in turn, additional expectations caused added work for student athletes: "Well, in general, black females or black athletes, they are expected to perform better than nonblack athletes. ... So it does put you under a bit more pressure training-wise because you don't want to let people down. ... [As a black person] you're viewed as if you should be running certain times, you should be winning all the races—and that's just because I'm half black!"

Black women student athletes are bombarded with stereotypes that create anxiety around the athletic work they are expected to deliver. As a result of racial and gender stereotypes, they feel added pressure to work harder both on and off the field.

ACADEMIC WORK

Participants in this study generally brought to light the academic adjustments and challenges they experienced, particularly frustration with the lack of academic advising and mentorship and persistent stereotypes. The majority reported that their academic work was hindered due to a lack of or subpar academic advising. One student shared, "I feel like my GPA is lower than most people's only because [in my] first year ... the academic advisors steered me in the wrong direction. They told me things that weren't true. ... They put me into a higher calculus [class] and I didn't need to be in that level. ... They also put me in a higher physics class, and I think that really threw me and hurt my GPA. ... But I'm still being positive about medical school."

One student related how inadequate academic advising delayed her educational progress: "I've had negative experiences with administration and academic advising in particular. I would have graduated by now, but I'm still here because of advice that I've received. I just feel like [academic advising is] very impersonal. I felt rushed. They don't care. It's all about statistics. They don't want to help the student or get to know you. … I took courses I didn't need when I could have gone on the path that I wanted to, to get where I wanted to be. But the academic advisor didn't take that into consideration." Subpar and lack of academic advising was often cited as the main reason behind the challenges the participants experienced in academic work. This recurrent theme was a notable finding, particularly because poor academic guidance led to additional years in university, additional tuition payments, unwanted academic major changes, and frustration and dissatisfaction. The effects of poor guidance were evident as a number of participants floundered or participated in unwanted courses or programs and moved back and forth between career paths.

Only a small portion of participants discussed the racial makeup of the academic advising staff at their institutions, noting that the staff members were not persons of colour. This aligns with research findings that show that when black students reside on campuses at which they are underrepresented, they not only feel isolated from peers and professors, but also feel isolated from the staff members who are trained and tasked with helping with academic concerns (Museus & Ravello, 2010).

Some participants mentioned that they sought out less traditional forms of support and guidance, from family members—particularly females such as mothers and aunts—rather than academic advisors. This finding supports previous research (Margolis & Romero, 2001) that found that black female students used alternative support networks when traditional networks were unavailable, inaccessible, or insufficient. The finding that black female student athletes utilized family members for academic and all-round support was striking, especially because most interview participants also reported that they were the first in their families to attend postsecondary education. This fact has implications for the type of advice that relatives can give regarding the university experience. Although parents and relatives who did not attend higher education will try to provide the best possible advice, they likely will not possess the cultural capital to adequately direct their children or family members. Although most universities implement academic achievement programs specifically for student athletes, gaps in receiving adequate collegiate advisement—with regard to determining appropriate classes, maintaining an adequate course load, understanding GPA and scholarship requirements, and setting career goals—remain an issue.

Most of the women in the study also indicated that they experienced a lack of mentorship. Almost all participants said that the lack of personal role models and mentors had an impact on their academic experience and work. This finding supports previous studies that found that black women in particular have a difficult time securing mentorship relationships (Benjamin, 1997; Ellis, 2001;

Jordan-Zachery, 2007; Sule, 2009). As stated by Carroll (1982) over 30 years ago, "Black women have had to develop themselves on their own, with no help, in order to 'make it' in academic institutions. This has taken its toll on black women in all areas of life and work" (p. 119). This is still the case today. Thus, black women have very few models or champions to encourage and assist them in their academic work and career preparation.

Along with limited and poor academic guidance and lack of mentorship, working against stereotypes in the academic realm was cited as a common challenge by participants. The continued existence of racial stereotypes (e.g., of blacks as intellectually inferior) was a notable theme in their university academic experience. They reported that race played a part in their academic experience and created an added dimension to their academic work. One participant stated, "I don't know if this is just because of where I grew up, but I felt that, especially as a black student athlete, I had to prove myself. I wanted to make sure that everyone knew I wasn't just here because I could play basketball. I want everyone to know that I can do well both athletically and academically. So that was always a personal pressure. ... I wanted people to know that I deserved to be there just as much as any other person."

Similarly, another woman expressed the added pressure of having to prove herself academically:

> I feel like you have to prove yourself more [when you're a black female student athlete]. ... I feel that you definitely have to prove yourself, not so much in the athletic aspect, more so as a student. ... I kind of have to work my butt off even more because they're expecting me to be [less academically inclined]. ... And so, I feel the need to maintain the [positive] ideas people have of me. ... I don't think most white athletes think about things like that. They might be the star of the team and they may have to worry about different little underlying academic things, but there are certain unwritten rules, unwritten thoughts, that are for a black athlete particularly. ... [Black athletes] need to prove to people that we're not just here for sports. ... Anyhow, I try not to pay attention to [negative stereotypes]. ... You have to just overcome it, right?

Participants noted that they were confronted with overt and covert stereotypes. The stereotypes suggested that black students were poor, academically unprepared, and not qualified to be in higher education. This was similar to the "proving process" described in previous scholarship (Myers, 2002; White, 2007; Woods, 2001). James (1997) also found that black students needed to prove themselves in order to demonstrate that they deserved a place in their chosen field. However, although the women in my study reported that they had added pressure as a result of having to prove themselves, they appeared to accept the proving process as a fact of life.

COMMUNITY WORK

The majority of participants in this study noted a lack of involvement in activities and socialization outside of their sport and academic commitments. There was a consensus among the participants that managing time outside sports and maintaining good grades alongside athletic commitments was difficult and that they were not able to enjoy the kind of social life and community work involvement that the general student population experienced. Involvement in volunteer organizations, program-affiliated associations, and educational events was restricted due to a lack of time and energy. One participant said:

> I tried to get involved. Some people can make it work. Some girls on our team are part of other little community groups. I haven't [become involved] because I find it hard to balance school and sports. Also, the amount of reading that I do compared to other people is obviously more. … So it has been hard to find time to get involved. … But I'm looking to volunteer outside of the school community and make time for that when the season is over. [Volunteering outside school is] a little easier and more flexible than some of the school activities. … I find those who aren't a part of sports have more time to participate in those sorts of groups because, for them, that's their extracurricular activity.

Similarly, another participant stated, "I had signed up for the Black Student Association this year, but I was never able to make it out to any of the events or meetings because of practice or I was too tired from practice. So volunteering at events as part of the ASA [African Student Association] during my first year was [all that I accomplished]. Other than that, I haven't been [involved in any nonathletic groups]."

These findings align with previous studies that found that student athletes compromised their social activities as they progressed through university and attempted to balance academic and athletic responsibilities (Miller & Kerr, 2002). Though the majority of women discussed their lack of involvement, a number of women spoke of various ways that they chose to get involved outside athletics within the university and the surrounding community. They reported that they got involved in order to give back to the community, to build relationships, and to network for their future goals. One participant said, "I feel like I set myself up for this because, in high school, I was on an awkward number of committees and things. Presently, I'm on the varsity board, I'm on the house board, I'm on the social board, I play two varsity sports, I have my full course load, and I also signed up to be a mentor. I think the things I learn from these groups will be helpful in my future." Another respondent discussed her involvement in a number of campus organizations:

> Every year, one of my really good friends … puts on a cultural show. … It's full of dancing and singing and the performing arts. I've helped out with that every year. There is also the Black Student Association and the Caribbean Student Association, and I do stuff with those groups. I guess that's part of my social time. I'm still working [too]. I can [include these types of activities on my resume]. I'm not just going to the movies or watching TV. … I'm doing something productive. I can kind of label it. I'm helping others, so it works.

In order to navigate the challenges in getting involved in community work, a number of participants chose to get involved when they were not participating in their sports. One woman shared how she became involved during the off-season: "I'm involved with a lot of humanitarian and social services organizations. … I help in the soup kitchens. I'm really interested in community service. During the season, I don't have enough time, so I do it once the season is over." For some participants, involvement outside of athletics was further limited by their part-time employment during the academic year. Most respondents felt it was important to foster social outlets and relationships and contribute to community work outside their circle of teammates and other athletes, but again, their unyielding schedules often thwarted their attempts to get involved.

This finding with regard to community work was not unique to the black female student athlete experience, as studies have found other racialized and nonracialized groups have had similar experiences. In previous studies, researchers found that athletic participation restricts involvement and leaves little time for exploring other aspects of academic and co-curricular experiences (Ferrante, Etzel, & Lantz, 1996; Miller & Kerr, 2002); however, the majority of students in this study did not appear to be overly concerned with their restricted social involvement even though they valued interactions with teammates and friends as well as community involvement. This finding was similar to those of previous studies (Blinde, 1989; Miller & Kerr, 2002; Parham, 1993) in which participants disclosed the sacrifices they made in their social lives and their feelings that university athletics inhibited their social development, leaving them with few interests outside sports. The athletes in my study also stated that these sacrifices were worth it. Almost all of the participants stated that if they had to make the choice over again, they would still choose to be a student athlete.

Part-Time Work

Working while attending school is a reality for most Canadian postsecondary students, whether it is during the summer or school year. According to Statistics Canada data (Marshall, 2010), 9 in 10 students work part-time during the school year. Full-time students who are employed work an average of 16 hours per week, while part-time students work more than 30 hours per week. Female students are 25% more likely to be employed during the school year (Marshall, 2010). A number of student athletes in this study were employed during the academic year and found the athletic funding-employment nexus to be a concern.

To win and maintain an athletic scholarship in Canada, student athletes must maintain a particular grade point average. Scholarships are renewed or cancelled on a yearly basis. Although this may keep athletes on their academic toes, it can also create financial and psychological stress when an athlete unintentionally or unexpectedly falls fractions below the required GPA and loses funding for the year. The minimal distribution and volatility of Canadian athletic scholarships have led student athletes to take up academic year employment. The majority of students in the study did not receive financial assistance on the basis of their athletic participation; thus, a number of them worked in an array of part-time positions, as these women explained:

> "I'm a lifeguard and a swim instructor. … I have a good part-time job now and I get paid well, and I can pay my tuition."

> "[I have been asked to join club teams and city leagues outside of school], but I've always [said], 'I have to waitress; I'm sorry.' Now I wish I would have taken the opportunity because I would have been so much more advanced in the sport. If I didn't have to work I would have tried something like that … maybe club [sport], or maybe I could have travelled for [sport]. All the girls on the team have been to Spain, England—travelled internationally."

> "If I had a full scholarship or something like that, I probably wouldn't be working. I'm working to pay for stuff that the scholarship doesn't cover."

"Yeah, I think I could have done better in track, but I feel like the fact that I have to work throughout the year has had more of an influence on my performance. ... I work part-time and I live on my own, so all of my bills are on me to pay. It just adds more stress, so even if I'm not working, I'm always stressing about the fact that I might not make my rent, or I might not be able to eat. So that's really hard, trying to adjust how much school work or practice was worth sacrificing to be able to pay my bills."

"When I was working almost full-time hours, I didn't have time to socialize. It was work, rugby, and school. Now I have time because I'm kind of working just part-time hours. ... When I was trying to get in 20 to 30 hours a week working [outside of school], plus training and going to school, it was a pretty rough year. I was tired all the time."

This finding brings to the forefront a new subgroup of student athletes—the employed student athlete. The employed student athlete appears to be a phenomenon unique to the Canadian context, as athletic funding is far less plentiful than in the US. It is not possible to make race- and gender-based comparisons of Canadian student athletes' part-time employment due to the lack of research in this area at this time.

FUTURE WORK IN SPORT

When asked about their transition following postsecondary education and their career objectives, the participants in this study discussed general vocational goals, sport-related career aspirations, employment prospects as professional athletes, nonathletic career aspirations, athletic retirement, and challenges of career planning.

The majority of the participants identified several possible career goals, but very few described themselves as seriously committed to any particular vocational path. Their ideas were vague, and they vacillated between numerous potential careers: "Right now I'm still a bit unsure; I think at this point I'm leaning more towards something like the research field"; "Well, I hope to get my master's in social work. The plan is to go into the program when I'm finished here, I think." Another participant said, "Sometimes when I get good grades I think about possibly applying to [medical] school. I think that I'd like to do a master's degree too. But I don't think right away. I actually have ambitions to start my own company ... and I would like to start there. That's where I see my career path going."

The uncertainty about their careers could be due to the lack of academic guidance and mentorship that a number of participants experienced at university. Some participants stated that the lack of black or racialized mentors made navigating the university and post-university terrain more challenging. The lack of guidance may have led to academic and, in turn, vocational insecurities and uncertainty (Museus & Ravello, 2010). Their lack of commitment to a particular career path might also be the result of role engulfment which occurs when one aspect of a person's identity or role supersedes others (Adler & Adler, 1991). It is possible that these women were so focused on their identities and roles as black student athletes that this identity dominated their time, and they did not make space to explore their identities and roles as future non-student athletes. Research suggests that while a student athlete can invest in both the student and athlete role simultaneously, if they invest more in the student role, it may facilitate the exploration of nonsport careers (Lally & Kerr, 2005). Further, it is possible that some participants found it difficult to commit to a particular career path as they were struggling with their identity as their sport retirement approached. It is unclear whether the participants' racial identity had an impact on this role engulfment. There is a lack of research examining the interplay of race, role engulfment, and career choice, making it difficult to infer the impact of these intersections.

These student athletes' lack of well-defined career plans is consistent with previous findings that collegiate student athletes have poor career-planning skills (Adler & Adler, 1991; Lally & Kerr, 2005; Parham; 1993). The participants in my study had limited or vague awareness of their nonsport vocational interests. They were more confident in their declarations that they no longer had sport-related career objectives.

A few participants had clear ideas about their vocational preferences and future goals. They had identified their career goals on entering university and had chosen undergraduate degree programs to reach those objectives. One participant stated, "I plan to become a teacher. I'm just going to take a few years off to try [professional rugby] and see if that works. If it doesn't pan out, then I've always wanted to be a teacher. ... I didn't even realize that I wanted to be a teacher when I was in high school, but coming into university and realizing how the curriculum is structured and how certain things are omitted from classes, I want to be able to change that atmosphere." Another stated, "I want to be a business lawyer. I want to do law and combine it with an MBA, which I know is going to be really difficult, but I want to be able to do it. I like law, and I also like business. So, I want to be able to have the combination of both." A number of interviewees elected to pursue careers in the competitive fields of medicine and engineering. This handful of women who had a clear career plan that they were strongly committed to exhibited a fierce single-mindedness as they prepared for their careers. They did not hesitate about their entrance into these competitive programs. A few of these participants noted that their drive to excel in these challenging and competitive academic fields was partially fuelled by their desire to disprove negative racial stereotypes about black mediocrity and athletic stereotypes of the "dumb jock." Most of these women did not have an alternative or backup plan.

A couple of participants identified their interest in sport-related work. One participant shared her vision: "I would like to work in any job related to sports. Even if it's management at a sports store, or a sports bar manager, or maybe even owning something like that, even like managing a professional team and a semiprofessional team or going overseas and working with a team like that. That would be pretty awesome for me." This participant was also the only one who referred to the possibility of working in coaching. This is not surprising, given the lack of women coaches in Canada (Kerr & Ali, 2012). Sport Canada reports, "The number of women trained as coaches and actively coaching—particularly in high-performance contexts—remains persistently low. The limited information available regarding women in other roles, notably within the governance of sport organizations or as technical leaders and officials, indicates that the experiences and skills of women are not being optimized in these domains either" (Government of Canada, 2015). It has been found that the proportion of women and racialized women in North America who advance to leadership and senior roles in sport is comparatively small (Canadian Association for the Advancement of Women and Sport and Physical Activity, 2016). Thus, the small number of racialized women noting aspirations of sport leadership was predictable.

Increasing the number of women and especially racialized women in coaching, particularly at the upper levels of Canadian sport, is important for female empowerment and decreasing the gender gap in sport (Kidd, 2013). Increasing the number of women of colour in coaching would further legitimize sport as an antiracist and equity-focused arena and would encourage more women of colour to take up sport and sport leadership.

Two other interviewees discussed their intentions to work as professional athletes postgraduation. One woman stated, "Looking ahead five years, the major focal point of my life—hopefully, playing professional—and after ten years, near the end of my career, hopefully I'll have settled down by then and figured out what I want to do." A few women were hopeful for a professional athletic career, but a number of them noted that although they initially had aspirations of pursuing professional and amateur athletic careers on entering university, those views had dissipated as they were confronted with information regarding the funding of women's sports, the lack of ethnoracial diversity in professional sports, and statistics on female athletes going professional. They now dismissed the possibility of athletic careers. One respondent stated, "I see my sport career basically ending [when I graduate]. Yeah, basically I'll be done by then. I'm not doing something amazingly spectacular in volleyball, so I'll just end it." Another woman said, "I feel like it was the best decision for me to get a university degree. I really wanted to play university basketball, and it was my dream to play university basketball, but that's done." Another participant described coming to the realization that she would go no further than university sport competition: "Back in the day, I did think soccer was everything and that I could go somewhere, and I had a lot a confidence. … At the end of the day, a sports career is one of the shortest careers you can have. … You're lucky to make two Olympics."

A number of participants indicated that as they progressed through university athletics, they became less serious about pursuing amateur or professional athletic careers due to the discourses surrounding the lack of funding, diversity, and opportunities for professional women's sport in Canada and the short duration of athletic careers. They abandoned aspirations of positions on national teams and contracts with professional clubs as they viewed them as unattainable, particularly due to their race and gender. Despite competing at elite regional and national levels, all but two participants acknowledged that amateur or professional careers were unlikely. While student athletes are becoming increasingly realistic about the probability of professional sport careers (Brown, Glastetter-Fender, & Sheldon, 2000; Brown & Hartley, 1998), male student athletes express greater confidence in a sports career than females (National Collegiate Athletic Association, 2016). Currently there is no available research examining race and gender and how they influence an athlete's confidence in a national or professional sports career. The lack of ambiguity most women felt about their decision to leave competitive sport as an activity or career was also apparent from the narratives. Most players discussed a redefinition of their relationships to sport; this was most commonly expressed as comments about "moving on," "understanding a professional career in sports is unlikely," or being "done."

The women mentioned a variety of occupational destinations and professions, such as physician, social worker, engineer, teacher, lawyer, researcher, and biochemist. Nonetheless, when discussing the future, although the place of sport in their lives would change when they left school, all of the participants were adamant that it would remain a part of their lives.

Regardless of the numerous challenges and adjustments that the participants had to make in the athletic, academic, and social realms, the majority of women in this study valued their academic and athletic experiences. Most participants were satisfied with their experiences and felt that the trade-offs they had made in order to compete were acceptable or more than acceptable.

CONCLUSION

The interviews for this study provided black women collegiate athletes with a space to talk freely about their experiences. Black women have been silenced intentionally and unintentionally by their lack of a space to share their experiences. In this study they were able to share examples of how they made work adjustments and navigated people's expectations and how structural forces were exerted on them.

The results of this study hold several implications for practice that institutions and individuals may consider in order to improve student development, the student experience, and student-to-professional career transitions for black Canadian female student athletes. One disconcerting finding was that many participants who selected a career path had not developed mature, viable career plans and they only had one path in mind, with no consideration of alternative career options. More focus must be placed on assisting student athletes in their vocational planning and preparation. Because employees will change careers multiple times during their lives, career planning and alternative vocational interests are more important than ever (Lyons, Schweitzer, & Ng, 2015).

Given the importance of mentoring for people of colour in higher education and for professional development, further study is needed on mentorship and race in the Canadian context. A lack of mentoring may have implications for women's future education and employment. The underrepresentation of black female students in Canadian higher education and the lack of mentorship that was evidenced in this study point to a need for student affairs personnel and student athletes themselves to implement mentoring programs for black female student athletes. Such initiatives, whether university led or student led, could address the unique concerns of these athletes and further connect the small black communities on university campuses.

Difficulties with academic advising were an almost universal experience for participants in this study, which may have numerous negative implications for their future studies and employment. Traditional advising programs should be complemented by innovative approaches to assist students' academic development, especially targeting student athletes and student athletes of colour. Mandatory academic advising sessions for student athletes during each academic term might also prove helpful. Student affairs personnel could develop annual workshops directed at each academic year or each phase of the university experience. Providing yearly experience workshops might help students progress academically and reduce transition challenges. Creative programmatic efforts should be implemented early to ensure the success of student athletes in both their university and post-university lives.

This study highlights the need for policy changes concerning funding and scholarships for student athletes. To support athletes who are sacrificing their time to represent their university, institutions should increase funding to at least cover room and board in addition to tuition and fees so that these students do not have to take on additional employment or worry about the yearly renewal of their athletic aid.

This study found that student athletes have an early realization that sport careers are unlikely for them, but their vocational planning is weak. It is critical for career counsellors and other student-support staff to encourage student athletes to realistically examine various occupational paths.

This study on black Canadian female student athletes' experiences shed light on the challenges and benefits the women encountered in their athletic work, academic work, and planning for future careers and the coping strategies they used to navigate personal, social, and cultural identities within the university setting. These identities included race, gender, athletic status, student status, and employment status. As these identities intersected, they revealed areas in which the women experienced additional challenges in their university athletic experiences and professional development—areas in which, for example, male or nonracialized student athletes might experience privilege. As women, they have less power than men in a patriarchal society. As black women, they have less power than white men and women in a Eurocentric society. The added confines of female athleticism enhanced these various challenges.

In addition to encouraging more explicit discourses around race and ethnicity, as well as the challenges that are specific to black women athletes in the sport and work arena, systemic changes are needed to improve the sport-related work environment for women. Though there appears to be a movement at the institutional level to empower women through sport while simultaneously preparing them for an array of postsecondary careers, further research utilizing an intersectional approach is needed to understand the lived experiences of athletes of colour in Canada.

KEY READINGS

Bruening, J., Armstrong, K., & Pastore, D. (2005). Listening to the voices: The experiences of African American female student athletes. *Research Quarterly for Exercise Sport*, 76(1), 82–100.

Carter-Francique, A., & Flowers, C. (2013). Intersections of race, ethnicity and gender in sport. In E. A. Roper (Ed.), *Gender relations in sport* (pp. 73–93). Boston: Sense Publishers.

Lally, P., & Kerr. G. (2005). The career planning, athletic identity, and student role identity of intercollegiate student athletes. *Research Quarterly for Exercise and Sport*, 76(3), 275–285.

DISCUSSION QUESTIONS

1. Why is it important to recognize and explore the multiple realities of women's work in sport in Canada?

2. What work-related benefits and challenges exist for black women in Canadian university sport?

3. One student athlete said of her experience with school work, athletic practice, and employment, "When I was working almost full-time hours, I didn't have time to socialize. It was work, rugby, and school. Now I have time because I'm kind of working just part-time hours." What is your opinion of the trade-offs this student athlete describes? What are some of the benefits and challenges of being an employed student athlete?

4. A number of student athletes discussed the differences in athletic work expectations for black women in comparison to nonblack women. One participant stated, "I guess there is an expectation. They always expect you to be super athletic or super fast. They don't expect that from the white athletes." Discuss the causes of this phenomenon and its implications.

5. What role have mentors played in your career or employment? Did you actively seek a mentor, or did you find a mentor after you were already established in your studies or career?

REFERENCES

Adler, P., & Adler, P. (1991). *Backboards and blackboards: College athletes and role engulfment.* New York: Columbia University Press.

Benjamin, L. (Ed.). (1997). *Black women in the academy: Promises and perils.* Orlando: University of Florida Press.

Blinde, E. (1989). Unequal exchange and exploitation in college sport: The case of the female athlete. *ARENA Review, 13*(2), 110–123.

Brown, C., Glastetter-Fender, C., & Sheldon, M. (2000). Psychosocial identity and career control in college student-athletes. *Journal of Vocational Behaviour, 56*(1), 53–62.

Brown, C., & Hartley, D. L. (1998). Athletic identity and career maturity of male college student athletes. *International Journal of Sport Psychology, 29*(1), 17–26.

Bruening, J., Armstrong, K., & Pastore, D. L. (2005). Listening to the voices: The experiences of African American female student athletes. *Research Quarterly for Exercise Sport, 76*(1), 82–100.

Canadian Association for the Advancement of Women and Sport and Physical Activity. (2016). *Women in sport: Fueling a lifetime of participation. A report on the status of female sport participation in Canada.* Retrieved from https://www.caaws.ca/e/wp-content/uploads/2016/03/FWC_ResearchPublication_EN_7March2016.pdf

Carroll, C. (1982). Three's a crowd: The dilemma of the black women in higher education. In G. Hull, P. Scott, & B. Smith (Eds.), *All the women are white, all the blacks are men, but some of us are brave* (pp. 115–128). New York: Feminist Press.

Chinn, B. (1991). *The academic, athletic, and social experiences of Canadian interuniversity student-athletes.* Master's thesis, University of Alberta, Edmonton.

Corbett, D., & Johnson, W. (1993). The African American female in collegiate sport: Sexism and racism. In D. Brooks & R. Althouse (Eds.), *Racism in college athletics: The African American athlete experience* (pp. 179–204). Morgantown, WV: Fitness Information Technology.

Crenshaw, K. (1991). Mapping the margins: Intersectionality, identity politics, and violence against women of color. *Stanford Law Review, 43*(6), 1241–1299.

Curtis, J., & McTeer, W. (1990). Sport involvement and academic attainment in university: Two studies in the Canadian case. In L. Velden & J. Humphrey (Eds.), *Psychology and sociology of sport: Current selected research* (pp. 177–191). New York: AMS Press.

Danylchuk, K. (1995). Academic performance of intercollegiate athletes at a Canadian university: Comparisons by gender, type of sport and affiliated faculty. *Avante, 1*(2), 78–93.

Danylchuk, K., & MacLean, J. (2001). Intercollegiate athletics in Canadian universities: Perspectives on the future. *Journal of Sport Management, 15*(4), 364–379.

Delgado, R. (2011). Rodrigo's reconsideration: Intersectionality and the future of critical race theory. *Iowa Law Review, 96*(4), 1247–1288.

Ellis, E. (2001). The impact of race and gender on graduate school socialization, satisfaction with doctoral study, and commitment to degree completion. *Western Journal of Black Studies, 25*(1), 30–46.

Engstrom, C., & Sedlacek, W. (1991). A study of prejudice toward university student-athletes. *Journal of Counseling and Development, 70*(1), 189–193.

Engstrom, C., Sedlacek, W., & McEwen, M. (1995). Faculty attitude toward male revenue and nonrevenue student-athletes. *Journal of College Student Development, 36*(3), 217–227.

Ferrante, A., Etzel, E., & Lantz, C. (1996). Counseling college student-athletes: The problem, the need. In A. Ferrante, E. Etzel, & J. Pinkney (Eds.), *Counseling college student athletes: Issues and interventions* (pp. 1–17). Morgantown, WV: Fitness Information Technology.

Gabay, D. (2013). *Race, gender and interuniversity athletics: Black female student-athletes in Canadian higher education.* Unpublished doctoral dissertation, University of Toronto.

Government of Canada. (2015). *Actively engaged: A policy on sport for women and girls.* Retrieved from https://www.canada.ca/en/canadian-heritage/services/sport-policies-acts-regulations/policy-actively-engaged-women-girls.html

Humber, W. (2004). *A sporting chance: Achievement of African Canadian athletes.* Toronto: National Heritage Books.

Hyatt, R. (2003). Barriers to persistence among African American intercollegiate athletes: A literature review of non-cognitive variables. *College Student Journal, 37*(2), 260–274.

James, C. (1997). Contradictory tensions in the experiences of African Canadians in a faculty of education with an access program. *Canadian Journal of Education, 22*(2), 158–174.

Jordan-Zachery, J. (2007). Am I a black woman or a woman who is black? A few thoughts on the meaning of intersectionality. *Politics and Gender, 3*(2), 254–263.

Kerr, G. & Ali, B. (2012). *Perceived barriers to achieving gender equity in Canadian interuniversity sport: Perspectives of athletic directors, 12*(2), 1–7. Retrieved from http://www.coach.ca/files/CJWC_APRIL2012_EN_1.pdf

Kidd, B. (2013). Where are the female coaches? *Canadian Journal for Women in Coaching, 13*(1), 1–9. Retrieved from http://www.coach.ca/files/CJWC_FEB2013_EN.pdf

Lally, P., & Kerr. G. (2005). The career planning, athletic identity, and student role identity of intercollegiate student athletes. *Research Quarterly for Exercise and Sport, 76*(3), 275–285.

Lyons, S., Schweitzer, E., & Ng. E. (2015). How have careers changed? An investigation of changing career patterns across four generations. *Journal of Managerial Psychology, 30*(1), 8–21.

Margolis, E., & Romero, M. (2001). "In the image and likeness…": How mentoring functions in the hidden curriculum. In E. Margolis (Ed.), *Hidden curriculum in higher education* (pp. 79–96). London: Routledge Falmer.

Marshall, K. (2010). Employment patterns of postsecondary students. *Perspectives on Labour and Income, 11*(9), 5–17. Statistics Canada Catalogue no. 75–001–XIE. Retrieved from http://www.statcan.gc.ca/pub/75-001-x/2010109/pdf/11341-eng.pdf

Miller, P., & Kerr, G. (2002). The athletic, academic and social experiences of intercollegiate student-athletes. *Journal of Sport Behaviour, 25*(4), 346–366.

Miller, P., & Kerr, G. (2003). The role experimentation of intercollegiate student athletes. *The Sport Psychologist, 17*(2), 196–219.

Museus, S. D., & Griffin, K. A. (2011). Mapping the margins in higher education: On the promise of intersectionality frameworks in research and discourse. *New Directions for Institutional Research, 151,* 5–13.

Museus, S. D., & Ravello, J. (2010). Characteristics of academic advising that contribute to racial and ethnic minority student success at predominantly white institutions. *NACADA Journal, 30*(1), 48–58.

Myers, L. (2002). *A broken silence: Voices of African American women in the academy.* Westport, CT: Bergin & Garvey.

National Collegiate Athletic Association. (2016). NCAA GOALS study (Growth, opportunities, aspirations, and learning of students in college). Retrieved from http://www.ncaa.org/about/resources/research/ncaa-goals-study

Parham, W. (1993). The intercollegiate athlete. *Counseling Psychologist, 21*(3), 411–429.

Person, D., Benson-Quaziena, M., & Rogers, A. (2001). Female student athletes and student athletes of color. *New Directions for Student Services, 93,* 55–64.

Schell, L. (1999). *Socially constructing the female athlete: A monolithic media representation of active women.* Eugene: University of Oregon Publications.

Sellers, R., Kuperminc, G., & Alphonse, D. (1997). The college life experiences of African American women athletes. *American Journal of Community Psychology, 25*(5), 699–719.

Sport Canada. (2012) *Canadian sport policy 2012.* Ottawa: Canadian Heritage. Retrieved from http://canadiansporttourism.com/sites/default/files/docs/csp2012_en_lr.pdf

Suggs, W. (2001). Left behind: Title IX has done little for minority female athletes, while white women have made significant gains. *Chronicle of Higher Education, 48*(14), 35–37.

Sule, V. T. (2009). Black female faculty: Role definition, critical enactments, and contributions to predominately white research institutions. *NASPA Journal About Women in Higher Education, 2*(1), 93–121.

USPORTS. (2018a). About the brand. Retrieved from https://usports.ca/en/about/the-brand

USPORTS. (2018b). Member universities. Retrieved from https://usports.ca/hq/member-universities

USPORTS. (2018c). *Policies and procedures 40—Eligibility.* Retrieved from https://usports.ca/uploads/hq/By_Laws-Policies-Procedures/2018/EN/Policy_40.10.1_to_40.10.6_Eligibility_Rules_%282018-2019%29.pdf

USPORTS. (2018d). *Policies and procedures 50—Athletic financial award.* Retrieved from https://usports.ca/uploads/hq/By_Laws-Policies-Procedures/2018/EN/Policy_50_Financial_Awards_%282018-2019%29.pdf

White, D. (2007). "Matter out of place": Ar'n't I a woman? Black female scholars and the academy. *Journal of African American History, 92*(1), 5–12.

Wilson, T. (2008). *Women who endure: A grounded theory study of black female former student-athletes.* Doctoral dissertation, Capella University, Minneapolis, Minnesota.

Woods, R. (2001). Invisible women: The experiences of black female doctoral students at the University of Michigan. In M. Reitumetse & A. Green (Eds.), *Sisters of the academy: Emergent black women scholars in higher education* (pp. 105–115). Sterling, VA: Stylus Publishing.

CHAPTER 12

The Public Women of Canada: Women in Elected Office

Jocelyne Praud, Alexa Lewis, and Jarod Sicotte

INTRODUCTION

In her book *Femmes publiques*, historian Michelle Perrot (1997) points out that in the French language, a "public woman" is usually a prostitute, while a "public man" is a man whose official position enables him to participate in running public affairs and exercising political power—in other words, a politician. Interestingly, in the English language, the expression "public man" has a broader meaning as it refers to a man with a high public profile, be he a politician, intellectual, or artist. A "public woman," however, is still a prostitute, though this meaning appears to have been less common in English than in French. In any event, the enduring sexist distinction[1] between a public man and a public woman in Canada's two official languages signals that in the political sphere, men have been viewed as legitimate, normal, and welcome actors and women as illegitimate, abnormal, and out of place.

In democratic systems such as Canada's, elected representatives have worked tirelessly to raise important social and economic issues and developing legislation to address them. Given the initial dearth of women among elected representatives, it is not surprising that issues specifically affecting women were neglected for a long time. Nonetheless, following the feminist mobilization of the 1960s and 1970s, more women were able to get elected to legislatures. In their new place of work, these women began to draw attention to the challenges faced by women as mothers and workers and advocate for laws that would put women on equal footing with men in the family and the workforce. For example, in the late 20th century, laws designed to bring about greater equality in hiring, pay, promotion, benefits, and working conditions, as well as laws providing assistance to women for childcare, maternal leave, employment insurance, health care, and housing, were passed in the federal, provincial, and territorial legislatures. Clearly such important laws have enabled women to work and support themselves and their dependents. While not all women elected representatives are necessarily interested in working on women's issues or in agreement about them, it remains that having a substantial number of women working in the executive, legislative, judicial, and administrative branches of government as ministers, legislators, judges, lawyers, and other public servants helps to ensure that laws pertaining to women's equality and associated policies are implemented and improved upon.

Using an intersectional perspective, this chapter focuses on the public women of Canada, including the diverse women who have been elected to public office at the federal, provincial, and territorial levels despite exclusionary norms concerning the characteristics that elected representatives are expected to exhibit. The chapter is divided into two sections. The first section examines how the centuries-old private/public split and associated sexual division of labour conceived by ancient Greek philosophers such as Plato and Aristotle have led to the exclusion of those lacking the required sex, gender, race, ethnicity, class, sexual orientation, or physical abilities from the political sphere.[2] In Canada, women were legally barred from voting in federal elections until 1918—that is, 30 years before Asian Canadians, 32 years before Inuit women and men, and 42 years before Indigenous Peoples with Indian status. Furthermore, although Canadian women in all their diversity have increased their numerical presence in federal, provincial, and territorial legislatures, not one of these democratic institutions presently reflects the actual sex, racial, and ethnic composition of the Canadian population, indicating the continued influence of exclusionary norms. To take the example of today's federal House of Commons, which has been described as Canada's "most diverse Parliament ever" (Desmarais, 2018), important representational gaps persist, especially when it comes to women. Although women constitute just over half of the Canadian population, they hold only a quarter of the seats in the House. Visible minorities represent 21% of the Canadian population and 16% of members of Parliament (MPs). Indigenous people represent 5% of the population and 3% of MPs (Desmarais, 2018, paras. 14, 23, 24).

The second section surveys how the Internet and social media have impacted Canadian politics and, in particular, how they have been used to unleash misogynist, racist, and homophobic attacks on elected representatives who deviate from the conventional mold of the white, heterosexual, male politician of British or French ancestry—in other words, mainly sexual minorities and women, including visible minority and Indigenous women. This finding echoes Jenaro, Flores, and Frías's (2018) extensive review of the academic literature on cyberbullying among adults, which highlights that "females, sexual minorities, and other ethnic minorities" as well as "certain professional groups, such as politicians, are … at greater risk for cyberbullying" (pp. 113, 118). Consequently, while a diversity of Canadian women have been able to increase their presence as elected representatives in the previously men-only political sphere, they are still not fully accepted as legitimate political actors performing important work for society, as indicated by the cyberbullying that they have been subjected to in recent years.

THE EXCLUSION OF WOMEN FROM POLITICS

The Private/Public Divide

The ancient Greek philosophers' conception of the world as split into two separate realms, with women and men performing distinct roles in their assigned realm, provided a powerful justification for the subordination of women to men and their exclusion from politics. In ancient Greece, these two realms were identified as the *oikos*, or the private sphere of production and reproduction, and the *polis*, that is, the city or public sphere. In the oikos, slaves were to produce the basic necessities of life (production), and women were to bear and rear children (reproduction). Although the oikos was the realm of women, slaves, and children, the manager and ruler of the oikos was the adult male citizen—the "man of the house," so to speak. In addition to being responsible for the oikos, the male citizen represented the interests of the household in the public realm, as the statesman (Coole, 1993; Okin, 1979). It is important to point out that this private/public divide was rooted in the dominant political theory of the day.

Aristotle (384–322 BCE) justified this divide in his work *Politics*, stating that men were naturally suited to be active in the public realm and rule over the less rational segments of the population (women, slaves, and children) given men's superior rational and intellectual capacities. Women, on the other hand, were naturally destined to the private realm due to their reproductive functions and irrational tendencies (Coole, 1993; Okin, 1979). For this father of Western political thought, the biological (sex) and constructed (gender) differences between women and men clearly demonstrated women's natural inferiority to men and justified women's confinement to the private sphere and exclusion from the public sphere and public affairs.

This point of view was hegemonic for centuries, and many early liberal democratic thinkers, such as Jean-Jacques Rousseau as expressed in his treatise on education, *Émile* (1762), believed that women were naturally confined to the private sphere due to their child-bearing capacities and supposed emotional propensities. This viewpoint remained largely unchallenged until the late 18th and early 19th centuries, with British thinkers such as Mary Wollstonecraft in *A Vindication of the Rights of Woman* (1792) and John Stuart Mill in *The Subjection of Women* (1869) arguing that women should have the same civil and political rights and educational opportunities as men (Coole, 1993; Okin, 1979).

Deeply influenced by the ideas of Aristotle, most of the leading thinkers and leaders who came after him perpetuated the notion that only a select group of men could be involved in public affairs or politics. In the 19th century, as representative democracies began to emerge in the West, laws were passed granting political rights—specifically the rights to vote and to run for election—to the select few men perceived to have the capacities to exercise such rights and, in turn, denying them to those perceived to lack such capacities.

Women, men without property, and men from different racial and ethnic backgrounds were identified as unfit for political rights and excluded from politics. In Canada, the specific age, sex, citizenship, and class attributes that voters and candidates (and thus elected representatives) were expected to have had already been codified into law by the founding colonies in the first half of the 19th century, prior to Confederation in 1867. While the achievement of universal suffrage in 1960 formally ended the **de jure** (legal) exclusion of Canadian women and other groups from politics, it did not end their **de facto** (actual) exclusion from politics.

De Jure and De Facto Exclusion of Canadian Women from the Political Sphere

Reiterating the legal restrictions in place in the colonies that came together to form the new Dominion of Canada, article 41 of the 1867 British North America Act, Canada's first constitutional act, specified that men who were

British subjects—that is, born or naturalized in Britain and its colonies and dominions—and property owners of 21 years of age were entitled to vote. In brief, all adult women, men without property, and men born outside the British Empire were legally excluded from voting and running for elected office. These various legal disqualifications were gradually lifted, starting with property qualifications at the beginning of the 20th century, sex right after World War I, and British nationality when the 1946 Canadian Citizenship Act was passed (Elections Canada, 2017a, 2017b).

Following several decades of mobilization by suffragists and social reformers across the country, female British subjects over the age of 21 obtained the right to vote in federal elections in 1918 and the right to run for federal office the following year.[3] While 1921 is the year when women were able to vote and run as candidates and also when Agnes Macphail became the first and only woman to win a federal seat in the Ontario riding of Grey South East, 1960 is the referential year for actual universal suffrage in Canada since Indigenous people no longer had to relinquish their Indian status in order to cast a vote in a federal election. The first time a First Nations woman, Ethel Blondin-Andrew, won federal office was in 1988, and a slew of "firsts" for women from diverse ethnocultural and racial backgrounds happened in the 1990s and early 2000s.[4] The 67-year gap between Macphail's election and Blondin-Andrew's victory highlights the need to analyze the extent to which women have been able to work as elected representatives from an intersectional perspective; the same can be said for Libby Davies, the first female member of Parliament (Vancouver East, 1997–2015) to come out as a lesbian. As another example of the need for intersectional analysis, 1993 is the year in which Canada saw its first (white) female prime minister, Kim Campbell, as well as its first two black women elected as members of Parliament, Jean Augustine and Hedy Fry. These examples suggest that while Canadian women's formal acquisition of political rights gradually put an end to their de jure exclusion from the political sphere, women, in particular diverse women, are still unable to exercise their right of eligibility for office to the same extent as men due to a variety of factors, including pervasive expectations about what politicians are supposed to look like and access to funding. The fact that, to date, neither the House of Commons nor the provincial and territorial legislatures are gender balanced indicates that de facto practices, such as the reluctance of party officials to really look for women candidates and their propensity to dismiss qualified women as not tough or competent enough, continue to prevent women from working in politics.

As table 12.1 indicates, since 1921, when only four women ran as candidates, women's overall numerical representation in the House of Commons has

Table 12.1: Women in the House of Commons since 1917

Election year	Number of women elected	% of women MPs
1917	0/235	0
1921	1/235	<1
1925	1/245	<1
1926	1/245	<1
1930	1/245	<1
1935	2/245	1
1940	1/245	<1
1945	1/245	<1
1949	0/262	0
1953	4/265	2
1957	2/265	1
1958	2/265	1
1962	5/265	2
1963	4/265	2
1965	4/265	2
1968	1/264	<1
1972	5/264	2
1974	9/264	3
1979	10/282	4
1980	14/282	5
1984	27/282	10
1988	39/295	13
1993	53/295	18
1997	62/301	21
2000	63/301	21
2004	65/308	21
2006	64/308	21
2008	69/308	22
2011	76/308	25
2015	88/338	26

Source: Adapted from Young, 2013, table 13.1, p. 256, and Canada, Library of Parliament, 2018.

progressed at an excruciatingly slow pace even though by 1993 the proportion of women candidates had increased over a hundredfold, with 476 women contestants (Canada, Library of Parliament, 2018).[5] Women had to contest no less than 20 federal elections before finally obtaining 10% of the federal seats in 1984. Following a brief period of successive gains in the late 1980s and early 1990s, during which their presence gradually increased to 20%, women's overall representation then stalled at 21% to 22% throughout the first decade of the 21st century. Modest gains were made in the 2011 and 2015 elections, with women winning respectively 25% and 26% of the seats in the House of Commons. Since it took close to 90 years for women to obtain a quarter of the seats in the House of Commons, one wonders whether it will take another 90 years for them to win half the seats and achieve parity with men.

Table 12.2 reveals that for the past four decades, women's legislative representation has not evolved uniformly across Canada's ten provinces and three territories. For example, in the smaller legislatures of the Northwest Territories,

Table 12.2: Women in Provincial and Territorial Legislatures in the 1980s, 1990s, 2000s, and as of 2018 (%)

Legislatures	1980s	1990s	2000s	As of 2018
Alberta	8	19	21	33
British Columbia	11	27	29	39
Manitoba	12	19	28	25
New Brunswick	7	16	15	22
Newfoundland & Labrador	6	4	17	25
Northwest Territories	13	8	11	11
Nova Scotia	2	10	23	33
Nunavut	–	5	5	27
Ontario	5	18	29	40
Prince Edward Island	6	19	22	19
Quebec	7	18	30	42
Saskatchewan	8	22	19	26
Yukon	19	18	32	37

Source: Adapted from Boesveld, 2018; Fraser, 2018; Ghoussoub, 2017; Legislative Assembly of Nunavut, 2018; Prince Edward Island Coalition for Women in Government, 2018; Valiante, 2018; Young, 2013, table 13.3, p. 258.

Prince Edward Island, and New Brunswick, women have remained grossly underrepresented, with under or just above 20% of the seats even today. Slow but steady progress is observable in Newfoundland and Labrador, Saskatchewan, and Manitoba, where as of 2018 women hold a quarter of the seats. Women have the highest proportion of seats (over 30%) in the Yukon, Nova Scotia, and four of the most populated provinces—Alberta, Ontario, Quebec, and British Columbia. Carbert's (2009) finding that urban ridings are more likely to elect women than rural ridings helps to explain why Alberta, Ontario, Quebec, and British Columbia, which have densely populated cities and thus more urban ridings, have a higher proportion of women representatives. In Yukon and Nova Scotia, the urban riding explanation is not as pertinent as the proactive role of parties in recruiting and getting women elected, specifically the New Democrats and Liberals in Nova Scotia and the three territorial parties in Yukon (Carbert & Black, 2013; Tukker, 2016).

Notwithstanding these more encouraging developments, including the presence of 39%, 40%, and 42% women among the members of the newly elected Legislative Assemblies of British Columbia, Ontario, and Quebec, it remains that, to date, none of the provincial and territorial legislatures are gender balanced.

Nonetheless, it is also important to note that women of colour and Indigenous women have made numerical gains in recent years, especially at the federal level.[6] For example, Young (2013) points out that "minority women's representation doubled between 1993 and 2004, from under 4 percent of the members of the Commons up to over 8 percent in 2004" and that "in 2004, minority women comprised 40 percent of all minority MPs, a better rate than we find for non-minority women" (p. 263). Echoing Young's observation, Tolley (2015, para. 5) highlights that the election of 15 visible minority women and 3 Indigenous women to the House in 2015 means that the proportion of women working as federal representatives is still higher among visible minority MPs (32%) and Indigenous MPs (30%) than among white MPs (25%).[7] Although these statistics are encouraging, they also indicate that gender parity is still not a reality, be it for visible minority, Indigenous, or white women MPs, hence the need to examine the various factors that can explain the sex imbalance observable in the different groups of MPs.

Explaining Women's Persistent Underrepresentation

Feminist scholars such as O'Neill (2015), Young (2013), and others have used the supply-and-demand explanatory framework developed by Norris and

Lovenduski (1995) to shed light on the perennial underrepresentation of women in Canadian politics. This framework emphasizes the importance of "supply" factors that encourage or discourage individual women from contesting political office as well as "demand" factors that encourage or discourage political parties from searching for and nominating women candidates. Although the framework acknowledges the important role of organizations such as the non-partisan Equal Voice, which works tirelessly to bring more women into politics across Canada, its main focus is on political parties as they remain the primary gatekeepers of the political sphere that decide whether to nominate a candidate or not.

Among supply factors to consider are the educational, professional, financial, and networking resources that aspiring politicians need and also the gender norms or "expectations regarding appropriate female and male public and private roles" in place in Canadian society (O'Neill, 2015, p. 27). Although in the 21st century more Canadian women than ever before have access to these resources, discriminatory practices and gendered expectations often end up deterring them from embarking on a political career. Indeed, while women have surpassed men in many fields of university education—including law and business, the fields most conducive to a political career—they are still less likely to work in these male-dominated sectors, which can be quite impervious, if not hostile, to women workers (O'Neill, 2015; Statistics Canada, 2015). Despite their educational achievements, women also earn less money than men overall (World Economic Forum, 2016). Last but not least, while gender norms and roles have changed considerably in Canada since women acquired political rights, as O'Neill (2015) states, "A political candidate who is the mother of small children is still likely to raise more eyebrows among the public and some party members than one who is the father of small children" (p. 27). In light of all of the above factors, it is not surprising that women are not as inclined as men to put themselves forward as candidates.

Demand factors focus on political parties and how they come to recruit candidates. Considerations influencing the recruitment decisions of parties include the electoral system as well as candidates' chances to win office. In Canada's single-member plurality electoral system, which is used in all national, provincial, territorial, and municipal elections, parties can only present one candidate in each riding, and candidates simply need to obtain a plurality of votes (the highest number) instead of a majority (more than half of the votes) to get elected. Because of these two features, parties have been reluctant to select candidates who do not have the same characteristics as previously victorious contestants, the majority of whom have been privileged white men. As noted by O'Neill (2015), despite their recent efforts to put forward a diversity of candidates,[8] federal parties (excluding the Bloc Québécois) are still more likely to run men in winnable ridings and women in unwinnable ridings. This overview of supply-and-demand factors clearly highlights the continued influence and relevance of powerful exclusionary norms regarding the involvement of women in Canadian politics.

In Canada and many other countries, the private/public divide led to the legal exclusion of women and other groups from politics. The very slow increase in the presence of elected women representatives at the federal, provincial, and territorial levels observable over the past four decades can be interpreted not so much as evidence of the inclusion of women in the political sphere, but rather as evidence of the continued resistance to diverse women politicians and thus their perennial exclusion from politics.

WOMEN IN ELECTED OFFICE IN THE AGE OF THE INTERNET AND SOCIAL MEDIA

The Rise of Social Media in Canadian Politics

The importance of the media in politics has been magnified by the growing popularity of online platforms. In the 20th century traditional media, namely newspapers, radio, and television, came to assume an increasingly central role in Canada's electoral politics, with political parties and candidates relying on them to communicate their messages to citizens and citizens deriving crucial political information from them. The rise of the Internet and social media platforms such as Twitter, YouTube, and Facebook means that in the 21st century political parties, politicians, and citizens have used not only traditional media, but also new social media to communicate and gather political information. In her article on the growth of what she calls "digital party politics," Small (2017) identifies the 2004 federal election as "Canada's first real Internet election" (p. 389) due to the extensive use of the Internet by Canadians as well as federal parties and candidates. Curry (2011) calls the 2011 federal election "Canada's first social media election" due to the parties' significant reliance on social media platforms. Clearly, establishing a social media presence has become essential today not only for political parties and their leaders, but also for anyone interested in a political career. As a case in point, 80% of federal MPs use Twitter and 75% have Facebook accounts (Patten, 2013, p. 24). Not surprisingly, politicians with the highest public profiles, such as party leaders, have the most Twitter followers and Facebook fans. While the increasing use of social media in the political sphere can enhance interactions between parties and politicians on the one hand and citizens on the other, as well as the latter's civic engagement and voter turnout, it can also have drawbacks, one of the most troubling being the cyberbullying of politicians in general and women politicians in particular.

Cyberbullying in Canadian Politics

The phenomenon of cyberbullying has, of course, risen with the increasing popularity of the Internet and social media. While traditional bullying occurs when a perpetrator confronts a victim face-to-face, **cyberbullying** is a "derogatory act carried out intentionally by sending or posting harmful material on social networks to cheat or tarnish anybody's image in [the] real world" (Sarna & Bhatia, 2015, p. 677). In their study, Sarna and Bhatia present two types of cyberbullying: direct and indirect. Direct cyberbullying may be defined as sending "disrespectful/abusing material in the form of text, images, videos, and audios to harass/torture individuals directly" (p. 677). Indirect cyberbullying seeks to harass individuals through actions such as spreading "false rumors, lies, etc. concerning them, tagging their embarrassing images, [and refusing] to socialize with the victim" (p. 677). According to Sarna and Bhatia, such indirect attacks are typically more harmful as their increased visibility may damage the targeted person's standing. However, with the rise of social media platforms such as Twitter, even attacks that are directly aimed at a specific individual may be viewed by the general public. Therefore, all cyberbullying and bullying in general has many negative effects since the dissemination of any detrimental and incorrect information may undermine an individual's reputation and job (p. 678).

As high-profile persons who, as part of their work, are regularly called on to take public stands and make decisions about sensitive issues and who depend on popular support to get re-elected and thus be able to continue to do their work, politicians are prime targets of cyberbullying via social media. Women, especially diverse women, who are quite new to the political sphere are particularly susceptible to cyberbullying. What is quite troubling about the cyberbullying of women politicians is that it can very well prevent them from doing the work that they were elected to do and also deter other women from choosing this profession, which can have repercussions not just on the women representatives themselves, but also on the previously ignored constituencies whose interests they have chosen to speak up for.

The effect of cyberbullying in the Canadian political sphere can be highlighted through the story of Sandra Jansen, a member of the Legislative Assembly (MLA) of Alberta who crossed the floor from her former Progressive Conservative Party (PCP) to join the governing New Democratic Party (NDP). A candidate in her PCP's leadership race, in November 2016 Jansen quit the party and the race due to harassment and bullying (Wood, 2016).[9] Rather than leave the political sphere altogether, Jansen chose to join the NDP. Following this move, Jansen rose on the floor of the Assembly and gave an impassioned speech about her experiences with cyberbullying and harassment (McConnell, 2016). She called her colleagues to action, giving examples of her own experiences following her change of party. Some of the demeaning comments Jansen received on Twitter and Facebook included: "Dead meat"; "Sandra should stay in the kitchen where she belongs"; "Fly with the crows, and get shot"; and "Dumb broad. A good place for her to be is with the rest of the queers" (McConnell, 2016, para. 3). As a result of these comments and veiled threats, a temporary protection unit was assigned to Jansen. This type of harassment, Jansen warned, is quickly becoming normalized in the public sphere and could have a deterring effect on the political involvement of women, particularly younger women. In her words, "Our daughters are watching us [and] they are watching the challenges facing women in politics today; imagine if we let that poison become normalized or if our daughters forego the political arena all together" (McConnell, 2016 [embedded video]). Sadly, cyberbullying is not isolated to Sandra Jansen. Online attacks occur constantly, to politicians from all walks of life.

On a 2016 CBC broadcast of the news program *At Issue* titled "Hateful Tweets," hosted by Peter Mansbridge, federal politicians read some of the demeaning tweets that they have received. Unlike the sassy quips that typically come to mind, these tweets often advocate violence and target politicians for their sex, gender, race, ethnicity, or sexual orientation, not their actions. Most of these tweets are too violent and inappropriate to repeat here. Ruth Ellen Brosseau, a young NDP MP from Quebec, was made famous for her involvement in the social media pseudoscandal "Elbowgate," the May 2016 incident in which Prime Minister Justin Trudeau elbowed Brosseau while attempting to bring the Conservative whip to his seat in the House of Commons. One online response to her was, "You're a goddamn joke," she read (Mansbridge, 2016, 3:14). Hateful tweets are not just isolated to the younger generation, as illustrated by attacks on federal Green Party leader Elizabeth May. In response to May speaking out against cyberbullying, she received comments such as, "Women aren't special. If you can't take the hate, get out of Parliament" (4:58). While academic studies on cyberbullying among adults have put forward different statistics showing that women are more likely to be victims of cyberbullying than men (Jenaro, Flores, & Frías, 2018), it is important to mention that men are not immune to cyberbullying, as a tweet received by Ontario MP Michael Chong, a popular candidate for the Conservative Party leadership, indicated: "Michael Chong is a Chinese spy. No Asians in the Party. If you like inclusivity so much, why don't you go back to China?" (9:47). It is important to note that cyberbullying does not simply involve sexist and racist attacks; victims have also been targeted because of their religion, sexual orientation, Indigenous ancestry, and appearance. Take, for instance, Maryam Monsef, the current federal Minister for Women and Gender Equality. Despite her dedication to improving the experience of women in Canada, this immigrant from Afghanistan and inspiring young politician is often attacked for her background and appearance. One tweet captures the spirit of attacks she has received: "I'd like to see Muslim Monsef's homely head on a pike pole planted outside Parliament Hill" (3:39). Other examples include Ontario's former openly gay Premier Kathleen Wynne, who has been "bombarded on social media by homophobic [and] sexist abuse" (Crawley, 2016), and Indigenous Manitoba MLA Nahanni Fontaine, whose "campaign … was filled with vicious verbal abuse and social media attacks" (Martin, 2016, para. 3). The experiences of Monsef, Wynne, Fontaine, and others suggest that while any politician may be cyberbullied, women politicians from diverse backgrounds are especially vulnerable to cyberbullying.[10] It even appears that the more an elected representative deviates from the archetypal white, heterosexual, male politician of British or French origin, the more likely that individual is to be subjected to demeaning and even violent online abuse.

A number of the tweets read on the *At Issue* broadcast are quite troubling as they do not stop at expressions of dislike, but typically advocate violence against the targeted politician, especially when the politician is a woman. Panellist Jennifer Ditchburn, the editor of the online magazine *Policy Options*, described the attacks as "quasi-violent. … [They are] a specific kind of attack against women where [they] are saying, 'Okay, I don't like you and also, I want to do something bad to you'" (Mansbridge, 2016, 6:32). With the rapid rise of social media, this kind of violence against women may soon become normalized if not addressed. While these attacks occur against politicians of all walks of life, women may be increasingly deterred by them due to their frequency and violent nature.

The **cyberharassment** of women politicians, including attacks and violent threats, demonstrates that in contemporary Canada, there is still a profound unease with women occupying positions of power in the political sphere and being involved in the running of public affairs, and that in 2018 misogyny is well and alive in Canada. The "women + power = discomfort" equation advanced by Bashevkin (2009) in her book *Women, Power, Politics: The Story of Canada's Unfinished Democracy* rings eerily true today even though both the federal cabinet and the provincial cabinet of British Columbia currently have a parity of women and men ministers. At this point in time, it seems that the enhanced visibility of women as provincial premiers[11] and federal ministers may even account for the recurrent cyberbullying of women in politics. It also seems that the numerical gains of visible minority and Indigenous women may account for online attacks directed at federal MPs Jenny Kwann and Bardish Chagger and Manitoba MLA Nahanni Fontaine. More research needs to be conducted on the cyberharassment of Canadian politicians, including those who do not fit the traditional mold of the white, heterosexual, male politician of British or French ancestry. As several women politicians and journalists have observed, the online abuse of women in politics is likely to deter women from considering a political career and thus perpetuates the exclusion of women from the political sphere. As highlighted before, the fewer women working as elected representatives, the less attention issues of concern to women are likely to receive. Women's retreat from politics and public service is particularly worrisome because it can also lead to the undermining and possible dismantlement of the laws and policies that have enabled women as a whole to work and support themselves and their dependents. Appointing a gender-balanced and diverse cabinet is definitely a step in the right direction. However, more concrete steps need to be taken to counter cyberbullying and the misogyny it spurs out and to ensure that all of Canada's present and future public women are effectively welcome as rightful political actors no matter their race, ethnicity, or sexual orientation.

CONCLUSION

While women have achieved significant milestones in Canadian politics—one of the most recent ones being the election in 2015 of Jody Wilson-Raybould as the MP for the federal riding of Vancouver Granville and her subsequent appointment as the first Indigenous justice minister—as well as numerical gains in federal, provincial, and territorial legislatures, they remain blatantly underrepresented in these democratic institutions. The fact that, to date, none of these elected bodies have reached gender parity indicates that women politicians and, in particular, diverse women politicians are still being excluded from the political sphere. Initially, exclusion was both de jure, with class, sex, and racial restrictions legally imposed on political rights, and de facto, with influential norms identifying politics as the sole domain of white, heterosexual men of British or French origin. Since 1960, when Indigenous people were no longer required to give up their Indian status in order to vote in federal elections, exclusion of diverse women from politics has continued in its de facto form. Even today, as Canada stands as one of the few countries in the world with a diverse, gender-balanced federal cabinet (though not a gender-balanced House of Commons), it is alarming that the Internet and social media are being used to target women politicians with sexist, racist, and homophobic comments and threaten them with violence. Such attacks, which aim at framing women as illegitimate, aberrant outsiders who have no place in politics, must be addressed by Canadian legislators as ad hoc individual coping strategies are unlikely to bring about long-lasting normative changes. In this respect, it would be quite instructive for legislators to examine the experiences of different foreign nations in effectively enhancing gender equality in politics and addressing sexist norms.

According to the Gender Quotas Database (International Institute for Democracy and Electoral Assistance, 2018), about half of the world's countries have an electoral quota designed to bring about greater gender balance in their national legislatures, and in 51 of those countries the law mandates that seats either be reserved for women or that parties present a parity of women and men.[12] As noted by Dahlerup and Freidenvall (2005), the objective of electoral quotas, particularly those mandated by law, is not only to quickly boost the number of women candidates and elected representatives, but also to trigger more egalitarian public perceptions of women's worth and capabilities in the private and public spheres. Instructively, Anglo-Saxon countries such as the United States, Canada, and Australia, which are strongly committed to individual rights, merit, and representation, have been reluctant to adopt mandatory gender quotas even though they have far fewer women in their national legislatures—only 19.5%, 26%, and 28.7%, respectively—than Rwanda and Bolivia, which have 61.3% and 53.1% women in their national legislatures (Inter-Parliamentary Union, 2018).[13] Going beyond numbers, research by Burnet (2012) as well as by Beaman, Pande, and Cirone (2012) reveals that in Rwanda and India, the implementation of compulsory gender quotas has altered citizens' views of politics as solely a men's domain. As the cyberbullying of Canadian elected representatives is showing no sign of subsiding, the adoption of a legislated electoral quota to foster greater gender balance and diversity in Canada's democratic institutions appears to be a crucial step in the normalization and acceptance of women in all their diversity as legitimate actors in Canadian politics. Last but not least, such a legal provision, especially if combined with campaigns that aim at educating young children and youth about the important work that women have done and continue to do in the political sphere, would help combat misogyny, foster greater acceptance of women politicians, and greatly contribute to establishing women represent-atives as Canada's effective and legitimate public women on par with Canada's public men.

NOTES

1. By highlighting this sexist semantic distinction, we seek to expose how prejudicial atti-tudes toward sex trade workers have been used to undermine women aspiring to pur-sue a career in politics. Furthermore, in this chapter on women politicians and elected representatives, the terms *politics* and *political sphere* are understood narrowly as encompassing elections to formal democratic institutions such as legislatures.

2. While we recognize the multitude of barriers facing those who do not fit the mold of the white, heterosexual, male politician of British or French ancestry, including gen-der identity, class, and physical ability, we focus mainly on how sexism, racism, and homophobia continue to hinder the entry of diverse women into the political sphere.

3. In 1917 the Military Voters Act and Wartime Elections Act gave women serving in the military and those with a male relative fighting in World War I the right to vote at the federal level. At the provincial level, women first received the rights to vote and run for office in 1916 in Alberta, Saskatchewan, and Manitoba; 1917 in British Columbia; 1918 in Nova Scotia; 1922 in Prince Edward Island; 1925 in Newfoundland; and 1940 in Quebec. Ontario granted women the right to vote in 1917 and to run for office two years later, and New Brunswick did so in 1919 and 1934 (Elections Canada, 2017b). For in-depth historical analyses of women's struggles for political rights in Canada, see Cleverdon (1974) and Bacchi (1983).

4. See Young (2013, p. 254) on the firsts achieved by Canadian women at the federal level as well as the articles in Trimble, Arscott, and Tremblay (2013) on the firsts achieved at the provincial, territorial, and municipal levels.

5. For the numbers of women who ran in all federal elections since 1921, see Canada, Library of Parliament (2018).

6. More research needs to be conducted specifically on the legislative representation of visible minority and Indigenous women at the provincial and territorial levels.

7. The decrease from 40% to 32% can be attributed to the addition of 30 seats to the House of Commons as of 2015 (Tolley, 2015, para. 5).

8. As Everitt (2017) notes, when it comes to the recruitment of diverse federal candidates, the Liberal Party and especially the New Democratic Party have been more proactive than the Conservative Party.

9. Danna Kennedy-Glans, a former Progressive Conservative MLA, also quit the leadership race on the grounds that Alberta politics had become too polarized and antagonistic to centrist viewpoints (Anderson, 2016, para. 20).

10. Federal MPs Jenny Kwann and Bardish Chagger also received hateful tweets (Mansbridge, 2016).

11. Although no province currently has a woman premier, all three territories and all provinces but four (Manitoba, Saskatchewan, Nova Scotia, and New Brunswick) previously had a woman premier.

12. The main gender quota types are compulsory reserved seats (whereby seats can only be held by women), legislated electoral gender quotas (requiring all parties to present gender-balanced candidate slates), and voluntary party quotas (whereby political parties specify the percentage of women candidates they intend to present in upcoming elections). See International Institute for Democracy and Electoral Assistance, 2018.

13. Regarding the presence of women in national legislatures worldwide, the Inter-Parliamentary Union (2018) ranks Rwanda and Bolivia as first and third, and the United States, Canada, and Australia as 102nd, 60th, and 50th. While the United States and New Zealand do not have any mandatory voluntary gender quotas in place and Ireland recently passed a law requiring parties to include a minimum of 30% women and men candidates, some of the more left-leaning Canadian, Australian, and British parties have voluntary quotas (International Institute for Democracy and Electoral Assistance, 2018).

KEY READINGS

Equal Voice. (2017). Retrieved from https://equalvoice.ca/

Harell, A. (2017). Intersectionality and gendered political behaviour in a multicultural Canada. *Canadian Journal of Political Science*, *50*(2), 495–514.

International Institute for Democracy and Electoral Assistance, Inter-Parliamentary Union, and Stockholm University. (2018). Gender quotas database. Retrieved from http://www.idea.int/data-tools/data/gender-quotas

Trimble, L., Raphael, D., Sampert, S., Wagner, A., & Gerrits, B. (2015). Politicizing bodies: Hegemonic masculinity, heteronormativity, and racism in news representations of Canadian political party leadership candidates. *Women's Studies in Communication*, *28*(3), 314–330.

Trimble, L., Arscott, J., & Tremblay, M. (Eds.). (2013). *Stalled: The representation of women in Canadian governments*. Vancouver: UBC Press.

DISCUSSION QUESTIONS

1. What are the main challenges facing diverse women politicians in Canada today? What policies need to be implemented to enable them to overcome these challenges?
2. Why and to what extent is cyberbullying of women politicians likely to deter diverse women from considering a career in politics?
3. What short-, medium-, and long-term strategies can be effective in countering cyberbullying?
4. Should Canada adopt a law to require federal political parties to present an equal number of women and men candidates, reflecting the diversity of the Canadian population? Why or why not?

REFERENCES

Anderson, D. (2016, November 8). Donna Kennedy-Glans and Sandra Jansen drop out of Alberta PC leadership race. *CBC News*. Retrieved from http://www.cbc.ca/news/canada/calgary/sandra-jansen-donna-kennedy-glans-drop-out-1.3842548

Bacchi, C. L. (1983). *Liberation deferred? The ideas of the English Canadian suffragists, 1977–1918*. Toronto: University of Toronto Press.

Bashevkin, S. (2009). *Women, power, politics: The story of Canada's unfinished democracy*. Don Mills, ON: Oxford University Press.

Beaman, L., Pande, R., & Cirone, A. (2012). Politics as a male domain and empowerment in India. In S. Franceschet, M. L. Krook, & J. M. Piscopo (Eds.), *The impact of gender quotas* (pp. 208–226). New York: Oxford University Press.

Boesveld, S. (2018, June 6). Surprise result from Doug Ford's win: There are now more women in Queen's Park. *Chatelaine*. Retrieved from https://www.chatelaine.com/news/ontario-election-women/

Burnet, J. (2012). Women's empowerment and cultural change in Rwanda. In S. Franceschet, M. L. Krook, & J. M. Piscopo (Eds.), *The impact of gender quotas* (pp. 190–207). New York: Oxford University Press.

Canada, Library of Parliament. (2018). History of federal ridings since 1867: Women candidates in general elections—1921 to date. Retrieved from https://lop.parl.ca/About/Parliament/FederalRidingsHistory/hfer.asp?Language=E&Search=WomenElection

Carbert, L. (2009). Are cities more congenial? Tracking the rural deficit of women in the House of Commons. In S. Bashevkin (Ed.), *Opening doors wider: Women's political engagement in Canada* (pp. 70–92). Vancouver: UBC Press.

Carbert, L. & Black, N. (2013). Electoral breakthrough: Women in Nova Scotia politics. In L. Trimble, J. Arscott, & M. Tremblay (Eds.), *Stalled: The representation of women in Canadian governments* (pp. 135–153). Vancouver: UBC Press.

Cleverdon, C. L. (1974). *The woman suffrage movement in Canada* (2nd ed.). Toronto: University of Toronto Press.

Coole, D. (1993). *Women in political theory* (2nd ed.). Boulder, CO: Lynne Rienner.

Crawley, M. (2017, January 25). Premier Kathleen Wynne bombarded on social media by homophobic, sexist abuse. *CBC News*. Retrieved from http://www.cbc.ca/news/canada/toronto/kathleen-wynne-twitter-abuse-1.3949657

Curry, B. (2011, March 27). Canada's first social media election is on, but will people vote? *Globe and Mail*. Retrieved from https://www.theglobeandmail.com/news/politics/canadas-first-social-media-election-is-on-but-will-people-vote/article574263/

Dahlerup, D., & Freidenvall, L. (2005). Quotas as a "fast track" to equal representation for women: Why Scandinavia is no longer the model. *International Feminist Journal of Politics*, 7(1), 26–48.

Desmarais, A. (2018, June 1). Diversifying Canada's most diverse Parliament. *IPolitics*. Retrieved from https://ipolitics.ca/article/diversifying-canadas-most-diverse-parliament/

Elections Canada. (2017a). The evolution of the federal franchise. Retrieved from http://www.elections.ca/content.aspx?section=vot&dir=bkg&document=ec90785&lang=e

Elections Canada. (2017b). A history of the vote in Canada. Chapter 2: From a privilege to a right, 1867–1919. Retrieved from http://www.elections.ca/content.aspx?section=res&dir=his&document=chap2&lang=e#a27

Everitt, J. (2017). Where are the women in Canadian political parties? In A.-G. Gagnon & A. B. Tanguay (Eds.), *Canadian parties in transition* (4th ed., pp. 296–315). Toronto: University of Toronto Press.

Fraser, E. (2018, September 25). New Brunswick voters send 11 female MLAs to legislature. *CBC News*. Retrieved from https://www.cbc.ca/news/canada/new-brunswick/new-brunswick-election-female-mlas-1.4835184

Ghoussoub, M. (2017, May 11). 111 women ran in BC's election, just 34 were elected. *CBC News*. Retrieved from http://www.cbc.ca/news/canada/british-columbia/111-women-ran-in-b-c-s-election-just-34-were-elected-1.4111156

International Institute for Democracy and Electoral Assistance, Inter-Parliamentary Union, and Stockholm University. (2018). Gender quotas database. Retrieved from http://www.idea.int/data-tools/data/gender-quotas

Inter-Parliamentary Union. (2018). Women in national parliaments: Situation as of 1st June 2018. Retrieved from http://www.ipu.org/wmn-e/classif.htm

Jenaro, C., Flores, N., & Frías, C.P. (2018). Systematic review of empirical studies on cyberbullying in adults: What we know and what we should investigate. *Aggressive and Violent Behavior, 38*, 113–122. doi.org/10.1016/j.avb.2017.12.003

Legislative Assembly of Nunavut. (2018). Members of the legislative assembly. Retrieved from http://www.assembly.nu.ca/members/mla

Mansbridge, P. (Host). (2016, December 1). Hateful tweets. *At Issue* [Television panel]. Canadian Broadcasting Corporation. Retrieved from http://www.cbc.ca/player/play/822542403674

Martin, N. (2016, June 6). MLA says her office threatened with phone call. *Winnipeg Free Press*. Retrieved from https://www.winnipegfreepress.com/local/mla-says-her-office-threatened-with-phone-call-383671751.html

McConnell, R. (2016, November 22). Impassioned Sandra Jansen calls on legislature to stand against misogyny. *CBC News*. Retrieved from http://www.cbc.ca/news/canada/edmonton/impassioned-sandra-jansen-calls-on-legislature-to-stand-against-misogyny-1.3863097

Norris, P., & Lovenduski, J. (1995). *Political recruitment: Gender, race, and class in the British Parliament*. Cambridge, UK: Cambridge University Press.

Okin, S. M. (1979). *Women in Western political thought*. Princeton, NJ: Princeton University Press.

O'Neill, B. (2015). Unpacking gender's role in political representation in Canada. *Canadian Parliamentary Review*, (Summer), 22–30. Retrieved from http://revparl.ca/38/2/38n2e_15_ONeill.pdf

Patten, S. (2013). Assessing the potential of new social media. *Canadian Parliamentary Review, 36*(2), 21–26. Retrieved from http://www.revparl.ca/36/2/36n2_13e_Patten.pdf

Perrot, M. (1997). *Femmes publiques*. Paris: Textuel.

Prince Edward Island Coalition for Women in Government. (2018). How does PEI compare? Percentage of women in provincial, territorial and national legislatures. Retrieved from https://www.peiwomeningovernment.ca/

Sarna, G., & Bhatia, M. (2017). Content-based approach to find the credibility of user in social networks: An application of cyberbullying. *International Journal of Machine Learning and Cybernetics, 8*(2), 677–689.

Small, T. (2017). Two decades of digital party politics in Canada: An assessment. In A.-G. Gagnon & A. B. Tanguay (Eds.), *Canadian parties in transition* (4th ed., pp. 388–308). Toronto: University of Toronto Press.

Statistics Canada. (2015). Table 9: Percentage of women among university graduates, by field of study, Canada, 1992 and 2008. Retrieved from https://www150.statcan.gc.ca/n1/pub/89-503-x/2010001/article/11542/tbl/tbl009-eng.htm

Tolley, E. (2015, November 26). Visible minority and Indigenous members of Parliament. *The Samara Blog.* Retrieved from http://www.samaracanada.com/samarablog/blog-post/samara-main-blog/2015/11/26/visible-minority-and-indigenous-members-of-parliament

Tremblay, M. (2013). Hitting a glass ceiling? Women in Quebec politics. In L. Trimble, J. Arscott, & M. Tremblay (Eds.), *Stalled: The representation of women in Canadian governments* (pp. 192–213). Vancouver: UBC Press.

Trimble, L., Arscott, J., & Tremblay, M. (Eds.). (2013). *Stalled: The representation of women in Canadian governments.* Vancouver: UBC Press.

Tukker, P. (2016, November 8). After election, Yukon boasts 2nd-highest proportion of female MLAs. *CBC News.* Retrieved from https://www.cbc.ca/news/canada/north/yukon-election-women-mlas-first-nations-1.3842656

Valiante, G. (2018, October 6). After election, Quebec leads Canada in women in office: Analysts. *CTV News.* Retrieved from https://montreal.ctvnews.ca/after-election-quebec-leads-canada-in-women-in-office-analysts-1.4124053

Wood, J. (2016, November 17). Sandra Jansen crosses floor to NDP benches. *Calgary Sun.*

World Economic Forum. (2016). The global gender gap report 2016: Canada. Retrieved from http://reports.weforum.org/global-gender-gap-report-2016/economies/#economy=CAN

Young, L. (2013). Slow to change: Women in the House of Commons. In L. Trimble, J. Arscott, & M. Tremblay (Eds.), *Stalled: The representation of women in Canadian governments* (pp. 253–272). Vancouver: UBC Press.

CHAPTER 13

Women, Aesthetic Labour, and Retail Work: A Case Study of Independent Fashion Retailers in Toronto

Deborah Leslie and Taylor Brydges

INTRODUCTION

Retail work is the largest sector of employment in Canada (Coulter, MacEwen, & Rawal, 2016). Like other interactive service occupations, it is characterized by precarious working conditions, including low pay, unpredictable hours, and a constant need to perform emotional or aesthetic labour (Warhurst & Nickson, 2007; Warhurst, Nickson, Witz, & Cullen, 2000). Emotional and aesthetic labour refer to the requirement that women adopt a certain personality and appearance as part of the job. This form of labour is highly gendered. In 2015, 59% of retail workers in Ontario were female, and nowhere is this more prominent than in fashion retail (Coulter et al., 2016). Compared to other products, fashion involves gendered performances. In the case of women's fashion boutiques, retail workers are required to perform and display appropriate codes of femininity, including a feminine appearance. In fashion retail, the product being sold—in this case, clothing—is literally worn on the body, and becomes part of a woman's gendered identity. Retail work also relates to divisions of race and class. Retail workers are predominantly white and middle class, and workers of colour are often subject to ethnic and racial discrimination (Coulter et al., 2016). The intersections of gender, race, and class are therefore central to retail work in women's fashion boutiques. *Intersectionality* refers to the notion that different identities—related to gender, race, class, and sexuality—are not separate or discrete. They cannot be simply added to one another or layered on top of one another. Rather, they intersect and blur into one another (Crenshaw, 1991). The experience of one changes another, making the effect of different subjectivities transformative.

This chapter examines the nature of employment in independent women's fashion boutiques. Drawing on the literature on aesthetic labour, it explores the ways in which working in independent fashion retail differs from employment in mass market chain stores for women's apparel, and the implications for the nature of women's work. While labour practices in independent women's fashion boutiques allow owners and employees to carve out greater space for autonomy and self-expression compared to chain store employees, this chapter examines how the work incorporates a heavy emphasis on individual aesthetics and design sensibilities and the unstable and precarious nature of this work.

The chapter draws on 35 semistructured interviews conducted between 2008 and 2015 with female retail owners, managers, and employees of independent fashion boutiques in Toronto. Interviews were one to two hours in length and were digitally recorded, transcribed, and coded according to themes. Retail establishments included small stores selling both new and vintage clothing in downtown neighbourhoods (including Queen Street West, Ossington Avenue, and Dundas Street West).

Many boutiques are concentrated in and around the arts and cultural district of Queen West. Over the last 20 years, this neighbourhood has become a primary destination for hip alternative retailers in the city, with the district recently being declared one of the "coolest in the world" (Remsen, 2014). However, as the neighbourhood has become increasingly expensive, some independent retailers have chosen to move one block north to Dundas Street West (Brydges, 2013). The Dundas West neighbourhood slowly began to undergo transformation around 2010, with the gradual expansion of independent retailers, restaurants, and cafés alongside the long-standing Portuguese establishments in the area (Brydges, 2013). Some retail businesses also shifted to Ossington Avenue, another emerging independent retail and restaurant quarter (Lontoc, 2015).

The first part of the chapter explores the nature of aesthetic labour. The second section examines women's aesthetic labour in the retail sector, highlighting the need for brand conformity in corporate chain stores, and the gendered nature of bodily performances. The third section explores the nature of work and aesthetics in alternative retailing, which includes small independent fashion boutiques, and examines how work in those boutiques is less controlled, leaving more room for a self-imposed aesthetic. In this setting, close relationships between female workers and customers can form. Finally, despite the heavy emphasis placed on autonomy and aestheticized labour, the chapter highlights the distinct ways in which this work remains risky and precarious.

AESTHETIC LABOUR

The notion of aesthetic labour derives from Hochschild's (1983) classic work on **emotional labour**, which she defines as "the management of [one's own] feeling to create a publicly observable facial and bodily display" (p. 7). Emotional labour is particularly important in interactive service occupations such as retail, hospitality, call centres, and health care (McDowell, 2009). In these sectors, workers are hired for personality traits such as adaptability, professionalism, and friendliness (Warhurst et al., 2000). As this work involves managing deep feelings and emotions (Hochschild, 1983), organizations create rules to prescribe what constitutes appropriate emotional engagement between employees and customers (Warhurst & Nickson, 2009). Employees are encouraged to appear positive at all times, waging what Hochschild (1983) refers to as a "war of smiles" (p. 127).

The literature on emotional labour contributes greatly to an understanding of how working women's feelings are appropriated and managed in the service sector. However, some researchers suggest that the literature on emotional labour tends to neglect the importance of the body (Warhurst & Nickson, 2007, 2009; Warhurst et al., 2000; Witz, Warhurst, & Nickson, 2003). As a result, others use the term *aesthetic labour* to foreground the "embodied capacities and attributes possessed by workers" (Warhurst et al., 2000, p. 4). *Aesthetic labour* refers to "how the corporeality, not just the feelings, of employees are organizationally appropriated and transmuted for commercial benefit. This embodiment is intended to appeal to the senses of customers, creating affective service-interaction based, typically, on having employees perceived to be 'good looking' or simply having the 'right look'" (Warhurst & Nickson, 2009, p. 386). It is argued that customer interaction depends as much on "styles of the flesh" as it does on manufactured feelings (Butler, 1990).

In service workplaces, symbolic values are attached to female workers' bodies. These values are a manifestation of a particular social location (Bourdieu, 1993). As Witz, Warhurst, and Nickson (2003) note, "embodied dispositions ... are not equally distributed socially, but fractured by class, gender, age and racialized positions or locations" (p. 41). These identities intersect, influencing who is hired for particular jobs. Embodied dispositions include ways of walking, talking, standing, and feeling (Witz et al., 2003), and refer to patterns of language and dress as well as manners, style, and the size and shape of the body (Warhurst et al., 2000). These dispositions vary by gender, class, race, sexuality, and other modalities.

For example, in their work on a London hotel, McDowell, Batnitzky, and Dyer (2007) find that gender, nationality, clothing style, and skin colour all figure prominently in recruitment. Employers hold stereotypical assumptions about who is appropriate for particular kinds of work, whether that be having the physical strength necessary for particular jobs or corresponding to acceptable versions of masculinity and femininity (McDowell et al., 2007). These assumptions are manifest in the allocation of individuals (with different embodied and social characteristics) to different positions.

Gendered and racialized assumptions about who is appropriate for particular kinds of work run through the fashion industry, which employs a large number of women but is known for a dearth of ethnic and racial minorities. The majority of fashion designers, models, journalists, retail buyers, and merchandising managers are white (Friedman, 2015). Women constitute the majority of fashion school student bodies and the industry's labour force (Business of Fashion, 2016, 2017). However, women are more likely to be found in entry-level creative positions, while male designers historically and presently dominate the highest positions in many of the most influential global fashion brands.

Workers undergo a process of "interpellation," whereby they are influenced by a particular ideology (Althusser, 1972, p. 174). Employees feel called to particular jobs and come to recognize themselves in these positions. Identities are not inherent to the individual, but are constituted in social interactions, including at work (McDowell et al., 2007).

Service work is unique in that it entails an interaction with a customer, who also holds ideas about who is appropriate for particular jobs. There is therefore a process of dual interpellation, whereby workers have to look the part and be perceived as appropriate by both customers and managers. Employees must conform to beliefs about the suitability of different types of work for people with differently classed, gendered, and raced bodies (McDowell et al., 2007).

While employers recruit and hire workers with the appropriate social and bodily characteristics, they further develop these dispositions to fit the brand and identity of their organization. They do this through training and monitoring, as well as through discipline and reward systems designed to ensure that employees adopt a particular style of service (Warhurst & Nickson, 2007). Workers are instructed in how to act, dress, and stand and what to say. This is particularly the case in retail work, where retail organizations play an important role in constructing workers' gendered, classed, and racialized identities.

AESTHETIC LABOUR IN FASHION RETAIL

Similar to other interactive service workers, retail workers are recruited on the basis of ascribed characteristics related to gender, age, class, race, and ethnicity (Adkins, 1995; Pettinger, 2004). In a survey of retail workers in Ontario, Coulter, MacEwen, and Rawal (2016) found that gender is the most important factor that determines who is hired in retail work, and that women's perceived attractiveness is particularly important in who gets hired. They found that race and ethnicity also come into play, with some employers tending to hire predominantly white or Asian workers. In fact, their 2015 survey found that 82% of retail workers in Ontario were white.

Like other female-dominated sectors, retail salaries are low, varying in Ontario from about $14 to $25 an hour. The lowest salaries go to cashiers, 86% of whom are women in Ontario, and sales and service workers, 59% of whom are women (Coulter et al., 2016). A high percentage of retail workers are employed part-time. In 2015 only 13% of retail workers were unionized (Coulter et al., 2016). Gender segregation is a key issue in this sector. Men are often hired for full-time stockroom or management positions, while women are hired on a part-time basis for customer service jobs (Coulter et al., 2016). Female sales assistants tend to serve female customers and to sell products that are culturally coded as "female" (Pettinger, 2005). Pettinger (2005) argues that this is most clearly illustrated in clothing, where garments are highly gendered as well as categorized by age and class.

Fashion retailing involves particular attention to performance and the body (Leslie, 2002). As Entwistle (2000) suggests, "Fashion is about bodies: it is produced, promoted and worn by bodies. It is the body that fashion speaks to and it is the body that must be dressed in almost all social encounters" (p. 1). Compared to other retail employees, fashion workers are more likely to work in order to procure a store discount to purchase clothes, muddying distinctions between work and consumption (Leslie, 2002; Pettinger, 2005).

Store policies dictate guidelines concerning weight and appearance, and employees are often expected to wear the products they sell (Leslie, 2002). As Pettinger (2005) puts it, "In modelling the stock for sale, workers are implicated in the sales environment as consumers as well as workers and their gendered identities are an important part of this. This relies on 'aesthetic labour,' an investment of skill, knowledge, time, money and energy into performing femininity" (pp. 474–475). The worker signifies what is fashionable and how the consumer will look in the "right" clothes (Pettinger, 2004).

Women who work in clothing retail often follow a sales routine that involves greeting the customer within a specified period of time and asking questions about what they are looking for. They provide product information, take items to the changing room, and suggest add-on sales.

Employees are trained in how to position their bodies in space. They are not allowed to sit, slouch, or lean on counters (Leslie, 2002). There are clear parallels with the catwalk and photographic modelling, where women are expected to stand and pose for hours. The company often dictates accessories, including jewellery, makeup, and hair style (Pettinger, 2005).

Ultimately, women's physical capital is converted into economic capital by service employers, who use embodied attributes as a source of competitive advantage (Warhurst & Nickson, 2007). As Entwistle and Wissinger (2006) put it, "Workers' bodies are harnessed to sell the organization's image, literally by embodying it" (p. 775). This is especially the case with women's bodies. Thus, *aesthetics* refers both to corporate hardware—including product design and the physical environment of the store—and to human hardware, including female workers' bodies (Pettinger, 2004).

Research indicates that styles of embodiment vary by retail brand. Rather than simply recruiting aesthetic labour, employers seek physical qualities that are aestheticized in particular ways and in keeping with the store brand.

Hall and Van den Broek (2012) extend this argument, dividing women's clothing stores into three categories: boutique style stores, which are very style conscious but not very cost conscious; mass market stores, which are both style and cost conscious; and value fashion shops, which are cost conscious but not very style conscious. They conclude that the regulation of appearance and aestheticized labour is greatest in boutique stores, which rely on higher levels of personal service. In these environments, there are very specific clothing policies for employees, designed to promote the store's clothing. Female workers receive extensive training in appearance and presentation in order to develop aesthetic skills. This is reflected in employee appraisals, which reward success in these areas.

Ironically, Hall and Van den Broek (2012) find that although aesthetic demands are heaviest on workers employed in fashion boutiques, these employers do not pay a premium wage. Managers claim that workers benefit by being associated with a desirable brand and having access to store discounts. Control rests with management, and the work remains highly precarious. As Hall and Van den Broek (2012) argue, "Rather than an emerging labour aristocracy, aestheticizing labour strategies are, first and foremost, managerial strategies in which employers define the aesthetic attributes they want and the terms of their commodification" (p. 100).

AESTHETIC LABOUR IN INDEPENDENT FASHION RETAILING IN TORONTO

Aesthetic labour varies by brand, type of store, and geography. Pettinger (2004) finds that urban stores tend to have a more racially and ethnically diverse workforce than suburban stores. Similarly, urban stores often sell brands marketed as more "cutting edge" or "alternative," and employees are expected to embody this image. Pettinger concludes, "Not only do aestheticized labour demands vary between organizations, geography affects taste for fashion and the precise market niche is subtly different in different places" (p. 179).

These differences between brand, market segment, and geography raise questions about women's aesthetic labour in smaller, independently owned fashion boutiques. These stores sell highly aestheticized products and demand considerable aesthetic knowledge and labour; however, they are not controlled by a larger corporate entity or brand.

In recent years, there has been a polarization in the fashion industry. At one end of the spectrum, there has been growth in national and international chains marketing "fast fashion," a system whereby firms copy the latest trends from fashion runways and transform them into lower-cost versions (Reinach, 2005). The idea is to sell designer-inspired high fashion at an accessible price. Products are often of lower quality and designed to be discarded after a few wearings. Product ranges are heavily branded and sold according to a chain/franchise model.

At the other end of the spectrum, there has also been growth in small independent women's fashion boutiques (Crewe & Forster, 1993; Leslie, Brydges, & Brail, 2015). These stores offer higher quality and design-oriented goods, made in smaller batches. Independent fashion boutiques sell both new and used or retro clothes. Often these are combined in the same shop, indicating a blurring of these categories. Independent retailers cultivate closer relationships with manufacturers and consumers. Many stores sell the work of local designers, and tend to be associated with bohemian downtown neighbourhoods, known for alternative retailing experiences, rather than malls or main streets.

Similar to chain stores, these alternative retailers are highly gendered (Leslie et al., 2015). Stores are often started by a female entrepreneur with an eye for fashion. In some cases, retail shops are owned by a designer and provide an out- let for showcasing her designs, as well as the work of other local designers. The owner of the store often works on the sales floor, getting to know the aesthetic preferences of her customer base. In some cases, owners hire additional female staff to assist them. In these situations, worker and owner work alongside one another. Assistants are often local fashion design students completing intern- ships or recent graduates.

Small independent boutiques are dominated by women. A majority of own- ers, workers, and consumers are white. There are parallels here with designer fashion, as well as with "indie" culture more generally, including independent fashion and music. These sectors are characterized by a culture of whiteness (Berlatsky, 2015; Sahim, 2015).

Self-Imposed Aesthetic Labour

In this section, we draw on interviews with female owners, managers, and employees of independent fashion boutiques in Toronto to consider the ways that they reflect broader trends in aesthetic labour. As this section will demonstrate, aesthetic labour in independent fashion retailers is different in several ways. First, it tends to be self-imposed by women, rather than dictated by a corpor- ate entity. Second, it relies on higher levels of female-oriented customer service. Finally, despite differences, retail employment in small independent boutiques remains precarious for female employees, albeit in unique ways.

In corporate or chain fashion retail stores, employees are expected to follow their employer's style. This can include requiring employees to follow scripts or mapping out where they stand in the store (Witz et al., 2003). In the corporate retail context, rigid policies also dictate acceptable aesthetic and bodily character- istics in order to have employees represent the store appropriately (Leslie, 2002).

How do employees conduct themselves in the absence of a broader corporate or brand aesthetic? In the case of small independent fashion boutiques, women have to take responsibility for managing their bodies and their look. Women's bodies may not be prescribed in relation to a corporate image, but employees still have to adhere to aesthetic codes and look the part, which entails having the appropriate cultural capital. *Cultural capital* refers to the social and cultural assets an individual holds, which may be related to education, knowledge, style, and dress (Bourdieu, 1993). In the case of fashion retail, this includes knowledge of fashion trends and names in the business, as well as wearing fashionable clothes and having a sense of style (Entwistle, 2006).

In the case of alternative retailers, it is the individual female entrepreneur (who is often also a retail employee herself) who must create and manage her own style. This is a much more individual and idiosyncratic process. Female owners adopt a self-governed and personal aesthetic and translate it into a retail space. As one owner noted, "The store is my style. The only thing I can offer is my taste. I wouldn't know how to do it any other way." Fashion and aesthetic labour are described as a labour of love, as self-driven and a manifestation of an individual's unique talents and sense of self. Another female owner said, "This is what I'll do forever. People sometimes ask what I will do if this doesn't work out. I can't imagine anything else. It is engrained in my brain. ... I love fashion. I love style. I love people. I love the fast pace. It's totally me."

Unlike chain stores, where there is a higher degree of dissonance between the aesthetic the female worker is forced to adopt and her own personal style, in independent retailing, one's aesthetic sensibility and aesthetic labour are in greater alignment. In turn, this can become a source of pride for owners, as one boutique owner explained: "The most rewarding aspect of running my own business has been the reception to the store. Whenever I have someone come in and say that they love this place, or that it is their favourite shop in the city, or how they love the clothes in here and that no one else in Toronto has them, it is really rewarding."

When hiring employees, owners reported that it was important that their shop clerks share their interest in fashion in addition to being capable on the retail floor. One store owner looked for these characteristics when hiring: "The girls that work in the store have to be independent, ... honest and self-motivated, because they often work alone. Most of them are young and are either in a fashion program or figuring out what they want to do. They have to have a knowledge of fashion, but also, they have to be really interested in it."

In independent retailers, women working on the shop floor must curate and qualify aesthetic goods as well as embody alternative styles and aesthetics and display their knowledge of fashion on their bodies. Tacit aesthetic knowledge is thus a key requirement (Entwistle, 2006). This is knowledge that can only be learned by observing, doing, or being embedded in dense cultural networks and sources of information about the latest trends. As Entwistle (2009) notes, this is "an embodied knowledge; worn on the body of those who calculate it and 'travelling' with them along global networks. That fashion's tacit aesthetic knowledge is embodied through style is not surprising: here we have a market concerned *with*, and oriented *towards*, bodies" (pp. 162–163; emphasis in original). During interviews, retailers also discussed the importance of women dressing well and looking stylish, both when they were in the shop and on the street, and were aware of how their style can serve as inspiration to their customer, who is often interested in their expertise.

Interestingly, while alternative retailers are more flexible in terms of accepted styles for their female staff, it is still important that everyone on the shop floor represent the brands carried by the store and the overall aesthetic. As one manager noted, "We expect the staff to wear [the brand] while at work, like ... a uniform. We give employees a clothing allowance each season. If someone is new, they might be stuck wearing the same thing every day, but we [other employees] share with them if we have something we don't wear anymore. Some of the younger staff really like the clothing, but it isn't their personal style. So, they dress one way at work and a little differently afterwards." Thus, as in chain stores, workers have to wear store merchandise even if it doesn't mesh with their own personal identity.

The aesthetic and style of a shop is not accidental, but rather is carefully crafted and maintained. As one retailer describes, she always feels like she is working: "Whether it's reading the latest magazines, following blogs, or being out at parties, it may not seem like work, but it's hugely important to the business."

Alternative retailers must also demonstrate and maintain their aesthetic online. Social media is a very important tool for independent retailers, as this woman shop owner explained: "I'm on ... Instagram, Twitter, Facebook all day long. I have over 800 Instagram photos. It's important to be very, very active and make it worth someone's time to check out your profile. You have to make that connection between social media and your customer. I have people come into the store who say ... it's because of something they've seen online." Aesthetic labour is thus not confined to the store, but stretches into other times and spaces, including online (Hracs & Leslie, 2013). In this sense, owners (and their employees who assist them in staying on top of social media) are forced to be "always on" (Entwistle & Wissinger, 2006). Unlike corporate workers who can walk away from their job at the end of the day, independent female retail owners and workers cannot necessarily distance themselves from the need to perform a particular aesthetic or style.

It is not enough to merely create a cool and alternative aesthetic. This image must be validated and affirmed by others in the fashion community. Many alternative independent retailers reported regularly attending fashion and arts events in the city, such as Toronto Fashion Week or charity galas. Being featured as one of the best dressed in the city in the society pages of a local newspaper or fashion magazine that reports on these events can further the image of the retailer and her store. As one owner noted, "We do not use traditional advertising, but we've been blessed with a lot of press, which has really helped our brand. People come in and say it is because they saw us in [the magazines] *Flare* or *Toronto Life*."

Therefore, garnering a reputation for style extends aesthetic labour beyond the boundaries of the sales floor into all aspects of one's everyday life. To be successful, these women must become "entrepreneurs of the self" (Entwistle & Wissinger, 2006). Individuals become their own "micro-structures," which means constant self-monitoring (McRobbie, 2002). The development of this kind of style presence in the local scene helps an alternative retailer to "stand out in the crowd" (Hracs, Jakob, & Hauge, 2013). This strategy distinguishes them from other retailers in a competitive retail landscape.

Therefore, like branded chain retailers, independent female owners and their employees engage in a highly aestheticized form of labour. However, unlike chain store employees, this aesthetic labour is more autonomous. Employees must monitor their own look and image, and they do this in a wide variety of spaces.

Building Personal Relationships with Customers

The self-service model has become increasingly common among corporate retailers. Many consumers have become accustomed to shopping alone or with minimal intervention from sales staff. In alternative retailers, highly personalized customer service is a key source of value and distinction (Leslie et al., 2015).

In interviews, retailers and their employees described establishing close long-term relationships with their female customers, a majority of whom are white and middle class. They employ a number of strategies to cultivate loyalty, such as exclusive events, customer appreciation parties, and occasional gifts with purchase. Most important, however, is honest and supportive customer service. Employees argue that it is crucial to build long-term relationships with their female clientele. As one boutique manager explained, "We nurture our customers. ... We have an incredibly loyal clientele and we have made friends with lots of them. ... Because we design, make, and sell everything ourselves, we have a lot of freedom to make our customers happy. For example, we can accept a return of an item that has been worn if we feel like that's going to make the customer happy." As evidence that this strategy can be successful, one owner estimated that her customer base is made up of 85% repeat customers, including some customers who have shopped at the store for over 20 years.

Unlike corporate retailers, independent boutiques cultivate especially close relationships with female consumers in their surrounding area. One retailer stated, "People in the neighbourhood are very big supporters of small businesses. They are anticorporation in many cases. With the galleries, the creativity, you feel like it's an artistic place. The looks you see here, you wouldn't see in other parts of the city."

Building on this, another interviewee described the sense of community in alternative fashion neighbourhoods: "Many customers live in this neighbourhood. They're conscientious and want to support Canadian fashion. They like that on the way home you can stop by the store and see what's new, and then go to the grocery store and pick up bread and then head home."

Retailers also connected the customer service experience with positive affective bonds between women. Interacting with customers and helping them find clothing that they love is one of the most rewarding aspects of running their fashion retail establishment. One retail owner described the emotions this involves: "It might be easy to think, 'Am I making a difference in the world? People are just buying clothing and I'm taking their money.' But they are living their lives in our clothing, and it makes them feel good about themselves and gives them that confidence. That's important to me."

Independent retailers are thus characterized by high levels of personal service and knowledge, often acquired through training in accredited fashion design schools. Women invest a lot of emotional labour in crafting close long-term relationships with their female clientele, particularly in the surrounding neighbourhood.

Precarious Employment

While a career as an alternative or independent retailer involves high levels of embodied aesthetic knowledge and can provide the opportunity for a greater degree of freedom and autonomy, this work remains extremely precarious. Precarious employment is characterized by job instability, insecurity, a lack of protection, and social and economic vulnerability. There are clear parallels here with other forms of creative work.

Given that the majority of interviewees had no previous experience or education related to retail or running their own business, their lives are defined by insecurity. As one female owner reflected, "Starting your own business is so risky. You think, 'I work for myself, I'll make my own hours, I'll be my own boss.' It isn't glamorous. It's harder than you think. … I don't have any business degrees. I have art degrees. I'm learning … but it comes with a lot of mistakes."

A lack of assistance and mentorship contributes to the precariousness of this work. One boutique owner recounted, "I'm just one person. I manage the admin for the store, I set up, I merchandise, I run the events. … I don't have anyone to help or guide me. Sometimes I think about where the business could be now if I had support. I can only go for so long."

An average day in the life of an alternative retailer sheds light on just how many tasks must be completed on a regular basis. While these tasks are not necessarily unique to independent retailing, it is important to keep in mind that all of these tasks are the responsibility of one (or occasionally a few) individuals running the store, whereas in corporate retail, there are myriad people involved. As one female shop manager described,

> I come in and open the store. I tidy and organize the merchandise to make sure it looks great. When a customer comes in, that is the top priority. If I'm not helping a customer, I'm planning window displays, following up with customers or designers, researching brands, answering emails and making orders. The store will soon have a men's section, so I'll be organizing that, tagging new clothes that come in. … Then there is blogging, as well as going on Twitter and Instagram. There's just so much that needs to be done. And then within each task, there are subtasks that need to be completed.

Given the hectic schedules and demands placed on the individual retailer, burnout is a significant challenge for women. As a result, some interviewees described uncertainty about their future in retail. One retailer noted that an additional challenge of working in retail is that no matter how good a job one may be doing, the business is still reliant on unpredictable consumer spending patterns: "I don't think I want to be in retail forever. … It's a difficult industry. You can't predict what a day or a week or a month or a year looks like. You are dependent on people's spending habits. If someone is going to cut corners, it's probably going to be on clothes. Everyone is aware of their dollars and cents these days. … It is really hard when the store isn't doing as well as it could be."

Income is thus unpredictable for the owners, and a majority of female staff are paid low salaries. It is not uncommon for retail employees to work at least one other job in addition to their retail work. The second job is typically at a bar or restaurant so women can work evenings or on days when the retail shop is closed.

Some employees we interviewed were also preparing to launch their own fashion label. Boutique employees indicated that they perceived their employers to be flexible and supportive of their other paid work compared to corporate retail, for example, allowing them to come in early or late or change shifts at the last minute. Employees who are also students value this flexibility when school is busy, such as during exams.

Women working in independent fashion boutiques share many characteristics with women working in chain stores. Both forms of employment are precarious, albeit in differing ways. Like other forms of fashion retail, income can be low and unpredictable. Unlike other forms of fashion retail, the individual bears higher responsibility and risk and is forced to take on a greater array of roles. This can lead to high levels of stress and anxiety, particularly for female retail owners who are unsure about their ability to continue in this career path.

CONCLUSION

All retail workers perform aesthetic labour. Nowhere is this more pronounced than in women's fashion retail, where the selling of fashion products is intimately connected to the body. Fashion retail workers are recruited for their embodied physical and social characteristics, including their gender, race, and class. Once hired, women are subject to strict training regimes and policy scripts, which prescribe everything from behaviour to dress and movement.

The nature of aesthetic labour differs according to store brand, market segment, and location. In small independent women's fashion boutiques there is usually only one location and one or two owners with a handful of female employees. Like "indie" enterprises more generally, owners and workers tend to be white and middle class. All actors work together on the shop floor, blurring roles. In such circumstances, aesthetic labour, while very important, is more autonomous and self-directed. Female workers and owners carve out a more independent identity. In the process of selling, they draw on high levels of embodied tacit aesthetic knowledge and brand expertise. Unlike chain store employees, however, the aesthetic labour demands of boutique owners extend well beyond the geography of the sales floor to encompass online spaces, fashion shows, and gala events.

Women who work in independent chain stores cultivate closer and longer-term relationships with female consumers, particularly in surrounding upscale, white neighbourhoods. While subject to low pay and higher risk and insecurity, independent retailers face unique forms of precarity, including increased levels of responsibility and a constant need to multitask.

The desire to start one's own independent retail business, or to work for one, is a response to precarious labour markets as well as a component of them. A growing number of young women are seeking out more creative and independent careers in the service sector (Ocejo, 2010). Many female interviewees, particularly those who were highly educated and under 35, faced a tight labour market with limited job opportunities. Female entrepreneurship is a response to these challenges. In starting small shops or labouring in them, they are participating in new forms of gendered aesthetic labour, offering new possibilities for creativity and fulfillment, as well as new forms of exploitation and control of women.

KEY READINGS

Coulter, K., MacEwen, A. & Rawal, S. (2016). *The gender wage gap in Ontario's retail sector: Devaluing women's work and women workers*. Retrieved from https://revolutionizingretail .files.wordpress.com/2012/06/the-gender-wage-gap-in-ontarios-retail-sector-devaluing-womens-work-and-women-workers.pdf

Leslie, D. (2002). Gender, retail employment and the clothing commodity chain. *Gender, Place and Culture, 9*(1), 61–76.

Leslie, D., Brydges, T., & Brail, S. (2015). Qualifying aesthetic values in the experience economy: The role of independent fashion boutiques in curating slow fashion. In A. Lorentzen, K. Topso Larsen, & L. Schroder (Eds.), *Spatial dynamics in the experience economy* (pp. 88–102). New York: Routledge.

Pettinger, L. (2004). Brand culture and branded workers: Service work and aesthetic labour in fashion retail. *Consumption Markets & Culture, 7*(2), 165–184.

Pettinger, L. (2005). Gendered work meets gendered goods: Selling and service in clothing retail. *Gender, Work and Organization, 12*(5), 460–478.

DISCUSSION QUESTIONS

1. To what extent is aesthetic labour gendered? What different forms of gendered aesthetic labour do men and women perform across the economy? How does gender intersect with race, ethnicity, class, and sexuality in different forms of aesthetic labour?

2. How does aesthetic labour differ between fast-fashion chains targeted at women and independent fashion retailers?

3. How is aesthetic labour changing in an era of social media, and how are women in particular impacted by these shifts? What are the impacts of having to perform aesthetic labour in a wider array of times and spaces and being "always on"?

4.   How is the growth of small independent businesses like boutiques, restaurants, craft breweries, and bakeries a response to the precarious labour market, particularly for young female workers? How do these new forms of female entrepreneurship lead to new forms of precarity?

REFERENCES

Adkins, L. (1995). *Gendered work: Sexuality, family and the labour market.* Buckingham, UK: Open University Press.

Althusser, L. (1972). Ideology and ideological state apparatuses: Notes towards an investigation. In *Lenin and Philosophy and Other Essays* (pp. 121–176). New York: Monthly Review Press.

Berlatsky, N. (2015, April 2). Why "indie" music is so unbearably white. *New Republic.* Retrieved from https://newrepublic.com/article/121437/why-indie-music-so-unbearably-white

Bourdieu, P. (1993). *The field of cultural production: Essays on art and literature.* New York: Columbia University Press.

Brydges, T. (2013). *Redefining retail: A case study of independent fashion retailers in Dundas West, Toronto, Canada.* Research paper, Department of Geography and Planning, University of Toronto.

Business of Fashion and McKinsey and Company. (2017). The state of fashion 2017. *Business of Fashion.* Retrieved from https://www.businessoffashion.com/articles/intelligence/10-fashion-trends-define-agenda-2017

Butler, J. (1990). *Gender trouble: Feminism and the subversion of identity.* New York: Routledge.

Coulter, K., MacEwen, A., & Rawal, S. (2016). *The gender wage gap in Ontario's retail sector: Devaluing women's work and women workers.* Retrieved from https://revolutionizingretail.files.wordpress.com/2012/06/the-gender-wage-gap-in-ontarios-retail-sector-devaluing-womens-work-and-women-workers.pdf

Crenshaw, K. (1991). Mapping the margins: Intersectionality, identity politics, and violence against women of color. *Stanford Law Review, 43*(6), 1241–1299.

Crewe, L., & Forster, Z. (1993). Markets, design, and local agglomeration: The role of the small independent retailer in the workings of the fashion system. *Environment and Planning D: Society and Space, 11*(2), 213–229.

Entwistle, J. (2000). *The fashioned body: Fashion, dress and modern social theory.* London: Sage.

Entwistle, J. (2006). The aesthetic economy of fashion buying. *Current Sociology, 54*(5), 704–724.

Entwistle, J. (2009). *The aesthetic economy of fashion: Markets and value in clothing and modelling.* Oxford, UK: Berg.

Entwistle, J., & Wissinger, E. (2006). Keeping up appearances: Aesthetic labour in the fashion modelling industries of London and New York. *Sociological Review, 54*(4), 774–794.

Friedman, V. (2015, February 11). Fashion's racial divide. *New York Times*. Retrieved from https://www.nytimes.com/2015/02/12/fashion/fashions-racial-divide.html

Hall, R., & Van den Broek, D. (2012). Aestheticising retail workers: Orientations of aesthetic labour in Australian fashion retail. *Economic and Industrial Democracy*, *33*(1), 85–102.

Hochschild, A. (1983). *The managed heart: Communication of human feeling.* Berkeley: University of California Press.

Hracs, B. J., Jakob, D., & Hauge, A. (2013). Standing out in the crowd: The rise of exclusivity-based strategies to compete in the contemporary marketplace for music and fashion. *Environment and Planning A*, *45*(5), 1144–1161.

Hracs, B. J., & Leslie, D. (2013). Aesthetic labour in creative industries: The case of independent musicians in Toronto, Canada. *Area*, *46*(1), 66–73.

Leslie, D. (2002). Gender, retail employment and the clothing commodity chain. *Gender, Place and Culture*, *9*(1), 61–76.

Leslie, D., Brydges, T., & Brail, S. (2015). Qualifying aesthetic values in the experience economy: The role of independent fashion boutiques in curating slow fashion. In A. Lorentzen, K. T. Larsen, & L. Schroder (Eds.), *Spatial dynamics in the experience economy* (pp. 88–102). New York: Routledge.

Lontoc, R. (2015, June 11). A fashionista's guide to the best shopping on Ossington. *Post City Toronto*. Retrieved from http://www.postcity.com/Eat-Shop-Do/Shop/June-2015/A-fashionistas-guide-to-shopping-Ossington/

McDowell, L. (2009). *Working bodies: Interactive service employment and workplace identities.* Oxford, UK: Wiley-Blackwell.

McDowell, L., Batnitzky, A., & Dyer, S. (2007). Division, segmentation and interpellation: The embodied labours of migrant workers in a Greater London hotel. *Economic Geography*, *83*(1), 1–25.

McRobbie, A. (2002). Clubs to companies: Notes on the decline of political culture in speeded up creative worlds. *Cultural Studies*, *16*(4), 516–531.

Ocejo, R. E. (2010). What'll it be? Cocktail bartenders and the redefinition of service in the creative economy. *City, Culture and Society*, *1*(4), 179–184.

Pettinger, L. (2004). Brand culture and branded workers: Service work and aesthetic labour in fashion retail. *Consumption Markets & Culture*, *7*(2), 165–184.

Pettinger, L. (2005). Gendered work meets gendered goods: Selling and service in clothing retail. *Gender, Work and Organization*, *12*(5), 460–478.

Reinach, S. (2005). China and Italy: Fast fashion versus prêt à porter. Towards a new culture of fashion. *Fashion Theory: The Journal of Dress, Body & Culture*, *9*(1), 43–56.

Remsen, N. (2014, September 5). Mapping out the 15 coolest neighborhoods in the world. *Vogue*. Retrieved from http://www.vogue.com/slideshow/fifteen-coolest-street-style-neighborhoods

Sahim, S. (2015, March 25). The unbearable whiteness of indie. *Pitchfork*. Retrieved from https://pitchfork.com/thepitch/710-the-unbearable-whiteness-of-indie/

Warhurst, C., & Nickson, D. (2007). Employee experience of aesthetic labour in retail and hospitality. *Work, Employment & Society, 21*(1), 103–120.

Warhurst, C., & Nickson, D. (2009). "Who's got the look?" Emotional, aesthetic and sexualized labour in interactive services. *Gender, Work and Organization, 16*(3), 385–404.

Warhurst, C., Nickson, D., Witz, A., & Cullen, A. M. (2000). Aesthetic labour in interactive service work: Some case study evidence from the "new" Glasgow. *Service Industries Journal, 20*(3), 1–18.

Witz, A., Warhurst, C., & Nickson, D. (2003). The labour of aesthetics and the aesthetics of organization. *Organization, 10*(1), 33–54.

CHAPTER 14

From the Woman's Page to the Digital Age: Women in Journalism

Andrea Hunter

INTRODUCTION

Women have been making a living in journalism since the 1800s. Through their work they have made a significant contribution to women's rights, and at the same time, the evolution of women's role in our society is reflected in the growing role of women journalists as reporters and, to a more limited extent, as editors, producers, and executives. This chapter traces the history of women's participation in journalism; their advocacy on women's issues such as suffrage, education, and health; their entry into higher levels of print and broadcast media; and the sexism and harassment that women journalists have faced.

Journalism is a vital part of democracy, and thus journalists play a special role in society. Journalists act as "watchdogs" by questioning what politicians, business leaders, and other influential figures are doing in the world. Journalists often think of their work as a public service. They hope their reporting will help people make informed choices, whether it be deciding who to vote for in the next election or if they should try a new medical drug on the market. Journalists want to shine light on important stories that may otherwise go unnoticed and highlight injustices in the world. Investigative journalists in particular work to uncover problems and issues that need to be addressed. Journalists also help draw our attention to the wider world around us, putting themselves in conflict zones, covering wars, famines, and natural disasters. As Nicole Cohen (2016) writes,

"Journalism is a form of communication essential for meaningful participation in democratic life. Although today most journalism is produced as a commodity for private profit, in its ideal form it contributes to public discourse and debate, enables citizens to hold those in power to account, and provides space for debate about how to organize political, economic, and social life" (p. 7).

Journalists are especially important in today's "information society" (Hassan, 2008), where there is seemingly no end to news to be found on the Internet and social media. It can be difficult to distinguish between what is "fake news" (opinion) and what is "real news" (balanced, unbiased reporting). In this age of information overload, it is important to have trained journalists who try to take a fair and balanced approach to their reporting so that we are not inundated with one-sided stories and opinion masquerading as fact. Because of the vital role that journalism plays in society, it is also important to have people from diverse backgrounds working in newsrooms as reporters, editors, and managers. Who journalists are and where they come from affect what stories and issues they see as important. For this reason, it is important to have women as well as men represented in all aspects of journalism work.

While today anyone with an Internet connection can have a public platform for their ideas, pre-Internet journalists were gatekeepers who had a large say in what information made it into the public sphere through television, radio, and newspapers. Where this chapter begins, in the late 1800s and early 1900s, newspapers were the only type of media that existed. They were highly influential and extremely popular: in 1901 there were 112 newspapers in Canada and the number of newspapers in circulation every day exceeded the number of families in the country. This high circulation of newspapers was a "sure sign that Canada's first mass medium had arrived" (Rutherford, 1982, p. 5).

If you were to open up one of these first newspapers looking for female journalists, you would find most of them in the women's pages. Here you would read about the latest fashion, social events, or domestic issues that were deemed of interest to and acceptable reading for women. There were only a couple dozen women working as journalists at that time. Today, however, women can be found integrated into all aspects of media organizations, reporting on hard-hitting news alongside their male colleagues. Female journalists are in the field covering breaking news. They can be found at protests, in war zones, covering fires, or anywhere outside the newsroom where news is happening. They are editors overseeing newsrooms and assigning stories. To a lesser extent, they are managers, making big-picture decisions for news organizations. While there are still women who write about fashion and other lighter issues reminiscent of the women's pages over a century ago, some of the most recognized and award-winning Canadian journalists who cover breaking news and do investigative reporting, including political reporters and foreign correspondents, are women. Overall there has been a move toward gender parity with respect to the number of women working in journalism, their earnings, and the positions of power they occupy in news organizations. Yet female journalists still face many of the same challenges their predecessors did, including managing a work/life balance and childcare expectations, glass ceilings, and sexist treatment (Byerly, 2011; Smith, 2015).

THEORETICAL APPROACHES TO UNDERSTANDING WOMEN'S WORK

This chapter will use a feminist political economy lens to examine women's experience in journalism. This approach is concerned with power—who has it and who does not. It shines a light on women's role in society, particularly their work, paying attention to work that is largely taken on by women in present-day society, such as childcare and running the household. This work is often unpaid and therefore not recognized when governments and nations calculate their net worth (Waring, 1988). The feminist political economy approach argues that work such as childcare, meal preparation, laundry, and all the other seemingly small day-to-day chores that women do should be recognized as important and valuable work that ensures that our society can keep functioning. It also calls attention to the fact that much of this work still falls to women today, particularly childcare.

This chapter will also draw on the theory of **structuration** (Giddens, 1984; Mosco, 2009): the idea that we live within set social structures like norms, traditions, and moral codes that both constrain and enable us. We live under these structures and act accordingly, but at the same time we also have the power to influence them through our own individual will or "agency." Structuration finds its roots in Karl Marx's philosophy that "we do make history, but not under conditions of our own making" (Mosco, 2009, p. 185). We have agency—the ability to influence our surroundings—but we are born into social situations that we did not construct ourselves. Marx was thinking primarily about social class and whether people were born into the working class or elite, but this concept can be used to discuss other types of privilege, such as gender, race, and sexuality.

One critique of the political economy approach is that it has not paid enough attention to how other factors, such as gender and race, intersect with class (Mosco, 2009). Using structuration allows the political economist to address these issues, as well as others, such as age and sexuality. While a feminist political economy approach that uses structuration pays particular attention to gender, it has much in common with an intersectional approach in that it can be used to consider how race, age, sexuality, and other social conditions work together to shape women's experience.

The impact of the work of the first female journalists and the journalists who would come after them can be understood as fitting within the theory of structuration. As you will see through this chapter, female journalists through the years have been constrained by social conventions and norms that they also changed as they moved into journalism organizations in greater numbers.

THE WOMAN'S PAGE AND WOMEN'S PROGRAMMING: THE PERSONAL AND THE POLITICAL

When women first began working as journalists in the late 1800s and early 1900s both their political rights and the expectations of how they should live their lives were radically different from today. They could not vote or be elected to political office. Many people opposed higher education for women, as the overwhelming expectation was that women's place was at home, as wives and mothers (Freeman, 1989; Kay, 2012). As Kay (2012) describes, "There was a strong prejudice against women professionals and a matching belief that no woman should work after marriage. The image of a woman at home was the measure of respectability" (p. 3). The few dozen women who worked as journalists in Canada around 1900 were seen as "audacious" and as making a "political statement" (p. 3). Most of these first female journalists were hired to work on the women's pages. Although there were a few exceptions, such as Kit Coleman, who covered the Spanish-American conflict in the late 1800s for the *Toronto Mail*, for most part female journalists steered clear of "hard news," such as business and politics (Freeman, 1989).

The impetus to hire women in a time when working outside the home was generally frowned upon was financial. Newspapers were moving from being funded by political parties to becoming full-fledged businesses that depended on advertising for their survival. Women were hired specifically to draw in female readers. As Lang (1999) notes, "Not only would the female subscriber boost sales, but her allegiance would be especially attractive to advertisers. Women now purchased many of the commodities formerly produced in the home, and manufacturers acknowledged the increasing importance of housewives as consumers" (p. 32). Some of these writers became wildly popular.

Answering questions from readers about etiquette was an integral part of the women's pages, and these journalists garnered huge followings of readers who looked to them for advice on what to wear, how to act in social situations, and how to think about their role in the world (Lang, 1999). These female journalists were very aware of why they had been hired and that they were expected to appeal to a wide group of female readers. Newspapers were businesses that were trying to reach mass audiences of all classes. To contextualize what these women were doing in terms of structuration and agency, they were not supposed to ruffle any feathers, but many did resist prevailing social norms, using this space to advocate for women's rights, including suffrage and higher education. They saw themselves as teachers and the women's pages as a sort of university. They often tried to convince their editors that women were interested in more than just domestic issues. As Kay (2012) writes, "Born in the Victorian age, they walked a fine line with editors and readers between representing the new woman, open-minded and venturesome—which they were—while at the same time maintaining conventional societal norms that promoted marriage and motherhood as a woman's true calling" (p. 4).

For example, Kate Simpson Hayes, who wrote under the pseudonym Mary Markwell for the *Manitoba Free Press*, "praised a woman's place within the domestic sphere and venerated the role of wife and mother" in her writing (Kay, 2012, p. 20). But she was also a single mother who had left her husband and supported her children by working outside the home. Many of these women would also write carefully about the changes that were starting to occur in society, advocating for change in some areas, and being more hesitant in others. Journalist Kit Coleman, who was politically conservative and reluctant to support a woman's right to vote, also advocated that there was more to life for women than simply waiting to get married. As she wrote to one of her readers, "I do not believe girls should remain at home waiting till husbands claim them. There is plenty of work at hand, and plenty of aims in life besides marriage, which is, of course, a good, healthy institution, but not the end of a woman's life" (Fiamengo, 2008, p. 23).

Others, however, were more overtly political, advocating for women's rights not only at home but in the wider world. Flora MacDonald Denison, who wrote for the *Toronto Sunday World*, has been described as "perhaps Canada's most radical feminist," a woman who tirelessly "propagandized on behalf of women's suffrage" (Fiamengo, 2008, p. 6). But even those who did not overtly advocate for women's rights would often insert political messages into topics that were otherwise benign. While today we might not associate fashion journalism with the political, as Freeman (2011) writes, when women wrote about fashion in the late 19th century they were often concerned with women's health. They saw their role as educating women about healthy and comfortable ways of dressing, "warning them about the dangers of tight-lacing corsets, or other dubious practices" (p. 43). Still, many felt they had to be cautious when advocating for healthy dress codes. As newspapers were businesses that depended on advertising dollars, these fashion writers "did not encourage an outright revolution in women's attire" (p. 43).

Being a journalist at that time was not a lucrative profession, and many women worked second jobs or freelanced, writing stories for other newspapers on the side (Freeman, 1989; Kay, 2012). While some came from well-to-do backgrounds, others were from working-class families, often beginning their working lives as teachers and then moving into journalism as a place to flex their writing muscles and take on a different sort of teaching. These women faced many of the same struggles as women journalists do today, particularly how to balance family expectations with a busy working life. In describing the 16 women who formed the first Women's Press Club in Canada in Toronto in 1904, Kay (2012) notes that only one among them was married with children. The others either never married, were married but with no children, or were divorced—three things that were very unusual for the time. As we will see later in this chapter, although social expectations of women are radically different today, contemporary female journalists still struggle with balancing family with work and unfair expectations that women should shoulder the bulk of childcare responsibilities.

We can draw parallels between the first women who worked in newspapers and the first women who worked in broadcasting in the 1930s and 1940s. These first broadcast journalists were hired specifically to create women's programming, but at the same time often advocated for women's rights. Elizabeth Long played a prominent role in developing women's programming and training female journalists at the CBC. In describing the journalists hired by Long, Freeman (2011) writes, "They juggled nostrums about homemaking and child-rearing with information on women's rights in Canada and abroad. Modern-day feminists might find their approach to their listeners, mostly housewives and mothers, somewhat patronizing; yet, under her direction, they promulgated feminist views to a broad yet diverse audience, keeping in mind the constraining social attitudes towards homemakers at the time and being careful not to push them beyond their own limits and uncertainties" (p. 121).

These early 20th-century women journalists took their role as teachers seriously. One of the people Elizabeth Long hired in 1939 was Mattie Rotenberg, the first woman to graduate with a PhD in physics from the University of Toronto. In her radio programs she tried to convey the importance of science to homemakers, emphasizing that science and homemaking were intertwined. The title of her first broadcast, "College in the Kitchen," is a clear indication that education was top of mind for her. Rotenberg said that in her first broadcast she tried to show women how connected the daily chore of cooking is to scientific inventions. The alarm clocks that housewives used to time baking, for example, were complex inventions that people in earlier times did not have (Freeman, 2011).

GLASS CEILINGS

Throughout the second half of the 20th century, women continued to become more entrenched in newsrooms as they moved out of the women's pages and onto the front pages. Slowly the number of female journalists in both print and broadcasting began to inch up. A study comparing statistics from 1975 to 1995 found a 7% increase in female print reporters over that 20-year span, with a total of 962 women working in dailies by 1995. In broadcasting there was a larger increase—17%—with a total of 486 women working in television by 1995 (Robinson, 2008; Robinson & Saint-Jean, 1998). But rather than simply looking at numbers, it is also important to look at what kind of jobs women were doing. Robinson (2008) notes that over that 20-year time period, there was an increase in women taking on higher-level positions. In 1975 most women were working as reporters, jobs at the bottom of the newsroom hierarchy, but by 1995 women were more evenly spread out in all the areas of newsrooms. They worked as reporters, but also as editors and managing editors. While it was an improvement to have women working in different positions, overall there were still far more men than women working in newsrooms.

Today, the most recent statistics show that while gender parity, in terms of number of women employed, has been reached for lower-level jobs, women are still underrepresented at the highest levels of management (Byerly, 2011; Robinson, 2005, 2008). As Hong (2012) describes, "Women are more likely to hit a 'glass ceiling' when it comes to getting senior management positions in journalism, and are less likely to be assigned to cover high-profile stories" (para. 1). It is troubling that women are underrepresented in the highest ranks. As Young and Beale (2013) write, "While near parity in some news roles seems to indicate a step forward, men, not women, remain largely in decision-making positions in top-level leadership of the country's main media" (p. 110). Newspapers, they say, fare worse than broadcasting, pointing out that there has not been a female editor-in-chief of the *Globe and Mail* and there have been only a few senior news leaders at the *Toronto Star*. In Quebec Lise Bisonnette ran *Le Devoir* from 1990 to 1998 and the *Montreal Gazette* appointed its first female editor-in-chief, Joan Fraser, in the early 1990s, a position currently held by Lucinda Chodan. In broadcasting, Young and Beale (2013) point to several examples of women in higher positions, including one that goes back to the early part of the last century, when Nelly McClung was the first woman to have a seat on the CBC's board of governors (1936–1942). There have also been several other high-profile women in positions of power, such as Trina McQueen, who in the late 1980s and early 1990s was the first woman to become the vice president of news, current affairs, and Newsworld for the CBC (now known as the CBC News Network). Later, in the early 2000s, she became the first female president and chief operating officer of CTV. There are also more recent examples, such as Jennifer McGuire, who is the general manager and editor-in-chief of CBC News, as well as Wendy Freeman, who in 2010 became the president of CTV News. Despite these examples, it is still mostly men who are in high positions of power in the news media.

So far this chapter has focused mainly on women who work in newsrooms, in jobs that provide steady income and benefits. Almost 15% of Canadian journalists are self-employed freelancers (Skelton, 2013). This is precarious and often poorly paid work. Most freelancers in Canada are women. As Smith (2015) writes about print freelancing, "Freelancing is an unstable, powerless sort of intellectual piecework done mostly in Canada by women, while editorial work at the highest and best-paid levels of the daily newspaper business is still done mostly by men" (p. 12).

The journalism industry in Canada and many other parts of the world has been going through an economic crisis, struggling to find lucrative business models in an Internet era when many readers expect to access information, including news, online for free. Newspaper subscriptions and sales have fallen dramatically. Journalism organizations that rely on advertising have also been hard hit, especially newspapers (McChesney & Pickard, 2011). The lucrative advertising dollars from classifieds that newspapers have traditionally depended on have migrated to free online services like Kijiji and Craigslist (Grueskin, Seave, & Graves, 2011). Since the 2008 financial crisis, in North America in particular, there have been many layoffs and closures, and freelance budgets have been cut. In this economic climate freelance journalists have been turning to sites such as Kickstarter and Indiegogo to raise money to offset travel and living expenses while they cover stories that they then hope to sell to mainstream media.

In Canada female journalists have been crowdfunding to cover stories they feel are not getting enough coverage in mainstream media, or starting their own independent publications to do the same. Often these stories have to do with women's issues, parenting, and human rights (Hunter, 2015, 2016).

CONTEMPORARY CHALLENGES

In study after study examining the contemporary challenges that women face when considering careers as journalists, the difficulty of balancing work and family comes up repeatedly (Smith, 2015). Journalism is not usually a job with regular, predictable hours. Even if a journalist's shift is scheduled to end at five o'clock, if an interviewee is not available until after that a journalist will not just pack up and go home, but will feel pressure to stay until the story is done. Journalists often work long hours to make sure a story gets published or on air. Journalism can be an unpredictable job. Journalists may have to travel at a moment's notice to cover a crisis abroad, return early from a holiday, or forego a weekend to cover breaking news. If women journalists have children in school or daycare who need to be picked up at a certain time, the uncertainty of the job can cause stress. It can also cause journalists to turn down assignments that could further their careers because they need to care for their children and other family members. Several studies have found that female journalists cite family obligations as interfering with their work and their ability to rise through the ranks. Robinson (2005) found that childcare arrangements and other family obligations interfered with 42% of women's work schedules. Looking specifically at managers, Barber and Rauhala (2008) found that 80.5% of women journalists believe the news business makes family commitments, such as caring for children, difficult. Aldridge (2001) found similar results in her study of print journalists—children and high-ranking positions were not symbiotic: "When asked about balancing work and home life nearly all the other women spontaneously linked their achievement to their not having children; one woman who had reached the level of managing editor stated flatly: 'I think that that kind of assignment is probably not compatible with young children kicking around'" (p. 618). A study on journalists in Quebec found that female journalists were more likely than males to be unmarried and not have children (Saint-Jean, 2000). Smith (2015) notes that it seems as if nothing much has changed in this respect for women over the generations. The female journalists in her study "seemed to feel powerless when it came to articulating their own workplace needs for flexibility, and they generally conceded an inevitability about gender roles on the job and at home" (p. 202). While the decision to have or not to have children was crucial to women as they considered advancing in their careers, men were not seen as having to make the same decisions. Smith found that not only do women journalists think about leaving their jobs after having children, but they also think about leaving their jobs *before* having children. They recognize that the demands of the job are extremely difficult when paired with the expectations that will be put on them when they have children.

It is useful to think about the work/life balance issue faced by women journalists in terms of structuration and ask why they are expected to take on the bulk of childcare. Why are the same social expectations not put on men? Looking at this from a feminist political economy standpoint, why is the work of childcare that is mostly done by women not recognized as "work"? Why are women expected to take on the bulk of *unpaid* household work? Social supports need to be put in place for women who want to work outside the home and also have children. In many parts of Canada there is a lack of such social supports as affordable daycare. Gender expectations for men also need to change, so that women and men see themselves as equal caregivers when it comes to raising children.

Although women have been integrated into journalism organizations as reporters, producers, and, to a lesser extent, managers, they still face very visible struggles for equality, including harassment from the public. A particularly shocking example of sexism and misogyny began in 2015. As the CBC reported on May 14 of that year, "For months now, television reporters across the country, including many CBC journalists, have been dealing with the vulgar phenomenon—in which someone shouts 'f--k her right in the p---y' into a microphone or camera during a live taping" (CBC News, 2015). These journalists feel directly attacked, degraded, and harassed while trying to do their job. As another example of harassment that female journalists face, *Toronto Star* columnist Heather Mallick has said that she is regularly subjected to sexist backlash that has affected her to the point where she does not answer her phone in the newsroom to avoid the "same guys yelling at me" (Canadian Journalism Foundation, 2017). She has also had to block readers online who have sent her death threats. As she described, "It's been pretty unpleasant and it's isolated me as a journalist. So now I don't speak as much, except in my columns. I just read, I take things in, but I communicate much less than I used to" (Canadian Journalism Foundation, 2017). It is difficult to say with certainty why this happens to female journalists, other than to speculate that some men feel threatened by women having a voice in the public sphere. While some of the men who have jumped in front of women's cameras to yell obscenities likely saw what they were doing as a harm-less joke—it did start as a spoof in the United States on a fake news show—it is highly distressing to the women involved. As CBC videographer Holly Caruk described, she felt embarrassed and threatened when her interview with a father with two small children was interrupted in this way, as well as in an interview she was doing with high school students about a fundraiser: "Everybody laughed. ... It felt embarrassing and off-putting. ... This was something that felt very tar-geted to me as a woman and very threatening" (CBC News, 2015).

GENDER AND DIVERSITY

The argument is often made that it is important to have women working as jour-nalists because women bring a different perspective and point of view to the news. This was certainly the feeling of the first editors and producers who hired women at newspapers and broadcast outlets. As Fleras (2003) writes, "Male-controlled media have defined what was newsworthy because of their monopoly of power to make decisions regarding what to emphasize and what to ignore" (p. 312). Some contend that these male-controlled structures under which journalists work are not easily changed and that individual journalists do not have much agency to influence what happens in newsrooms, which have their own fixed cultures and routines (Craft & Wanta, 2004). They caution that increasing the number of women working in newsrooms may not make much of a difference, pointing out that "women in traditionally masculine workplaces such as politics, business, and journalism, often confront pressure (either real or perceived) to conform to masculine styles of speech, behavior, and interaction" (Goodyear-Grant, 2013, p. 118). Some studies have found that there is no difference in how men and women cover news. Other scholars argue that having more women working as journal-ists will in fact change the content of news and "may result in less masculin-ist reporting, for a uniquely female way of doing the news—one that is more sensitive to gender issues and the portrayal of political women—may gradu-ally emerge" (Goodyear-Grant, 2013, p. 115). Studies that have looked at how male and female politicians are portrayed differently in the media have found that women are subjected to gendered coverage (Goodyear-Grant, 2013). News reports about female politicians will often bring up the fact that they are also mothers, overtly or implicitly indicating that their political careers may interfere with their parenting responsibilities or vice versa. Men generally do not get this type of coverage. Some researchers say that the way to end this type of gen-dered coverage is to increase the number of women working in the media. Smith

(2015) writes that women can change what we think of as news. In her study of female print reporters she found that "many participants challenged the male news agenda, writing about gender, class, ability, and race-based issues and even demanding men tackle 'women's issues'" (p. 209).

Many media organizations in Canada take diversity seriously in their hiring practices and mandates, acknowledging that it is very important to have a diverse newsroom as individual journalists do have an effect on the breadth of stories that are covered. Diversity is a central part of the mandate of the Canadian Broadcasting Corporation/Radio-Canada, which means that programming should "reflect Canada and its regions" and "reflect the multicultural and multi-racial nature of Canada," in accordance with the 1991 Broadcasting Act (CBC/Radio-Canada, n.d., "Mandate").

Reflecting on what it means to fulfill this mandate, the CBC states on its website, "Our diversity and inclusion vision is to be the media leader in draw-ing on the wealth of unique Canadian perspectives to shape our content, work-place and workforce" (CBC/Radio-Canada, n.d., "Diversity and Inclusion"). In Quebec, the newspaper *La Presse* started a diversity internship program with the goal of better reflecting Quebec society ("Quatre stagiaires," 2017). Clearly, jour-nalism organizations feel that who they have working as journalists influences what makes it into the news and what does not. As one former print journalist put it, "What filters through your own life experience is what ends up in the paper" (Smith, 2015, p. 209).

CONCLUSION

The first female journalists were born at a time when the epitome of being a respectable female was to become a mother and wife. By venturing into work outside the home and advocating for suffrage and more independence for women, including the freedom to dress in less restrictive ways, these women were work-ing within social structures that certainly influenced and constrained them, but they were also working to change these social structures through their own indi-vidual agency. This continued throughout the 20th century and into the 21st century as women became more established in journalism. While there is still gender inequality at the highest levels, women have been changing expectations, both in terms of gender roles and what counts as news, ever since their predeces-sors first made it onto the women's pages.

It is important to look at the experiences of women in journalism through a feminist political economy lens and recognize that there is still an assumption that women will take on the bulk of childcare, whereas men are not as burdened by this expectation (Smith, 2015). A feminist political economy approach also draws our attention to gendered news coverage, particularly of politicians, and how news stories often focus on female politicians' family responsibilities more than men's (Goodyear-Grant, 2013). Again, the hidden assumption in this kind of coverage is that women need to be concerned about childcare and men do not, at least not to the extent that it would interfere with their career.

Structuration is a useful theory to bring into political economy to examine how factors such as gender, race, age, and sexuality impact our experience of the world. While these issues have historically been left out of a political economy approach, political economists are increasingly recognizing that their approach must be more intersectional. As Young and Beale (2013) point out, there needs to be more research that examines particularly how race intersects with women's experiences in newsrooms. We know that as a whole "Canadian newsrooms continue to lack racial diversity, with racialized and indigenous groups still significantly underrepresented" (Young & Beale, 2013, p. 116). In her study of female print journalists Smith (2015) noted that the career paths of the journalists she studied appeared to be "influenced in multiple, fluid, and often hidden ways by other characteristics as they intersect with gender. Assumptions about these characteristics, such as age, race, parenthood status, and class, further complicate the shaping of participants' experience in their workplaces" (p. 201). Some of the younger participants in her study felt that they were treated differently because of their age, including being flirted with by male interviewees or having a senior male reporter assigned to help them cover a potentially "dangerous" story. In these cases, age and gender work together to define their experience. There is an opportunity in academic research to examine more closely, from an intersectional approach, how variables such as age, sexuality, disability, gender, and socioeconomic background work together to define people's experiences and, in turn, what they bring to the newsroom. As the media is one important way that Canadians engage with the world around them and is often influential in defining the political agenda, it is imperative that we have a better understanding of who is making the news.

Women have made great strides in this profession since they first put pen to paper in the women's pages almost two centuries ago. Their experience as women in journalism intersects with the social class they were born into, their racialized status, and age (Smith, 2015), and there is much more work to be done to make journalism a more diverse and equitable profession.

KEY READINGS

Byerly, C. M. (2011). *Global report on the status of women in the news media.* Washington, DC: International Women's Media Foundation.

Canadian Journalism Federation. (2017). *No safe space: Harassment of women in media* [Video file]. Retrieved from https://www.youtube.com/watch?v=G31rbpbu1ks

Kay, L. (2012). *The sweet sixteen: The journey that inspired the Canadian women's press club.* Montreal & Kingston: McGill-Queen's University Press.

Young, M. L., & Beale, A. (2013). Canada: The paradox of women in the news. In C. M. Byerly (Ed.), *The Palgrave international handbook of women and journalism* (pp. 109–121). Basingstoke, UK: Palgrave MacMillan.

DISCUSSION QUESTIONS

1. What types of obstacles and discrimination do female journalists face today, and how would you compare this to the first female journalists' experiences?

2. Why does it matter if there are female journalists?

3. If you were a journalist, how would your own particular perspective (gender, race, social class, sexuality, and so on) influence what kind of stories you would want to report on?

4. How does harassment of women journalists relate to other trends of violence against women that you've observed or are aware of? Have you experienced or witnessed anything similar? What do you think is the underlying cause of this, and what can be done about it?

5. What social structures constrain or enable you in your life? What underlying conditions are those structures related to (age, race, and so on)? Do you feel that you have adequate personal agency?

REFERENCES

Aldridge, M. (2001). Lost expectations? Women journalists and the fall-out from the Toronto newspaper war. *Media, Culture and Society, 23*(5), 607–624.

Barber, M., & Rauhala, A. (2008). The Canadian news directors study: Demographics and political leanings of television decision-makers. *Canadian Journal of Communication, 30*(2), 281–292.

Byerly, C. M. (2011). *Global report on the status of women in the news media.* Washington, DC: International Women's Media Foundation.

Canadian Journalism Foundation. (2017). *No safe space: Harassment of women in media* [Video file]. Retrieved from https://www.youtube.com/watch?v=G31rbpbu1ks

CBC News. (2015, May 15). FHRITP phenomenon: CBC journalists share "mortifying" experiences. *CBC.ca*. Retrieved from http://www.cbc.ca/news/canada/fhritp-phenomenon-cbc-journalists-share-mortifying-experiences-1.3072191

CBC/Radio-Canada. (n.d.). Diversity and inclusion at CBC/Radio-Canada. Retrieved from http://www.cbc.radio-canada.ca/en/explore/jobs/diversity-and-inclusion-at-cbc-radio-canada/

CBC/Radio-Canada. (n.d.). Mandate. Retrieved from http://www.cbc.radio-canada.ca/en/explore/mandate/

Cohen, N. (2016). *Writers' rights*. Montreal & Kingston: McGill-Queen's University Press.

Craft, S., & Wanta, W. (2004). Women in the newsroom: Influence of female editors and reporters on the news agenda. *Journalism and Mass Communication Quarterly, 81*(1), 124–138.

Fiamengo, J. (2008). *The woman's page: Journalism and rhetoric in early Canada*. Toronto: University of Toronto Press.

Fleras, A. (2003). *Mass media communication in Canada*. Toronto: Nelson.

Freeman, B. (1989). *Kit's kingdom: The journalism of Kathleen Blake Coleman*. Ottawa: Carleton University Press.

Freeman, B. (2011). *Beyond bylines: Media workers and women's rights in Canada*. Waterloo, ON: Wilfrid Laurier University Press.

Giddens, A. (1984). *The constitution of society: Outline of the theory of structuration*. Cambridge, UK: Polity.

Goodyear-Grant, E. (2013). *Gendered news: Media coverage and electoral politics in Canada*. Vancouver: UBC Press.

Grueskin, B., Seave, A., & Graves, L. (2011). *The story so far: What we know about the business of digital journalism*. New York: Columbia University Press.

Hassan, R. (2008). *The information society*. Cambridge, UK: Polity Press.

Hong, J. (2012). Women still face hurdles in Canadian media. *Ryerson Journalism Research Centre*. Retrieved from http://ryersonjournalism.ca/2013/04/29/women-still-face-hurdles-in-canadian-media-researc-finds/

Hunter, A. (2015). Crowdfunding independent and freelance journalism: Negotiating journalistic norms of autonomy and objectivity. *New Media & Society, 17*(2), 272–288.

Hunter, A. (2016). "It's like having a second full-time job": Crowdfunding, journalism and labour. *Journalism Practice, 10*(2), 217–232.

Kay, L. (2012). *The sweet sixteen: The journey that inspired the Canadian women's press club*. Montreal & Kingston: McGill-Queen's University Press.

Kaye, J., & Quinn, S. (2010). *Funding journalism in the digital age: Business models, strategies, issues and trends*. New York: Peter Lang.

Lang, M. (1999). *Women who made the news: Female journalists in Canada, 1880–1945*. Montreal & Kingston: McGill-Queen's University Press.

McChesney, R., & Pickard, V. (2011). *Will the last reporter please turn out the lights.* New York: New Press.

Mosco, V. (2009). *The political economy of communication* (2nd ed.). London: Sage.

Quatre stagiaires font leur entrée dans la salle de rédaction. (2017, July 11). *La Presse.* Retrieved from http://www.lapresse.ca/arts/medias/201707/11/01-5115074-quatre-stagiaires-font-leur-entree-dans-la-salle-de-redaction.php

Robinson, G. (2005). *Gender, journalism and equity: Canadian, US and European perspectives.* Cresskill, NJ: Hampton Press.

Robinson, G. (2008). Feminist approaches to journalism studies: Canadian perspectives. *Global Media Journal, 1*(1), 123–136.

Robinson, G., & Saint-Jean, A. (1998). Canadian women journalists: The "other half" of the equation. In D. Weaver (Ed.), *The global journalist* (pp. 349–370). Cresskill, NJ: Hampton Press.

Rutherford, P. (1982). *A Victorian authority: The daily press in late nineteenth-century Canada.* Toronto: University of Toronto Press.

Saint-Jean, A. (2000). L'apport des femmes au renouvellement des pratiques profession-nelles: Le cas des journalistes. *Recherches féministes, 13*(2), 77–93.

Skelton, C. (2013, August 19). No fewer journalists today than 10 years ago: Statistics Canada. *Vancouver Sun.* Retrieved from https://vancouversun.com/news/staff-blogs/no-fewer-journalists-today-than-10-years-ago-statistics-canada

Smith, V. (2015). *Outsiders still: Why women journalists love—and leave—their newspaper careers.* Toronto: University of Toronto Press.

Waring, M. (1988). *If women counted: A new feminist economics.* San Francisco: Harper Collins.

Young, M. L., & Beale, A. (2013). Canada: The paradox of women in the news. In C. M. Byerly (Ed.), *The Palgrave international handbook of women and journalism* (pp. 109–121). Basingstoke, UK: Palgrave MacMillan.

CHAPTER 15

Equity Shifts in Firefighting: Challenging Gendered and Racialized Work

Susan Braedley

INTRODUCTION

In the words of a Swedish observer, "Firefighting is the last bastion for … men suffering from chronic male hubris" (Kuchler, 2008). Firefighting is an occupation that embodies a "muscular working class manhood … commonly employed as a highly significant mobilizing cultural ideal intended to invoke cross-class recognition and solidarity regarding what counts as a man" (Beasley, 2008, p. 90). Yet, coexisting with white masculine dominance and privilege (Braedley, 2009), fire services are also becoming more equitable for women and people from racialized groups. This chapter draws on fieldwork from two studies completed between 2007 and 2016, including work observations at 27 fire halls in 8 fire services; 140 interviews with workers from 11 Canadian urban and suburban fire services in British Columbia, Manitoba, Ontario, New Brunswick, and Nova Scotia; and interviews with municipal officials responsible for employment equity in 11 cities. The chapter outlines how and why employment equity improvements have been difficult to achieve in this occupation despite continual scandals and calls for change. Yet changes are being made, thanks to media attention, court battles, pressure from activists, and, more recently, mobilization within the firefighting community.

The daily and nightly work of firefighters includes a wide range of tasks, including doing drills and training, maintaining equipment, and responding to a wide variety of emergency calls. About half of all calls are for emergency medical response; other frequent calls are to assist with car accidents, fires, stuck elevators, suicides, and much more. In the course of their work, firefighters lift and manoeuvre heavy objects, such as bringing a gurney into an apartment up a narrow flight of stairs. They move and carry injured and immobile bodies. They use heavy power tools to cut open vehicles, rescue people from confined and dangerous spaces, and put out fires by dragging, placing, and manipulating heavy hoses that spread water and fire-suppressing chemicals. They support other emergency workers, such as police and paramedics, at 911 calls. In some municipalities they may also do other work, such as inspecting buildings for fire safety, providing public fire safety education, working on community projects to address hoarding, and checking on shut-in and elderly community members. The work is highly varied. Firefighters work in small teams, usually of four firefighters who work together consistently. On any shift, a fire hall may have one team or many teams, who work for either 24- or 12-hour shifts.

Few women work in firefighting. While the argument is made that women are not physically capable of some of the work, it is also the case that equipment, strategies, and modes of response have been developed with a particular male body in mind—a tall body of significant weight and upper-body strength. Considering employment equity for women in firefighting requires us to think beyond questions of how to include women in male-dominated occupations and consider whether and how work can be redesigned to allow and encourage a variety of different bodies and subjectivities to participate.

The chapter begins with a description of the feminist political economy approach taken in this analysis and used extensively in many Canadian studies of women and work. Next, employment equity is defined as deployed in the Canadian context. Then, drawing from research data, the case of fire services is presented with attention to four dimensions that are both necessary to achieving employment equity and often overlooked: bodies, material environments, culture, and employment equity measurement.

STUDYING GENDER AND WORK: FEMINIST POLITICAL ECONOMY'S INTERSECTIONAL LENS

This analysis is guided by feminist political economy, a lens that understands gender, race, class, ability, age, sexuality, and indigeneity as intersecting social relations that shape inequalities (Luxton, 2006). Further, these social relations shape and are shaped by economics, politics, culture, and ideology. This means that inequities must be examined and understood within their historical and geographic context. Feminist political economists always ask, Who benefits from these inequalities and how? Who pays for them, and how? Further, feminist political economy asks us to find and identify tensions or contradictions in these relations. These points of contradiction offer opportunities to challenge inequities and advocate for change.

This approach complements, but is not the same as, approaches to intersectionality that developed initially within feminist, antiracist legal studies (Bilge, 2010). Rather than beginning with concerns about identity and related inequalities, feminist political economy emphasizes a methodological approach that traces the connections between and among relations of domination and oppression, including the dynamics of global capitalism, to reveal how these relations penetrate our most intimate daily lives. Further, it demonstrates how people's different problems and struggles for emancipation around the world are connected in many ways. This approach requires us to imagine a freedom beyond achieving civil rights or human rights for particular groups in unique jurisdictions. We need to understand that until all are free, none of us are free (Davis, 2016).

Canadian feminist political economists have taken up issues of women, gender, and work using this distinctive intersectional approach. This literature includes analyses of gendered labour market segregation (Armstrong, 1996), gendered and unequal unpaid work in the household (Luxton, 1980), the racialization of gendered and undervalued work (Arat-Koç, 2006), and conditions of work in feminized and racialized employment (Baines, 2008; Das Gupta, 2009; Teeple Hopkins, 2017). The role of the state in shaping gender equity has received analysis, especially in terms of paid and unpaid work (Bakan & Koybashi, 2007; Brodie & Bakker, 2008), as has women's economic security (Cohen & Pulkingham, 2009). Feminist political economists have also produced studies on women's overrepresentation in precarious work (Fudge & Strauss, 2013), gendered work in Indigenous communities (Kuokkanen, 2011), and transgender people and work (Irving, 2015).

Further, feminist political economists have used their intersectional approach to examine workplace issues, including understandings of skill (Armstrong, 2013), occupational health and safety (Braedley, Owusu, Przednowek, & Armstrong, 2017), union organizing (Coulter, 2013; Das Gupta, 2009), and other related topics. These authors show that gender, racialization, class, and other social relations penetrate our understandings not only of which bodies do what work, but also how that work is understood, organized, and valued.

Central to these analyses is a challenge to traditional views that work considered appropriate for women (tasks related to the domestic sphere, care work, and work requiring fine manual dexterity) is less skilled and of less value than work that has been considered men's work. Further, feminist political economy has challenged the practices that shape what work people do and the value of that work based on race, immigration status, indigeneity, ability, or other factors. While feminist political economists have worked on the question of pay equity (Armstrong, 2007), they have not devoted significant attention to the challenges of employment equity in **masculinized work**, addressed below.

WHAT IS EMPLOYMENT EQUITY?

Employment equity is a particularly Canadian term, attributed to Judge Rosalie Abella, who introduced it in the landmark *Equality in Employment: A Royal Commission Report* (Abella, 1984; Agócs, 2014). It was employed as an alternative to the US government's use of the term *affirmative action*, which had triggered backlash (Bakan & Koybashi, 2007). In 1986 the government of Canada proclaimed the Employment Equity Act, which aimed to achieve workplace equality for four historically disadvantaged groups: women, visible minorities, Aboriginal[1] Peoples, and persons with disabilities. The act addressed three barriers to employment. First, no one should be denied employment for reasons beyond their ability to do the work. Second, special measures may be necessary to improve employment opportunities for people from the designated groups. Third, employers are required to make "reasonable accommodation" in the workplace for legitimate differences between groups.

The federal policy does not apply to all employers in Canada, however. Since 1984, federal, provincial, and municipal governments have sometimes addressed employment inequities and at other times reacted to employment equity backlash. In most workplaces, employment equity is only partially guaranteed, sometimes by human rights legislation, sometimes only by voluntary policy initiatives. As of 2017, Quebec is the only province with its own employment equity legislation.

In many cases, employment equity policies and practices prescribe an equal treatment approach, designed to encourage and free up labour market competition, while ignoring questions about discriminatory working conditions. This approach treats everyone the same, appeasing those who are concerned that women and minorities get jobs ahead of white men—so-called reverse discrimination. But this approach ignores systemic discrimination. In the long period since the federal legislation was enacted, significant employment equity policy variation has remained in Canadian jurisdictions and in public sector employment. Employment inequities in many occupations in Canada have been well documented (Abu-Laban & Gabriel, 2002; Grundy & Smith, 2011), including dimensions of gender (Braedley, 2009; Creese & Beagan, 2009), racialization (Teelucksingh & Galabuzi, 2007) and sexuality (Drydakis, 2009). Many barriers remain to employment equity in Canada.

EMPLOYMENT EQUITY AND FIRE SERVICES

Policing, the military, and firefighting have well-earned reputations as white, **heteronormative**, masculinist labour forces. These public services are also distinctive in that their goals are aligned with the maintenance of state power and private property interests (Braedley, 2015; Gordon & Stewart, 2006). Scandals related to employment inequities are common in these services, with reports of discriminatory hiring practices, barriers to promotion, and harassment.

Professional fire services provide an excellent case study of employment equity problems. Women are more underrepresented in firefighting than in policing or the military. The 2011 National Household Survey indicated that women held 1,195 of 31,830 firefighter positions, or just under 4%, and 110 of the 2,310 chief and senior officer positions, or just under 5% (Statistics Canada, 2011). Aboriginal people and visible minorities make up a tiny percentage of firefighters, and most municipalities do not keep track of fire services' workplace diversity. Where women and other underrepresented groups are employed by fire services, employment inequity scandals have emerged with disconcerting regularity. For example, long-standing concerns about racism in the Halifax fire service yielded a complaint to the Nova Scotia Human Rights Commission in 2007, which was settled through a difficult out-of-court reconciliation process in 2013. In British Columbia, reports of extreme sexual harassment in several cities made international news headlines in 2004 and again in 2006. In 2007 and again in 2009 a firefighter in Pemberton, British Columbia, launched a human rights complaint about discrimination and harassment due to his sexuality (Mackin, 2011). In 2011, a firefighter in Windsor, Ontario, launched a lawsuit against her employer, alleging sexual harassment by her superiors and a hostile work environment (CBC News, 2011). In 2015, a CBC investigation into sexual harassment and discrimination at Canadian fire services found evidence of systemic sexism throughout the industry.

Workers deserve to be free from harassment and discrimination in their workplaces, but this freedom is insufficient to ensure employment equity.

Employers often focus on strategies to include underrepresented groups through recruitment, hiring, and diversity training as their answer to addressing discrimination and harassment. But these measures have not produced employment equity. It is also necessary to identify how sexism, racism, heterosexism, ableism, ageism, and other inequitable social relations have shaped occupational material environments (buildings, equipment, uniforms) and normative orders (rules, rituals, cultural norms) so that these structures and relations can be changed. Whether or not these changes to working conditions are "reasonable accommodation" remains a question of politics.

In fire services, inequitable social relations are evident everywhere. In what follows, illustrations from research reveal the complexities of employment inequities in Canadian fire services and the challenges inherent in making change.

BODIES AT WORK: GENDER AND RACIALIZATION

In many jobs, bodies matter. Miners lift and handle heavy tools; personal support workers shift, lift, and move the people they care for; surgeons require excellent eye-hand coordination. Bodily capacities to physically handle job demands are key to job performance. In firefighting, the benchmark for physical capacity is the ability to rescue another firefighter from a fire. This requires not only physical strength but speed and aerobic capacity while wearing a full set of gear that weighs at least 20 kilograms.

This benchmark is important to firefighters' trust in one another, but it has proved difficult to assess. The required pre-employment physical fitness testing is very controversial and has resulted in court battles. Prospective firefighters must train for, pay for, and pass this test before being considered for a position, as described by an Aboriginal woman firefighter in Ontario:

> I wanted to be a firefighter. I loved the physicalness and the adrenaline and everything. I tried [to pass the test] for about five years. ... Every time they had a big recruitment I would go. The first time ... you go hand over hand and it was sliding because I couldn't grip anymore. ... Finally I did it, but [I took too long]. They told me to come do it over at the end. But also in the cart pull—I weigh 125 [pounds] soaking wet—so I'm trying to pull this skid and it weighs 200 [pounds], and the laws of physics weren't working in my favour. Everybody's cheering me on, and saying, "Don't stop" and I'm like, "I won't!" I was pulling for all I was worth. ... You have to pass it all and I had failed the

hand over hand, [so] I went and hired a personal trainer. Now, I wasn't making a whole lot of money, so it was a personal sacrifice to invest in a personal trainer. … We worked on the upper body and then I went back and I did it. … And every time I went through the recruitment process, people said, "Oh, you won't have any problem because they're trying to hire women and minorities." … That kinda bothered me, because it hasn't worked to my benefit.

This test is important not only to firefighters, but to all those concerned about employment equity in Canada. It became the focus of a legal battle regarding physical capacity testing, biological sex categories (male/female), and gender (masculine/feminine/nonbinary). In 1999, the Supreme Court of Canada made a historic decision in the *Meiorin* case, rejecting the government of British Columbia's argument that the existing firefighter fitness test was a valid occupational requirement for firefighters (*British Columbia (Public Service Employee Relations Commission) v. BCGSEU*, 1999). The court ruled that the test, based on measurements of male physiological aerobic capacity rather than job performance, was in violation of the Canada Human Rights Act. The court ordered that these differences must be accommodated by employers, unless they prevent safe, effective work performance. The Supreme Court judgment insisted that employers take into account women's characteristics when setting workplace standards (Cox & Messing, 2006, p. 33). This decision has had an impact on employment standards for all public safety work, but there are ongoing debates about occupational physical requirements for firefighting.

This decision was important in that it acknowledged biological differences in strength and aerobic capacity between most women and most men (Cox & Messing, 2006). The difference in physical size and strength among women as a group, and among men as a group, is bigger than the difference between men and women (Connell, 2002). Most women do not have the physical or aerobic capacities of most men, but these differences are relatively small (Messing & Kilbom, 1998). The *Meiorin* decision has raised as many questions as it has resolved. What is the relationship between sex or gender, physical capabilities, bodily differences, and the capacity to perform certain kinds of work? What accommodations and adaptations to work standards can be made while also ensuring safe, effective work? What are the limits to accommodation and adaptation?

Fire services' individualized pre-employment fitness tests were instituted to address critiques of previous height and weight requirements that barred most women, some men, and some ethnicities from firefighting (Cox & Messing, 2006).

Since the *Meiorin* decision, changes have been made to the tests, but they remain problematic. For example, the tests specify what must be done and how tasks must be performed. These tests measure and emphasize bodily capacities of strength and speed, which are more common in men, while de-emphasizing or ignoring flexibility, agility, and endurance, which are more common in women and also important in performing firefighting work (Messing, Lippel, Demers, & Mergler, 2000). Further, the test uses equipment that was designed for bodies that are taller and heavier than many women and men. This disadvantages some racialized groups that tend to smaller physical frames than caucasians. Arguably, the norm of white masculinity remains woven into the determination of what counts as a physical fitness level sufficient to the work of firefighting.

Many firefighters have been opposed to the testing changes, including women and visible minority firefighters. A white woman firefighter interviewee from Ontario stated, "They lowered the standards in order to get more women on the job. … They definitely dropped the standards." For these firefighters, the changes were not understood as accommodations, but as lowered standards that might imperil safety. These workers were proud that they had met the previous standard. They wanted others to understand that they were as fit as any other firefighter and had not been hired due to their minority-group status. For these firefighters, any change was a reduction in those standards. A male visible minority firefighter in Ontario explained, "I've always said, if you can pass all the tests and you can meet all the standards, then I've got no problems with that. But don't ever lower the standards just because you want minorities and women on the job. Look at me. [If] I couldn't get on the job, I wouldn't expect you to hire me."

Promisingly, despite backlash, there have been many initiatives to encourage firefighter applications from women, visible minority and racialized groups, Aboriginal Peoples, persons with disabilities, and LGBTQ2S[2] communities, particularly in Canada's urban fire services. As one example, a Toronto Fire Service recruitment and training initiative won international recognition for increasing the numbers of women and nonwhite students in preservice firefighter education (City of Toronto, 2011). In the period from 2012 to 2016, of 119 new fire prevention and public education staff at Toronto Fire Services, 33% were women or members of visible minority groups. In 2015/2016, 37% of operations[3] firefighter recruits were also from designated underrepresented groups (Pegg, 2017). But retaining these new recruits depends on other initiatives and changes to confront the masculinized and whitened working environment of firefighting.

MASCULINIZED AND WHITENED: BUILDINGS, EQUIPMENT, AND UNIFORMS

Firefighting environments, equipment, and uniforms make it difficult for women and some men to perform on the job. Just as we understand that success in tennis, golf, cycling, scuba diving, and many other sports is predicated on having equipment that fits and is designed for the bodies of the people who use it, so too is this true in occupations where physical performance is essential to safe, effective job performance. Yet, whether it is the height of the step into a fire truck, the balance and distance between the handles on a chainsaw, the design of the safety clothing, or the organization of bunks for overnight shifts at the fire hall, every aspect of fire services seems to have been designed for a 6-foot or taller, 200-pound man. As Cox and Messing (2006) state, "Work environments and task protocols in jobs typically held by men are generally designed with the average Caucasian man's physique in mind" (p. 25).

In addition, firefighters sleep, eat, shower, and exercise on the job, in work environments that historically have been designed on the model of military barracks. Most fire halls in the research projects discussed here had one shower room, communal sleeping areas, and no sex-specific bathrooms.

Women firefighters had a lot to say about these issues. A white woman firefighter from Manitoba said, "Nothing fits me properly, and everything is mostly just too big—the safety equipment, the uniforms, the adjustment positions for the steering wheel and pedals on the truck. It's my job to make myself fit, and I do my best. But it wouldn't take a rocket scientist to design something better." Her peer from Ontario explained, "I put up the gender sign when I go to shower or use the bathroom, so [the men will] stay out. I work out when they aren't in the gym area. We dragged a cot into an equipment room so I don't have to sleep with the rest of them. I don't mind. Sometimes I need a break from them."

As there are very few women in firefighting, women firefighters do not often work together. They are often the only woman working in their fire hall during their shift. As the "exception" to the rule of masculine bodies, they are usually left to adapt on their own. The physical environment offers fewer challenges to men from underrepresented groups, but does not provide an inclusive work environment. No matter their gender, those who may require privacy for personal care or sleeping (due to gender, trauma, a health concern, or religious beliefs that proscribe nudity in front of others) or for religious observances, such as daily prayer, are not likely to be easily accommodated in firefighting workplaces. The organization of space reflects the history of sex, gender, race, and class in firefighting.

A HOMOSOCIAL, HOMOPHOBIC BROTHERHOOD: THE BASIS OF CULTURE

An assistant fire chief in Manitoba laid out the basis for fire hall culture, linking the close family-like relationships to firefighting's mentorship model for training, its stable work teams that form platoons, the shift work that supports socializing off the job because it is so different from most people's work schedules, involvement in sports (which was a common interest among most of the 140 firefighters interviewed in this research), and the collegiality:

> It's like a family. It's almost like we've got the young kids and the older siblings that are raising them up … It creates enjoyment coming to work because they actually look forward to it, because … I'm with my friends. … They're all my colleagues—all my friends per se are at work. … So, this gives them … a bit of a family, a belonging. They're very proud of their platoons. … [They] have an attachment to it. They sort of show it, like … when they have the golfing things or any of the stuff they have—platoon, interplatoon baseball games. And they're very proud in that. So I like that. … [When] they come to work, they're respectful of their colleagues. They also don't want to let their colleagues down.

Add to these dynamics a constant awareness among firefighters that workers will face potentially life-threatening circumstances during the course of their work and must rely on each other for their safety. Although there are exceptions, most firefighter crews operate as a collective or team, both in their regular duties, such as training and cleaning vehicles and buildings, and their other activities while on the job, such as meal preparation, dining, exercise, or leisure activities. This model of work organization is co-constituted by the culture and the relative homogeneity of the firefighters' social locations. Most firefighters are Canadian born and raised and have some background in athletics or sports. Many come from families with many members who work in fire services, policing, or the military. As one white male firefighter from Nova Scotia explained, "You won't find too many firefighters who didn't grow up playing hockey, and lots of us still play. Nowadays you meet firefighters with university degrees and all that, but they're still boys from the neighbourhood. They know how to get along here."

In work observations conducted over nine years and four provinces, this fire hall culture was palpable in 24 of the 27 fire halls included in the study. Other researchers have also noted this dynamic, not only in Canada, but also in US and UK fire services (Chetkovich, 1997; Regehr, Dimitropoulos, Bright,

George, & Henderson, 2005; Ward & Winstanley, 2006). This kind of social engagement has been described as **"homosocial"**: a social relationship rooted in a preference for same-sex social (not sexual) relationships. The term is used most often in reference to men (Flood, 2008). In fire halls, this homosociality shapes bonds or a brotherhood (Braedley, 2010) that encompasses trust, loyalty, and teamwork.

At most of the fire halls included in this research, this brotherhood was reinforced by often continual exchanges and interjections of sexist and homophobic language. Firefighters encouraged, teased, and directed each other through comments that associated women and homosexuality with weakness, fear, or a poor work ethic, and associated men, manliness, and male genitals with courage, strength, and other positive traits. Phrases such as "don't be a girl," "hitch your skirt up," "what are you, queer?" and "get a pair" were frequently used by workers and generally considered as humorous, harmless commentary. When asked about this talk, firefighters showed awareness of its negative implications. As a white male firefighter in Ontario said, "If my wife or kids heard me talk like this, I'd be in big trouble. I don't talk like this outside of work. It's just the way it is here. I know it's idiotic." A visible minority male firefighter in British Columbia agreed: "It doesn't mean anything, we're just fooling around. We don't do it in front of the public."

Exceptions are important in research that aims for change. In 2015, during a full week of observations at one fire service, researchers noted a total absence of sexist, homophobic, or racist language. Observations were made of the dynamics among the different crews that worked various shifts, involving 32 firefighters and five chiefs of various ranks at two fire halls in one municipality. All the operations firefighters were men, mostly white and Canadian born.[4] Further, this was a fire service with high morale and close-knit crews.

How can this research exception be understood? Feminist political economy turns our attention to the political, economic, and social conditions involved. Due to this municipality's rapid population growth, surging economy, and geographic expansion, the fire service had grown rapidly. As a result, it had a large cohort of workers with less than 10 years of experience. Many of these newer firefighters had significant postsecondary education, had travelled extensively, and had grown up in ethnically diverse neighbourhoods. Further, in a newly constructed fire hall, the fire service stocked safety equipment to fit smaller bodies, had sex-specific washrooms, and offered sufficient space for firefighters to have some privacy during their working days and nights.

This fire service had made these changes due in part to the availability of economic resources in a prosperous, growing city. It was noted that the municipal government environment had many women in positions of leadership in public services, who had advanced an equity agenda. Clearly there was political support for these changes and expenditures. Further, the fire service had hired several energetic deputy chiefs who showed leadership on equity issues. The many new positions allowed these new leaders to hire those they believed would help to bring about progressive change in the workplace culture. No doubt stimulating these initiatives were public pressure and media reports about sexual harassment scandals in fire services, a situation that was considered an embarrassment. Only some of these conditions were available in other municipalities included in this research. Employment equity requires not only commitment, knowledge, and shifts in perception, but material resources and political support.

EVADING THE CHALLENGES OF MATERIAL ENVIRONMENT AND CULTURE: THE EQUITY SIDE DOOR

Although lacking the budgets, political support, or priority-setting necessary to address their cultural barriers to employment equity, many municipal fire services have found other ways to make improvements. These methods involve employing underrepresented groups in work that does not involve responding to emergency calls or working in the fire halls. As a result, in many fire services there are now two pathways open to women and racialized workers in fire services. The first pathway is a side door to management.

Until recently, all fire services personnel other than clerical workers began and established their careers as firefighters who were employed in emergency response work in fire halls, known as "operations." However, women without operations experience have been appointed to assistant chief and deputy chief positions in some fire services. It is these hires that may account for the slightly higher percentage of women in senior fire services positions than in firefighter positions in the 2011 National Household Survey (Statistics Canada, 2011). Women are being hired from other kinds of jobs inside and outside fire services, such as human resources, finance, and emergency dispatch. Because they are not hired for operations firefighting, these women bypass the physical fitness test. A white woman assistant chief in British Columbia explained what the process of gaining acceptance without a firefighting background is like: "I was an outsider and I was put into this position. I was aware of the challenges—that the staff in the fire halls are not going to accept me in a chief's role because of the fact that I haven't earned it and come through the fire hall. ... I've worked really hard and I have been accepted. I'm kind of like the favourite chief now."

Although these hires improve the numbers of women and the public image of fire services, gendered inequities lurk within this progress. Some women in deputy or assistant chief positions reported that they earn less than men of the same rank in the same service. Unlike their male counterparts, they had not been provided with a vehicle or gear and were not included on the 24/7 coverage schedule to assume command with other chiefs. In other cases, women chiefs from nontraditional backgrounds were fully included and compensated.

A second side door is opened for women and other members of designated groups who were successful in gaining positions as operations firefighters, but did not want to stay in them. These workers applied for positions in fire prevention, training, or other non-operations positions as soon as opportunities arose. These jobs tend be daytime, five days a week, and can be a better fit for those with childcare responsibilities. But, perhaps more significantly, they remove these workers from the oppressive material and cultural environment of the fire hall. As one firefighter, who left operations after two years and now works for the same fire services in a training position, explained, "Don't get me wrong. I liked the work. But I got tired of it. There were the assholes and the apologists and whatever. But mostly, I could never relax. … I wasn't really [accepted as] a firefighter because I'm a black gay man. I was backing into the closet, and I was only partly out at work, anyway."

Improving the numbers of underrepresented group members in the fire service is an insufficient strategy toward employment equity. Opening a side door to management and moving qualified firefighters through a side door to non-operations positions are employment equity measures with contradictory consequences. Both moves improve the numbers of underrepresented groups, while at the same time they ignore or evade the need to change the inequitable material and cultural conditions of fire hall life. This contradiction may reinforce, rather than challenge, fire services' white, masculine, heterosexual norms by putting "others" in specific roles, thus potentially shaping a sex, gender, and racialized division of labour in the fire service.

ACCOUNTING FOR EMPLOYMENT EQUITY

It should now be clear that employment equity requires shifts in how we consider and address issues of bodies, material environments, and workplace culture, as well as equitable hiring processes and compensation. But understanding how employment equity is measured and assessed is also important. Some fire services, and the municipalities that operate them, have begun to keep track of employment equity, in keeping with policy changes at the provincial or, more often, municipal level.

When this research project began in 2007, most municipalities and fire services did not maintain records on employment equity. This is still the case in many Canadian cities. Although policies may encourage services to make improvements, there are often no requirements for services to measure or monitor progress. But some cities have taken action to set targets and measure progress across all municipal departments, including fire services.

In Canada, in keeping with the 1986 federal legislation that set the direction for employment equity across the country, employment equity targets are set by determining what proportion of the population of women, visible minorities, Aboriginal Peoples, and persons with disabilities are available for work in a particular region and have recent, relevant education or experience in their occupation of choice. These proportions are often reduced further, as some employers may have justifiable restrictions on the pools from which they recruit. For example, some employers are required to show preference for candidates who are Canadian citizens.

This labour market availability is derived from Statistics Canada data (Statistics Canada, 2016) using the specific National Occupational Coding information used in collating census data. The result is that targets are well below population percentages. For example, one municipal official, an equity services manager in Manitoba, indicated, "We don't aim for 50% women like the population, because labour market availability for women is 30.5%, and we've hit 29.5% at the city, so we've improved."

This measurement process aims to produce employment equity in specific workplaces, but taking into account only those identified as available and trained in a particular field directs attention away from the root causes of many employment inequities. Left out are considerations of why some populations and groups have a lower percentage of people available for work. For example, why are smaller proportions of women, Aboriginal people, and people with disabilities available for work in many regions than in the general population? These wider questions about why some groups remain unemployed or underemployed cannot be asked or answered using available census data. Feminist political economy helps us to raise these important questions, however, by directing attention to the political, economic, and social conditions in which employment equity struggles occur.

CONCLUSION

Drawing on research on Canadian fire services, this chapter has revealed four of the key challenges to employment equity in masculinized occupations, including, in particular, intersections of sex, gender, race, and sexuality. These challenges evoke critical questions about how work is accomplished, organized, and valued; how workers access, experience, and do their work; and how employment equity can be achieved.

First, this chapter showed that assumptions about sex, gender, and racialization are intertwined with understandings and measurements of bodily capabilities and capacities that affect safe, effective work. Yet genuine differences among and between gendered and racialized bodies challenge some notions of equality that ignore these embodied differences. Second, this research demonstrated that material environments matter, in that they enable and disable bodies, while also reflecting gendered and cultural norms. Changes to material environments are expensive to address, and often require new technologies, techniques, and tools, and complete shifts in how work is accomplished.

Third, culture matters in shaping who is included in workplaces and how. Changing culture can be facilitated by a generational turnover in personnel and other shifts, but in an occupation like firefighting where the culture produces many positive benefits for mainstream workers, initiatives toward change are often resisted.

Fourth, employment equity measurements are central in determining what counts as equity, and whose equity counts. Accepted methods for establishing employment targets ignore the systemic discrimination that keeps women and other underrepresented groups from labour market availability for many jobs.

Finally, the research data discussed here show that changes are being made. Some changes can have contradictory or paradoxical consequences, with limits to employment equity arising from advances. Masculinized occupations present specific challenges to employment equity that go well beyond addressing problems with recruitment, hiring, discrimination, and harassment, but these are not insurmountable.

Change is happening, albeit slowly and unevenly. Public pressure and political will are critical factors in spurring change. Progressive leadership in fire services and firefighters' unions is also an important factor, including from white men who have positioned themselves as allies in struggles for employment equity. Financial commitments are required to ensure changes to equipment, buildings, and training, including training that supports work groups to become more inclusive. Further, research findings that demonstrate how firefighting work can be accomplished by different bodies are being used, but there is much research that still needs to be done.

Can firefighting work be altered to support inclusion of a wider range of workers? In fact, this is already being done. Firefighters whose strength and fitness have declined due to aging or chronic conditions are accommodated in operations firefighting, but only to a certain point. It seems entirely possible that firefighting could be more inclusive by making changes to each of the areas mentioned here. But there are limits to inclusiveness, yet to be precisely determined. It is difficult to imagine persons with disabilities such as severe deafness or vision impairment or profound physical disability doing this work. Fitness and strength remain central, although mechanical and technological innovation may make these factors less of an issue in future. Thus, employment equity needs to be a continual direction, rather than a destination that can be totally described in advance.

NOTES

1. Editor's note: Various terms have been used to denote the people of Canada's First Nations, Metis, Innu, and Inuit communities, and their use has evolved over time. *Indigenous* and *Aboriginal* are both used in federal legislation and publications. Similarly, a variety of terms are used to designate gender, sexual orientation, and race. All of these terms may have different social, historical, and individual connotations for different people. For example, Canadian employment equity legislation uses *Caucasian* and *visible minority*, whereas individuals in those groups may refer to themselves as *white*, *black*, *brown*, *people of colour*, and so on. The terms used in this chapter are those chosen by the study participants and used in Canadian legislation, including *Aboriginal*. Elsewhere in the book the term *Indigenous* is used.

2. Lesbian, gay, bisexual, trans, queer, two-spirited.

3. Operations are the firefighters who work in direct emergency response work, and this is by far the largest single group of professional firefighters in Canada. In some jurisdictions, firefighters work solely in divisions that do inspections, training, or other tasks and are not involved in operations.

4. The researchers were a caucasian Canadian-born woman professor, assisted in one case study by a black non-Canadian-born male doctoral student. Since we had witnessed overt racism and sexism at other sites, we did not believe our positionality was a strong factor in this case.

KEY READINGS

Agócs, C. (2014). The making of the Abella Report: Reflections on the thirtieth anniversary of the report of the Royal Commission on Equality in Employment. In *Employment equity in Canada: The legacy of the Abella Report* (pp. 13–28). Toronto: University of Toronto Press.

Braedley, S. (2015). Pulling men into the care economy: The case of Canadian firefighters. *Competition and Change, 19*(3), 264–278.

Cox, R., & Messing, K. (2006). Legal and biological perspectives on employment testing for physical abilities: A post-*Meiorin* review. *Windsor Yearbook of Access to Justice, 24*, 23–53.

DISCUSSION QUESTIONS

1. How do normative ideas and assumptions about gender and race affect how work is organized and accomplished?

2. Does gender matter in terms of physical capacity to do some kinds of work? If so, how? If not, why not? How can perceived gender limitations be addressed to shape improvements in employment equity?

3. What kinds of employment equity strategies have had perverse or contradictory consequences in masculinized work? Which strategies hold more promise?

4. Backlash is always a consequence of employment equity change. How should it be handled or addressed?

REFERENCES

Abella, R. S. (1984). *Equality in employment: A Royal Commission report.* Ottawa: Minister of Supply and Services.

Abu-Laban,Y., & Gabriel, C. (2002). *Selling diversity: Immigration, multiculturalism, employment equity, and globalization.* Toronto: Broadview Press.

Agócs, C. (Ed.). (2014). The making of the Abella Report: Reflections on the thirtieth anniversary of the report of the Royal Commission on Equality in Employment. In *Employment equity in Canada: The legacy of the Abella Report* (pp. 13–28). Toronto: University of Toronto Press.

Arat-Koç, S. (2006). Whose social reproduction? Transnational motherhood and challenges to feminist political economy. In K. Bezanson & M. Luxton (Eds.), *Social reproduction: Feminist political economy challenges neo-liberalism* (pp. 75–92). Montreal: McGill-Queen's University Press.

Armstrong, P. (1996). The feminization of the labour force: Harmonizing down in a global economy. In I. Bakker (Ed.), *Rethinking restructuring: Gender and change in Canada* (pp. 29–54). Toronto: University of Toronto Press.

Armstrong, P. (2007). Back to basics: Seeking pay equity for women in Canada. *Labour and Industry, 18*(2), 11–32.

Armstrong, P. (2013). Puzzling skills: Feminist political economy approaches. *Canadian Review of Sociology/Revue canadienne de sociologie, 50*(3), 256–283.

Baines, D. (2008). Race, resistance, and restructuring: Emerging skills in the new social services. *Social Work*, *53*(2), 123–131.

Bakan, A. B., & Koybashi, A. (2007). Affirmative action and employment equity: Policy, ideology and backlash in the Canadian context. *Studies in Political Economy*, *79*, 139–160.

Beasley, C. (2008). Rethinking hegemonic masculinity in a globalizing world. *Men and Masculinities*, *11*(1), 86–103.

Bilge, S. (2010). Recent feminist outlooks on intersectionality. *Diogenes*, *57*(1), 58–72.

Braedley, S. (2009). A ladder up: Ontario firefighters' wages in neoliberal times. *Just Labour*, *14*, 129–149.

Braedley, S. (2010). Accidental health care: Masculinity and neoliberalism at work. In S. Braedley & M. Luxton (Eds.), *Neoliberalism and everyday life* (pp. 136–162). Montreal: McGill-Queen's University Press.

Braedley, S. (2015). Pulling men into the care economy: The case of Canadian firefighters. *Competition and Change*, *19*(3), 264–278.

Braedley, S., & Luxton, M. (2010). Competing philosophies: Neoliberalism and the challenges of everyday life. In S. Braedley & M. Luxton (Eds.), *Neoliberalism and everyday life* (pp. 3–21). Montreal: McGill-Queen's University Press.

Braedley, S., Owusu, P., Przednowek, A., & Armstrong, P. (2017). We're told, "Suck it up": Long-term care workers' psychological health and safety. *Ageing International*, *43*(1), 1–19.

British Columbia (Public Service Employee Relations Commission) v. BCGSEU, [1999] 3 S.C.R. 3.

Brodie, M. J., & Bakker, I. (2008). *Where are the women?: Gender equity, budgets and Canadian public policy*. Ottawa: Canadian Centre for Policy Alternatives.

CBC News. (2011, December 11). Windsor firefighter sues over sexual harassment. Retrieved from www.cbc.ca/news/canada/windsor/story/2011/01/10/wdr-city-fire-lawsuit.html

Chetkovich, C. (1997). *Real heat: Gender and race in the urban fire service*. Brunswick, NJ: Rutgers University Press.

City of Toronto. (2011, September 3). Toronto Fire Services receives prestigious international award. Retrieved from http://wx.toronto.ca/inter/it/newsrel.nsf/bydate/AE8B9AC6F8BF8B2F852578E9004258DC

Cohen, M. G., & Pulkingham, J. (2009). *Public policy for women: The state, income security, and labour market issues*. Toronto: University of Toronto Press.

Connell, R. W. (2002). *Gender*. Cambridge, UK: Polity Press.

Coulter, K. (2013). Raising retail: Organizing retail workers in Canada and the United States. *Labor Studies Journal*, *38*(1), 47–65.

Cox, R., & Messing, K. (2006). Legal and biological perspectives on employment testing for physical abilities: A post-*Meiorin* review. *Windsor Yearbook of Access to Justice, 24*, 23–53.

Creese, G., & Beagan, B. (2009). Gender at work: Strategies for equality in neoliberal times. In E. Grabb & N. Guppy (Eds.), *Social inequality in Canada: Patterns, problems, and policies* (5th ed., pp. 224–236). Toronto: Prentice Hall.

Das Gupta, T. (2009). *Real nurses and others: Racism in nursing.* Halifax: Fernwood.

Davis, A. Y. (2016). *Freedom is a constant struggle: Ferguson, Palestine, and the foundations of a movement.* Chicago: Haymarket Books.

Drydakis, N. (2009). Sexual orientation discrimination in the labour market. *Labour Economics, 16*(4), 364–372.

Flood, M. (2008). Men, sex and homosociality: How bonds between men shape their sexual relations with women. *Men and Masculinities, 10*(3), 339–359.

Fudge, J., & Strauss, K. (2013). *Temporary work, agencies and unfree labour: Insecurity in the new world of work.* Abingdon, UK: Routledge.

Gordon, T., & Stewart, T. (2006). *Cops, crime and capitalism: The law and order agenda in Canada.* Halifax: Fernwood Press.

Grundy, J., & Smith, M. (2011). Evidence and equity: Struggles over federal employment equity policy in Canada, 1984–95. *Canadian Public Administration, 54*(3), 335–357.

Irving, D. (2015). Performance anxieties: Trans women's un(der)-employment experiences in post-Fordist society. *Australian Feminist Studies, 30*(83), 50–64.

Kuchler, T. (2008, August 6). Anti-gay bigotry spans European cultures. *EU Observer.* Retrieved from http://euobserver.com/879/26567

Kuokkanen, R. (2011). From Indigenous economies to market-based self-governance: A feminist political economy analysis. *Canadian Journal of Political Science, 44*(2), 275–297.

Luxton, M. (1980). *More than a labour of love: Three generations of women's work in the home.* Toronto: Women's Press.

Luxton, M. (2006). Feminist political economy in Canada and the politics of social reproduction. In K. Bezanson & M. Luxton (Eds.), *Social reproduction: Feminist political economy challenges neo-liberalism* (pp. 11–44). Montreal: McGill-Queen's University Press.

Mackin, B. (2011, December 27). Wait begins for Pemberton human rights verdict. *The Whistler Question.* Retrieved from https://www.whistlerquestion.com/wait-begins-for-pemberton-human-rights-verdict-1.1283136

Messing, K., & Kilbom, Å. (1998). Identifying biological specificities of relevance to work-related health. In K. Messing, Å. Kilbom, & C. Thorbjornsson (Eds.), *Women's health at work* (pp. 99–120). Solna, Sweden: National Institute of Working Life.

Messing, K., Lippel, K., Demers, D. L., & Mergler, D. (2000). Equality and difference in the workplace: Physical job demands, occupational illnesses, and sex differences. *NWSA Journal, 12*(3), 21–49.

Pegg, M. (2017). *Toronto Fire Services diversity, recruitment and inclusion plan update.* Report for Action CD18.2. Toronto: Toronto Fire Services.

Regehr, C., Dimitropoulos, G., Bright, E., George, S., & Henderson, J. (2005). Behind the brotherhood: Rewards and challenges for wives of firefighters. *Family Relations, 54*(3), 423–451.

Statistics Canada. (2011). National household survey: Data table, occupations (99–012 X2011033). Ottawa: Statistics Canada.

Statistics Canada. (2016). Employment equity technical guide. Retrieved from https://www.canada.ca/en/employment-social-development/services/employment-equity/tools/technical.html

Teelucksingh, C., & Galabuzi, G. E. (2007). Working precariously: The impact of race and immigrant status on employment opportunities and outcomes in Canada. In T. Das Gupta, C. E. James, R. C. A. Maaka, G.-E. Galabuzi, & C. Anderson (Eds.), *Race and racialization: Essential readings* (pp. 202–208). Toronto: Canadian Scholars' Press.

Teeple Hopkins, C. (2017). Work intensifications, injuries and legal exclusions for paid domestic workers in Montréal, Québec. *Gender, Place and Culture, 24*(4), 1–12.

Ward, J., & Winstanley, D. (2006). Watching the watch: The UK fire service and its impact on sexual minorities in the workplace. *Gender, Work and Organization, 13*(2), 193–219.

CHAPTER 16

Women in Manufacturing: Challenges in a Neoliberal Context

June Corman

INTRODUCTION

Prior to changes to Canadian employment laws, corporations could selectively choose the composition of their workforce. This discriminatory employment practice enabled employers in sectors such as mining, forestry, construction, and steel and in other heavy manufacturing plants to hire men—mostly white men—into jobs that offered good pay, benefits, and pension plans in post–World War II Canada. Women were hired for less financial compensation in light manufacturing plants such as food and rubber processing.

When women gained access to good jobs in male workplaces in the 1980s, union agreements and government protections meant that women who were hired by steel, industrial manufacturing, and mining companies were commonly entitled to the same pay, benefits, and pensions as men. The women who were lucky enough to get these jobs were able, as men had been for decades, to support their families, donate to charities, pay taxes, and build communities in many ways. Access to these jobs and experiences on the job, though, were often fraught with difficulties. For example, women miners entered a male domain with an infused culture of masculinity at the mine face and in management practices (Mercier, 2011). Provincial regulations in Ontario changed in 1978 to allow women to work underground, but mine managers were still hesitant to hire women. Inco in Sudbury waited until 1992 to send the first woman underground. Sudbury women miners, like women in other sectors, were motivated by higher wages and were prepared to cope with physically hard work and sexual harassment to gain financial independence (Keck & Powell, 2008). These experiences were typical of women hired at nontraditional workplaces (Woodhall & Leach, 2010).

Initiatives to hire women into these well-compensated jobs coincided with a downturn in demand for these products, efforts to decrease labour costs, and, in some cases, depletion of mineral resources (Fonow, 2003; Gibbs, Leach & Yates, 2012; Luxton & Corman, 2001; Mercier 2011). Employment at the two big Hamilton steel mills fell from over 23,000 in 1980 to under 8,000 in 2017 (G. Howe, president of USW Local 1005, personal communication, 2017). Similarly from 2001 to 2015 Ontario lost 43,000 auto industry jobs (CBC, 2015). Those last hired, including most of the women, were the first to lose their jobs. Only 5% of unionized steelworkers at Stelco were women in 2017 (G. Howe, personal communication, 2017), and in 2016 only 19.9% of motor vehicle manufacturing in Canada was done by women (Statistics Canada, 2018). Decisions of corporate executives, who responded to the relentless pursuit of greater profits by closing, downsizing, or relocating mills, plants, and mines, decimated local economies and deprived those who lost jobs of their livelihood. Neither individual effort on the floor nor collective resistance could help women keep their jobs.

This chapter uses three case studies to examine the vulnerabilities for women of hiring practices, compensation packages, and downsizing or discontinuing production in the manufacturing sector: (1) the Hilton Works steel plant in Hamilton, Ontario, (2) John Deere Welland Works in Welland, Ontario, which made small agricultural and landscaping equipment until it closed in 2009, and (3) a rubber plant in southern Ontario that makes rubber products for cars.

Intersectional feminism directs our attention to how the interplay between "sociocultural categorizations such as gender, ethnicity, race, class, sexuality, age/generation, dis/ability, nationality, mother tongue and so on ... produce different kinds of societal inequalities and unjust social relations" (Lykke, 2010, p. 50). In a capitalist system, variations in gender, race, class, and place of residence generate differences in chances for success in life (Bennholdt-Thomsen & Mies, 1999). In the context of people working in manufacturing in Ontario, this framework directs attention to several observations: white men have had better access to the best jobs in manufacturing compared to women and racialized groups; younger age linked to lower seniority has caused vulnerability for women to workforce reductions and low-tier pay; after plant closures, working-class women of all ages face fragile futures; and disabilities attributed to the work process further compound financial hardships. In all three cases presented here, in the context of capitalist production practices, maximizing profits for the benefits of owners overrode considerations of the impacts of these decisions on the women and men employed at their plants (Corman, Duffy, & Pupo, 2012).

HILTON WORKS STEEL PLANT, HAMILTON, ONTARIO

The Hilton Works steel plant (owned by Stelco/US Steel) is a useful example of the difficulties facing women who aspire to jobs in heavy manufacturing as this plant was the first in Ontario to hire women. Since 1945 steel companies in Hamilton insisted on male mill workers until they were forced to end discrimination against women applicants. Rising employment levels at Hilton Works in the 1970s generated thousands of female applicants for these high-paying jobs, but the company systematically ignored women applicants (Luxton & Corman, 2001).[1] To force change, interested women joined with USW (United Steelworkers) Local 1005 to build a campaign to target Stelco management. Their complaint to the Human Rights Commission was successful and, in the summer of 1980, Hilton Works began hiring women into many types of jobs in the steel plant, from preparing ingredients to making molten steel to employment in the end units, where steel sheets are rolled in preparation for shipping. Hired into these most prestigious working-class jobs in Hamilton, women had access to high wages, generous benefit packages, pensions, and good health and safety provisions. As a single mother explained after she accepted the job at Hilton Works, "Getting that job made it possible for me to support myself and my kids adequately" (Luxton & Corman, 2001, p. 60). Another typical woman at the plant reminisced after being laid off, "It was the best job I ever had, the best job I could imagine having. The best pay, of course. But it was also a job where I could be a skilled worker" (Luxton & Corman, 2001, p. 93).

These benefits offset the disadvantages of the hot, dirty, and tiring work process and motivated women to challenge the masculine workplace culture that a largely white male workforce had constructed over the decades. In response to attitudes such as this expressed by a male steelworker, "It takes a real man to work here" (Luxton & Corman, 2001, p. 83), the women's committee and the union launched a second campaign to change both management practices and plant floor behaviour. The campaign was designed to legitimize women's presence and reduce the sexism they experienced as part of the backlash against their hiring. As one of the earliest initiatives of this nature in a North American steel mill, this campaign to normalize women's work in a steel mill provided precedents for those in other male preserves to follow.

The Women Back Into Stelco Campaign levelled the playing field for women and men applicants and legitimized women's work in the mill. Yet the drastic reductions in this workforce over the next 37 years, from 12,809 in 1979 to 520 unionized steelworkers in 2017, meant few women or men of any background had access to starting their work life at these jobs. Given their low seniority, most of those women who were hired were laid off in times of retrenchment, first under Stelco ownership, and then under the direction of US Steel. Those few women who qualified for retirement then found their pension and benefits vulnerable after US Steel bought the plant in 2008 (Corman & Walsh, 2011) and then again under the 2017 contract negotiated with US Steel (Craggs, 2017). Uncertainty increased once more when Bedrock Industries, a private-sector company, bought the plant in June 2017 (Zochodne, 2017). As Gary Howe, president of USW Local 1005, lamented in June 2017, "We have approximately 26 women working as 1005 members out of a total of 520 members. So that is 5 percent. Not very good" (G. Howe, personal communication, 2017). In 2017 none of the women occupied positions on the union executive, and the women's committee was no longer mentioned on the union website.

The availability of jobs at this steel plant is uncertain as the future now relies on decisions made by CEOs of Bedrock Industries (Zochodne, 2017). USW Local 1005 continues to organize to protect these jobs and to ensure pensions and benefits for 9,000 retirees (McNeil, 2017). The 2018 free trade negotiations between Canada and the United States have created a perilous climate for steel producers because the US government imposed tariffs on some Canadian steel products, prompting retaliatory tariffs by the Canadian government. As a woman steelworker explained, "We've lost so much already and we need to take a stand now or we will lose it all. ... If we don't stop it, we're going to see our entire standard of living eroded away."

JOHN DEERE WELLAND WORKS IN WELLAND

Even after the successful Human Rights Commission ruling in 1980, the workforces in many heavy manufacturing plants in Ontario, such as automotive factories and other assembly plants, remained predominantly white and male. John Deere Welland Works, a manufacturer of all-terrain vehicles and loaders, hired its first women on the floor in 1987, and never exceeded 15 women out of a unionized (Canadian Auto Workers) workforce at the high of 6,000 employees. Throughout this time period, women never occupied an executive position in the union.

In 1987 John Deere posted a notice at employment help centres that it would accept applications from women for positions such as welders, painters, and loaders at its plant in Welland. At this time, only men were employed in the three main phases of production: welding small John Deere products, painting the equipment a bright green, and loading products for transport.

A woman welder explained that at that time only four women joined the workforce. One of the first women hired explained that she applied without any hope of actually being hired even though she had the qualifications: "I started at John Deere in 1987, 22 years ago. I had worked at Gencorp Rubber, now named Henniges. John Deere had a notice that they were going to start hiring women. I put my name in. I was the perfect candidate. I didn't think I would be hired [but I was]. Then I had to make a choice. I just felt like doing it. I gotta admit, the difference in pay made possible what I have today." John Deere never seriously recruited women applicants, and even as late as 2002 only nine women were on the shop floor. Of the fifteen women working at John Deere in 2008, an employee explained that "one is in her fifties, at John Deere for 25 years; a lot of the girls were in their late thirties and early forties; and one was probably 30."

When women were hired at the plant, management insisted that new hires receive less pay for the same work done by senior workers and, as a consequence, newly hired women and men received much less financial compensation than more senior male workers. A woman welder explained, "They have the old guys making between $27, $26, rising to $35, $40 [an hour] depending on bonus; the young guys, or the medium, Tier 2, from around $22, raising to $25; and us at $11, raising to $21.50, all depending on the year in which you were hired." Even with annual raises, those newly hired could never reach the pay levels enjoyed by others, as a woman welder explained: "The guys that were hired prior to my group made double the money I did. When I got hired, we were on a tier system where it took us six years to get up to full wage for our hiring group. I never would match the money some of these baby boomer guys were making." Senior men appreciated that they benefited from their early year of hire. According to a very senior male welder, "Those who held jobs prior to the 1998 system were given a factor—any money you make, you multiply it by the factor. That would put us with high seniority about 50% or 60% higher than the others working beside us, sometimes higher."

The contrast in men's and women's salaries was especially visible within families. A man in his fifties explained that under the **tiered pay** plan introduced in 1998/1999, he, his son, and his daughter all received different pay packages because each had been hired in a different year, with his daughter being hired last.

"There were three in my family working there. I was at the top rate as if [no concessions] ever happened. When new people come in, such as my daughter, it would take six years for her to get to the top of her rate." His daughter and others hired in her cohort in Tier 3 would never reach the rate achieved by either her father (on the most lucrative plan) or her brother (in Tier 2) doing the same work.

A young woman welder explained how she felt working next to a man who was doing the same work for twice the pay: "It was very degrading, standing beside the same person doing the same job, earning like $10 less an hour. That really, really hurt me." She felt even more bitter when men drew the pay difference to her attention: "I was looking at my pay stub, and some guy very sarcastically said, 'Did ya want help taking this home?' I blew up at him. I know it was a joke, but it hurt. I thought that was very cruel." The sizable pay differential "felt like a stab in the back."

Not only were new hires, both women and men, paid less per hour than the more senior workforce, the new team bonus program, the Continuous Improvement Pay Plan (CIPP), tied the amount of bonuses to the level of hourly pay, further disadvantaging junior employees and almost all the women. A disadvantaged woman welder explained, "They were all 30-year guys. They had that job so down to a T that they eliminated three guys. Now they're doing six-man work with three guys. Each guy was getting a $15,000 to $20,000 bonus every six months. Unheard of. My whole time there, I think I only made $2,000 extra in six months." As a man in a privileged team explained, "I was probably the highest-paid person in John Deere for the simple reason that I was in a three-man team, and I understood CIPP. We made unbelievable money."

Even tiered pay and other concessions made by the workforce were not sufficient to protect Canadian jobs as John Deere looked for prospects to reach higher profit margins by lowering labour costs. In September 2008 the company announced the closure of the Welland operation with the shift of production to underutilized plants in the United States and to low-wage workers in newly built facilities in Mexico (Pupo, Duffy, & Corman, 2013). As demand for products was strong and employment had been at consistent levels for a decade, the shutdown of the John Deere plant was a devastating shock. Tom Napper, then president of the local union, explained, "We were at the top of production; everything was going great. They were making money and we just finished bargaining. So we knew all of the ins and outs of the place."

Many expressed feelings of being betrayed by a company to which they had devoted the best years of their lives to make a respected, valued, and quality consumer product (Pupo, Duffy, & Corman, 2013). This betrayal by John Deere by closing the plant severed their pride in being John Deere employees.

Contrary to their assumptions, being profitable had not mattered. Making quality product had not mattered. For women and men alike, the closure indicated that their efforts over all these years were not valued and hence, in retrospect, for many, had been meaningless outside of their instrumentality for making a living. Many spoke angrily about this abrogation of the assumed employment contract. They had upheld their side of the bargain by managing the physical consequences of heavy work and working as required year after year.

The jobs at John Deere had meant that all workers could provide materially for their families with a solid paycheque, benefits, and pension entitlement. Now not only could they not support their families, but those jobs were also lost forever to the Welland labour market, meaning that the next generation in Welland would never have access to these good jobs. Women had proven that they could weld alongside men, but those women who worked at John Deere and others may never again have the opportunity to do so.

Finding other good jobs was next to impossible. These women and men joined a long line of desperate people who were searching for the elusive job that they hoped could provide a living wage and a retirement package (Duffy, Corman, & Pupo, 2015). Even lower-paid jobs were hard to secure because the shutdown had triggered a cascade of business closures (warehouses, suppliers, retail outlets, and restaurants) that deprived their workers of employment. All these disenfranchised people were thrown into a labour market that contained no relevant jobs for their experience level. Steel and auto plants were not hiring, and most other jobs paid less, with few benefits or pension entitlement. Some women tried to retrain, but even those who managed to certify as, for example, home care workers or social service workers ended up with less pay, fewer benefits, and less pension entitlement than when they worked as welders at John Deere.

Sylvia is a case in point. She welded at John Deere for 10 years prior to the closure announcement. This good job was very important to her as she supported her invalid husband, who had lost his job at Atlas Steel. The job at John Deere had given her access to benefits to pay for his costly medication. Strategizing how to secure another job with benefits while still at John Deere, Sylvia returned to school to finish her diploma in social services and then started working in this field while still continuing her shifts at the plant. At that time she saw herself as organized and realistic, with a plan to support herself and her husband: "I gave myself grieving time and then moved forward." Like so many others, 18 months after the closure Sylvia despaired that she still did not have permanent work or a benefit plan. This woman who had seen herself as competent and motivated while at John Deere reported, "I am beaten up, punched, and kicked around."

In contrast, more senior employees, all men, who had enjoyed the highest pay and most favourable bonus-heavy jobs had been able to save money from their healthy paycheques. Their pension entitlement meant that they could live their senior years in ease. For young and middle-aged women and men, the closure damaged their household finances in the near future, through lack of good jobs and, extending into their senior years, through lack of pension entitlement. John Deere's decision to close the plant resulted in the loss of opportunity for these younger and middle-aged women and men to provide for their families in ways that their old male comrades had enjoyed for decades (Corman, Duffy, & Pupo, 2017).

RUBBER PLANT IN NIAGARA

In contrast to Hilton Works and John Deere, the rubber plant in Niagara had always employed women, although the workforce gradually became half male as other employment opportunities vanished for men in the Niagara region. Men who lost their jobs at Atlas Specialty Steels and other plants competed alongside women for what had been mostly women's work. Intensified competition for these jobs coincided with the downsizing of the workforce from a high of 1,100 unionized workers to only 300 at the time of the plant's closure in 2011 (Johnson & Benner, 2011). Given the decrease in employment opportunities, the ethnic composition of the plant remained unchanged and continued to be dominated by workers of European ancestry.

From the founding of the plant, various work processes were solely allocated to men or to women. The first step of the production process—the chemical mixing room—was dominated by men who were paid a couple of dollars per hour more. These men worked with hazardous chemicals to create liquid rubber. As a senior woman explained, "We have the mixing department and all these years it's been men. And it's kind of their domain. It was a very dirty area. They had long-term health effects because they were breathing in carbon and smoke. It was heavy work, so the women didn't want to go in there." Once mixed, the liquid rubber flowed through the plant and was processed by employees, largely women, using specialized equipment at work stations. Men monopolized the heavy presses, while women almost exclusively did the finishing work. As a woman who worked on the line relayed, "You know, for women, small parts, putting in inserts and, for guys, … working big presses."

By the time of the closure announcement, men's jobs were still largely segregated, though a couple of women did work in mixing. Describing the workforce at this time, a woman on the line reported, "There are some jobs where it's still mostly guys where they mix the rubber. Not many women like that job. There are probably physical demands, heavy and physical, and dirty. And millwrights, actually no women. I never see any electrician women either. We had a couple of supervisor women before, but most of the supervisors are guys." In contrast, there was much less segregation on the women's side of the plant as men worked along with women in jobs that used to be women's preserve. A middle-aged woman explained how men had moved into what had been women's work: "There is a mixture of women and men pretty well in joining and finishing. ... We kind of mixed the jobs. Now it doesn't matter. She can do, he can do. One shift is guy on that job, next shift is woman on that job." Involvement in the union, though, remained a male preserve with the exception of one or two women on the executive over the last 20 years.

In contrast to most other local employment options for women, the workforce at the rubber plant was unionized and had guaranteed recall rights, benefits, regulated working conditions, and access to a pension to provide financially for their household through their senior years. For those who could take the dust, repetitive motion, and rotating night shifts, the trade-offs were worthwhile. The pay, tied to the particular job, was twice the minimum wage but less than financial compensation packages at heavy industry sites. Contrasting employment conditions with those with less or better rewards, a rubber plant worker earning $20 an hour explained, "You're gonna get more than $10, but we're not gonna make the $32 like GM [General Motors] guys. Never gonna happen." Because women had formed the majority of the workforce at the rubber plant, benefits that could be associated with seniority (pay, bidding for jobs, order of layoffs, and recalls) were not structured along gender lines. Molly is a typical example of women who had successfully supported their families through their work at the plant. She had raised and supported her children with little assistance from her ex-husband. The paycheque, at double minimum wage combined with overtime, meant she could afford a mortgage on a modest house and pay other essential day-to-day expenses. Eyeglass, dentist, and prescription benefits covered her children's needs. As the years progressed, holiday entitlement increased from a legislated two weeks to the top grade of five weeks of paid vacation.

On March 1, 2011, Littlejohn and Company rationalized production of the consortium of previously Henniges-owned rubber plants by announcing the closure of the Welland operation effective in the fall of 2011. Looking for ways to maximize profits for shareholders, management reallocated production to existing facilities throughout Canada, the United States, and Mexico

(Johnson & Benner, 2011). Operating with the logic of an economic system based on profit, Littlejohn was focusing on investor profits. These decisions had total disregard for the women and men who had devoted years of their lives to this plant and were dependent on these jobs for their livelihoods. Decent jobs had permanently vanished from a labour market that offered little comparable work for subsequent generations of women. Closing what the employees knew to be a profitable plant, and hence wreaking havoc on their lives and removing job opportunities for their children, created disdain among workers for the US decision-makers.

During the last six months of the plant's operation, US corporative executives required the rubber workers to increase output and make quality product. Tempting though it would have been to sabotage production, women emphasized that they went to work with their heads held high and would not be reduced to the "despicable behaviour of those executives" who made the call to close the plant. Many women who had worked at Henniges expressed the same sentiment as one who stated, "American corporate executives did dirty work in their job by closing the plant, but we are not losing our pride by doing dirty work on the job. We'll show them."

The closure meant that though all workers lost the opportunity to work at the plant, the financial consequences of job loss varied in terms of pension benefits and access to other jobs. Older, more senior women and men retired on full pension; others in their early to late fifties with slightly less seniority would eventually receive monthly pension payments but no benefits; and the large third group, mostly in their forties with least seniority, would receive a lump sum pension payment five years after the closure. Many explained their nervousness about bearing responsibility for investing this money without the experience of pension fund managers. The job had meant financial stability, and now job loss meant, for many, a very insecure and precarious old age. A woman who was typical of those her age explained, "I'd been there for 35 years. I was planning on retiring from there when I was 60 something. I find it hard. I was 54 when the plant was shut down. Who's going to hire you when you're 54? What do you do after being in a factory for 35 years? It's hard to find something else when they see that you were born in 1957."

Not only was age an issue, but workers also confronted the reality that their job skills were only marginally in demand, if at all. Given the absence of good jobs, few women were able to transition directly from their job at the plant to another comparable good job. Rather, those who eventually found factory jobs worked at physically demanding labour processes for three-quarters of their previous pay. No one expected these jobs to be long term, and although pension plans were in place, all were too old to work the requisite number of years to be eligible even if their employment was extended. Less fortunate women found employment in the precarious sector, either in retail work at outlets such as the Dollar Store, in the tourist industry as cleaners, or as security guards at factories or malls. These jobs paid at or just above minimum wage and had no benefits or pension plans. As a woman who found a minimum-wage job explained, "I really don't know how people are going to survive. How the hell is somebody going to buy a house at the price that they are now, making $11 an hour? If you have kids, oh my God, you can't even afford to pay the mortgage payment with all the other bills. What are they going to do? I have no idea. Somebody better do something."

Job searches were also complicated because of lingering health problems that women had contracted at the plant, such as repetitive strain injuries. Common to the production process, almost everyone reported injuries to their wrists, arms, and shoulders for themselves and their coworkers. These women remained at the plant despite the certainty of developing repetitive strain injuries. Sacrificing their health was part of the trade-off for good pay, benefits, and a monthly pension at retirement. The company could not fire an employee who was unable to do a job due to a repetitive strain injury occurring at work. Those employees could receive workers' compensation payments and then be transferred to a different sort of job. An older woman, interviewed while she was still employed at the plant, explained, "I have an injury and I've filed an incident report. You put in an incident report each time. You tell them when it started getting sore. They keep it on file. So eventually when you have to go to the doctor, compensation has to cover it because you've been telling them it's sore. I've worked 17 years. Eventually I'm going to have a serious injury. It builds up." In her case, though, the condition may not manifest until after the closure, and then she could be deprived of a claim to workers' compensation through the rubber plant. After Littlejohn pulled up stakes and left town, these health conditions, directly attributable to employment, hindered the women's ability to be hired into other jobs. Employers did not want to take on the liability of people who had previously sustained repetitive strain injuries.

The large number of single mothers who worked at the plant were particularly vulnerable to ruin with the closure. With financial responsibility for their children, these mothers had worked 12-hour shifts, both days and nights, and incurred repetitive strain injuries to give their children the same opportunities as those growing up in two-parent homes. Losing their jobs, which had offered permanent, full-time employment, benefits, and good pay, meant that sole-support mothers lost their ability to support their families as few other comparable jobs were available. As a single female rubber worker explained, "Look at my situation. I'm single. A lot of people say, if a woman loses her job, big deal, she's got a husband. The husband will take care of her. Not in my case." Another reported a succession of many jobs after the closure, including standing in a cold room, reaching down for newly killed chickens, and then hanging the birds up for processing.

The job at the rubber plant had meant financial stability, and now job loss meant a very insecure and precarious future. The closure eliminated their jobs, and thus their income-providing resource. In addition, since their bodies were consumed by factory work, they were unfit for similarly paid employment at other locations and even, for some, for minimum-wage work. Now, in their forties and fifties, the job was gone, the paycheque was gone, and their bodies were permanently weakened. A woman who was laid off from the rubber plant described her despair at going from being gainfully employed to unable to provide: "At this point it's day by day. At times there's even suicidal thoughts because I just feel like my life, I've failed. I had it all once. Now I have nothing. Dirt. I know that I'm not the only person going through this. Now I sit here and I call it my dungeon. I can't go out. I got no money to go out."

DISCUSSION AND CONCLUSION

With the closures of the John Deere Welland Works and the rubber plant as well as the massive downsizing of Hilton Works, women and men workers felt betrayed by the companies. At these plants, management had expected those on the labour side of the capital-labour relationship to make a long-term commitment such that they would return to the plant to work consistently day in and day out, year after year. And the workers had done so. These people had committed the best years of their lives to these plants and were prepared to invest 30 to 40 years in these companies. In exchange, the employees expected a reciprocal commitment. Yet the owners of the steel mill, the John Deere plant, and the rubber plant did not honour this tacit commitment; they acted without any consideration for their dedicated employees or their communities. At each site workers had reluctantly accepted concessions and still had continued to produce quality products in hopes that such measures would safeguard their jobs. Many spoke angrily about this abrogation of the assumed employment contract. A woman ex-rubber worker explained, "I've worked in that place for 34 years. I feel that they should feel responsibility to make sure that I'm capable of taking care of myself when I retire. Corporations should take full responsibility for their employees. They should be making sure that those people are well taken care of."

Neoliberal regimes and corporate restructuring encourage an international division of labour with manufacturing jobs moving to locales that offer the lowest production cost. In this globalized context, women experience harsh corporate decision-making in full force as the location of manufacturing jobs and who gets hired into these jobs are entirely decided by private-sector companies. The Welland-based factories and US Steel Hilton Works were a small part of very large corporations located outside Canada, with assets scattered throughout the world. With access to dispersed production facilities, executives could trim costs and increase revenues of the parent corporation by selling certain production facilities or transferring production to lower-cost plants within the corporation. In these and other cases, the interests of the parent corporation took precedence over the interests of the individual factories, particular employees, or the communities hosting the production facilities. The decisions to abandon factories led directly to loss of jobs and resulted in few options for these displaced workers to support their families, with the result of diminished incomes, dismal livelihoods, dislocated families, and community disruption.

In this southern Ontario context, after job loss workers confronted an employment reality where their job skills were only marginally in demand, and the labour market was devoid of other good jobs. Women working in plants had gained valuable experience, but these skills were not directly transferable to service sector work. Those employers had plenty of younger women with service sector experience to hire for these precarious retail and tourism jobs. To compound this economic fragility, these laid-off workers were left to provide and care for their families in a neoliberal climate of cutbacks to services (Fuatai, 2016). Not only was their income diminished, but government services in many fields were not keeping up with demand.

In 1980, at the time of the Human Rights Commission ruling, a future could be imagined with women and men working side by side in high-paid manufacturing jobs, each of them earning enough to provide for their families and support their communities. Instead, massive downsizing of good working-class jobs in Canada has resulted in continued workplace segregation, an associated wage gap of 87% in 2016, and few opportunities for women and men to secure reasonable livelihoods (Israel, 2017). In 2016 women were only 28% of the workforce in heavy and light manufacturing, and the proportion of manufacturing jobs held by women had stagnated without increase from 2001 to 2016 (Women in Manufacturing Working Group, 2017). A future of such promise was never realized; few women entered nontraditional manufacturing jobs, and those who invested their time and energy into these jobs often lost them due to downsizing and were cast into a labour market unwelcoming to those their age and with their skill set.

Like the downsizing of the Hamilton steel industry from 1980 to 2018, the closures of the John Deere and rubber plants in Welland are a clear indication of the vulnerability of working people to the dictates of corporate management. This devastation is repeated time and again in communities around the world as the logic of the capitalist economic system bases production decisions on profit maximization. The reach of these disruptions around the globe and the depth of consequences are so massive that individuals are left feeling defeated and hopeless.

Politicians of all stripes claim to represent "the people," as is evident in the rhetoric of US president Donald Trump and Ontario premier Doug Ford. These politicians, in their attempts to claim "the people," offer confused and disoriented analyses of the causes of and solutions to economic hardships. People are searching for answers. These politicians are not providing policies that will create a just and fair society. Nor are reasonable answers available in the popular press. Now is the time for unions, political parties, and other social movements to develop and promote real alternatives and then mobilize people—all disenfranchised people—to be active in politics and engaged in their communities at all levels.

NOTE

1. Up to events in 2001, material from this section is taken from Luxton and Corman (2001). Other research is from original unpublished work by Ann Duffy, Norene Pupo, and June Corman.

KEY READINGS

Gibbs, H., Leach, B., & Yates, C. (2012). *Negotiating risk, seeking security, eroding solidarity: Life and work on the border.* Halifax: Fernwood.

Lahiri-Dutt, K. (Ed.). (2011). *Gendering the field: Towards sustainable livelihoods for mining communities.* Canberra: ANU E Press.

Luxton, M., & Corman, J. (2001). *Getting by in hard times: Gendered labour at home and on the job.* Toronto: University of Toronto Press.

Sugiman, P. (1994). *Labour's dilemma: The gender politics of auto workers in Canada, 1937–1979.* Toronto: University of Toronto Press.

DISCUSSION QUESTIONS

1.   What are the trade-offs for women who do dirty, hot, and heavy work in a factory setting?

2.   Why is job loss due to factories closing devastating to women?

3.   In what ways could the market economy be restructured into an alternative economic system that prioritizes people's needs rather than the compulsion to maximize profits?

REFERENCES

Bennholdt-Thomsen, V., & Mies, M. (1999). *The subsistence perspective: Beyond the globalised economy.* London: Zed Books.

CBC. (2015, January 27). Auto industry hits young families hardest, study finds. *CBC News.* Retrieved from www.cbc.ca/news/canada/windsor/auto-industry-decline-hits-young-families-hardest-study-finds-1.2932795

Corman, J., Duffy, A., & Pupo, N. (2012). Overlooking the workers: Community leaders' perspectives on plant closures and economic recession. In L. M. Aguir & C. J. Schneider (Eds.), *Researching amongst elites: Challenges and opportunities in studying up* (pp. 121–140). Burlington, VT: Ashgate.

Corman, J., Duffy, A., & Pupo, N. (2017). Inequality and divisions on the shop floor: The case of John Deere Welland Works. In S. Ross & L. Savage (Eds.), *Labour under attack: Anti-unionism in Canada* (pp. 52–67). Halifax: Fernwood.

Corman, J., & Walsh, C. (2011). Their struggle is our struggle. *Canadian Dimension, (45)3,* 21–22.

Craggs, S. (2017, June 1). New contract means wins for Stelco workers, but pain for retirees. *CBC News.* Retrieved from www.cbc.ca/news/canada/hamilton/steelworkers-hear-agreement-1.4140671/

Duffy, A., Corman, J., & Pupo, N. (2015). Family finances: Fragility, class and gender. *Canadian Review of Sociology, 52*(2), 222–231.

Fonow, M. M. (2003). *Union women: Forging feminism in the United Steelworkers of America.* Minneapolis: University of Minnesota Press.

Fuatai, T. (2016, February 2). Labour activists fight devastating cuts to Ontario's health services. *Rabble.* Retrieved from rabble.ca/news/2016/02/labour-activists-fight-health-cuts-queens-park/

Gibbs, H., Leach, B., & Yates, C. (2012). *Negotiating risk, seeking security, eroding solidarity: Life and work on the border.* Halifax: Fernwood.

Israel, S. (2017, March 08). StatsCan on gender pay gap: Women earn 87 cents to men's dollar, Canadian women still more likely to work in traditionally "female" occupations. *CBC News.* Retrieved from www.cbc.ca/news/business/statistics-canada-gender-pay-gap-1.4014954/

Johnson, D., & Benner, A. (2011, March 2). Henniges closing Welland, 300 people losing jobs. *St. Catharines Standard*. Retrieved from www.stcatharinesstandard.ca/2011/03/01/henniges-closing-in-welland-300-people-losing-jobs/

Luxton, M., & Corman, J. (2001). *Getting by in hard times: Gendered labour at home and on the job*. Toronto: University of Toronto Press.

Lykke, N. (2010). *Feminist studies: A guide to intersectional theory, methodology and writing*. New York: Routledge.

Keck, J., & Powell, M. (2008, December 17). Women into mining jobs at Inco: Challenging the gender division of labour (part 4 of 5). *Women in Mining*. Retrieved from www.republicofmining.com/2008/12/17/women-into-mining-jobs-at-inco-challenging-the-gender-division-of-labour-%E2%80%93-jennifer-keck-and-mary-powell-part-4-of-5/

McNeil, M. (2017, June 7). Local 1005 approves new contract: Obstacle cleared for Bedrock Industries. *Hamilton Spectator*. Retrieved from www.pressreader.com/canada/the-hamilton-spectator/20170607/281487866320499

Mercier, L. (2011). Bordering on equality: Women miners in North America. In K. Lahiri-Dutt (Ed.), *Gendering the field: Towards sustainable livelihoods for mining communities* (pp. 33–48). Canberra: ANU E Press.

Pupo, N., Duffy, A., & Corman J. (2013). Facing plant closure: Workers and their unions in times of crisis. Paper presented at American Sociology Conference, New York.

Statistics Canada. (2018). Data tables, 2016 census. Industry–North American industry classification system (NAICS) 2012(427A), class of worker (5a), labour force status (3), age (13a) and sex (3) for the labour force aged 15 years and over in private households of Canada, provinces and territories, census metropolitan areas and census agglomerations, 2016 census—25% sample data.

Women in Manufacturing Working Group. (2017). Women in manufacturing critical to Canada's competitiveness. (n.p.): Canadian Manufacturers and Exporters.

Woodhall, J. R., & Leach, B. (2010, Fall). Who will fight for us? Union designated women's advocates in auto manufacturing workplaces. *Just Labour: A Canadian Journal for Work and Society, 16*, 44–58.

Zochodne, G. (2017, September 29). Turnaround specialist takes 100-year-old Stelco public, months after it came out of creditor protection. *Financial Post*. Retrieved from https://business.financialpost.com/investing/stelco-ipo

CHAPTER 17

The Nonprofit Sector: Women's Path to Leadership

Agnes Meinhard and Mary Foster

INTRODUCTION

Canada's nonprofit sector, the second-largest in the world per capita, comprises some 170,000 nonprofit organizations,[1] including 86,000 charities (Faul, 2015). **Nonprofit organizations** are independent, voluntarily constituted, self-governing organizations that are prohibited from distributing profits to their stakeholders. They deliver myriad services to segments of the population that are not adequately served through the open marketplace or by the government (Salamon & Anheier, 1996). They range from food banks, women's shelters, children's aid societies, and immigrant service organizations to environmental protection agencies, opera companies, and sporting societies. Many of these organizations are composed mainly of women, led by women, and governed by boards that are predominantly made up of women. In the 1990s the National Action Committee on the Status of Women counted approximately 700 feminist organizations on its membership list, many of which represented hundreds of additional women's organizations (Meinhard & Foster, 2003). Studies in the United States in the 1980s and 1990s estimated that as many as 50% of organizations may be gender-segregated women's organizations (McPherson & Smith-Lovin, 1982, 1986; Popielarz, 1999). Since the per capita number of nonprofit organizations in Canada and the United States is roughly equal (4.5 per thousand people), it is fair to speculate that the ratio of women's organizations might be similar.

Despite the pervasiveness of women's nonprofit organizations, there has been little research focusing on them, although in the waning years of the 20th century, women's nonprofit organizations did attract some scholarly attention, particularly in the United States. However, there is no consensus across studies as to what exactly constitutes a "women's organization." This label had been applied to three types of organizations: (1) women who come together to achieve any type of goals, (2) women who come together to work on women's issues, and (3) people, regardless of sex, who come together to work on women's issues.

The most common use of the term *women's organizations*, or variations such as *women's associations*, *women's clubs*, and *women's nonprofit organizations*, refers to organizations run by women, for women. For example, Riordan (2000) defines *women's organizations* as "specific sites for the articulation of women's needs and the application of women's solutions" (p. 64). While McPherson and Smith-Lovin (1986) include only organizations that serve women exclusively, others limit the term to feminist groups concerned primarily with the status of women and their rights (Clemens, 1999). A subset of these include only "separatist" organizations in this category, such as **radical feminist** groups (Staggenborg, 1995). Others encompass both feminist and nonfeminist organizations (Bordt, 1997; Tyyskä, 1998), and some include organizations that are not exclusive to women, but are predominantly composed of women (Selle, 2001).

In the first Canadian comprehensive study of women's organizations, we categorized any organization with a female executive director and a governing board whose composition was at least two-thirds female as a women's organization (Meinhard & Foster, 2003). We based our decision on a growing body of literature (reviewed below) that attests to differences in management and leadership behaviours that women display compared to men and their impact on organizations, regardless of the specific mission of the organization.

BRIEF HISTORICAL BACKGROUND OF CANADA'S NONPROFIT SECTOR

The earliest recorded nonprofit organization in Canada, the Hotel Dieu, was established in Quebec City in 1658 under the auspices of the Roman Catholic Church. It gave sustenance to the poor, the sick, and the injured. In 1688, two more organizations were established: Le Bureau des Pauvres [The Office of the Poor] in Quebec City, created and run by volunteers through citizen donations to feed and clothe the poor; and La Maison de la Providence [Providence House], established in Montreal to house and educate young girls from poor families.

Because it was run by nuns and served girls, it may be considered the first women's organization in Canada.

Despite nonprofit organizations being part of the earliest history of Canada, this group of organizations only became recognized as a separate sector in the 1980s. It wasn't until the forging of the welfare state following World War II that nonprofit organizations, in partnership with the federal and provincial governments, became a key element in the provision of social services for Canadians. More nonprofit organizations were created in the two decades between 1970 and 1990 than in the seven preceding decades. They provided work for an increasing number of people. In the 1960s and 1970s, federal programs such as Opportunities for Youth harnessed the energy of young Canadians who were rejecting the corporate culture of the times. This occurred in tandem with increasing numbers of young female university graduates entering social service professions and finding employment in the rapidly growing nonprofit sector. The 1990s saw a retrenchment in government funding across all provinces, resulting in a slowing of the growth of the nonprofit sector and eventually the creation of new forms of social benefit organizations. These organizations, most often referred to as social enterprises, generate profits while pursuing social goals.

At the beginning of the 21st century, the nonprofit sector was a significant source of employment for Canadians. Two million people (11.1% of the labour force) work in this sector, accounting for approximately 8.1% ($106 billion) of Canada's GDP (Faul, 2015). However, this is a misleading figure, as 13 million volunteers (45% of the population 15 years of age and older) contribute more than two billion hours of volunteer labour. This is equivalent to more than one million full-time jobs and is worth $21 billion calculated at minimum wage. There is no significant difference in the rate of volunteering between men and women (National Survey of Giving, Volunteering and Participating [NSGVP], 2000).[2] Approximately three-quarters of the two million employees in the nonprofit sector are women, although women comprise only 47% of Canada's labour force. According to the 2016 labour force figures, approximately 8.2 million women and 9.1 million men are gainfully employed (Statistics Canada, 2016). Thus, 1.5 million out of 8.2 million or 18% of employed women work in the nonprofit sector compared to just 500,000 out of 9.1 million or 5% of employed men. This is another example of gender segregation by occupation. Nevertheless, the nonprofit sector provides women with more organizational leadership opportunities than any other sector.

According to the 2017 Canadian Nonprofit Sector Salary and Benefits Study commissioned by Charity Village, 71% of chief executive jobs at nonprofits are filled by women (Portage Group, 2017). By the first decade of the 21st century, 21% of Canada's largest nonprofits had women at the helm (Veldhuis, 2011) as opposed to only 7.5% in the corporate sector in 2011 and only 9.4% in 2018 (Rosenzweig & Company, 2018). Despite this, there is still a gender wage gap. On average, women make 90% of what men do in nonprofit organizations, but at the highest levels there is a yawning gap of 20%. This reflects in part the propensity for men, if they do work in the sector, to work for the larger organizations that can afford to pay higher salaries (Portage Group, 2017).

WOMEN'S NONPROFIT ORGANIZATIONS

The rapid rate of organizational growth evidenced in the 1960s and 1970s abated by the mid-1980s, but the decades since have nevertheless seen a steady net growth rate of nonprofit organizations. Although numbers are unavailable, there is no reason to believe that the growth of women's organizations has not kept pace, at around 50%.

In Canada, women's paid work before the 20th century was largely restricted to activities that mirrored domestic work; thus, most employed women worked as servants, cooks, launderers, dressmakers, seamstresses, and milliners. At the beginning of the 20th century, there was a sharp increase in the number of women who worked outside the domestic realm as factory workers, teachers, nurses, and sales personnel. Nonetheless, in the early 1900s only 14% of women—most of whom were unmarried—were engaged in paid work. They constituted 13% of the paid labour force (Connelly, 2015). The activities of the rest of the women were restricted to the domestic realm and family farm. Volunteering was one of the few ways in which women were able to contribute directly to society. The associations they joined and formed exposed them to the public issues of the day and helped them develop administrative, management, and leadership skills. While volunteerism played a liberating role in the lives of many Canadian women who did not work outside the home, the experience of immigrant women and women of colour was different. Most came to Canada as domestic workers with even fewer public privileges and extra-domestic opportunities. Thus, the groups they formed focused on their own fair treatment (Wharton-Zaretsky, 2000).

At first women volunteered with existing benevolent societies, such as the Red Cross and the Salvation Army, that were managed and funded by men. Because participation was encouraged but control was withheld women were still "kept in their place" (Kaminer, 1984). Working on the front lines, women gained keen insight into what was really needed. However, in an atmosphere of "hegemonic masculinity" they were barred from organizational decision-making. **Hegemonic masculinity** refers to a culturally idealized form of masculinity that "embodies society's most valued way of being a man" (Hechavarria & Ingram, 2016, p. 245), associated with competitiveness, aggressiveness, and risk-taking. Juxtaposed to this is **emphasized femininity**, an idealized form of female behaviour characterized by altruism, compassion, and caring, buying into a patriarchal bipolarization supporting male dominance, especially in the workplace (Ahl & Marlow, 2012; for a good review of this concept see Hechavarria & Ingram, 2016).

Frustrated, women in North America began forming their own associations, and by the second half of the 19th century they were administering organizations in the fields of philanthropy, the arts and sciences, and social reform (Clemens, 1999). Women continued to volunteer in benevolent societies, but as the nonprofit sector grew and more organizations were formed by women, gender segregation in the nonprofit sector became a reality in the 20th century to the extent that women in North America "rarely belong to male-dominated groups, and are less likely to belong to integrated groups than to female-dominated ones" (Popielarz, 1999, p. 239). In two studies on nonprofit organizations conducted almost two decades apart (1982 and 1999), US researchers found that half of the organizations studied were exclusively female as opposed to only 20% to 22% that were exclusively male. Men were much more likely to belong to mixed-gender organizations (McPherson & Smith-Lovin, 1982; Popielarz, 1999). While the rate of volunteering does not differ between the genders, two-thirds of women volunteers are members of women's organizations, while slightly over half of volunteering men belong to exclusively male organizations (Popielarz, 1999). Women continue to join women's organizations even as large national nonprofit organizations are opening their doors to women.

HISTORICAL REVIEW OF THE ROLE OF WOMEN'S NONPROFIT ORGANIZATIONS IN CANADA

As mentioned above, one of the first nonprofit organizations, La Maison de la Providence, was an organization run by women mainly for the housing and education of young women. There are many more examples in early Canadian history of women's organizing that provided succour to the needy. The work was carried out by both women in religious orders and laywomen organizing church sisterhoods to raise funds for food and medicine and the construction of schools and hospitals (Martin, 1985). Women volunteers were not only providing social services and health care to the needy, but also organizing national associations with the aim of improving society, for example, the Women's Christian Temperance Union (1874) and the National Council of Women (1893). Because immigrant and other minority women often felt unwelcome in mainstream organizations, they formed their own groups and organizations (Middleton, Ambrose, & Mitchinson, 2014). As early as 1840, black women in Ontario and Nova Scotia formed all-female benevolent societies to help fugitives from slavery (Sadlier, 1994) and ensure fair treatment in their communities (Wharton-Zaretzky, 2000). Black women's organizations continue to provide services, including educational, legal, and financial support, in their communities. Similarly, women from other ethnic groups organized to provide programs and educational opportunities in their communities. One of the earliest of these groups was the National Council of Jewish Women of Canada (modelled after the National Council of Women in the United States), founded in 1897 and "dedicated to identifying Jewish and non-Jewish community needs and providing leadership, energy, and financial resources to bring about meaningful changes" (National Council of Jewish Women of Canada, n.d.). Another example of an early 20th-century women's organization was the Chinese Empire Ladies Reform Association (1903), whose mandate was to "pioneer feminist movements for Chinese women" (Victoria's Chinatown, n.d.). Today we bear witness to a multitude of women's organizations representing the ethnic and cultural mosaic of Canada.

Women's nonprofit organizations have been a source of social capital for women. *Social capital* refers to the networks of interconnection that allow groups, communities, and societies to provide for the needs of their members. Organizations are venues for bonding and bridging social capital. Women's organizations, with their informal structures, are predominantly places to bond with other women, gain support from them, and learn from them in an atmosphere of trust and safety. As women's organizations have a tendency to collaborate with other organizations, they also serve a bridging role. Through these collaborations, an organization can offer many women contacts in the outer community to improve their own social positions and create ties that can work for the betterment of society.

By 1912 approximately one in eight Canadian women were volunteering in women's organizations, and thus, these organizations became a significant social force in Canada (Middleton et al., 2014). At a time when they were still disenfranchised, membership in these organizations gave women a modicum of power by voicing their concerns publicly (Strong-Boag, 1976).

The role of women's organizations in gaining rights for women is unquestionable. What is less well known is their role in the passage of legislation for social reform that affected society as a whole, not just women. In the late 19th and early 20th centuries this was challenging because without representation in Parliament and the clout of a vote, their social reform agendas failed to become high-priority issues with parliamentarians. It became clear that in order to have any impact on legislation, women would have to gain the vote. The Toronto Women's Literary Guild was formed in 1877 for the express purpose of gaining rights for women in all spheres of life, including the political. In 1883 it was renamed the Toronto Women's Suffrage Association (Strong-Boag, 2016). In 1891 the powerful Women's Christian Temperance Union of Canada joined the struggle for suffrage, and by 1918 women citizens in all Canadian provinces, with the exception of Quebec and First Nations women, were enfranchised. The women of Quebec had to wait until 1940, and First Nations women until 1960, for the privilege to vote (Strong-Boag, 2016).

The second wave of feminism that was sweeping the continent in the late 1960s and 1970s led to official recognition of women's concerns for equal rights in all aspects of life by the government of Canada. Three decisions marked this recognition: first, in 1972 the federal government underwrote a conference organized by the National Action Committee on the Status of Women dedicated to effecting change in the status of women in Canada; second, the government created the office of the Status of Women Canada with a mandate to "coordinate policy with respect to the status of women and administer related programs" (Government of Canada, 2018); and finally and most importantly, in 1985, after protests by women's groups, a clause guaranteeing equal rights for women and men in Canada was enshrined in the Canadian Charter of Rights and Freedoms. These legitimating actions by the government further spurred the proliferation of women's organizations. Today, in Canada as in other parts of the world, there are thousands of women's organizations, large and small, supporting causes and providing services that are important not only to women, but also to society as a whole. Attitudes toward work and social values that were in the past exclusive to feminist organizations are now commonplace in most organizations.

There seems to be a reciprocal relationship between the nonprofit sector and the empowerment of women. As this brief historical exposé suggests, women's nonprofit organizations were a means for women to fight for both the rights of others and their own rights, which served to empower them. In a large cross-national study using the 1999 United Nations Gender Empowerment Measure (GEM), Themudo (2009) found that countries with greater women's empowerment also had the largest nonprofit sectors. Themudo correspondingly found that as the GEM score in a country increases, so does the size of the non-profit sector. His research indicates that Canada has the fourth-highest GEM score (only the Scandinavian countries scored higher) among 38 nations from every continent, both rich and poor, and it has the second strongest nonprofit sector (2009, p. 674).

PREFERENCE FOR PARTICIPATING IN WOMEN'S ORGANIZATIONS

There are both extrinsic and intrinsic factors that can explain why women prefer and continue to volunteer in women's organizations. In the past, extrinsic factors played a large role. In many organizations, membership was closed to women. For example, Kiwanis and the Lions Club, both international service organizations, opened their membership to women only in 1987. In the gender-neutral organizations that accepted women, leadership was usually male and women were not included in decision-making or leadership positions—an effective glass ceiling was in place (Gibelman, 2000).

Intrinsic factors are based in various theories of volunteering. The most frequently cited reason given for volunteering is a desire to "help others" or "give back to the community" (Carter, 1975; Duchesne, 1989; NSGVP, 2000). While this may be an important reason for "doing good," it is not necessarily a sufficient cause for joining an organization. There are tangible rewards in joining an organization. These include both affective incentives, for example, making friends, acquiring status, and being esteemed (Flynn & Webb, 1975), and instrumental incentives, for example, acquiring skills and building social capital (Flynn & Webb, 1975; Masi, 1981). Joining an organization also provides opportunities for social catharsis—the sharing of positive or negative emotions—and collective identification with a good cause (Duchesne, 1989).

These intrinsic factors may be particularly germane in explaining women's affiliation with all-female organizations. The experience gained in nonprofit organizations prepared many women for the job market (Flynn & Webb, 1975; Kaminer, 1984; Masi, 1981). Women's organizations have provided opportunities to gain leadership and management skills in top administrative positions that are seldom available in mixed settings, even in organizations in which women are a majority (Clemens, 1999; Kaminer, 1984; Masi, 1981; Popielarz, 1999). Unconstrained by existing expectations of hierarchical, task-oriented male leadership styles (Kanter, 1977), women were able to practice the more inclusive and process-oriented leadership that has by now been recognized as essential to modern organizations by many organizational researchers (DeAngelis, 2014; Eagly, 2013; Zenger & Folkman, 2012).

UNIQUE CHARACTERISTICS OF WOMEN'S NONPROFIT ORGANIZATIONS

From an organizational perspective, women's nonprofit organizations display some unique characteristics. Three areas in which research has indicated differences are relationships with the organizational environment, leadership and internal relationships, and organizational structure.

Relationships with the Organizational Environment

Women's organizations around the world have been acknowledged as a "driving force in local action" (Eurofound, 1993, p. 86), changing "the face of social service provision" (Riordan, 2000, p. 65). Despite this, their survival is often precarious. Underfunded and understaffed (Riordan, 2000), they are considered marginal to mainstream economic and social development. In much of the world, women's organizations lack support from governments and philanthropic agencies "because their work, which genuinely seeks to empower the powerless, is potentially challenging to those in power" (Riordan, 2000, p. 67).

In Canada, women's organizations are not perceived to be prestigious targets for donors. Earlier research found that aiding marginalized members of society, which many women's groups do, does not register in the consciousness of major donors and corporate leaders (Bradshaw, Murray, & Wolpin, 1996; Useem, 1987). Even large philanthropic gifts made by women are not directed to women's organizations ("Why Is Fundraising Difficult for Women's Organizations?" 1999). In 2010 the bulk of philanthropic giving went to religious organizations (40%); health, hospitals, education, and universities (25%); social services (11%); and international organizations (8%; Turcotte, 2012). Although a significant proportion of social service, international, and advocacy organizations would fall under the category of women's organizations, they would still account for a very small percentage of donations, mirroring earlier research (Useem, 1987). With fewer overlapping board memberships, women's organizations are further disadvantaged, unable to access philanthropic networks (Moore & Whitt, 2000). Paradoxically, the more precarious an organization's funding, the scarcer the resources that are available for fundraising. Thus, women's organizations are very dependent on governments for funding.

In a series of studies between 2002 and 2009 investigating women's non-profit organizations, we found that with respect to the changing socioeconomic environment, women's organizations were more sensitive to the growing gaps between haves and have-nots as the social welfare net was tightened in the late 1990s, and were much more likely than other nonprofit organizations to criticize and agitate against the cutbacks. This is not surprising, as women's organizations had laid the foundations of the modern welfare state (Clemens, 1999). Feeling vulnerable, especially in an atmosphere of increased competition for dwindling dollars, they were more pessimistic about the future. They feared that their clients were undervalued and their needs were not a priority for funding by the government or private donors.

Leadership and Internal Relationships

Ever since women entered the workplace in large numbers, and especially as they have slowly moved up the organizational ladder, there has been an explosion of research on the leadership qualities of women as opposed to men (as reviewed by Tillapaugh & Haber-Curran, 2017). The expectation that there would be differences in leadership styles is rooted in gendered socialization of boys and girls in home and school settings, and also tangentially through media and the toys they play with. Boys at play are expected to be competitive, hierarchical, and independent, whereas girls are encouraged to be nurturing and relationship oriented (Tannen, 1990). A recent study by MacPhee and Prendergast (2018) has affirmed that the passage of time has not changed the differential socialization patterns of boys and girls. Gender socialization affects values linked to leadership preferences: girls value helping others (self-transcendence) more highly, and boys value being in charge (self-enhancement) more highly (Aelenei, Darnon, & Martinot, 2017). However, a direct link between these differences in socialization and organizational leadership is difficult to establish because tendencies ingrained by socialization are often superseded by situational exigencies in the workplace (Kanter, 1977). This notwithstanding, there is some evidence to indicate that these socialized behaviours carry over to the organization (Fondas, 1997).

Recent meta-analyses of research on this topic (Eagly, 2013) indicate that while in aggregate there are differences between men and women on several management measures, these differences are small with very wide individual variation. There are some areas, however, in which women are consistently different. Women are more likely than men to be democratic, process-oriented,

transformational leaders who value information-sharing and collaboration (Bass, Avolio, & Atwater, 1996; Eagly, 2013; Helgesen, 1990; Rosener, 1990, 1995). Not only are women more likely to be transformational leaders, but when they use **transactional** styles, they tend to use positive, reward-based incentives, whereas men rely more on negative, threat-based incentives (Desvaux, Devillard-Hoellinger, & Meaney, 2008).

While there may be little to differentiate men and women in terms of their leadership styles, especially in gender-neutral organizations where there is pressure to conform to entrenched leadership styles, there are clear differences in women's values and attitudes (Eagly, 2013). Women hold social values that are more supportive of the welfare of others both individually and universally (Adams & Funk, 2012; Halpern & Parks, 1996; Schwartz & Rubel-Lifschitz, 2009). They tend to deal more fairly with their clients (Dawson, 1997) and are consistently more cooperative in negotiations, as reported in a meta-analysis by Walters, Stuhlmacher, and Meyer (1998). They are also more open in their communications, sharing information more readily (Deal, 2000).

Three things stand out from this overview: (1) The findings that leadership behaviours are contextually contingent leads to the conclusion that in settings where women are in the majority, the small differences found in leadership styles will be more pronounced and readily observable, (2) more open communications and information-sharing lead to different work processes and relationship patterns, and (3) women leaders are well placed in organizations where they can act for the public good.

Organizational Structure

Given their focus on process and relationships, it is not surprising that women eschew the hierarchical, more authoritarian structures developed by men, preferring more informal structures that provide open communications and rapid access to information and support (Barnato & Peele, 2006). In a recent Canadian study, Coombs (2018) suggests that women are still contesting the dominant organizational discourses in the nonprofit sector.

The earliest women's organizations of the late 19th century deliberately avoided hierarchical structures (Clemens, 1999) for more collectivist ones (Bordt, 1997). In time, unable to resist the forces of institutionalization, many women's nonprofits abandoned the pure collectivist organizational form that government and private funders found difficult to relate to, and adopted hybrid structures that were less formalized and more inclusive, consensual, and empowering (Bordt, 1997; Lott, 1994). This contrasts with observations that, in general, nonprofit organizations have more formalized structures (Marsden & Cook, 1994). Currently there is no research to indicate the proportion of women's organizations that employ less formal hybrid structures, but in our study of women's nonprofit organizations (Meinhard & Foster, 2003) we found that 51% of the women's organizations in our sample had highly informal, nonhierarchical structures. Even in mixed-gender technology-based companies, the higher the representation of women in the organization's founding period, the lower the formalization and bureaucratization evident in later years (Baron, Hannan, & Burton, 1999). Because of the changing nature of work, newer organizational behaviour textbooks are promoting less rigid, decentralized structures that allow for greater information-sharing and collaboration.

This internal openness of structure coincides with more frequent collaborations by women's organizations with other nonprofit organizations, irrespective of size, revenue sources, mandate, and community (Foster & Meinhard, 2005; Meinhard & Foster, 2003). Other research highlights the embeddedness of women's organizations in a network of community agencies (Stewart & Taylor, 1997; Yasmin, 1997). Historically, collaboration with other organizations was critical in achieving suffrage (Clemens, 1999) and, more recently, in establishing a national daycare program in Finland (Tyyskä, 1998).

Interestingly, the successes of women's nonprofit organizations with collaboration did not extend to the corporate sector. With the bulk of their revenue coming from governmental sources, the steep cuts in government funding did not result in successful revenue diversification by women's organizations from government to corporate funders, as it did with gender-neutral ones (Meinhard & Foster, 2003). This may have been the result of their lack of board connections or insistence by women's organizations on maintaining their open structures instead of adopting a more corporate structure.

CONCLUSION

Nonprofit organizations have provided women with significant opportunities to develop leadership and management skills. Historically, women had been excluded from the workforce because of strongly held cultural norms about appropriate female roles. Even as these norms softened in the 20th century, senior management and decision-making authority usually resided with men. Thus, one of the few places where women could develop executive skills was in the nonprofit sector.

Women's nonprofit organizations evolved with their own unique culture-collectivist focus, flat hierarchies, and emphasis on process and communication, as well as a passion for promoting civil society and ameliorating social issues. Because these organizations tended to be smaller, underfunded, and focused on marginalized populations and issues, they had to learn to collaborate with others. They became experts at building and maintaining relationships not only with organizations serving similar populations, but also with diverse organizations.

Now in the 21st century, the for-profit sector seems to be mirroring some of the attitudes, values, and passions of women's nonprofit organizations. In terms of the ideal management model, command, and control, the traditional male model has fallen out of favour and instead some of the characteristics and attitudes more often seen in female leaders—compassion, communication, collaboration—have become valued. In particular, interorganizational collaboration is a significant feature of doing business successfully in today's world (Kiron, 2017). As Kanter (1994) presciently pointed out, "The ability to create and sustain fruitful collaborations gives companies a significant competitive leg up" (p. 96). Perhaps, as Rosener (1995) suggests in her book *America's Competitive Secret: Utilizing Women as a Management Strategy*, corporations should increase the number of women in leadership positions, because they have more experience and skill in developing collaborative relationships.

A further shift in corporate culture is that more and more companies have expanded their mandates from a limited focus on profits and shareholder value to embrace triple bottom line accounting that considers social, environmental, and financial concerns. Corporate social responsibility is now a core value of most organizations. It may be manifested informally by supporting and encouraging employee volunteer activities or through a more formal integration with core business, whole divisions, and teams devoted to corporate citizenship with significant investment in social programs (Foster, Meinhard, Berger, & Krpan, 2009). Could it be a blessing in disguise that because women had to develop their own unique management styles through their work in volunteer organizations without the influence of men they are more prepared to be successful in leadership roles in the complex 21st century? Perhaps the time is ripe for a re-examination of these issues.

NOTES

1. There are several terms in use to describe nonprofit organizations and the nonprofit sector, including *voluntary, civil society, third-sector,* and *nongovernmental* organizations.

To avoid confusion this chapter uses the term *nonprofit organizations* to include all of these types of organizations.

2. The NSGVP (2000) and the National Survey of Nonprofit and Voluntary Organizations (Highlights of the NSNVO, 2003) are the only comprehensive studies of the nonprofit sector conducted in Canada. Although they are somewhat dated, there is no reason to believe that their findings have changed substantially in the intervening years.

KEY READINGS

Eagly, A. H. (2013). Women as leaders: Leadership style vs. leaders' values and attitudes. In *Gender and work: Challenging conventional wisdom; Research symposium*. Cambridge, MA: Harvard Business School. Retrieved from http://www.hbs.edu/faculty/conferences/2013-w50-research-symposium/Documents/eagly.pdf

National Survey of Giving, Volunteering and Participating. (2000). *Motivations and barriers to volunteering*. Retrieved from http://www.imaginecanada.ca/sites/default/files/www/en/giving/factsheets/motivations_and_barriers_to_volunteering.pdf

National Survey of Nonprofit and Voluntary Organizations. (2003). Imagine Canada Sector Source. Retrieved from http://sectorsource.ca/sites/default/files/resources/files/nsnvo_summary_english.pdf

Themudo, N. S. (2009). Gender and the nonprofit sector. *Nonprofit and Voluntary Sector Quarterly, 38*(4), 663–683. doi:10.1177/0899764009333957

DISCUSSION QUESTIONS

1. If a study focused on women's nonprofit organizations today, what would the key research questions be? How would they add to the findings presented in this chapter?

2. Collaboration seems to be more important in the work environment today than it used to be. Why do you think this is the case? What role, if any, have women played in these changes?

3. Corporate social responsibility is a much more prominent core value of corporations than it used to be. How do you think women's greater involvement in both nonprofit and the corporate sectors may have contributed to this trend?

REFERENCES

Adams, R., & Funk, P. (2012). Beyond the glass ceiling: Does gender matter? *Management Science, 58*(2). doi.org/10.1287/mnsc.1110.1452

Aelenei, C., Darnon, C., & Martinot, D. (2017). Boys, girls, and the school cultural environment: Teachers' judgment and students' values. *Journal of Social Psychology, 157*(5), 556–570. doi:10.1080/00224545.2016.1243514

Ahl, H., & Marlow, S. (2012). Exploring the dynamics of gender, feminism and entrepreneurship: Advancing debate to escape a dead end? *Organization, 19*(5), 543–562.

Barnato, A., & Peele, P. (2006). How do female and male faculty members construct job satisfaction? In *Biological, social, and organizational components of success for women in academic science and engineering: Report of a workshop.* Washington, DC: National Academies Press.

Baron, J. N., Hannan, M. T., & Burton, M. D. (1999). Building the iron cage: Determinants of managerial intensity in the early years of organizations. *American Sociological Review, 64*(4), 527–547.

Bass, B., Avolio, B., & Atwater, L. (1996). The transformational and transactional leadership of men and women: An extension of some old comparisons. *Applied Psychology: An International Review, 45*, 5–34.

Bordt, R. L. (1997). *The structure of women's nonprofit organizations.* Bloomington & Indianapolis: Indiana University Press.

Bradshaw, P., Murray, V., & Wolpin, J. (1996). Women on boards of nonprofits: What difference do they make? *Nonprofit Management and Leadership, 6*, 241–254.

Carter, N. (1975). *Trends in voluntary support for non-governmental social service agencies.* Ottawa: Canadian Council on Social Development.

Clemens, E. S. (1999). Securing political returns to social capital: Women's associations in the United States, 1880s–1920s. *Journal of Interdisciplinary History, 29*(4), 613–639.

Connelly, M. P. (2015). Women in the labour force. *The Canadian Encyclopedia.* Toronto: Historica Canada. Retrieved from http://www.thecanadianencyclopedia.ca/en/article/women-in-the-labour-force/

Coombs, M. (2018). *Women, learning, and charitable leadership in Canada.* Doctoral dissertation, Ontario Institute for Studies in Education, University of Toronto.

Dawson, L. M. (1997). Ethical differences between men and women in the sales profession. *Journal of Business Ethics, 16*(11), 1143–1152.

Deal, J. J. (2000). Gender differences in the intentional use of information in competitive negotiations. *Small Group Research, 31*(6), 702–724.

DeAngelis, T. (2014). Venus rising? *American Psychological Association, 45*(2), 32. Retrieved from http://www.apa.org/monitor/2014/02/venus.aspx

Desvaux, G., Devillard-Hoellinger, S., & Meaney, M. C. (2008, December). A business case for women. *McKinsey Quarterly, 4*, 26–33. Retrieved from https://www.forbes.com/2008/10/03/business-women-economics-lead-cx_1003mckinsey.html#293a906f2d5d

Duchesne, D. (1989). *Giving freely: Volunteers in Canada*. Statistics Canada, Labour Analytic Report, Catalogue no. 71–535, no. 4. Ottawa: Minister of Supply and Services.

Eagly, A. H. (2013). Women as leaders: Leadership style vs. leaders' values and attitudes. In *Gender and work: Challenging conventional wisdom; Research symposium*. Cambridge, MA: Harvard Business School. Retrieved from http://www.hbs.edu/faculty/conferences/2013-w50-research-symposium/Documents/eagly.pdf

Eurofound. (1993). *Annual report of the European Foundation for the improvement of living and working conditions, 1992*. Luxembourg: Publications Office of the European Union. Retrieved from https://publications.europa.eu/en/publication-detail/-/publication/32b04073-ed65-4ab7-923f-cf1d1e404b53

Faul, S. (2015). The charitable and nonprofit sector in Canada. *Imagine Canada*. Retrieved from https://pillarnonprofit.ca/sites/default/files/resources/storyofthenonprofitsector_14jan15-2.pdf

Flynn, J. P., & Webb, G. E. (1975). Women's incentives for community participation in policy issues. *Journal of Voluntary Action Research*, *4*(3-4), 137–145.

Fondas, N. (1997). Feminization unveiled: Management qualities in contemporary writings. *Academy of Management Review*, *22*(1), 257–282.

Foster, M., & Meinhard, A. (2005). The diversity of revenue sources among voluntary organizations in Canada. *Nonprofit Management and Leadership*, *16*(1), 43–60.

Foster, M. K., Meinhard, A. G., Berger, I. E., & Krpan, P. (2009). Corporate philanthropy in the Canadian context: From damage control to improving society. *Nonprofit and Voluntary Sector Quarterly*, *38*(3), 441–466.

Gibelman, M. (2000). The nonprofit sector and gender discrimination: A preliminary investigation into the glass ceiling. *Nonprofit Management and Leadership*, *10*(3), 251–269.

Government of Canada. (2018). *Status of Women Canada*. Retrieved from https://swc-cfc.gc.ca/abu-ans/who-qui/index-en.html

Halpern, J. J., & Parks, J. M. (1996). Vive la différence: Differences between males and females in process and outcomes in a low-conflict negotiation. *International Journal of Conflict Management*, *7*(1), 45–60.

Hechavarria, D. M., & Ingram, A. (2016). The entrepreneurial gender divide. *International Journal of Gender and Entrepreneurship*, *8*(3), 242–281. doi:10.1108/IJGE-09-2014-0029

Helgesen, S. (1990). *The female advantage: Women's ways of leadership*. New York: Doubleday.

Highlights of the National Survey of Nonprofit and Voluntary Organizations. (2003). Ottawa: Statistics Canada. Retrieved from http://sectorsource.ca/sites/default/files/resources/files/nsnvo_summary_english.pdf

Kaminer, W. (1984). *Women volunteering*. Garden City, NY: Anchor Press.

Kanter, R. M. (1977). *Men and women of the corporation*. New York: Basic Books.

Kanter, R. M. (1994). Collaborative advantage: The art of alliances. *Harvard Business Review*, *72*, 96–108.

Kiron, D. (2017). Why your company needs more collaboration. *MIT Sloan Management Review*, *59*(1), 17–19. Retrieved from https://sloanreview.mit.edu/article/why-your-company-needs-more-collaboration/

Lott, J. T. (1994). Women, changing demographics and the redefinition of power. In T. Odendahl & M. O'Neill (Eds.), *Women and power in the nonprofit sector* (pp. 155–183). San Francisco: Jossey-Bass.

MacPhee, D., & Prendergast, S. (2018). Room for improvement: Girls' and boys' home environments are still gendered. *Sex Roles*, *80*(6), 1–15. doi:10.1007/s11199-018-0936-2

Marsden, P. V., & Cook, C. R. (1994). Organizational structures. *American Behavioral Scientist*, *37*(7), 911–930.

Martin, S. (1985). *An essential grace: Funding Canada's health care, education, welfare, religion and culture*. Toronto: McClelland & Stewart.

Masi, D. A. (1981). *Organizing for women: Issues, strategies, and services*. Lexington, MA: Lexington Books.

McPherson, J. M., & Smith-Lovin, L. (1982). Women and weak ties: Differences by sex in the size of voluntary organizations. *American Journal of Sociology*, *87*(4), 883–904.

McPherson, J. M., & Smith-Lovin, L. (1986). Sex segregation in voluntary associations. *American Sociological Review*, *51*(1), 61–79.

Meinhard, A., & Foster, M. (2003). Differences in the response of women's voluntary organizations to shifts in Canadian public policy. *Nonprofit and Voluntary Sector Quarterly*, *32*(3), 366–396.

Middleton, A., Ambrose, L., & Mitchinson, W. L. (2014). *Women's organizations*. Toronto: Historica Canada. Retrieved from http://www.thecanadianencyclopedia.ca/en/article/womens-organizations

Moore, G., & Whitt, J. A. (2000). Gender and networks in a local voluntary-sector elite. *Voluntas*, *11*(4), 309–328.

National Council of Jewish Women of Canada. (n.d.). Our history. Retrieved from http://www.ncjwc.org/about/our-history/

National Survey of Giving, Volunteering and Participating. (2000). Toronto: Canadian Centre for Philanthropy Research Program. Retrieved from http://www.imaginecanada.ca/sites/default/files/www/en/giving/factsheets/motivations_and_barriers_to_volunteering.pdf

Popielarz, P. A. (1999). (In)voluntary association: A multilevel analysis of gender segregation in voluntary organizations. *Gender and Society*, *13*(2), 234–250.

Portage Group (2017). *Canadian nonprofit sector salary and benefits report: Updated 2017*. (n.p.): Charity Village.

Riordan, S. (2000). Put your money where your mouth is! The need for public investment in women's organizations. *Gender and Development*, *8*(1), 63–69.

Rosener, J. B. (1990). Ways women lead. *Harvard Business Review*, *68*(6), 109–125.

Rosener, J. B. (1995). *America's competitive secret: Utilizing women as a management strategy.* Oxford, UK: Oxford University Press.

Rosenzweig & Company. (2018). *The 13th annual Rosenzweig report.* Retrieved from https://www.rosenzweigco.com/media-1/the-13th-annual-rosenzweig-report-on-women-at-the-top-levels-of-corporate-canada

Sadlier, R. (1994). *Leading the way: Black women in Canada.* Toronto: Umbrella Press.

Salamon, L. M., & Anheier, H. K. (1996). *The emerging nonprofit sector: An Overview.* New York: Room 400.

Schwartz, S. H., & Rubel-Lifschitz, T. (2009). Cross-national variation in the size of sex differences in values: Effects of gender equality. *Journal of Personality and Social Psychology, 97*(1), 171–185. doi:10.1037/a0015546

Selle, P. (2001). The Norwegian voluntary sector and civil society in transition: Women as a catalyst of deep-seated change. In K. D. McCarthy (Ed.), *Women, philanthropy and civil society* (pp. 109–152). Bloomington: Indiana University Press.

Staggenborg, S. (1995). Can feminist organizations be effective? In M. M. Ferree & P. Y. Martin (Eds.), *Feminist organization: Harvest of the new women's movement* (pp. 339–355). Philadelphia: Temple University Press.

Statistics Canada. (2016). Employment by industry and sex. Retrieved from http://www.statcan.gc.ca/tables-tableaux/sum-som/l01/cst01/labor10a-eng.htm

Stewart, S., & Taylor, J. (1997). Women organizing women: Doing it backwards and in high heels. In A. M. Goetz (Ed.), *Getting institutions right for women in development* (pp. 212–222). London: Zed Books.

Strong-Boag, V. J. (1976). *The parliament of women: The National Council of Women of Canada, 1893–1929.* Ottawa: National Museums of Canada.

Strong-Boag, V. J. (2016). *Women's suffrage in Canada.* Toronto: Historica Canada. Retrieved from http://www.thecanadianencyclopedia.ca/en/article/suffrage/

Tannen, D. (1990). *You just don't understand.* New York: Ballantine Books.

Themudo, N. S. (2009). Gender and the nonprofit sector. *Nonprofit and Voluntary Sector Quarterly, 38*(4), 663–683. doi:10.1177/0899764009333957

Tillapaugh, D., & Haber-Curran, P. (2017). *Critical perspectives on gender and student leadership.* Hoboken, NJ: Jossey-Bass.

Turcotte, M. (2012). *Charitable giving by Canadians.* Canadian Social Trends, Statistics Canada Catalogue no. 11–008–X. Ottawa: Statistics Canada. Retrieved from https://www150.statcan.gc.ca/n1/en/pub/11-008-x/2012001/article/11637-eng.pdf?st=V7fDXH4H

Tyyskä, V. (1998). Insiders and outsiders: Women's movements and organizational effectiveness. *Canadian Review of Sociology and Anthropology, 35*(3), 391–401.

Useem, M. (1987). Corporate philanthropy. In W. W. Powell (Ed.), *The nonprofit sector: A research handbook* (pp. 340–359). New Haven, CT: Yale University Press.

Veldhuis, C. (2011). Women and work in the nonprofit sector. *Charity Village*. Retrieved from https://charityvillage.com/Content.aspx?topic=Women_and_Work_in_the_Nonprofit_Sector#.WYjAPITyupo

Victoria's Chinatown. (n.d.). *Chinese Empire Ladies Reform Association*. Retrieved from http://chinatown.library.uvic.ca/index.html%3Fq=chinese_empire_ladies_reform_association.html

Walters, A. E., Stuhlmacher, A. F., & Meyer, L. L. (1998). Gender and negotiator competitiveness: A meta-analysis. *Organizational Behavior and Human Decision Processes*, *76*(1), 1–29.

Wharton-Zaretsky, M. (2000). Foremothers of black women's community organizing in Toronto. *Atlantis*, *24*(2), 61–71.

Why is fundraising difficult for women's organizations? (1999). *Nonprofit World*, *17*(5), 55.

Yasmin, T. (1997). What is different in women's organizations? In A. M. Goetz (Ed.), *Getting institutions right for women in development* (pp. 199–211). London: Zed Books.

Zenger, J. & Folkman, J. (2012). Are women better leaders than men? *Harvard Business Review*. Retrieved from https://hbr.org/2012/03/a-study-in-leadership-women-do

CHAPTER 18

Understanding the Work in Sex Work: Canadian Contexts

Kara Gillies, Elene Lam, Tuulia Law, Rai Reece, Andrea Sterling, and Emily van der Meulen

INTRODUCTION

We write this chapter as a group of people who support sex worker rights and justice, and who have been involved in the Canadian and international sex workers' rights movements for combined decades. Some of us also have direct experience working in the sex industry, which we draw on below to explicate the different labour conditions in various sex work sites and sectors. Central to this chapter is a framing of sex work as a form of labour. Derived by sex workers themselves, this framework has long been advocated for by allied activists, researchers, policy-makers, and others the world over. It was in 1979 or 1980 when sex worker activist Carol Leigh (1997) first coined the term *sex work* to redirect attention away from stigmatizing perceptions of women in the sex industry and toward a labour-based understanding of their activities. Today, the term is used not only to encompass a variety of sexual and erotic services performed in exchange for money or other compensation, some of which we discuss in this chapter, but also to acknowledge this exchange as labour.

To begin contextualizing and exploring this topic, we first outline what sex work is and who performs it. We then sketch the legal context of sex work in Canada, both before and after the *Canada v. Bedford* (2013) Supreme Court decision, to provide background on how laws and legal processes can impact sex workers' ability to work with safety and dignity. Next, we unpack issues related to human trafficking and attempt to disentangle the sex work/trafficking conflation; here, we engage in an intersectional analysis that pays particular attention to migrant and Indigenous workers, acknowledging the harsher criminalization and surveillance practices to which racialized women are subject. We then turn to an exploration of managers, employers, bosses, and other individuals who organize or facilitate the commercial exchange of sexual services (i.e., third parties). Employer/employee relationships are common in the sex trade, as they are in other industries and workplaces, but, due to prohibitions set out in the Criminal Code of Canada, most managerial activities are against the law if sexual services are involved. The chapter concludes by considering resistance and union organizing, culminating in a reflection on how sex workers' human and labour rights would be better realized through the decriminalization of their lives and work.

WHAT IS SEX WORK AND WHO ARE SEX WORKERS?

For many, the sex trade is an area of considerable intrigue and curiosity, in large part due to the clandestine and sexual nature of the work, and there are thus many assumptions, stereotypes, and mythologies about who is involved and what they do. One of the key questions that people ask is about the size and scope of the industry. Statistics on the number of sex workers in Canada, however, are largely unreliable as stigma and criminalization make it difficult to achieve an accurate count. Researchers have noted a reticence amongst sex workers to participate in studies (Shaver, 2005), and, accordingly, survey responses can sometimes be low; data derived from social service agencies tend to represent just the sex workers who access those services; and arrest statistics for prostitution-related offences only shed light on enforcement patterns, which typically target racialized, migrant, and/or street-based sex workers. Despite these various methodological challenges and data collection limitations, a wealth of credible qualitative and quantitative information has been compiled by researchers and sex worker organizations across Canada over the past three decades.

We know, for instance, that despite the ubiquitous references to street-based sex work in media and popular culture (indeed, the most frequent image representing sex work is a woman in high heels leaning into a car window), most sex work actually happens behind closed doors. In fact, between 80% and 90% of any given city's sex industry occurs in an array of indoor locations (Benoit & Millar, 2001; Benoit & Shumka, 2015). These workspaces can include sex workers' own homes or apartments as well as brothels, bars, hotel rooms, dungeons, bathhouses, massage parlours, strip clubs, and more. We also know that while there is a spectrum of genders represented in the industry—including cis and trans men, as well as genderqueer and gender non-conforming individuals—the majority of sex workers across sectors are cis and trans women. Recent research shows that 77% of sex workers identify as female, 17% as male, and 6% as another gender, making sex work a feminized form of labour upon which many women rely (Benoit & Shumka, 2015). Those who decide to engage in sex work do so for diverse reasons; for example, the hours can be flexible, and it is often relatively lucrative compared to other work that similarly does not require formal education or training (Sanders, O'Neill, & Pitcher, 2017). For women who live with a disability, are single mothers, are students, and/or have few mainstream qualifications, sex work can be a viable option to meet basic needs, supplement other income, or achieve economic security; however, for others, legal risks, social condemnation, physical constraints, and both race and age biases can make it a challenging form of work.

Given the wide variety of sex workers as well as sex work settings and establishments, there is accordingly an equally wide array of labour-based activities in which those involved in this industry engage. Indeed, sex workers offer services that include various sexual acts, but also companionship and conversation, specialized services, and gendered erotic performance, sometimes without direct contact with the customer, such as peep shows, video chat, and phone sex. Each sector of the industry demands different skills and knowledge: erotic dancers perform in front of large crowds; dominatrices must know how to inflict pain without harming or marking their clients, unless requested; and webcam workers must be familiar with video software and hardware. Workers across this diverse industry often engage in emotional labour (Hochschild, 1983; see also Milrod & Weitzer, 2012), and also develop important and valuable skill sets such as "reading" clients to assess potential problems as well as client needs and desires. Many of the labour-related skills that sex workers cultivate—like negotiation, marketing, branding, and interpersonal communication—are transferable to "mainstream" industries.

In this respect, sex industry businesses and workers share some similarities with those in other labour market sectors, but in a context of prohibitive regulation and criminalization. Independent escorts, for example, who manage all aspects of their business, including advertising, and screening and communicating with clients, mainly advertise their services on the Internet through personal websites, classified listings, and social media, and are thus well versed in online marketing and branding. Other escorts might prefer to work for an agency, which, like hair salons or modelling agencies, typically takes a percentage (20% to 50%) of sex workers' hourly rates in exchange for arranging meetings with clients, providing administrative and security personnel, employing and arranging drivers, and creating advertising and marketing materials (Bruckert & Law, 2013). Since 2014, however, advertising the sexual services of another person has been a criminal offence (see Sterling, 2018).

In spite of sex work being one of the few labour markets in which the gendered wage gap is reversed in women's favour, sex workers can earn widely varying incomes. Industry dynamics and income disparities are informed by the gendered, raced, and classed contours of beauty and "sexiness" (see, for example, Raguparan, 2018), as well as by the forms of discrimination and violence that cis and trans women in general face as a direct result of structural economic instability and other inequalities (Global Network of Sex Work Projects [NSWP], 2017). To illustrate, escorts' hourly rates generally range from $100 to $600. These variations in price are informed by geographic location, marketing approach, and race, age, body type, and other characteristics that are subject to discriminatory social bias. As a result, escorts whose rates are at the high end of the scale are predominantly white, class-privileged, cisgender women (Bernstein, 2007); in turn, racialized, trans, and Indigenous sex workers are more often excluded from managed indoor workplaces and are overrepresented in street-based work, exposing them to greater risk of violence from both police and predators who pose as clients (Krüsi, Belak, & Sex Workers United Against Violence, 2018). Thus, for sex workers, gender inequality, intersecting with other social oppressions such as racism, sexism, classism, homophobia, and transphobia, is directly connected to the feminization of poverty, sexual identity–based discrimination, and unfair and restrictive migration laws, which are in turn linked to sex work stigma (Feminists for Sex Workers, 2017). Further, criminalization fuels state and police surveillance and interventions that directly increase the numbers, and racial and class disproportionality, of women in conflict with the law (Benoit & Shumka, 2015).

In part because of these gendered social and legal inequities, feminists have long engaged in political and moral discussions about the exchange of money for sexual services, how it should be regulated, and its role in society, namely disagreeing over whether sex work is in and of itself exploitative or whether it should be seen as labour (see Bruckert & Hannem, 2013; Chapkis, 1997; Duggan & Hunter, 1995; Outshoorn, 2005). The purpose of this chapter is not to revisit these well-documented debates, but instead to advance a sex-work-as-work and labour rights perspective (see Durisin, van der Meulen, & Bruckert, 2018).

Given the rise of prohibitionist rhetoric and policy approaches in Canada and around the world, however, we would like to address a few key points: (1) it is imperative to acknowledge sex workers' agency and ability to speak and make informed decisions on their own behalf, even if they are faced with constrained or limited options; (2) moralistic notions and assumptions advanced by non–sex workers about what is best for sex workers, especially in terms of law and policy, can result in harm and human rights abuses; and (3) criminalizing sex workers' workplaces, their employers or managers, and/or their clients, as we explore in greater detail below, is antithetical to achieving labour rights and protections.

Some, however, take an opposing view and instead argue that sex workers are always-already victims who are unable to consent to engage in sex work (see, for example, Women's Equality Liberty Coalition, 2018), and that it is thus necessary to implement laws that criminalize the purchase of sex and its facilitation. Often referring to themselves as radical feminists or as sex work abolitionists, this approach has been widely critiqued by sex workers in Canada and around the world who have long fought to be recognized as legitimate labourers and for their work activities, work sites, and work relations to be governed and protected as such (Gall, 2012). Many scholars, too, have found significant fault with the criminalization of purchasing sexual services and other aspects of sex work (for a recent assessment, see Kingston & Thomas, 2018).

Of course these are not the only perspectives on sex work. Some socialist feminists and other neo-Marxists understand prostitution as a form of "survivalist labour" (Walkowitz, 2016, p. 192) through which working-class women creatively negotiate economic need. Conversely sex-positive feminists have seen sex work as "a heroic overcoming of gender norms, a high-water mark of autonomy and agency" (Showden, 2011, p. xvii). The sex-work-as-work perspective, reflecting Carol Leigh's coining of the term noted at the beginning of this chapter, can be seen as a middle ground that not only acknowledges the constraints of socioeconomic structures—including the dependence and compulsion of work under capitalism (Westcott, Baird, & Cooper, 2006)—but also women's capacity to exert agency.

But what about the general public more broadly? What does the average Canadian think about sex work? Although there is doubtless a mix of opinions reflecting Canada's diversity of political affiliations, religions, and socioeconomic strata, national public opinion surveys indicate that, since 2005, considerably fewer Canadians think that prostitution should be illegal compared to those who support decriminalizing sex work activities and allowing consensual adult prostitution (Lowman & Louie, 2012). Importantly, polls also indicate a

distinct lack of support for legislative approaches that emphasize criminalizing clients (Lowman & Louie, 2012), a legal framework that has been recently
adopted in Canada.

CANADA'S CURRENT LEGAL CONTEXT

In December 2013 the Supreme Court decided in *Canada v. Bedford* that existing
anti-prostitution laws were unconstitutional and that they violated sex workers'
rights as enshrined in the Canadian Charter of Rights and Freedoms. Instead of
protecting sex workers, the Court found that the laws "put the safety and lives
of prostitutes at risk" (*Canada [Attorney General] v. Bedford,* 2013, para. 1). Although the act of exchanging sex for money was not illegal prior to the *Bedford*
decision, three directly associated activities were criminalized: (1) keeping or
being found in a bawdy house, defined as a fixed location where prostitution
regularly occurs, such as a brothel, massage parlour, private residence, or even a
parking lot; (2) living on the avails (i.e., earnings) of someone else's prostitution;
and (3) communicating for the purpose of prostitution in public places. These
provisions were not uniformly enforced—racialized, Indigenous, transgender,
and working-class sex workers were disproportionately targeted by police, as was
anyone working on the streets. With its decision, the Supreme Court included
a 12-month stay, allowing Parliament one year to introduce new legislation, but
the Court explicitly stated that any new laws must be in accordance with sex
workers' Charter rights.

The Conservative Party of Canada, which comprised a majority government
at the time, considered sex work to be inherently exploitative and introduced Bill
C-36, the Protection of Communities and Exploited Persons Act (PCEPA), in
June 2014 to "denounce and prohibit the purchase of sexual services because it
creates a demand for prostitution" (PCEPA, 2014). The act evinced a gendered
violence framing: its preamble articulated prostitution as antithetical to "human
dignity and the equality of all Canadians" and as having "a disproportionate
impact on women and children" (2014). After a very fast deliberation and review process, PCEPA came into force on December 6, 2014, and ushered in an
amended legal framework for prostitution in Canada.

One of the key changes introduced by PCEPA was the removal of the word
prostitution from the definition of a bawdy house; however, police can still lay
bawdy house charges if the location is being used for "acts of indecency." Further, the former "living on the avails" offence was so-called "modernized" to
forbid receiving a material benefit that is derived from the commercial exchange

of sexual services. The communicating offence was likewise amended, and now forbids communicating for the purpose of selling sexual services next to a school, playground, or daycare. In addition to these legislative changes and updates, PCEPA introduced two brand-new laws. The first is a law that disallows knowingly advertising someone else's sexual services (sex workers who advertise their own services are immune from prosecution), and the second prohibits purchasing sexual services or communicating for that purpose, thus criminalizing clients while simultaneously prohibiting women from engaging in the communications required to give and receive sexual consent, which is a legal and ethical requirement for any sexual activity, commercial or otherwise.

Although PCEPA claims to protect sex workers, it has left them vulnerable to harms, as the new legislation retains many of the former provisions that were deemed unconstitutional by the Supreme Court, plus adds these two new offences. Because the laws are geared primarily toward prostitution, and policing efforts disproportionately target street-based activities, there are many groups of sex workers who are able to work with less government and policing interference, such as those who work indoors away from the prying eyes of the state or who engage in various activities that do not necessarily include sexual intercourse, for example pro-dominants (i.e., dominatrices). In Canada, pro-domination has long been considered a legal grey area as it involves a wide range of BDSM (bondage, discipline, sadism, masochism) and fetish services (Lindemann, 2011), but not necessarily prostitution. This may change as PCEPA modified the term *prostitution* to the more ambiguous "sexual services" and broadened the definition of a "weapon" to include items that are used to bind or tie someone up against their will. Women who work as pro-dominants are concerned that these changes may effectively criminalize aspects of their work and push the industry further underground (Big Susie's, 2014), even though communication and consent are central tenets of the job, as they are in other sex industry sectors (and indeed in non-commercial BDSM play as well; Pinsky & Levey, 2015).

In addition to the complex provisions set out in the federal Criminal Code, different municipalities also try to regulate and control massage parlours through various zoning and licensing bylaws (Laing, 2012; van der Meulen & Valverde, 2013). Women who work in massage parlours, for example, may have body rub licenses, holistic health licenses, or registered massage therapist licenses. As these licensing schemes can be overly onerous and restrictive, and can have disproportionately high licensing fees, other massage parlour owners and sex workers operate without a license to protect their privacy and avoid investigation from licensing inspectors and local law enforcement (Pivot Legal Society, 2006).

Stripping is similarly subject to prohibitive municipal regulations in Ontario, where cities established bylaws prohibiting touching shortly after lap dancing was introduced in the 1990s. Many erotic dancers, however, continue to offer lap dances because they are the principal source of income. In this context, management, security, and other staff often wilfully ignore dancers' interactions with customers in an effort to avoid legal liability—this not only offloads liability onto dancers but can also leave them to manage problems with customers on their own (Law, 2016). In these respects, the layering of municipal and criminal regulation can compound the harms faced by workers across the diverse sex industry.

HUMAN TRAFFICKING AND SEX WORK

Potential harms can be further exacerbated by immigration regulation and border service officers, who, in the name of detecting and preventing human trafficking, tend instead to create problematic conditions for sex workers. Despite the insistence of some media outlets, policy-makers, and nongovernmental organizations, sex work and human trafficking are two distinct phenomena (Agustín, 2006; De Shalit, Heynen, & van der Meulen, 2014; Durisin & Heynen, 2015). Numerous activists and academics have demonstrated that the conflation of sex work and trafficking has instigated a moral panic about sexual labour and migration and has informed anti-trafficking laws and actions in many countries (Kempadoo, 2012; Sanghera, 2005; Weitzer, 2007), while simultaneously neglecting forced labour and exploitation in other industries (Global Alliance Against Traffic in Women, 2007). It has been further shown that anti-trafficking campaigns and policies are inherently racist and sexist, designed to racially profile and control women's movement, whether across transnational borders or within nations (Maynard, 2015). In the contemporary context, trafficking is receiving increased global and domestic attention as a serious human rights violation, with many claims as to its frequency despite a dearth of supporting empirical evidence.

Canada is a signatory to the United Nations Protocol to Prevent, Suppress and Punish Trafficking in Persons, Especially Women and Children, and thus has a duty to prevent and combat trafficking within and across its borders. However, legal definitions and popular understandings of trafficking are varied and inconsistent; some common constructs include the coercive movement of people, any form of forced labour, and sex work itself, regardless of circumstances. This latter conflation of trafficking with sex work is buttressed by PCEPA's positioning of sex work as a form of de facto exploitation and is used to justify the criminalization and over-policing of sex workers, their clients, and third parties.

In many ways, the current preoccupation with trafficking is a social construct based on myths and morality with the goal of abolishing or prohibiting sex work (Doezema, 2010; Kempadoo, 2012; Weitzer, 2007). Within this construct, racialized women are seen as inherent victims unable to make informed decisions about their lives and work. Although this construct informs legal approaches, its moralistic, racist, and gendered underpinnings are evident in enforcement practices: "sex workers who are targeted in anti-trafficking investigations are labeled as victims but treated as criminals" (Canadian Alliance for Sex Work Law Reform [CASWLR] & Pivot Legal Society, 2016, p. 9).

While Canadian anti-trafficking policies and accompanying state interventions such as targeted policing and raids have a significant negative impact on all sex workers, migrant and Indigenous women are disproportionately affected. Thus, an intersectional analysis that considers the gendered, raced, and classed implications of these measures is particularly important. As the targets of aggressive policing, which is both caused and intensified by entrenched racist and colonial perspectives and policies, migrant and Indigenous workers face surveillance, harassment, arrest, detention, and, for migrants, deportation (Agustín, 2007; Lam, 2016, 2018; Weitzer, 2007). Indeed, as sex worker rights organization Butterfly (2016) has argued, "anti-trafficking measures … do not assist the people they claim to help. Instead, they endanger sex workers' lives and violate their human rights" (see also TAMPEP, 2015).

With regard to transnational migration, the recomposition of capital and international structural conditions under globalization has led to political, economic, and social imbalances between the Global North and South, and increased demand and opportunities for transnational migrant workers in informal and formal labour markets in Canada. Restrictive and discriminatory immigration policies, including some that explicitly bar temporary foreign workers from sex trade businesses, press migrant sex workers into illegalized immigration status and isolate them from social, health, and labour rights supports. For example, research has shown that women workers in massage parlours are more often racialized and immigrants (Kolar, Atchison, & Bungay, 2014), and their working conditions and ability to negotiate fees and condom usage with clients can vary considerably (Handlovsky, Bungay, & Kolar, 2012). Migrant sex workers, especially those without citizenship, are less likely to access support and services, can experience a high level of workplace violence, and are targets for harassment, abuse, and raids by law enforcement officers (Brock, Gillies, Oliver, & Sutdhibhasilp, 2000; Kempadoo, 2001; Lam, 2016; Migrant Sex Workers Project, 2015).

When considering intra-national migration, the trafficking discourse has largely focused on Indigenous women's domestic movement and travel for work. Indigenous scholar Sarah Hunt (2015) has been critical of this focus, suggesting that the trafficking framework reinforces power relations that represent Indigenous women as dependant on the colonial government and law to be "saved" and "protected" from physical and sexual violence. So far, this relationship of dependency has not worked in Indigenous women's favour and has, in fact, led to the perpetuation of colonial power relations. (p. 26)

Systemic and intersectional factors that lead to Indigenous women's migration from home communities to urban settings or across urban contexts are deeply rooted in historical and contemporary colonialism, including substandard education on reserves, insufficient and insecure housing, poor health care, lack of employment opportunities, and intergenerational trauma caused by Canada's residential school system (CASWLR & Pivot Legal Society, 2016).

Little attention is paid to the agency and self-determination that migrant and Indigenous women exercise when navigating the complex "push and pull" dynamics of international and domestic migration, or the myriad structural inequities and state policies that cause and complicate their experiences. For many, migration and travel for work represent opportunities for economic security or advancement, for breaking away from oppressive local conditions, and for improving one's quality of life (Agustín, 2006; Chimienti, 2010). Sometimes these favourable outcomes are achieved, and sometimes not. Often the intersecting oppressions that inform the decision to migrate or move to a new location for employment persist in the new context. The criminalization of multiple aspects of the sex trade contributes to this oppression for migrant and Indigenous women who sell or trade sex. Instead, migrant justice organizations, Indigenous activists, sex worker rights groups, and human rights advocates argue for harmful anti-trafficking agendas to be replaced by a social justice, migrant justice, and anticolonial approach to better address violations of migrant and Indigenous women's rights and safety.

MANAGERS, EMPLOYERS, AND OTHER THIRD PARTIES

Regardless of their migratory experiences, it is common for women in the sex trade to work for third parties such as managers or employers. Just like in other industries, a manager or boss in the sex trade provides administrative and infrastructure supports, including marketing, reception, screening calls, providing safe work sites, and security in exchange for a flat fee, a percentage of the worker's earnings, or compensation factored into the pay structure. This mutually beneficial arrangement is typically overlooked by our society, which instead reduces managers of sex workers to the racist and gendered caricature of the "pimp" (Bruckert & Law, 2013; Gillies, 2013; van der Meulen, 2010). In practice, however, many sex industry businesses (e.g., escort agencies, massage parlours, and dungeons) are run by women who are former sex workers themselves (Bruckert & Law, 2013); notably this is not the case for strip clubs, which, though relatively less criminalized and stigmatized, are more commonly run by men (Law, 2016). Likewise, the media and policy-makers construct managers and other third parties as exploitative predators and criminalize activities such as procuring and, in the majority of contexts, materially benefiting from another person's prostitution.

One such criminalized context is that of a "commercial enterprise" such as a massage parlour or an escort agency, upon which many women depend for a safe and sheltered workspace without paying costly overhead. Women who work in sectors such as erotic dance typically require the space, staffing, and infrastructure of a commercial enterprise to effectively deliver their services. While the Supreme Court *Bedford* decision led to a change in the legal definition of bawdy houses, sex workers, especially those who work together or for a third party (e.g., a manager), can still face various criminal charges, as can anyone who is at the location purchasing sexual services. This leaves many sex workers vulnerable and prevents them from being able to organize a union or advocate for their rights and protections under labour or other legislation.

The criminalization of managers and employers, then, can undermine both the quality of the employer-worker relationship and the worker experience. Managers and employers are forced to distance themselves from the sexual components of the job, resulting in unclear job expectations and compensation, lack of job training (including on occupational health and safety), and vague service expectations for clients that can lead to misunderstandings and conflicts with the workers (Pivot Legal Society, 2006). Like other workers, women in the sex trade experience incidents of unfair labour practices and substandard working conditions such as unpaid wages, safety hazards, excessive work hours, and discriminatory or deceptive hiring practices. Unlike other workers, however, most sex workers are unable to seek redress through provincial/territorial employment standards, occupational health and safety, or human rights legislation

(Pivot Legal Society, 2006; van der Meulen, 2012). This is due to the doctrine of paramountcy, which gives federal laws, including criminal sanctions against third parties, precedence over provincial/territorial legislation.

Moreover, most escorts and erotic massage providers are hired as independent contractors, precluding them from provincial labour protections, even if the criminal aspect of their employer's role is unknown or overlooked. Erotic dancers are also subject to this nebulous employment relationship and, as a result, must navigate working conditions that often involve expectations of unpaid labour, including stage shows and being continually visible to clients, discriminatory staffing practices informed by Euro-Western beauty norms that often exclude black women through racial "quotas," and sexual harassment (Law, 2016).

SEX WORK LABOUR ORGANIZING

As noted above, a key barrier to realizing sex workers' rights and safety in the workplace is the pervasive denial that sex work is legitimate work or work at all. Too frequently, sex work, especially when performed by women, is cast as a social or personal pathology and disconnected from the normative conception of work. **Organized labour** can play a role—and, to an extent, already has—in advancing the aims and goals of the international sex worker rights movement, that is, the end of unjust laws and the recognition of sex work as work (Clamen & Gillies, 2018; Clamen, Gillies, & Salah, 2013; van der Meulen, 2012). In Canada, several labour councils and unions have called for decriminalization and have officially recognized sex work as legitimate labour. Nationally, in 2001 the Canadian Union of Public Employees (CUPE) adopted a motion in support of decriminalization, and the following year the Canadian Labour Congress (CLC) passed a resolution to "consult within labour and the community to develop policies that provide supportive measures for sex trade workers" (Clamen, Gillies, & Salah, 2013, p. 125; see also CLC Solidarity and Pride Working Group & CLC Women's Committee, 2005).

Labour councils and unions have been important avenues for encouraging support for sex workers' rights. In 2014, the Ontario Public Service Employees Union (OPSEU) passed a resolution recognizing sex workers' rights to workplace safety and labour protections and advocated for decriminalization. OPSEU's Provincial Women's Committee (2015a, 2015b) went on to take a strong public stand in favour of total decriminalization of sex work. These actions were further solidified when, at the provincial level in 2016, CUPE Ontario committed to "support and resource sex workers' struggle for human and labour rights, condemn the criminalization of sex workers, support their labour organizations and harm reduction programs and support legal sex workers in accessing their labour rights" (CUPE Ontario, 2016, p. 17).

While we have seen increasing rhetorical support from some unions in Canada, there has been only one instance in which sex workers became officially unionized. This occurred in 1979 when the Canadian Association of Burlesque Entertainers was recognized as Local 1689 by the CLC (Sorfleet, 2005). Outside of Canada, sex workers have been much more successful at achieving unionization. In 1996 Australian workers in legal brothels in New South Wales and Victoria formed the first sex workers' union under the Australian Liquor, Hospitality and Miscellaneous Workers' Union. The next year dancers at San Francisco's Lusty Lady peep show unionized with the Service Employees International Union Local 790. In 2001 in the Netherlands the national sex worker organization De Rode Draad affiliated with the country's trade union confederation, and in 2002 sex workers in Great Britain formed a branch of GMB, the country's third largest union. Similarly, the Association for Women Prostitutes of Argentina is part of that country's largest trade union, the Central de Trabajadores Argentinos.

However, even in contexts (i.e., regions or work sectors) where it is unimpeded by criminalization, sex work unionization is not always a viable or desirable option. For example, in Canadian jurisdictions, labour laws generally restrict unionization to employees working for a single employer or at a single work site, and also exclude independent contractors. While many women in the sex trade might appreciate the entitlements of employee status (such as paid vacation, restrictions on work hours, and paid parental and other leaves), others may instead prefer the flexibility, autonomy, and other benefits of freelance work (van der Meulen, 2011). Professional associations and colleges are additional models for organizing and self-regulation; however, any move toward formal professionalization such as accreditation risks excluding the most marginalized workers, especially street-based and migrant workers. Sex work provides supports for many women who cannot or choose not to work in mainstream jobs (e.g., because they need to earn additional income to make ends meet on social assistance or disability payments, they have a physical or mental disability that presents challenges to being hired into conventional jobs, they need to occasionally supplement underemployment in a "mainstream" profession, or their qualifications are not applicable in Canada). Potential organizing mechanisms will therefore need to be flexible and involve minimal barriers to participation.

CONCLUSION

In the Canadian context, where aspects of sex work remain criminalized despite the groundbreaking Supreme Court *Bedford* decision in 2013, it is difficult for those in the sex trade to access labour rights and protections. Instead they are too often subject to punitive criminal law provisions that increase anti–sex work stigma and discrimination and can result in criminal charges for engaging in consensual sexual activities for financial or other remuneration. Moreover, criminalization precludes sex workers from accessing labour and human rights mechanisms that could address problematic workplace practices that disproportionately affect racialized, working-class, Indigenous, and migrant women, including discriminatory hiring and firing, and workplace sexual and racial harassment. By advancing an understanding of sex work as a form of work and sex workers as labourers, we can shift both public perception and state regulation away from problematic criminal justice interventions and toward health-, safety-, and labour-related policy approaches. Such a conceptual and procedural shift would benefit sex industry workers, their colleagues and coworkers, their clients and employers, and their friends and family.

This kind of labour-based conceptualization of sex work is not new; sex workers around the world, regardless of race, gender, citizenship, age, education level, and so on, have advocated for recognition of their self-determination and the acceptance of sex work as work (NSWP, 2013). A labour-based understanding of sex work is foundational to New Zealand's governmental approach to the sex industry. In 2003 New Zealand voted to decriminalize sex work and to develop a framework that "safeguards the human rights of sex workers and protects them from exploitation," as well as "promotes the welfare and occupational health and safety of sex workers" (Prostitution Reform Act, 2003, Part 1. s.3a,b). Rather than utilizing criminal law mechanisms, the New Zealand government worked with the country's national sex worker rights organization to develop labour and public health policies that would benefit sex workers and their clients (Abel, 2014). In years following decriminalization, sex workers in New Zealand reported decreased social stigma as well as increased occupational benefits and control over their work, including improvements to their safety and relationships with police, the ability to demand condom usage with clients, lower rates of sexually transmitted infections, and better access to sexual health services (Abel, Fitzgerald, Healy, & Taylor, 2010). In 2012 a New Zealand Parliament Library Research Paper concluded that while sex work is still a controversial topic in the country, "key evidence indicates that the decriminalisation of prostitution has impacted favourably on various aspects of sex work for many" (Bellamy, 2012, p. 10).

Labour activists, policy-makers, and others can look to the New Zealand model to discern what could be effectively implemented in the Canadian context. As this chapter has argued, of central importance to establishing sex workers' rights to safe and fair work is the sex-work-as-work conceptualization; without this social and political framework, laws and policies will continue to do more harm than good, especially for marginalized women who are already the targets of problematic surveillance, policing, and immigration policies and practices. A change in the laws in Canada is necessary, but so too is a social shift in understanding that sex workers are labourers deserving of the rights and protections applicable to all other workers.

KEY READINGS

Bruckert, C., Parent, C., & Robitaille, P. (2003). *Erotic service/erotic dance establishments: Two types of marginalized labour.* Ottawa: Law Commission of Canada.

Chapkis, W. (1997). *Live sex acts: Women performing erotic labor.* New York: Routledge.

Gall, G. (2016). *Sex worker unionization: Global developments, challenges, and possibilities.* London: Palgrave Macmillan.

Global Network of Sex Work Projects: http://www.nswp.org/

Kempadoo, K., & Doezema, J. (Eds.). (1998). *Global sex workers: Rights, resistance, and redefinition.* New York, NY: Routledge.

Leigh, C. (2004). *Unrepentant whore: Collected works of Scarlot Harlot.* San Francisco: Last Gasp.

Maynard, R. (2015, September 9). #Blacksexworkerslivesmatter: White-washed "anti-slavery" and the appropriation of black suffering. *The Feminist Wire.* Retrieved from http://www.thefeministwire.com/2015/09/blacksexworkerslivesmatter-white-washed-anti-slavery-and-the-appropriation-of-black-suffering/

DISCUSSION QUESTIONS

1. What did you know about sex work before reading this chapter, and where had this knowledge come from (e.g., friends, newspapers, TV shows, movies)? Discuss whether your thoughts have changed now that you have learned more about the sex industry.

2. What are some of the key social, legal, and political barriers and obstacles facing sex workers in Canada today? How can these be addressed?

3. Why do sex workers argue that it is problematic to conflate sex work and human trafficking? What are some of the impacts of this conflation on sex workers' advocacy efforts and labour rights?

4. In what ways is sex work similar to other types of work? Make a list of three different sex work sectors (e.g., escorting, stripping, street-based work, phone sex). Brainstorm the different types of work-related activities in which people in this sector engage (e.g., answering phone queries about the services offered, helping clean the work site, communicating with customers). Next, create a list of non–sex industry jobs where people would engage in these same types of activities.

5. Unions are important for establishing workplace rights and improving labour conditions. What are some things that unions can do to support workers in diverse sex industry sectors? What are some of the limits of unions?

RESOURCES FOR FURTHER INFORMATION: KEY SEX WORK ORGANIZATIONS IN CANADA

Action Santé Travesti(e)s et Transexuel(le)s du Québec (ASTTeQ) (Montreal)

Butterfly: Asian and Migrant Sex Workers Network (Toronto)

Canadian Alliance of Sex Work Law Reform

Émissaire (Longueuil)

FIRST (Vancouver)

Maggie's: Toronto Sex Workers' Action Project (Toronto)

Migrant Sex Workers Project (Toronto)

PEERS (Victoria)

Projet Lune (Quebec)

Prostitutes Involved, Empowered, Cogent Edmonton (PIECE) (Edmonton)

Prostitutes of Ottawa-Gatineau Work, Educate, Resist (POWER) (Ottawa)

Providing Alternatives, Counselling and Education (PACE) Society (Vancouver)

Rézo, projet travailleurs du sexe (Montreal)

Safe Harbour Outreach Project (SHOP) (St. John's)

Sex Professionals of Canada (SPOC) (Toronto)

Sex Workers Advisory Network of Sudbury (SWANS) (Sudbury)

Stella, l'amie de Maimie (Montreal)

Stepping Stone (Halifax)

Supporting Women's Alternatives Network (SWAN) (Vancouver)

Shift (Calgary)

Triple XXX (Vancouver)

Winnipeg Working Group (Winnipeg)

REFERENCES

Abel, G. (2014). A decade of decriminalization: Sex work "down under" but not underground. *Criminology and Criminal Justice, 14*(5), 580–592.

Abel, G., Fitzgerald, L., Healy, C., & Taylor, A. (2010). *Taking the crime out of sex work: New Zealand sex workers' fight for decriminalization.* Bristol, UK: Policy Press.

Agustín, L. M. (2006). The conundrum of women's agency: Migrations and the sex industry. In M. O'Neill & R. Campbell (Eds.), *Sex work now* (pp. 116–140). Cullompton, UK: Willan Publishing.

Agustín, L. M. (2007). *Sex at the margins: Migration, labour markets and the rescue industry.* London: Zed Books.

Bellamy, P. (2012, July). *Prostitution law reform in New Zealand.* Parliamentary Library Research Paper. Retrieved from https://www.parliament.nz/resource/en-NZ/00PLSocRP12051/c62a00e57bd36e84aed237e357af2b7381a39f7e

Benoit, C., & Millar, A. (2001). *Dispelling myths and understanding realities: Working conditions, health status, and exiting experiences of sex workers.* Victoria, BC: The Michael Smith Foundation for Health Research.

Benoit, C., & Shumka, L. (2015). Sex work in Canada. *University of Victoria.* Retrieved from http://www.understandingsexwork.ca

Bernstein, E. (2007). Sex work for the middle classes. *Sexualities, 10*(4), 473–488.

Big Susie's. (2014, June 30). Brief to the Standing Committee on Justice and Human Rights House of Commons Bill C-36 *Protection of Communities and Exploited Persons Act.* Retrieved from http://www.aidslaw.ca/site/wp-content/uploads/2014/09/LN-C36subm_Justice-27June2014-ENG.pdf

Brock, D., Gillies, K., Oliver, C., & Sutdhibhasilp, M. (2000). Migrant sex work: A roundtable analysis. *Canadian Woman Studies, 20*(2), 84–91.

Bruckert, C., & Hannem, S. (2013). Rethinking the prostitution debates: Transcending structural stigma in systemic responses to sex work. *Canadian Journal of Law and Society, 28*(1), 43–63.

Bruckert, C., & Law, T. (2013). *Beyond pimps, procurers and parasites: Mapping third parties in the incall/outcall sex industry.* Ottawa: University of Ottawa.

Butterfly. (2016, March). Stop the harm from anti-trafficking policies and campaigns: Support sex workers' rights, justice, and dignity. Retrieved from https://www.butterflysw.org/harm-of-anti-trafficking-campaign-

Canada (Attorney General) v. Bedford [2013] 3 SCR 1101.

Canadian Alliance for Sex Work Law Reform & Pivot Legal Society. (2016, October). *Joint submission for Canada's review before the UN Committee on the Elimination of All Forms of Discrimination against Women, 65th session.* Vancouver: Pivot Legal Society. Retrieved from http://tbinternet.ohchr.org/Treaties/CEDAW/Shared%20Documents/CAN/INT_CEDAW_NGO_CAN_25385_E.pdf

Canadian Union of Public Employees (CUPE) Ontario. (2016). *Action plan 2016: Privatization; Paving the way to poverty.* Retrieved from https://cupe.on.ca/wp-content/uploads/2016/07/2016-06-15-Action-Plan-2016-Final-Version-Ratified-by-members-at-convent-.pdf

Chapkis, W. (1997). *Live sex acts: Women performing erotic labor.* New York: Routledge.

Chimienti, M. (2010). Selling sex in order to migrate: The end of the migratory dream? *Journal of Ethnic and Migration Studies, 36*(1), 27–45.

Clamen, J., & Gillies, K. (2018). Will the real supporters of workers' rights please stand up? Union engagement with sex work in Canada. In E. M. Durisin, E. van der Meulen, & C. Bruckert (Eds.), *Red light labour: Sex work regulation, agency, and resistance* (pp. 305–316). Vancouver: UBC Press.

Clamen, J., Gillies, K., & Salah, T. (2013). Working for change: Sex workers in the union struggle. In E. van der Meulen, E. M. Durisin, & V. Love (Eds.), *Selling sex: Experience, advocacy, and research on sex work in Canada* (pp. 113–129). Vancouver: UBC Press.

CLC Solidarity and Pride Working Group & CLC Women's Committee. (2005, November). Sex trade discussion paper. CLC Solidarity and Pride Conference, Quebec City, Quebec.

De Shalit, A., Heynen, R., & van der Meulen, E. (2014). Human trafficking and media myths: Federal funding, communication strategies, and Canadian anti-trafficking programs. *Canadian Journal of Communication, 39*(3), 385–412.

Doezema, J. (2010). *Sex slaves and discourse masters: The construction of trafficking.* London: Zed Books.

Duggan, L., & Hunter, N. D. (1995). *Sex wars: Sexual dissent and political culture.* New York: Routledge.

Durisin, E. M., & Heynen, R. (2015). Producing the "trafficked woman": Canadian newspaper reporting on eastern European exotic dancers during the 1990s. *Atlantis: Critical Studies in Gender, Culture and Social Justice, 37*(2), 8–24.

Durisin, E. M., van der Meulen, E., & Bruckert, C. (2018). Contextualizing sex work: Challenging discourses and confronting narratives. In E. M. Durisin, E. van der Meulen, & C. Bruckert (Eds.), *Red light labour: Sex work regulation, agency, and resistance* (pp. 3–24). Vancouver: UBC Press.

Feminists for Sex Workers. (2017). Feminist manifesto in support of sex workers' rights. Retrieved from https://feministsforsexworkers.com

Gall, G. (2012). *An agency of their own: Sex worker union organizing.* Winchester, UK: Zero Books.

Gillies, K. (2013). A wolf in sheep's clothing: Canadian anti-pimping law and how it hurts sex workers. In E. van der Meulen, E. M. Durisin, & V. Love (Eds.), *Selling sex: Experience, advocacy and research on sex work in Canada* (pp. 269–278). Vancouver: UBC Press.

Global Alliance Against Traffic in Women. (2007). *Collateral damage: The impact of anti-trafficking measures on human rights around the world.* Bangkok, Thailand: Author. Retrieved from http://www.gaatw.org/Collateral%20Damage_Final/singlefile_Collateral Damagefinal.pdf

Global Network of Sex Work Projects. (2013). *Consensus statement on sex work, human rights, and the law.* Edinburgh, Scotland: Author. Retrieved from http://www.nswp.org/resource/nswp-consensus-statement-sex-work-human-rights-and-the-law

Global Network of Sex Work Projects. (2017). *Promoting health and human rights: Policy brief; Sex work and gender equality.* Edinburgh, Scotland: Author. Retrieved from http://www.nswp.org/sites/nswp.org/files/policy_brief_sex_work_and_gender_equality_nswp_-_2017.pdf

Handlovsky, I., Bungay, V., & Kolar, K. (2012). Condom use as situated in a risk context: women's experiences in the massage parlour industry in Vancouver, Canada. *Culture, Health and Sexuality, 14*(9), 1007–1020.

Hochschild, A. (1983). *The managed heart: Commercialization of human feeling.* Berkeley, CA: University of California Press.

Hunt, S. (2015). Representing colonial violence: Trafficking, sex work and the violence of law. *Atlantis: Critical Studies in Gender, Culture and Social Justice, 37*(2), 25–39.

Kempadoo, K. (2001). Women of color and the global sex trade: Transnational feminist perspectives. *Meridians, 1*(2), 28–51.

Kempadoo, K. (2012). From moral panic to global justice: Changing perspectives on trafficking. In K. Kempadoo, J. Sanghera, & B. Pattanaik (Eds.), *Trafficking and prostitution reconsidered: New perspectives on migration, sex work, and human rights* (pp. vii–xxxiv). Oxford, UK: Routledge.

Kingston, S., & Thomas, T. (2018). No model in practice: A "Nordic model" to respond to prostitution? *Crime, Law, and Social Change: An Interdisciplinary Journal,* 1–17. https://doi.org/10.1007/s10611-018-9795-6

Kolar, K., Atchison, C., & Bungay, V. (2014). Sexual safety practices of massage parlor-based sex workers and their clients. *AIDS Care, 26*(9), 1100–1104.

Krüsi, A., Belak, B., & Sex Workers United Against Violence. (2018). "Harassing the clients is exactly the same as harassing the workers": Street-based sex workers in Vancouver. In E. M. Durisin, E. van der Meulen, & C. Bruckert (Eds.), *Red light labour: Sex work regulation, agency, and resistance* (pp. 213–223). Vancouver: UBC Press.

Laing, M. (2012). Regulating adult work in Canada: The role of criminal and municipal code. In P. Johnson & D. Dalton (Eds.), *Policing sex* (pp. 166–184). New York: Routledge.

Lam, E. (2016). Inspection, policing and racism: How municipal by-laws endanger the lives of Chinese sex workers in Toronto. *Canadian Review of Social Policy/Revue Canadienne de Politique Sociale, 75,* 87–112.

Lam, E. (2018). *Behind the rescue: How anti-trafficking investigations and policies harm migrant sex workers.* Toronto: Butterfly. Retrieved from https://docs.wixstatic.com/ugd/5bd754_bbd71c0235c740e3a7d444956d95236b.pdf

Law, T. (2016). *Managing the "party": Third parties and the organization of labour in Ontario strip clubs.* Unpublished doctoral dissertation, University of Ottawa, Ottawa, Ontario.

Leigh, C. (1997). Inventing sex work. In J. Nagle (Ed.), *Whores and other feminists* (pp. 223–231). New York: Routledge

Lindemann, D. (2011). BDSM as therapy? *Sexualities, 14*(2), 151–172.

Lowman, J., & Louie, C. (2012). Public opinion on prostitution law reform in Canada. *Canadian Journal of Criminology and Criminal Justice, 54*(2), 245–260.

Maynard, R. (2015). Fighting wrongs with wrongs? How Canadian anti-trafficking crusades have failed sex workers, migrants, and Indigenous communities. *Atlantis: Critical Studies in Gender, Culture and Social Justice, 37*(2), 40–56.

Migrant Sex Workers Project. (2015). *Report on migrant sex workers justice and the trouble with "anti-trafficking": Research, activism, art.* Retrieved from http://www.migrantsex-workers.com/report.html

Milrod, C., & Weitzer, R. (2012). The intimacy prism: Emotion management among the clients of escorts. *Men and Masculinities, 15*(5), 447–467.

Outshoorn, J. (2005). The political debates on prostitution and trafficking of women. *Social Politics: International Studies in Gender, State and Society, 12*(1), 141–155.

Pinsky, D., & Levey, T. G. (2015). A world turned upside down: Emotional labour and the professional dominatrix. *Sexualities, 18*(4), 438–458.

Pivot Legal Society. (2006). *Beyond decriminalization: Sex work, human rights and a new framework for law reform.* Vancouver: Pivot Legal Society.

Prostitution Reform Act, 2003, Act of Parliament U.S.C. Wellington, New Zealand.

Protection of Communities and Exploited Persons Act (PCEPA), S.C. 2014, c. 25. Retrieved from http://laws-lois.justice.gc.ca/eng/AnnualStatutes/2014_25/page-1.html?wbdisable=true

Provincial Women's Committee, OPSEU. (2015a, December 4). Letter to the Minister of Justice to decriminalize sex work. Toronto: Author. Retrieved from https://opseu.org/news/letter-minister-justice decriminalize-sex-work

Provincial Women's Committee, OPSEU. (2015b, December 17). PWC marks International Day to End Violence Against Sex Workers. Retrieved from https://opseu.org/news/pwc-marks-international-day-end-violence-against-sex-workers

Raguparan, M. (2018). "The Paradox?!": Racialized and Indigenous sex workers' encounters within a capitalist market. In E.M. Durisin, E. van der Meulen, & C. Bruckert (Eds.), *Red light labour: Sex work regulation, agency, and resistance* (pp. 189–202). Vancouver: UBC Press.

Sanders, T., O'Neill, M., & Pitcher, J. (2017). *Prostitution: Sex work, policy and politics* (2nd ed.). Thousand Oaks, CA: Sage Publishing.

Sanghera, J. (2005). Unpacking the trafficking discourse. In K. Kempadoo, J. Sanghera, & B. Pattanaik (Eds.), *Trafficking and prostitution reconsidered: New perspectives on migration, sex work, and human rights* (pp. 3–24). Oxford, UK: Routledge.

Shaver, F. (2005). Sex work research: Methodological and ethical challenges. *Journal of Interpersonal Violence, 20*(3), 296–319.

Showden, C. R. (2011). *Choices women make: Agency in domestic violence, assisted reproduction, and sex work.* Minneapolis: University of Minnesota Press.

Sorfleet, A. (2005). *Sex workers' workbook: Where YOU regulate the sex industry.* Vancouver: $WE@&R! Retrieved from http://walnet.org/swear/SexWorkersWorkbook.pdf

Sterling, A. (2018). New risk-spaces, new spaces for harm: The effects of the advertising offence on independent escorts. In E. M. Durisin, E. van der Meulen, & C. Bruckert (Eds.), *Red light labour: Sex work regulation, agency, and resistance* (pp. 94–103). Vancouver: UBC Press.

TAMPEP. (2015, July). *TAMPEP on the situation of national and migrant sex workers in Europe.* Amsterdam, Netherlands: Author. Retrieved from http://www.nswp.org/sites/nswp.org/files/TAMPEP%20Briefing%20%20Paper%202015.pdf

van der Meulen, E. (2010). Illegal lives, loves, and work: How the criminalization of procuring affects sex workers in Canada. *Wagadu: A Journal of Transnational Women's and Gender Studies, 8,* 217–240.

van der Meulen, E. (2011). Sex work and Canadian policy: Recommendations for labour legitimacy and social change. *Sexuality Research and Social Policy, 8*(4), 348–358.

van der Meulen, E. (2012). When sex is work: Organizing for labour rights and protections. *Labour/Le Travail, 69,* 147–167.

van der Meulen, E., & Valverde, M. (2013). Beyond the Criminal Code: Municipal licensing and zoning bylaws. In E. van der Meulen, E. M. Durisin, & V. Love (Eds.), *Selling sex: Experience, advocacy, and research on sex work in Canada* (pp. 314–322). Vancouver: UBC Press.

Walkowitz, J. R. (2016). The politics of prostitution and sexual labour. *History Workshop Journal, 82*(1), 188–198.

Weitzer, R. (2007). The social construction of sex trafficking: Ideology and institutionalization of a moral crusade. *Politics and Sociology, 35*(3), 447–475.

Westcott, M., Baird, M., & Cooper, R. (2006). Reworking work: Dependency and choice in the employment relationship. *Labour and Industry, 17*(1), 5–17.

Women's Equality Liberty Coalition. (2018). Factum for the Intervener Women's Equality Liberty Coalition. Supreme Court of Canada Bradley Barton v. Her Majesty the Queen. Court File No. 37769.

GLOSSARY

collective bargaining: A process of negotiation between unions and employers used to reach agreement on new terms of employment—such as wages, maternity leave, or overtime—and resolve conflicts between the parties.

colonialism: A set of ideals stemming from control of a region or people by a greater power and promoting a dominant culture or perspective.

cyberbullying, cyberharassment: Sending or posting harmful or demeaning content about an individual or group over digital devices, on social media platforms, or in Internet forums. Examples include sexist, racist, or homophobic statements.

de facto: In fact; in reality. Example: the de facto exclusion of racialized people from voting even though their right to vote is guaranteed by law.

de jure: Based on laws. Example: the de jure exclusion of women from the right to vote, codified in laws about who can and cannot vote.

demographics: Statistical characteristics of populations, such as gender, age, race, and income.

deskilling: Devaluing or lowering people's education credentials, skills, and experience.

discouraged workers: Individuals who have given up on trying to find a job.

emotional labour: Managing one's own feelings and expressions on the job when interacting with customers, coworkers, and superiors. Examples include smiling, using a pleasant tone of voice, and complimenting others. The purpose of emotional labour may be to elicit a desired behaviour from customers or to protect one's job. It often involves concealing one's true feelings.

emphasized femininity: An idealized form of female behaviour characterized by altruism, compassion and caring, and buying into male dominance, especially in the workplace. Contrast with *hegemonic masculinity*.

employment equity: A uniquely Canadian approach to fair employment for women, visible minorities, Indigenous people, and persons with disabilities. Employment equity programs now often include LGBT individuals.

Employment Insurance: A financial support program for qualifying unemployed workers in Canada; called Unemployment Insurance prior to 1996.

equity: Equal, fair, and just treatment of women and men that is free from bias, such that they have equal chances to realize their potential. In Canada, *employment equity* is used as an alternative to the US term *affirmative action*.

gender: A social construct that describes differences in masculine and feminine traits and behaviours such as appearance, speech, and life choices. Traditionally limited to two distinct groups, male and female, but now expanded to include a spectrum of classifications and traits. Contrast with *sex*, which is biologically determined. Gender and sex often overlap, but not always.

gender norms: Prevailing expectations regarding women's and men's respective abilities and appropriate roles in the private and public spheres.

gender parity: Equality between women and men on specific measures such as income, workforce participation, and university graduation rates.

gendered division of labour: The division of labour in the household based on traditional gender roles.

global care chains: Networks of caregiving that extend from one country to another. Example: low-income women from the Global South who care for the children and households of upper- and middle-class families in the Global North.

Global North, Global South: Socioeconomic and political divisions of the world into two zones of more and less prosperous, developed, and stable nations. The Global North includes the United States, Canada, Europe, Australia, New Zealand, Japan, South Korea, and Taiwan. The Global South consists of Africa, Latin America, the Middle East, and other developing parts of Asia.

globalization: Business practices designed to increase profits by buying, selling, and manufacturing goods and marketing services internationally rather than only locally.

gross domestic product (GDP): The value of goods and services produced by a country.

harassment: Unwanted physical or verbal behaviour arising from power differentials between victim and perpetrator that offends or humiliates a victim and often persists over time; includes sexual harassment.

hegemonic masculinity: A culturally idealized form of masculinity that embodies society's most valued way of being a man, such as competitiveness, aggressiveness, and risk taking. Contrast with *emphasized femininity*.

heteronormativity: The notion that people are divided into clear male and female genders and that everyone in society is naturally heterosexual. Promotes heterosexuality as the preferred sexual orientation and is often associated with homophobia.

homophobia: Prejudice against or contempt for people who are homosexual or LGBT.

homosocial: Describes a social relationship rooted in a preference for same-sex social (not sexual) relationships. Usually used in reference to men.

interlocking framework of oppression: A theory that views relations of domination as structured via a system of interconnected race, class, and gender oppression.

intersectionality: A theoretical framework used to study oppression of marginalized groups in society by considering how social conditions such as gender, class, race, age, and ethnicity interact and combine to create oppression. Proponents of intersectionality underline that these conditions cannot be studied separately but must be considered in totality to fully understand how marginalization occurs.

labour force: For the purpose of government statistics, the labour force consists of people who are either working for pay or looking for paid work.

LGBT: Abbreviation for *lesbian, gay, bisexual, or transsexual.* Sometimes expressed with added letters such as *Q* for *queer* or *I* for *intersexual* (intermediate between male and female).

Live-in Caregiver Program (LICP): A federal program, operating from 1992 to 2014, that allowed a Canadian family to hire an international nanny. Nannies were required to live in their employer's home for at least two years, after which they could apply for Canadian permanent residency. Strongly criticized by feminist groups for exploitation of immigrant women by employers.

masculinized work: Work that is closely associated with abilities, subjectivities, and norms that are considered to be male, even if women make up much of the labour force. Examples: construction work, finance and accounting, medicine, police, firefighting, and military work.

minoritization: A process of marginalizing individuals. Emphasizes the role of the dominant group in creating a minority, rather than deficits in minoritized people, in contrast to the term *minorities.*

neoliberalism: A laissez-faire ("hands-off") approach by the government toward the economy and society. Assumes that the free market will regulate itself without government intervention and that people are responsible for their own welfare.

nonprofit organizations: Service organizations that are independent, voluntarily constituted, and self-governing, and are prohibited from distributing profits to their stakeholders.

oikos: In ancient Greece, the private sphere of production and reproduction in which women bore and raised children and slaves produced the basic necessities of life. Contrast with *polis,* the city or public sphere, in which men ran public affairs.

organized labour: Work organizations that represent the interests of unionized workers in trade unions, labour federations, and labour organizations that involve the participation of unionized workers such as health and safety committees, and other worker organizations that advocate on behalf of paid workers whether unionized or not.

othering: The practice of excluding and marginalizing people who don't fit the narrow definition of a dominant social group, such as labelling immigrants or people with disabilities as outsiders.

patriarchy: A system of social organization in which fathers rule the family, women and children are dependent on them, and males hold the majority of political and socioeconomic power.

precarious employment: Jobs characterized by uncertainty, a lack of guarantee of future work, and unpredictable hours.

racialization: The dynamic and complex process by which racial categories are socially produced by dominant groups in ways that entrench social inequalities. Term preferred by scholars and social justice activists over *visible minority status,* which is used by government agencies such as Statistics Canada.

radical feminists: Feminists who seek to actively abolish patriarchy and male supremacy. Contrast with *liberal feminists,* who believe that changes in laws will result in the erosion of patriarchy, thus changing gender roles and expectations.

seniority: Greater job status conferred by greater age, length of employment, or rank compared to employees of lesser status. Seniority correlates with higher salary, priority retention in case of layoffs, and other benefits.

sex: Biologically determined classification of people based on traits such as X and Y chromosomes and reproductive organs. Historically believed to be clearly divided between male and female; now understood by scientists to encompass a wider range of variations.

social capital: Assets that derive from our connections to other individuals, groups, and institutions. People who have more social capital have advantages like access to greater economic gains and increased authority.

social reproduction: The process of feeding, clothing, and restoring people on both a daily and generational basis, which usually occurs in private households. Social reproduction is a precondition for economic activity in the public sphere.

STEM: Abbreviation for *science, technology, engineering, and mathematics.*

structuration: A theoretical concept that looks at how individuals can assert agency and change the social structures they live under and, conversely, how the social structures we live under shape our lives.

systemic discrimination: Negative bias or disadvantage affecting particular groups of people that is structured into rules, habits, physical environments, cultures, organizations, and other aspects of society.

tiered pay: A pay structure based on paying new hires less than the current workforce for doing the same task.

time poverty: A lack of time for activities of daily life such as work, education, leisure, and self-care that directly impact socioeconomic status, health, and well-being. Especially impacts women due to the amount of unpaid household labour they are expected to do.

transactional leadership: A managerial command-and-control style of leadership in which compliance is promoted by awarding or withholding rewards, including the use of threats. Contrast with *transformational leadership.*

transformational leadership: A leadership style that nurtures, inspires, and empowers followers by articulating a clear vision, encouraging creativity, sharing information, and building team spirit. Contrast with *transactional leadership.*

underemployment: Working less than full-time or working at a job that is below a person's level of skills, education, or experience and cannot fulfill economic needs.

union: A worker association formed to represent the collective interests of workers in relations with their employer through the process of collective bargaining and the administration of a collective employment agreement.

visible minorities: A term used primarily by Statistics Canada to designate "persons, other than Aboriginal peoples, who are non-Caucasian in race or non-white in colour." Scholars and social justice advocates prefer the term *racialized people.*

WIL: Abbreviation for *work-integrated learning*—high school, college, and university on-the-job training programs. These programs are variously called *internships, practicums, placements,* or *co-ops.*

workers' compensation: Health care, rehabilitation, and salary replacement for workers who are injured, made ill, or disabled on the job.

CONTRIBUTORS

Sandra Acker is professor emerita in the Department of Social Justice Education at the Ontario Institute for Studies in Education at the University of Toronto. Her research focuses on women academics, changes in academic work, tenure practices, doctoral students, and the social production of academic research. She is a recipient of the 2014 Ontario Confederation of University Faculty Associations' Status of Women Committee Award of Distinction.

Pramila Aggarwal, PhD (ABD), recently retired from the Community Worker Program at George Brown College in Toronto, where she taught for 20 years. She is currently a visiting professor at the International Institute of Adult and Lifelong Education in Delhi, India. She has worked in Canada as well as internationally on issues of violence against women, antiracism, human rights, and community development. Her activism in Canada has centred on immigrant workers' rights.

Susan Braedley is an associate professor in the Department of Social Work at Carleton University.

Taylor Brydges is a postdoctoral researcher at Stockholm University and the University of Zurich. Her research explores economic competitiveness, innovation, and entrepreneurship in the cultural and creative industries, including the contemporary nature of work in the creative economy and the impact of digital technologies on patterns and spaces of labour and entrepreneurship. She is also interested in issues relating to sustainability and the circular economy, with a focus on the fashion industry.

June Corman is a professor of sociology at Brock University. Her research focuses on women and work, mainly in the areas of education, farm women, and industrial workers. She is the recipient of Brock's Rosalind Blauer Award for activities bringing attention to women and the Graduate Mentor Award, as well as the YWCA Woman of Distinction Award.

Anne Forrest is an associate professor of women's and gender studies at the University of Windsor. Her areas of interest are women and unions, collective bargaining, industrial relations theory, and organizational change. She has served her faculty association in many capacities, including as chair of the grievance committee and president.

Mary Foster is a professor of marketing at the Ted Rogers School of Management at Ryerson University. Through Ryerson's Centre for Voluntary Sector Studies, she has collaborated on research projects on women in voluntary organizations, donating behaviour, and the role of the voluntary sector in creating bridging and bonding social capital. Her other research interests include women in management, privacy and cyberbullying, the use and impact of social media, and the role of neuroscience in innovative management education.

Danielle Gabay, PhD, teaches in the Department of Sociology at Ryerson University. Her research focuses on equity and diversity in sport and education, as well as institutional culture and quality assurance in Canadian higher education.

Kara Gillies has been active in the sex workers' rights movement in Canada for over 25 years. She was a long-time member of Maggie's: Toronto Sex Workers' Action Project, and in 2003 she cofounded the Canadian Guild for Erotic Labour. Her advocacy focuses especially on the impact of criminal law on sex workers' personal, social, and workplace well-being.

Andrea Hunter was a journalist and producer with the Canadian Broadcasting Corporation for many years. She holds bachelor's and master's degrees in journalism from Carleton University and a PhD in sociology from Queen's University. Her research focuses on the political economy of journalism and social media from a feminist perspective.

Esther Ignagni is an associate professor in the School of Disability Studies at Ryerson University. She is a former community health worker and activist. Her academic training and work have been in public health, bioethics, and allied health fields, and she has conducted research with several health organizations. She combines her work in health with a disability rights analysis to explore the body as a site for evolving eugenics practice and the social production of impairment and disability.

Melanie Knight is an associate professor in the Department of Sociology at Ryerson University in Toronto. Her research interests are primarily focused on race, gender, and precarious employment; black women entrepreneurs; black collective economic and community initiatives; and racism and the discourse of enterprise. She is also involved in community initiatives addressing women and employment and is a faculty affiliate of the Centre for Labour Management Relations at Ryerson University.

Elene Lam has been involved with the international sex workers' rights movement for more than 15 years. She is the founder and director of Butterfly: Asian and Migrant Sex Workers Support Network, co-founder of the Migrant Sex Workers Project in Canada, and the former director of Hong Kong's Zi Teng, the Chinese sex worker rights organization. She is currently working on her doctorate at McMaster University.

Tuulia Law has been involved with sex work activism for a number of years. She is a former member of Sex Professionals of Canada, has been involved with Prostitutes of Ottawa-Gatineau Work, Educate, Resist (POWER), and currently works with strippers organizing in Toronto. She is also an assistant professor at York University, where she teaches in the criminology program. Her research interests include men who manage male sex workers, sexual assault prevention strategies by university administration and students, and critical victimology.

Deborah Leslie is a professor of geography at the University of Toronto. Most of her research focuses on the role of cultural industries in urban economic development. She also writes on the precarious nature of work in cultural industries. Most recently, she has been engaged in a collaborative project with Norma Rantisi investigating the path and place-dependent development of the Montreal circus.

Alexa Lewis holds an honours BA in political science (international relations and political theory) and has published work on civil resistance in the Middle East and the emergence of capitalist society.

Katherine Lippel is a professor of law and has held the Canada Research Chair in Occupational Health and Safety Law at the University of Ottawa Law Faculty, Civil Law Section, since 2006. She previously taught law for 25 years at the Université du Québec à Montréal. She was made a fellow of the Royal

Society of Canada in 2010, and in 2017 she was awarded the Social Sciences and Humanities Research Council Gold Medal, the council's highest award.

Agnes Meinhard is professor emerita of organizational behaviour and theory in the Ted Rogers School of Management at Ryerson University. She is also the founding director of Ryerson University's Centre for Voluntary Sector Studies, which conducts research on the role of nonprofit organizations and voluntary activity in society.

Linda Muzzin is a professor of higher education in the Department of Leadership, Higher and Adult Education, at the Ontario Institute for Studies in Education at the University of Toronto, with a cross-appointment in pharmaceutical sciences. Her research interests include college and university faculty, professional education and practice, and knowledge production from critical theoretical perspectives.

Leslie Nichols, PhD, is a public policy researcher and social justice advocate. She investigates the marginalization of women, immigrants, youth, and other groups in the Canadian workforce and the social, political, and economic forces that create inequality for those populations. Her publications include studies on topics such as women's time poverty, immigrant settlement, and immigrant youths' transition from education to employment.

Jocelyne Praud teaches in the Department of Political Studies at Vancouver Island University. She has published several journal articles and book chapters on gender and politics in Canada and France. Together with Sandrine Dauphin, she co-authored *Parity Democracy: Women's Political Representation in Fifth Republic France* (UBC Press, 2010). She also co-edited the bilingual collection *Mothering Canada: Interdisciplinary Voices* (Demeter Press, 2010) and edited a special issue on gender parity in politics for the journal *West European Politics* in 2012.

Stephanie Premji is an associate professor in the School of Labour Studies and the Department of Health, Aging, and Society at McMaster University. Her research examines health and safety issues among immigrant and racialized workers through a gender lens. She is the editor of *Sick and Tired: Health and Safety Inequalities*.

Susan Prentice is a professor in the Department of Sociology at the University of Manitoba. She works closely with provincial and national childcare advocacy groups.

Rai Reece is a professor in the Community Justice Services Program in the School of Social and Community Services at Humber College. Since 2005 she has been involved with antiprison work with prisoners and ex-prisoners. Her most recent co-publication in the *Canadian Journal of Criminology and Criminal Justice* examines harm-reduction practices in federal prisons. She holds a PhD in women's studies from York University and is the recipient of the 2018 Humber College Research Excellence Award.

Jarod Sicotte holds a BA in political science (political theory) from the University of Victoria and was the editor-in-chief of the undergraduate journal *OnPolitics* in 2017/2018.

Andrea Sterling has been involved with sex-working communities in Montreal and Toronto for over 10 years. She was a board member of Canada's oldest sex-worker-run organization, Maggie's: Toronto Sex Workers' Action Project, and also a member of Stella in Montreal. She is a doctoral student at the University of Toronto, where she is researching the various modes of regulation experienced by Canadian sex workers.

Vappu Tyyskä is professor emerita of sociology at Ryerson University, with graduate program affiliations in immigration and settlement studies and policy studies. Her major areas of research include immigrant families, youth, gender, and family relations. Her book *Youth and Society: The Long and Winding Road* is in its 3rd edition with Canadian Scholars.

Emily van der Meulen is an associate professor of criminology at Ryerson University. Her involvement in the sex workers' rights movement spans nearly 15 years. She is editor or co-editor of numerous books, including *Red Light Labour: Sex Work Regulation, Agency, and Resistance* (with Elya M. Durisin and Chris Bruckert, University of British Columbia Press, 2018) and *Making Surveillance States: Transnational Histories* (with Robert Heynen, University of Toronto Press, 2019).

INDEX

Abella, Rosalie, 182, 306

absolute poverty, 77–78

academic work

    black female athletes, 230–233, 240–241

    minoritized faculty. *See* minoritized

      faculty

Action Travail des Femmes case, 32

aesthetic labour

    corporate hardware, 274

    in fashion retail, 273–275

    human hardware, 274

    independent fashion retailing, 275–282

    interpellation, 272

    meaning of, 271

    nature of, 270, 271–273, 282

    self-imposed aesthetic labour, 276–279

    service workplaces, 271–272

    use of term, 271

affirmative action, 306

Afghan Women's Organization, 98

African Youth Charter, 138

age, 12, 14t, 332

ageism, 149

Alberta Works, 76

alternative retailers. *See* independent fashion

    retailing

America's Competitive Secret: Utilizing Women as a

    Management Strategy (Rosener), 351

ancient Greek philosophers, 249–250

Angus Reid Institute, 147–148

arbitration, 44

Aristotle, 249–250

Association québécoise des centres de la petite

    enfance, 169

At Issue broadcast, 258, 259

athletes. *See* black female athletes

athletic work, 227–230

Atlantic University Sport (AUS), 226

Augustine, Jean, 251

Australian Liquor, Hospitality and

    Miscellaneous Workers' Union, 371

Bedford case, 359–360, 364, 372

Bedrock Industries, 326

behavioural norms, 2

Bem Sex Role Inventory Test, 2

BHASE (business, humanities, health, arts,

    social science, and education) fields, 144–145,

    146t

Bill C-36, 364

binary fashion, 3

biological traits, 2

Bisonnette, Lise, 294

black female athletes

    academic work, 230–233, 240–241

    athletic work, 227–230

    career goals, 236–238, 240, 241

    community work, 233–235

    future work in sport, 236–240

    generally, 223–225, 240–241

    intersectionality, 225–226

    mentorship and role models, 231–232, 240

    part-time work, 235–236

    professional athletes, 238–239

    racial stereotypes, 229–230, 232–233

    research on student athletes, 224–225

    revenue-generating sports, 225

    support networks, 231

    U Sports, 225, 226–227

black female entrepreneurs

    branding of a business, 216–217

    complex relationship with

      entrepreneurship, 211

    creation of the black entrepreneur class,

      205–207

    generally, 203–204, 217–218

black female entrepreneurs (*Continued*)
 government statistics, 215
 "housewife," 210
 ideologies of race and gender, 204–205
 interlocking framework of oppression, 203
 low participation, notion of, 214
 multiculturalism, 216
 from nineteenth century onward, 209–214
 precarious employment, 208–209
 present-day context, 214–217
 reasons for participation, 215–216
 relegation to domestic work and nursing,
  207–208
 slavery, impacts of, 204–205
 twentieth-century Canadian immigration
  policies, 207–209
 underground economy, 212–213
black feminist scholarship, 5
Blondin-Andrew, Ethel, 251
Blues Legacies and Black Feminism (Davis), 213
bodies at work, 308–310
boutique stores. *See* fashion retail
brain drain, 101
breadwinner jobs. *See* unions and unionization
Breaking Anonymity, 187
British Columbia Government and Service
 Employees Union (BCGSEU), 31–32
Broadcasting Act, 298
Brosseau, Ruth Ellen, 258

Campbell, Kim, 251
Canada Health Act, 71
Canada Human Rights Act, 309
Canada Research Chairs, 183
Canada West Universities Athletic Association
 (CWUAA), 226
Canadian Association of Burlesque
 Entertainers, 371
Canadian Association of University
 Teachers, 179
Canadian Broadcasting Corporation/
 Radio-Canada, 298
Canadian census, 13, 139, 210
Canadian Charter of Rights and Freedoms

anti-prostitution laws, 364
 disabled workers, complaints of, 124
 equality rights, 345
 inclusion of women in, 24
Canadian Citizenship Act, 251
Canadian Employment Insurance Special
 Benefits, 143–144
Canadian Human Rights Act, 38, 123
Canadian Immigration Act of 1910, 207
Canadian Institute for Health Research, 62
Canadian Interuniversity Sport (CIS), 226
 See also U Sports
Canadian Labour Code, 147
Canadian Labour Congress, 33–40, 41, 370
Canadian Labour Force Survey, 82
Canadian Nonprofit Sector Salary and Benefits
 Study, 341–342
Canadian Survey on Disability, 118
Canadian Union of Postal Workers (CUPW), 42
Canadian Union of Public Employees (CUPE),
 39, 43, 44, 370–371
care crisis, 159
care work, 11, 73
Caribbean Domestic Scheme, 102, 103
Caring for Children Pathway Program, 166
caring occupations, 16–18
Caruk, Holly, 297
Cary, Mary Ann Shadd, 210
cashiering, 16–18
catering, 16–18
Chagger, Bardish, 260
Changing Academic Profession, 184–185
Charity Village, 341
child-bearing, 1, 40–42, 143–144
Child Care Advocacy Association of Canada, 170
Child Care Expense Deduction, 157
Child Care Human Resources Sector Council,
 163–164
childcare, 157
 alternatives to childcare crisis, 166–167
 Canada's childcare workforce, 161–166
 childcare centres, 165
 domestic childcare workers, 102–103,
  166–167

early childhood education and care
(ECEC). *See* early childhood education
and care (ECEC)
educational credentials, 169
family home childcare providers, 165
female-dominated field, 158
and freedom to work, 74
generally, 157–158
government, and affordable childcare, 87
intersectionality, 164
market-based service, 161
nannies, 166–167
no right to childcare services, 160
nonprofit childcare, 161
part-time work, 144
public policy change, 169–170
Quebec, 87, 144, 167–168
social movements, 168–170
social reproduction theory, 159–161
unionization, 169
childcare centres, 165
Chilly Collective, 187
Chinese Empire Ladies Reform Association, 344
Chong, Michael, 259
chromosomes, 2
chronic stress, 59–60
Citizenship and Immigration Canada, 98
class, 4, 74
cleaning occupations, 16–18
clerical occupations, 16–18
CN, 30, 32
Coleman, Kit, 290, 291
collective bargaining, 25, 26, 381
College of Early Childhood Educators, 169
colonialism, 7, 381
Commission des droits de la personne et des
droits de la jeunesse (CDPD), 61
community work, 11
community work, and black female athletes,
233–235
corporate restructuring, 335
corporatization, 191
country comparisons. *See* international
perspective

Criminal Code of Canada, 147, 360
crowding, 4
cultural capital, 276–277
CUPE. *See* Canadian Union of Public
Employees (CUPE)
CUPW. *See* Canadian Union of Postal Workers
(CUPW)
cyberbullying, 257–260, 261–262, 381
cyberharassment, 259–260, 381

Davies, Libby, 251
de facto, 381
de facto exclusion from politics, 250–254
de jure, 381
de jure exclusion from politics, 250–254
demographics, 139, 381
Denison, Flora MacDonald, 291–292
Department of Citizenship
and Immigration, 208
depression, work-related, 59
deskilling, 72, 97, 100–101, 141–142, 381
dignity on the job, 43–45
direct cyberbullying, 257
disability
body-mind differences, 112, 126
and care, relationship between, 125
defining disability, 112
Disability Studies framework, 111,
112–114, 117, 124–125, 131
eugenicist efforts, 115
forced unpaid labour, 115–116
human rights legislation, 123, 130
independent living (IL) model,
125–126
institutional labour, 115–116
personal support philosophy, 125
social model analysis, 113, 117, 124–125
sociopolitical approaches, 117
transinstitutionalization, 126–127
unemployment rate, 118
use of term, 111–112
See also disabled women
disability, work-related. *See* occupational health
and safety

Disability Studies framework, 111, 112–114, 117, 124–125, 131

disabled women
academic work, 187
accessibility issues, 122
accommodation issues, 122–123
attitudinal barriers, 123
career advancement, 120
decommodification of labour, 129–130
"disabled," use of term, 112
discrimination, 123
educational attainment, 119
employment statistics, 118–119
everyday work lives, 130–131
exclusion from the workplace, 118–124
expansion of scope of work, 124–126
feminist scholarship, 116–118
government assistance, 122
history of disabled workers, 114–116
horizontal segregation, 119–120
marginalization in relation to paid work, 119, 128
neoliberalism, 120–121, 127
postwork analyses, 128–130
poverty, 121–122
revolving door of discrimination, 127
unemployment, 85
and work, generally, 130–131
work and health, 128–129
work as containment, 126–127
See also disability

Disabling Barriers, Enabling Environments, 113–114

discouraged searchers, 69

discouraged workers, 69, 381

discrimination
attitudinal discrimination, 123
correction of past discrimination, 32–33
disabled women, 123, 127
and human rights legislation, 27–28
indirect discrimination, 28
reverse discrimination, 306
systemic discrimination, 55, 385

discriminatory employment practices, 4

diversity, 178
in media organizations, 297–298
in public office. See public women
and women's employment rate, 12

division of labour
gendered division of labour, 10–11, 382
(see also women and work)
international, in manufacturing work, 335

domestic labour, 1–2, 11

Domestic Scheme Program, 207

domestic workers, 11–12, 60–61, 102–104, 166–167, 207–208

Dominion Stores, 29, 35

double day, 11

double shifts, 104

dual-earner couples, 11

Duclos, Jean-Yves, 164

early childhood education and care (ECEC)
demographics, 163
female-dominated field, 158
generally, 158–159
job satisfaction, 164
quality of early childhood care, 165–166
turnover rate, 164
wage-improvement campaigns, 168–169
wages, 162–163

ECEC. See early childhood education and care (ECEC)

economic policies, 68

education
BHASE. See BHASE (business, humanities, health, arts, social science, and education) fields
childcare staff, 169
combining education and work, 140, 146
credentialism, 169
disabled workers, 119
postsecondary education, 177–178
Quebec, 182
and racialized women, 18
STEM. See STEM (science, technology, engineering, and mathematics) fields

and the workplace. *See* class
  young women, 144–146, 145t
Elbowgate, 258
elected representatives. *See* public women
elections. *See* politics; public women
Émile (Rousseau), 250
emotional labour, 271, 361, 381
emphasized femininity, 343, 381
employers of sex workers, 368–370
employment
  age, impact of, 12, 14t
  full-time employment, 15, 16t
  gender, impact of, 14t
  immigrant status, 14t, 15
  immigrant women, 95–96
  part-time employment, 15
  precarious employment, 9, 19, 79,
    100–101, 208–209, 280–282, 384
  race, impact of, 13–15, 14t
  survival employment, 96, 100
  underemployment. *See* underemployment
  unemployment. *See* unemployment
  young women, 138–140
  youth, 83–84
employment equity, 306, 381
  in fire services, 307–308, 315–316
  generally, 306–307
  legislation, 306 (*see also* Employment
    Equity Act)
  policies and practices, 306–307
Employment Equity Act, 13, 182
Employment Insurance (EI), 68, 74, 76–77,
  80–82, 381
employment insurance policies, 76–77
employment rate
  diversity, and women's employment
    rate, 12
  full-time, by gender, 16t
employment standards, 101–102
Employment Standards Act, 42
entrepreneurship
  black women. *See* black female
    entrepreneurs
  freelancers, 294
  independent escorts, 361

independent fashion retailing, 275–282
  precarious employment, 280–282
equal pay for equal work, 36–38
*Equality in Employment: A Royal Commission
  Report*, 306
equality of opportunity, 178
equity, 178, 382
Equity, Diversity, and Inclusion Action
  Plan, 184
erotic dancers, 366, 369, 370
escort agencies, 369, 370
essentialism, 177
ethnicity. *See* immigrant women; immigration
  and immigrant status; racialized women
Expert Panel on Women in University
  Research, 183
exploitation on the job, 101–102

Facebook. *See* social media
factory work, 55
faculty. *See* academic work
fairness, 31
family, 159
family home childcare providers, 165
family policy, 160–161
family status. *See* class
family-work balance, 143–144, 296
fashion boutiques. *See* fashion retail
fashion retail
  aesthetic labour, 273–275
  fast fashion, 275
  independent fashion retailing. *See*
    independent fashion retailing
  performance, and the body, 273–274
Federal Contractors Program, 182–183
female firefighters. *See* women firefighters
female job ghetto, 11
female journalists. *See* women journalists
femininity, 11, 343
feminist organizations, 339
feminist scholarship
  African American feminist scholars, 53
  disabled women, 116–118
  feminist political economy approach,
    289–290, 304–306

feminized education programs and careers, 144–146, 145t

Femmes publiques (Perrot), 247

field of intersectionality studies, 6

Filipino women, 102

fire services

    change as reduction in standards, 310

    employment equity, 307–308

    fire hall culture, 312–314

    fire halls, 311

    generally, 303–304

    homosocial culture, 313

    operations, 314, 318n3

    pre-employment physical fitness testing, 308–310, 314

    racism, 307

    research exception, 313–314

    sexual harassment, 307

    See also women firefighters

5Cs, 16–18

Fontaine, Nahanni, 259, 260

Ford, Doug, 336

foreign credentials, 100

Foreign Domestic Movement Program, 102

Fraser, Joan, 294

freedom to choose whether and how much to work, 73–75

freelancers, 294

Freeman, Wendy, 294

Fry, Hedy, 251

full-time employment, 15, 16t

GDP. *See* gross domestic product (GDP)

gender, 2, 382

    and employment, 14t

    and stereotypes. *See* gender stereotypes

    and the workplace, 4

gender binary, 5

gender differences

    cyberbullying, victims of, 258–259

    in employment, generally, 3–4

    freedom to choose whether and how much to work, 73–75

health impacts, 75

hours worked, 72–73

intersectionality approach. *See* intersectionality

part-time employment, 75, 75t

retraining, 75–76

salaries, 72–73

unpaid labour, 72–73

volunteering, rates of, 341

Gender Empowerment Measure, 345–346

gender equality, 24

gender gaps, 181–187

    academic leadership, 183–184

    country comparisons, 184–185

    found through qualitative research, 185–186

gender norms, 2, 143, 382

gender parity, 116, 382

Gender Quotas Database, 261

gender stereotypes, 44

gender wage gap

    manufacturing work, 327–328

    pay equity, 38–40

    unionized workplaces, 33–34, 38

gendered division of labour, 10–11, 382

General Motors (GM), 27, 30

glass ceiling, 18, 19, 184, 187, 293–295

glass cliff, 184, 187

glass escalator, 18

global care chain, 103–104, 382

Global North, 6, 7, 8, 382

    See also international perspective

global perspective. *See* international perspective

Global South, 6, 7, 102, 382

    See also international perspective

globalization, 141, 382

    definitions of, 6

    examples of, 6

    and women's work, 6–7

glossary of terms, 381–386

goods-producing sector. *See* manufacturing work

government policies, 68, 74, 169–170

Gradual Civilization Act, 7
grandmothers, 104–105
Great Depression, 76, 209
gross domestic product (GDP), 138, 382

harassment, 1, 52, 382
    cyberharassment, 259–260
    sexual harassment. *See* sexual harassment
Harmatiuk, Beatrice, 37–38
Harper government, 160–161
Hayes, Kate Simpson, 291
health
    disabled women, and work and health,
        128–129
    occupational health and safety. *See*
        occupational health and safety
    underemployment, impact of, 71–72
    unemployment, impact of, 71–72
health-care workers, 55–56
hegemonic masculinity, 343, 382
herstory, 189
heteronormative, 307, 383
Hilton Works steel plant, 325–326, 334
homophobia, 187, 383
homosocial, 313, 383
Hotel and Restaurant Employees and Bartender
    International Union, 37
Hotel Dieu, 340
hours worked, 72–73
household financial security, 70
household labour, 11, 12
Household Service Workers Scheme, 103
Human Development Consultants, 142
Human Resources and Skills Development
    Canada, 119, 146
human rights legislation, 24, 27–28, 123, 130
        See also Canadian Charter of Rights and
          Freedoms; specific legislation
human trafficking, 366–368

illness, 52–53
    See also occupational health and safety
immigrant women
    added burdens of, 105–106

deskilling, 72, 97, 100–101
domestic workers. *See* domestic
    workers
and employment, 14t, 15
employment standards, 101–102
employment statistics, 95–96
exploitation on the job, 101–102
gender, and immigration categories,
    99–100
illness and, 52–53
low-wage work, 80, 81t, 101
neoliberalism, impact of, 97–99
"pay the job, not the worker," 35
precarious employment, 100–101
sex workers, 368
social construction of, 96–97
survival employment, 96, 100
time poverty, 104–105
underemployment, 56
and unemployment, 79–82
unpaid household labour, 104–105
use of term, 97
view as less desirable, 97
and work, generally, 95–96
workers' compensation, 61
    See also immigration and immigrant
        status; racialized women
immigration and immigrant status
    and black women's work, 207–209
    economic immigration class, 99
    entering Canada as dependent, 99–100
    funding, cuts in, 98
    growth of immigrant population, 95
    intra-national migration, 368
    othering, 97
    and race, 80
    refugees, 100
    settlement services, 98–99
    skilled workers, 99
    social capital, 105
    transnational migration, 367
    See also immigrant women
Inco, 30
independent contractors, 370, 371

independent fashion retailing, 275–282, 282–283
　growth of, 275–276
　mentorship, lack of, 281
　personal relationships with customers,
　　279–280
　precarious employment, 280–282
　reputation for style, 279
　self-imposed aesthetic labour, 276–279
　social media, 278
　tacit aesthetic knowledge, 277–278
Indian Act of 1876, 7
Indigenous people
　childcare data, 164
　and colonialism, 7
　cultural assimilation, 7
　Indian Act of 1876, 7
　residential school system, 8, 190
　voting rights, 251, 261
　See also Indigenous women
Indigenous women
　academic work, 181, 186–187
　in Canada, generally, 7–8
　human trafficking, 368
　"pay the job, not the worker," 35
　in politics, 251, 254, 260–261
　sex workers, 368
　unemployment, 82
　unemployment rate, 82t, 83t
　violence against, 7–8
　voting rights, 345
indirect cyberbullying, 257
indirect discrimination, 28
institutional labour, 115–116
interlocking framework of oppression, 203, 383
International Labour Congress, 60
International Labour Organization, 140
international perspective
　electoral quotas, 261, 263n12, 263n13
　human trafficking, 366–367
　manufacturing, and international division
　　of labour, 335
　minoritized faculty, 184–185
　social imbalances, 367
　unemployment, 69
　women in politics, 261

International Union, United Automobile,
　Aerospace and Agricultural Implement
　Workers of America. See United Automobile
　Workers (UAW)
Internet
　cyberbullying, 257–260, 261–262
　cyberharassment, 259–260
　direct cyberbullying, 257
　indirect cyberbullying, 257
　"Internet election," 256
　journalism, 294–295
　social media, and politics, 256–257
interpellation, 272
intersectionality, 177–178, 190, 383
　black feminist scholarship, roots in, 5
　black women university athletes, 225–226
　childcare, 164
　development of, 5
　field of intersectionality studies, 6
　generally, 1–3
　main argument of, 5
　manufacturing work, 324–325
　and prevention, 54–56
　retail work, 269–270
　theory vs. method, 5–6
　to understanding women and work, 3–6
　women firefighters, 304–306
　workers' compensation, 57–62
intersex individuals, 2, 3
involuntary part-time employment. See part-
　time employment

Jansen, Sandra, 257–258
job segregation by gender, 27–29
job titles, 28, 52
Jodhan case, 124
John Deere Welland Works, 326–330, 334
journalism
　democracy, role in, 287–288
　economic crisis in Internet era,
　　294–295
　gender and diversity, 297–298
　generally, 287–289
　"information society," 288
　male-controlled structures, 297

pre-Internet journalism, 288–289

See also women journalists

Keynesian economics, 76

kin and community work, 11

Kiwanis, 346

knowledge production, 189–192

knowledges, 189–190

Kwann, Jenny, 260

La Maison de la Providence, 340–341, 343

labour force, 3, 10, 158, 383

labour market

discriminatory employment practices, 4

social categories, 5

structural factors, 4

laissez-faire capitalism, 9

language. *See* class

Le Bureau des Pauvres, 340

leadership, 348–349

legislative representation. *See* public women

LGBT, 383

LGBTQ

academic work, 188

homophobia, 187, 383

LGBT, defined, 383

LGBTQ movement, 2

unionized workplaces, 34

violence in the workplace, 60

lifting tasks, 52, 308

Lions Club, 346

Littlejohn and Company, 331–332

Live-in Caregiver Program, 102–103, 166–167, 383

location. *See* class

Long, Elizabeth, 292

low income cut-off (LICO), 78

low income measure (LIM), 78

low-income women, 77–79

See also poverty

low-wage work, 80, 81t, 101, 160, 273

MacDonald Hotel case, 37

Macphail, Agnes, 251

Madre, Odessa, 212

The Making of "Mammy Pleasant": A Black Entrepreneur in Nineteenth-Century San Francisco (Hudson), 213

Mallick, Heather, 296

managers of sex workers, 368–370

manufacturing work, 16, 323–325

corporate restructuring, 335

discussion, 334–336

Hilton Works steel plant, 325–326, 334

initiatives to hire women, 324

international division of labour, 335

intersectionality, 324–325

John Deere Welland Works, 326–330, 334

Niagara rubber plant, 330–334

single mothers, 333–334

tiered pay, 327–328

wage gap, 327–328

Women Back Into Stelco Campaign, 326

Market Basket Measure (MBM), 78

Markwell, Mary, 291

Marx, Karl, 289

masculinity, 11, 343

masculinized work, 306, 383

See also fire services; women firefighters

massage parlours, 365, 369, 370

maternity leave, 41–42

maternity rights, 40–42

May, Elizabeth, 258

McClung, Nelly, 294

McGuire, Jennifer, 294

McQueen, Trina, 294

Me Too movement, 147, 148

Meiorin case, 31–32, 309–310

men

and cyberbullying, 259

in female-dominated occupations, 18

gender expectations, 296

glass escalator, 18

masculinized work, 306

parental leave, 157

"public man," 247

and STEM fields, 145

use of term, 3

women's voice, threat of, 296–297

men (*Continued*)
   young men, 140
      See also gender differences
mental health, 59–60, 71
mentorship, 231–232, 281
Métropolitain, 30
Michener Centre, 114–115
military, 307
Mill, John Stuart, 250
minoritization, 178, 383
minoritized faculty
   academic leadership, 183–184
   academic work and gender, generally,
      177–178, 192–193
   chilly climates, 187, 193
   classic university careers, 179
   country comparisons, gender gaps, 184–185
   experiences of, 187–188
   gaps beyond gender, 186–187
   gender gaps, 181–187
   glass ceiling, 187
   glass cliff, 184, 187
   Indigenous women, 181
   instructor-student relations, 188
   and job security, 179
   knowledge production, 189–192
   metaphors of the academy, 187–188
   neoliberalism, 190–192
   new knowledges, 189–190
   organization of, 178–181
   overrepresentation of minoritized faculty,
      179–180
   qualitative research, gender gaps found
      through, 185–186
   second glass ceiling, 184
   service roles, 181
   sexual orientation, 187
   slow scholarship, 191
   social expectations, 180–181
Monsef, Maryam, 259
multiculturalism, 216
musculoskeletal disorders, 54, 57–59

nannies, 166–167
National Action Committee on the Status of
   Women, 339, 345

National Council of Jewish Women of
   Canada, 344
National Council of Women, 344
National Household Survey, 118, 307, 314
National Inquiry into Missing and Murdered
   Indigenous Women and Girls, 7–8
National Occupational Coding, 316
neo-Marxists, 363
neocolonialism, 8–9
neoliberalism, 9, 68, 76–77
   defined, 384
   disabled women, 120–121, 127
   immigrant women, 97–99
   international division of labour, 335
   in manufacturing work. *See*
      manufacturing work
   and minoritized faculty, 190–192
   postsecondary education, 192
   unions under, 141
   young women, 140–141
new economy, 9–10, 18
New Zealand, 372–373
Niagara rubber plant, 330–334
nonprofit organizations, 339, 384
      See also nonprofit sector; women's
         nonprofit organizations
nonprofit sector
   childcare providers, 161
   generally, 339–340
   historical background, 340–342
   nonprofit organizations, 339
   women's nonprofit organizations.
      See women's nonprofit
         organizations
nontraditional jobs, 52
nurses, 60, 207–208

Obama, Barack, 13
occupational health and safety
   generally, 51–54, 62
   health-care workers, 55–56
   intersectional analysis, and prevention,
      54–56
   intersectional analysis, and workers'
      compensation, 57–62
   intersectional framework, 53

mental health injuries, 59–60

musculoskeletal disorders, 54, 57–59

occupational cancer, 55

workplace stress, 59–60

occupational violence, 60

See also violence against women

occupations of Canadian women, 16–18, 17t

oikos, 249, 384

oil embargo, 9

older women

aging, and double standards, 12

immigrant grandmothers, 104–105

and poverty, 12

unemployment, 84–85

online attacks, 257–260

Ontario Federation of Labour, 41, 142

Ontario Human Rights Code, 27–28

Ontario Human Rights Commission, 45

Ontario Ministry of Labour, 60

Ontario Public Service Employees Union

(OPSEU), 370

Ontario University Athletics (OUA), 226

OPSEU. *See* Ontario Public Service Employees

Union (OPSEU)

Organization of the Petroleum Exporting

Countries (OPEC), 9

organized labour, 370, 384

See also unions and unionization

othering, 97, 384

Ottawa Police Association, 42

paid *vs.* unpaid labour, 11–12

parental leave, 157

Parry Sound Social Services, 42

part-time employment, 15

black female athletes, 235–236

gender differences, 75, 75t

lack of affordable childcare, 144

statistics, 67

unionized workplaces, 35

wages of, 71

young women, 140

patriarchy, 149, 384

pay equity, 38–40, 168–169

Pay Equity Task Force, 38

"pay the job, not the worker," 34–36

PCEPA. *See* Protection of Communities and

Exploited Persons Act (PCEPA)

person with a disability. *See* disabled women

Petites Mains (Little Hands), 54

physical demands of work, 37, 308–310

pink ghetto, 18

Pleasant, Mary, 213–214

policing, 307

polis, 249

political economy approach, 289–290,

304–306

politics

cyberbullying, 257–260, 261–262

social media, role of, 256–257

voting rights, 251

women in politics. *See* public women

Politics (Aristotle), 249–250

post-traumatic stress disorder, 60

postsecondary education, 177–178, 192

See also minoritized faculty

poverty, 77–78

absolute poverty, 77–78

disabled women, 121–122

low income cut-off (LICO), 78

low income measure (LIM), 78

low-income women, and unemployment,

77–79

Market Basket Measure (MBM), 78

and older women, 12

poverty line, 78

and precarious employment, 79

Quebec's childcare program, 168

relative poverty, 78

time poverty, 104–105, 385

precarious employment, 9, 19, 79, 100–101,

208–209, 384

pregnancy, 40–42

prevention, 54–56

private health insurance, 71

private/public divide, 249–250

pro-domination, 365

professional athletes, 238–239

Protection of Communities and Exploited

Persons Act (PCEPA), 364

provincial human rights legislation, 123
PSCA. *See* Public Service Alliance of Canada (PSCA)
psychological injuries, 57–58
psychosocial risks, 54
public office. *See* public women
public policies. *See* government policies
Public Service Alliance of Canada (PSCA), 39, 44–45
public women
    cyberbullying, 257–260, 261–262
    cyberharassment, 259–260
    de facto exclusion from politics, 250–254
    de jure exclusion from politics, 250–254
    exclusion of women from politics, 249–256
    generally, 247–249, 260–262
    House of Commons, representation in, 251–253, 252t
    Indigenous women, 251, 254, 260–261
    persistent underrepresentation, 254–256
    private/public divide, 249–250
    provincial legislative representation, 253–254, 253t
    "public woman" *vs.* "public man," 247
    racialized women, 254, 260
    social media, 256–257
    supply-and-demand explanatory framework, 254–256

qualitative research, 185–186
Quebec
    childcare program, 87, 144, 167–168
    chronic stress, as compensable injury, 60
    domestic income, 168
    domestic workers, 60–61
    employment equity legislation, 306
    girls' and women's education, 182
    La Presse, 298
    musculoskeletal disorders, 58–59
    Petites Mains (Little Hands), 54
    Quiet Revolution, 182
    voting rights, 345
    "worker," 60–61
Quebec Association of Child Care Centers, 169

Québec Common Front, 41–42
Quebec Student Sports Federation (QSSF), 226

race
    and employment, 13–15
    and immigration, 80
    mixed-race heritage, 13
    racialized workforce in mid-20th-century, 27
    service jobs, and racialized workers, 26
    as social construct, 13
    and the workplace, 4
    workplace racism, 45
    See also racialized women
racialization, 53, 384
racialized women, 79t
    academic work, 186–187
    athletes. *See* black female athletes
    black women. *See* black female entrepreneurs
    at bottom of occupational ladder, 53
    domestic workers. *See* domestic workers
    educational attainment, 18
    employment, and race, 13–15
    entrepreneurship. *See* black female entrepreneurs
    factory work, 55
    illness, 52–53
    immigrant status, impact of, 15
    labour market experiences, 53–54
    low-wage work, 80, 81t
    musculoskeletal disorders, 54
    patterns of employment, 13
    "pay the job, not the worker," 35
    in politics, 254, 259, 260
    public women, 259, 260
    racial harassment, 45
    racialized immigrant women. *See* immigrant women
    in traditionally male occupations, 18
    and unemployment, 79–82
    unemployment rate, 80
    unions, and breadwinner wages, 33
    women's nonprofit organizations, 344
    See also race

racialized workers. *See* race; racialized women

radical feminists, 340, 363, 384

Reagan, Ronald, 9, 190

recession, 69, 73

refugees, 100

relative poverty, 78

repetitive work, 54, 58

representation, 189

Réseau du sport étudiant du Québec (RSEQ), 226

Retail, Wholesale, and Department Store Union (RWDSU), 29, 35

retail work
    aesthetic labour. *See* aesthetic labour
    fashion retail. *See* fashion retail
    generally, 269–271
    intersectionality, 269–270
    low salaries, 273
    self-service model, 279

retraining, 75–76

reverse discrimination, 306

role models, 231–232

Rotenberg, Mattie, 292–293

Rousseau, Jean-Jacques, 250

Royal Commission on Equality in Employment, 182, 184

Royal Commission on the Status of Women in Canada, 24, 41, 182

rubber plant in Niagara, 330–334

RWDSU. *See* Retail, Wholesale, and Department Store Union (RWDSU)

safety. *See* occupational health and safety

salary differences, women *vs.* men, 72–73
    See also gender wage gap

"same or similar" test, 36–37

Second Career, 76

second shift, 11, 73

self-employment. *See* entrepreneurship

self-imposed aesthetic labour, 276–279

self-regulation models, 371

seniority, 24, 28–29, 32–33, 384

seniority districts, 28

Service Employees International Union (SEIU), 35, 371

service work
    aesthetic labour. *See* aesthetic labour
    interpellatin, 272
    overrepresentation of women, 11
    racialized workers, 26
    symbolic values of female bodies, 271–272
    unique aspects of, 272–273
    women and, 16

settlement services, 98–99

settler colonialism, 7

sewing, 54

sex, 2, 385

sex workers
    "acts of indecency," 364
    agency and self-determination, 368
    bawdy house, 364–365
    Bedford case, 359–360, 364, 372
    communicating offence, 365
    current legal context, 364–366
    earnings, 362
    emotional labour, 361
    employers, 368–370
    erotic dancers, 366, 369, 370
    escort agencies, 369, 370
    gendered social and legal inequities, 362–363
    human trafficking, 366–368
    immigrant women, 368
    independent contractors, 370, 371
    independent escorts, 361
    Indigenous women, 368
    indoor locations, 360–361
    legal brothels in Australia, 371
    "living on the avails" offence, 364–365
    managers, 368–370
    massage parlours, 365, 369, 370
    New Zealand, 372–373
    pro-domination, 365
    "prostitution," 364
    public attitudes, 363–364
    self-regulation models, 371
    sex work, described, 360–364
    sex work, use of term, 359
    sex work abolitionists, 363
    sex-work-as-work perspective, 363, 372

sex workers (*Continued*)

    survival employment, 363

    third parties, 368–370

    unionization, 370–371

    who sex workers are, 360–364

sexual assault, 147–148

sexual harassment, 147–149

    Canadian Labour Code definition, 147

    fire services, 307

    as gender discrimination, 43

    lawyers, role of, 44

    union representation and, 43–45

    young women, 147–149

    zero-tolerance policies, 44

single mothers, 74, 333–334

Sisters of the Yam: Black Women and Self-Recovery (hooks), 203

Skills Development, 76

slavery, 204–206

small business. *See* entrepreneurship

social capital, 105, 344, 385

social categories, 5

social class. *See* class

social conditions, 1, 4–5, 75, 77–85

social constructs, 2, 13

social expectations of women, 74, 180–181, 296

social media

    and alternative retailers, 278

    cyberbullying, 257–260, 261–262

    At Issue broadcast, 258, 259

    role in politics, 256–257

social model analysis, 113, 117, 124–125

social movements

    childcare crisis, 168–170

    Me Too movement, 147, 148

    Time's Up movement, 147

social policies, 68

social reproduction, 11, 77, 86, 125, 159–161, 385

social values, 11

social welfare, 9

socialist feminists, 363

sports. *See* black female athletes

the state, and gender equity, 305

Statistics Canada, 10, 12, 69, 83, 146, 147, 235, 316

Status of Women Canada, 345

Stelco, 30

STEM (science, technology, engineering, and mathematics) fields, 18, 19, 96, 145, 146t, 149, 385

stigmatization, 103

stress, 59–60

structural factors in labour market, 4

structuration, 289–290, 291, 296, 299, 385

student athletes. *See* black female athletes

The Subjection of Women (Mill), 250

substantive equality approach, 31–32

suffragists, 251, 345

supply-and-demand explanatory framework, 254–256

survival employment, 96, 100, 363

systemic discrimination, 55, 385

teaching professions. *See* academic work

Temporary Authorization Program, 102

Temporary Foreign Workers Program, 166

Thatcher, Margaret, 9, 190

tiered pay, 327–328, 385

time poverty, 104–105, 385

time-use studies, 11

Time's Up movement, 147

Toronto Fire Service, 310

Toronto Women's Literary Guild, 345

Toronto Women's Suffrage Association, 345

trades

    trade certificates, 145

    women instructors, 188

transactional leadership, 349, 385

transformational leadership, 349, 385

transsexual individuals, 3

Trudeau, Justin, 7, 258

Trump, Donald, 336

Truth and Reconciliation Commission of Canada, 8, 190

Twitter. *See* social media

U Sports, 225, 226–227

UAW. *See* United Automobile Workers (UAW)

UE. *See* United Electrical, Radio and Machine
  Workers Union (UE)
UFCW. *See* United Food and Commercial
  Workers (UFCW)
underemployment, 15–16, 56, 67, 385
  consequences of, 67–68
  core data, 69
  and deskilling, 72
  financial impacts, 70–71
  gender differences, 72–76
  generally, 85–87
  health impacts, 71–72, 75
  impacts of, 70–72
  intersecting social conditions, impact of,
    77–85
  meaning of, 67
  See also part-time employment;
    unemployment
underground economy, 212–213
unemployment
  consequences of, 67–68
  core data, 69
  disabled women, 85
  discouraged searchers, 69
  discouraged workers, 69
  duration of, in Canada, 70t
  employment insurance policies, 76–77
  financial impacts, 70–71
  gender differences, 72–76
  generally, 15–16, 85–87
  and global economic trends, 69
  health impacts, 71–72, 75
  immigrant women, 79–82
  impacts of, 70–72
  Indigenous women, 82
  intersecting social conditions, impact of,
    77–85
  low-income women, 77–79
  older women, 84–85
  racialized women, 79–82
  young women, 83–84
  See also unemployment rate
Unemployment Insurance Act, 41, 68
unemployment rate, 80t, 81t, 82t, 83t

data included in, 69
disabled Canadians, 118
disabled women, 85
discouraged workers, 69
official *vs.* "lived" rate, 69
racialized women, 80
women *vs.* men, 68
young men, 140
young women, 84
See also unemployment
Unifor. *See* United Automobile Workers (UAW)
unions and unionization, 25
  childcare staff, 169
  collective bargaining, 25, 26
  dignity on the job, 43–45
  disruption of past practices, 46
  equal pay for equal work, 36–38
  fair-pay practices, 33–40
  formal equality proposition, 30
  gender wage gap, 33–34
  generally, 23–26
  job segregation by gender, union support
    for, 27–29
  male demographics of union
    membership, 24
  maternity rights, 40–42
  under neoliberalism, 141
  Niagara rubber plant, 331
  part-time workers, 35
  pay equity, 38–40
  "pay the job, not the worker," 34–36
  protecting the breadwinner advantage,
    33–34
  public-sector unions, 24
  racial harassment, 45
  reform, 24
  seniority, 24, 28–29, 32–33
  sex workers, 370–371
  sexual harassment, 43–45
  substantive equality approach, 31–32
  union, defined, 385
  women doing men's work, 30–33
  women's access to breadwinner jobs,
    26–33

unions and unionization (*Continued*)
  women's access to breadwinner status,
    40–45
  women's access to breadwinner wages,
    33–40
  "women's issues," 25
  "women's work," 28–29, 39–40
  "workers' issues," 24
United Automobile Workers (UAW), 24, 27, 45
United Electrical, Radio and Machine Workers
  Union (UE), 24, 29
United Food and Commercial Workers
  (UFCW), 39
United Nations, 138
  Gender Empowerment Measure, 345–346
  human trafficking convention, 366
  UN Convention on the Rights of Persons
    with Disabilities, 112
United States, civil rights movement in, 2
United Steel Workers (USWA), 29, 44
universal health care, 71
university careers. *See* academic work
unpaid labour
  care work, 11, 73
  disabled workers, 115–116
  domestic labour, 1–2, 11
  freedom to choose whether and how much
    to work, 73–75
  gender differences, 72–73
  immigrant women, 104–105
  vs. paid labour, 11–12
  work-integrated-learning (WIL)
    positions, 141, 142–143
USWA. *See* United Steel Workers (USWA)

VALE, 30
A Vindication of the Rights of Women
  (Wollstonecraft), 250
violence against women
  Indigenous women, 7–8
  international convention, discussions re, 60
  in nontraditional jobs, 52
  nurses, 60
  workplace violence, 60

visible minority, 79, 186, 386
  and Canadian census, 13
  Employment Equity Act definition, 13
  glass ceiling, 18
  See also racialized women
voting rights, 251, 262n3, 345

wage gap. *See* gender wage gap
wage-improvement campaigns, 168–169
Walker, C. J., 211–212
Wardair case, 43
We Are Your Sisters: Black Women in the Nineteenth
  Century (Sterling), 204
white British women, 96–97
WIL. *See* work-integrated-learning (WIL)
  positions
Wilson-Raybould, Jody, 260
Wollstonecraft, Mary, 250
women
  glass ceiling, 18
  positive affective bonds between, 280
  "public woman," 247
  social conditions, 1, 4–5, 75, 77–85
  social expectations, 74, 180–181, 296
  social reproduction, 11, 77, 86, 125,
    159–161
  use of term, 3
  voting rights, 251, 262n3, 345
  See also gender differences; women
    and work
Women, Power, Politics: The Story of Canada's
  Unfinished Democracy (Bashevkin), 260
women and work
  age, 12
  diversity, and women's employment rate, 12
  future for, in Canada, 18–19
  gendered division of labour, 10–11
  general trend, in Canada, 8–12
  manufacturing sector. *See* manufacturing
    work
  occupations, 16–18, 17t
  service sector. *See* service work
  traditional jobs, 145–146
  unionization. *See* unions and unionization

women doing men's work, 30–33
    See also employment
Women Back Into Stelco Campaign, 326
women firefighters
    challenges, generally, 317–318
    employment equity, 315–316
    equipment, 311
    equity side doors, 314–315
    feminist political economy approach,
        304–306
    fire hall culture, 312–314
    improvements, 314–315
    intersectionality, 304–306
    Meiorin case, 31–32, 309–310
    non-operations positions, 315
    underrepresentation in fire services, 307
    uniforms, 311
    work environments, 311
    See also fire services
women journalists
    contemporary challenges, 295–297
    earlier history of, 290–293
    feminist political economy approach,
        289–290
    freelancers, 294
    generally, 298–299
    glass ceilings, 293–295
    structuration, 289–290, 291, 296, 299
    theoretical approaches, 289–290
    women's pages, 288–289, 290–293
    women's programming, 290–293
    work/life balance issue, 295–297
    See also journalism
women politicians. *See* public women
Women's Christian Temperance Union,
    344, 345
Women's Equality Liberty Coalition, 363
women's movement, 2, 182
women's nonprofit organizations, 339–340,
    342–343
    black women's organizations, 344
    donors and, 347
    and empowerment of women, 345–346

generally, 350–351
    historical review of role of, 343–346
    leadership, and internal relationships,
        348–349
    organizational environment, relationships
        with, 347–348
    organizational structure, 349–350
    preference for participation in, 346–347
    social capital, 344
    unique characteristics, 347–350
    volunteering, theories of, 346
    volunteering rates, 344
    See also nonprofit sector
Women's Press Club, 292
women's work. *See* women and work
work
    combining education and work, 140, 146
    differing experiences of, 1
    and health, 128–129
    paid *vs.* unpaid labour, 11–12
    and survival, 33
    unpaid labour. *See* unpaid labour
    use of term, 3
    See also women and work
work health and safety. *See* occupational health
    and safety
work-integrated-learning (WIL) positions, 141,
    142–143, 386
work/life balance. *See* family-work balance
workers' compensation, 57–62, 386
    application of compensation rules,
        61–62
    equitable access to, 57–61
    immigrant status, 61
"'Working for Nothing but for a Living': Black
    Women in the Underground Economy"
    (Harley), 212
workplace racism, 45
workplace stress, 59–60
workplace violence, 60
    See also violence against women
World Health Organization, 112
Wynne, Kathleen, 259

young women, 83–84
  BHASE fields, 144–145
  combining education and work, 140, 146
  definition of term, 137–138
  demographics, 138–140
  deskilling, 141–142
  employment patterns, 138–140
  exploitation, 142–143
  family-work balance, 143–144
  feminized education programs and
    careers, 144–146, 145t
  high school students, 146
  higher education, 144
  negative perceptions of, 141–143
  neoliberalism, 140–141
  part-time employment, 140
  "pink collar" fields, 144–145
  sexual assault, 147–148
  sexual harassment, 147–149
  and work, generally, 149
  work-integrated-learning (WIL)
    positions, 141, 142–143
  See also youth
youth, 137
  age and gender distribution, 138t
  employment patterns, 139t
  socioeconomic demotion, 142
  stereotypes, 142
  See also young women
Youth in Transitions Survey, 146